Rethinking Fundamental Theology

Rethinking Fundamental Theology examines central theological questions: about God, human experience and, specifically, religious experience; the divine revelation coming through the history of Israel and through the life, death and resurrection of Jesus; human faith that responds to revelation; the nature of tradition that transmits the record and reality of revelation; the structure of biblical inspiration and truth, as well as basic issues concerned with the formation of the canon; the founding of the Church with some leadership structures; the relationship between Christ's revelation and the faith of those who follow other religions. O'Collins concludes with some reflections on theological method.

Written with the scholarship and accessibility for which O'Collins is recognized and valued, this book will relaunch fundamental theology as a distinct and necessary discipline in faculties and departments of theology and religious studies around the world.

Gerald O'Collins S. J. is Adjunct Professor Australian Catholic University, Melbourne. Author or co-author of 62 published books and of hundreds of articles in professional and popular journals, he is widely known for his appearances on BBC and as a lecturer in many universities and colleges around the world.

Rethinking Fundamental Theology

Toward a New Fundamental Theology

Gerald O'Collins, S.J.

OXFORD
UNIVERSITY PRESS

OXFORD
UNIVERSITY PRESS

Great Clarendon Street, Oxford, OX2 6DP,
United Kingdom

Oxford University Press is a department of the University of Oxford.
It furthers the University's objective of excellence in research, scholarship,
and education by publishing worldwide. Oxford is a registered trade mark of
Oxford University Press in the UK and in certain other countries

Published in the United States of America by Oxford University Press
198 Madison Avenue, New York, NY 10016, United States of America

British Library Cataloguing in Publication Data
Data available

ISBN 978-0-19-967398-8

Links to third party websites are provided by Oxford in good faith and
for information only. Oxford disclaims any responsibility for the materials
contained in any third party website referenced in this work.

Preface

If this book were entitled *Rethinking Moral Theology: Toward a New Moral Theology*, it would more readily establish an instant conversation with many readers. They would perhaps want to know what claims to be 'new' about this particular work in moral theology. They might, of course, immediately guess that it addresses all kinds of contemporary issues coming from biology, ecological concerns, global economics, international relations, and so forth. Some prospective readers would be curious about the distinction, if any, to be drawn between moral theology and ethics—whether new or traditional. Obviously they intersect. But do they converge, more or less totally? Yet, all in all, *Rethinking Moral Theology* would, even at first glance, seem an intelligible project.

Rethinking Fundamental Theology, however, could readily appear an improbable project. While readers will know or at least have heard of moral theologians, have they ever met any of those who call themselves 'fundamental theologians'? Here some Roman Catholics might remember that the Second Vatican Council (1962–5) listed various branches of theology (*Decree on the Training of Priests*, 17) but never alluded to fundamental theology. To write a book on this topic might easily come across as descending into obscure territory and pandering to arcane interests.

Add too the fact that 'fundamental theology', whether old or new, continues, in my experience, to suggest to numerous people one of two extremes: (1) an irrational approach typical of rigid, even mindless 'fundamentalism', or else (2) the too rational approach of a 'foundationalism' that claims to secure triumphantly the foundations of Christian faith by 'demonstrating' the existence of God, the divine identity of Christ, and his creation of the enduring Church. It is desperately easy to confuse fundamental theology with fundamentalism, on the one hand, or foundationalism, on the other. But fundamental theology belongs at neither extreme.

As we shall see, (1) against fundamentalism a genuine fundamental theology cherishes the exercise of reason in various forms (in particular, historical reason, philosophical reason, and a thoughtful and faithful interpretation of the Bible) when it reflects on basic Christian beliefs. (2) In place of foundationalism, it proposes a more modest programme by dealing with objections to faith and making a rational case for the central claims of faith. These claims are not incoherent, and they can point to reasons in their support. Hence fundamental theology should not be caricatured, as if it were bent on producing knockdown arguments for basic truth claims and considered those who disagreed to be either knaves or fools.

Another caricature of fundamental theology portrays it as a peculiarly Roman Catholic enterprise, and even one that has been limited to Catholic departments and faculties in continental Europe. Here one should recall that the discipline arose primarily under Protestant and Anglican auspices in the eighteenth and nineteenth centuries (see Ch. 1 below). Unquestionably, major contributions to fundamental theology have come from Catholic scholars working in Europe: for instance, René Latourelle and his collaborators (by no means all of them Catholics) in the *Dictionary of Fundamental Theology* (Crossroad, 1994), Karl Rahner in *Foundations of Christian Faith* (Seabury Press, 1978), and those who produced in four volumes the *Handbuch der Fundamentaltheologie* (Herder, 1985–8). But, as we shall see in Chapter 1, such prominent Lutheran theologians as Gerhard Ebeling (1912–2001) and Wilfried Joest (1914–95) wrote in the area of fundamental theology during the twentieth century. Another Lutheran scholar, Wolfhart Pannenberg (b. 1928), was one of the authors for the *Handbuch der Fundamentaltheologie*. In the United Kingdom notable writers have addressed central concerns of fundamental theology, even if they do not necessarily invoke the name of that discipline. I think here, for example, of David Brown (*Tradition and Imagination: Revelation and Change* (Clarendon Press, 1999)) and Richard Swinburne (*Revelation: From Analogy to Metaphor* (Clarendon Press, 1992)). Outside Europe, for instance, in the United States and Canada, numerous scholars have taken up themes of fundamental theology: Catholics like Avery Dulles (*Models of Revelation* (Doubleday, 1983)), Francis Schüssler Fiorenza (*Foundational Theology: Jesus and the Church* (Crossroad, 1984)), Bernard Lonergan (*Method in Theology* (Herder and Herder, 1972)), and Robert Sokolowski (*The God of Faith and Reason: Foundations of Christian Theology* (Catholic University of America Press, 2nd edn. 1995)), and other Christians like William Abraham (*Crossing the Threshold of Divine Revelation* (Eerdmans, 2006)), George Mavrodes

(*Revelation in Religious Belief* (Temple University Press, 1988)), and Nicholas Wolterstorff (*Divine Discourse: Philosophical Reflections on Claims that God Speaks* (Cambridge University Press, 1995)).

Some readers know that, as well as collaborating over the years in works on fundamental theology, I have published three books in the area: *Foundations of Theology* (Loyola University Press, 1971), *Fundamental Theology* (Paulist Press, 1981), and *Retrieving Fundamental Theology* (Paulist Press, 1993). But my motive in writing *Rethinking Fundamental Theology* goes well beyond the desire to revise and update those earlier books. From the 1990s, fresh challenges and new developments have emerged for the agenda of fundamental theology: interreligious dialogue, for instance, has become an ever more pressing concern. Moreover, as the third millennium unfolds, even though the questions fundamental theology traditionally raised have in no way become outdated and irrelevant, the very existence of this discipline seems to be quietly threatened with non-existence. A quick check of the programmes listed by many departments and faculties of theology around the world shows how they fail to offer courses and seminars in fundamental theology. They may organize courses on the introduction to (systematic) theology, with revelation and faith prominent on the agenda. But neither the full scope of fundamental theology nor its name as a distinct discipline features on these programmes. The discipline needs to be relaunched.

One result of cancelling fundamental theology from the agenda or of never having given it a place on the programmes has been emerging in recent years. Chapter 1 will show how some philosophical theologians (of different Christian communities), while seemingly knowing nothing of fundamental theology and its inheritance, have moved in and partly filled a void left by a widespread demise of fundamental theology.

This book has been born out of a sense of the urgent need to preserve and renew the legacy of Avery Dulles, Gerhard Ebeling, René Latourelle, Karl Rahner, and other outstanding practitioners of fundamental theology. In a kind of intergenerational conversation, I want to develop further the insights and arguments gained from contact with these and other great exponents of fundamental theology. They set themselves to offer a faithful and reasonable account of basic Christian beliefs and 'give an account of their hope' (1 Pet. 3: 15).

Chapter 1 will clarify the origins of fundamental theology, reflect on its distinctive character when compared with apologetics, philosophical theology, philosophy of religion, and systematic theology, and propose the basic themes that provide fundamental theology with its proper identity: for instance, the existence of God, the human condition, the nature of divine self-revelation, the transmission of revelation through tradition, the inspiration of the Scriptures, and so forth.

Chapter 2 will address belief in the existence of a personal God and some pervasive objections to belief in God. Chapter 3 will reflect on the human condition and its potential openness to faith in the divine self-revelation. After examining four alternative views of the human condition, the chapter develops the theme of human beings as those who 'experience' (*homo experiens*).

Chapter 4 will explore revelation: first the 'general' revelation available through the order and beauty of the created world and the moral law 'written' on human hearts, as well as the faith which this 'general' revelation evokes. This chapter will then attend to the 'special' history of divine revelation (recorded in the Scriptures), investigating its means, its 'sacramental' structure (involving word and event), and its mediators (attending in particular to the task of discerning and evaluating the experience of prophets).

Chapter 5 will take up the function of Jesus Christ as the unsurpassable Revealer and the fullness of revelation. This involves reflecting on the Gospels' witness to his preaching of the kingdom, with particular attention paid to his parables, miracles, claims to a personal authority that put him on a par with God, and the 'trinitarian' face of his life and work. The chapter ends by distinguishing between revelation as past (foundational revelation), as present (dependent revelation), and as future (the consummation of revelation at Christ's second coming).

In Chapter 6, I plan to reflect on Jesus Christ as being Revealer and Revelation in his crucifixion and resurrection. What does the cross reveal about the identity of God? Why accept the resurrection and what it discloses about the tripersonal God?

Chapter 7 will turn to the faith that responds to the divine self-manifestation. Is such faith reasonable? What brings it about? In particular, this chapter will draw on the paradigmatic cases of movements to faith provided by John's Gospel.

Chapter 8 will examine what happened and happens when human beings, after experiencing in faith the divine self-revelation, handed on their experience in the living tradition of the Church. Tradition (in upper case), as process and content, needs to be distinguished from innumerable particular traditions (in lower case).

In Chapter 9, I will reflect on the nature of biblical inspiration. Both in the formation of the Bible and its use, we should distinguish between revelation and inspiration, and not succumb to the endemic temptation to identify them. That said, how might we describe biblical inspiration? Chapter 10 then takes up the closely related questions of biblical truth, the formation of the canon, and the interpretation of the Scriptures.

In Chapter 11, I will examine the founding of the Church and her basic structures. Did Christ intend to found the Church? What might be said about the emergence of triple ministry of bishops, priests, and deacons? That leads in Chapter 12 to reflection on the place of world religions in the history of revelation and salvation. The chapter interprets their situation within and through the universal presence of Christ and the Holy Spirit.

In the light of the previous chapters, Chapter 13 will investigate three 'styles' of theology and propose some basic guidelines for Christian theology—a task that belongs appropriately to fundamental theology.

Even as I complete this Preface and have not yet written the chapters that follow, I am aware that all of these chapters could be expanded to make a book in its own right. I will try to make each of the chapters coherent and convincing, but will need to be selective in the material that I assemble for their construction. Hence, at times positions and perspectives will be stated rather than supported by detailed argument. My hope is that this book as a whole will offer a new, satisfying, and coherent vision of fundamental theology, a vision that may serve to rethink and relaunch the discipline.

For various kinds of help in composing and completing this book I want to express my gratitude to John Begley, Stephen Connelly, Stephen Davis, Christiaan Mostert, John Martis, Alan Padgett, Tom Perridge, two anonymous readers for Oxford University Press, and the staff of the Dalton McCaughey Library (United Faculty of Theology, Melbourne). I dedicate this work to the members and staff of the Jesuit Theological College (both Jesuits and lay persons).

Gerald O'Collins SJ

Australian Catholic University
Melbourne
31 July 2010

Note for Paperback Edition

For this paperback edition a few corrections have been made. I am grateful for the reviews which have already appeared:

Thomas Cattoi, *Commonweal*, 13 July 2012, 35–6.
Peter Groves, *Expository Times* 123/7 (2012), 338–40.
Euan Marley, *New Blackfriars* 93 (2012), 617–18.
Clive Marsh, *Theology* 115 (2012), 358–9.
Alan Padgett, *Theological Studies* 73 (2012), 714–15.
Paul Richardson, *Church of England Newspaper*, 15 July 2011.

I hope to find a later occasion to enter into dialogue with these and other reviewers.

G. O'C., 31 January 2013.

Contents

Abbreviations

ABD	D. N. Freedman (ed.), *Anchor Bible Dictionary*, 6 vols. (New York: Doubleday, 1992).
Bettenson	H. Bettenson and C. Maunder, *Documents of the Christian Church* (3rd edn. Oxford: Oxford University Press, 1999).
CSEL	*Corpus Scriptorum Ecclesiasticorum Latinorum* (Vienna, 1866–).
DFTh	R. Latourelle and R. Fisichella (eds.), *Dictionary of Fundamental Theology* (New York: Crossroad, 1994).
DzH	H. Denzinger and P. Hünermann (eds.), *Enchiridion Symbolorum, definitionum et declarationum* (37th edn. Freiburg im Breisgau: Herder, 1991).
HFTh	W. Kern, H. J. Pottmeyer, and M. Seckler (eds.), *Handbuch der Fundamentaltheologie*, 4 vols. (Freiburg im Breisgau: Herder, 1985–8).
ND	J. Neuner and J. Dupuis (eds.), *The Christian Faith* (7th edn. Bangalore: Theological Publications in India; 2001).
Oxford Dictionary	F. L. Cross and E. A. Livingstone (eds.), *The Oxford Dictionary of The Christian Church* (3rd edn (rev.); Oxford: Oxford University Press, 2005).
par(r)	and parallel(s) in other Gospels
PL	*Patrologia Latina*, ed. J. P. Migne, 221 vols. (Paris, 1844–64).
TDNT	G. Kittel and G. Friedrich (eds.), *Theological Dictionary of the New Testament*, trans. G. W. Bromiley, 10 vols. (Grand Rapids, Mich.: Eerdmans, 1964–76).
TRE	G. Krause and G. Müller (eds.), *Theologische Realenzylopädie*, 36 vols. (Berlin: Walter de Gruyter, 1977–2004).

1

History, Terms, Identity, and Themes

If this book is to provide resources for rethinking, renewing, and even relaunching the theory and practice of fundamental theology, it needs to begin by clarifying the specific character of this branch of theology. By doing that, we will then be in a position to gather into a logical sequence the themes that fundamental theology addresses and that constitute its identity. Since, however, readers often cannot work up too much interest in a topic or even in a whole discipline unless they know where it has come from, let me first sketch the background of fundamental theology.[1]

---

[1] See R. Latourelle and R. Fisichella (eds.), *Dictionary of Fundamental Theology* (New York: Crossroad, 1994; hereafter *DFTh*); R. Rauser, *Theology in Search of Foundations* (Oxford: Oxford University Press, 2009); M. Seckler, 'Fundamentaltheologie: Aufgaben und Aufbau, Begriff und Namen', in *HFTh* iv. 451–514; R. Sokolowski, *The God of Faith and Reason: Foundations of Christian Theology* (orig. edn. 1982; Washington, DC: Catholic University of America Press, 1995); H. Wagner, 'Fundamentaltheologie', *TRE* xi. 738–52. The absence of any entry on fundamental theology in F. L. Cross and E. A. Livingstone (eds.), *The Oxford Dictionary of the Christian Church* (3rd edn. (rev.); Oxford: Oxford University Press, 2005; hereafter *Oxford Dictionary*) offers another, disturbing sign of how this discipline has been quietly marginalized or simply ignored in some or even many quarters. This dictionary contains, however, entries on the related enterprises of 'apologetics', 87–8, and 'natural theology', 1139.

Historical background

As Gerhard Ebeling pointed out, from the eighteenth century Protestant authors used such terms as 'foundations', 'fundamental doctrine', and even 'fundamental theology', as well as engaging with the issues and realities that corresponded to these terms. They did this against the background of those who had earlier responded to deists, agnostics, and atheists, by developing, in various ways, 'apologies' for 'natural religion' and 'revealed religion' in response to deists, agnostics, and atheists. An apologetical literature that argued for the existence of God, the divine identity of Christ, and his establishment of the Church went back even to the end of the sixteenth century. When nineteenth-century Roman Catholic scholars introduced 'fundamental theology' as a distinct discipline within theology, they were influenced by widespread concerns of Protestant theologians who included F. D. E. Schleiermacher (1768–1834).[2]

What Ebeling wrote in a long 1970 essay was confirmed five years later in an even more documented account by Heinz Stirnimann about the origins of fundamental theology. In particular, after a Catholic faculty of theology moved from Erlangen to the University of Tübingen in 1819, such leading figures as Johann Sebastian von Drey (1777–1853) and Franz Anton Staudenmaier (1800–56) drew from their Protestant counterparts various suggestions and even models for thinking in the area of fundamental theology. Much more than a merely apologetical, 'defensive' intention played a role here. Many shared the desire to construct a scientific introduction to theology, which would set out principles and methods to be followed in the doctrinal or dogmatic tracts that followed. This led some to compose encyclopedias that embodied a fundamental and a dogmatic vision and approach. From the mid-eighteenth century to the mid-nineteenth century, something similar happened among those dedicated to producing a *Fundamentalphilosophie* (fundamental philosophy), a term that gave its name to

---

[2] G. Ebeling, 'Erwägungen zu einer evangelischen Fundamentaltheologie', *Zeitschrift für Theologie und Kirche*, 67 (1970), 479–524; this essay was reprinted in his *Wort und Glaube*, iv (Tübingen: J. C. B. Mohr, 1995), 377–419; see also id., 'Fundamental Theology', in *The Study of Theology*, trans. D. A. Priebe (Philadelphia: Fortress Press, 1978), 153–65.

various books that aimed at establishing the basic principles and methods of philosophical knowledge.[3] Thus it was in dialogue with different currents of thought that Drey and his colleagues created a tradition which would continue to inspire Catholic professors of the Tübingen School. Those who later contributed to fundamental theology include Karl Adam, Josef Rupert Geiselmann, Walter Kasper, Hans Küng, and Joseph Ratzinger. Max Seckler, as one of the three co-editors of and a major contributor to the four-volume *Handbuch der Fundamentaltheologie* (1985–8), represents a recent highpoint.

When fundamental theology began to emerge in the eighteenth century, it had an immediate background, as we saw above, in the apologetics developed by Anglican, Catholic, and Protestant authors in response to the Enlightenment. A movement that started in seventeenth-century Europe and spread to North America and elsewhere, the Enlightenment typically resisted authority and tradition and aimed at deciding issues though the use of reason alone. In religious matters many representatives of this movement rejected divine revelation, miracles, and Christ's resurrection, could be strongly opposed to mainline Christian beliefs, and in some cases doubted or denied the existence of a personal God.[4] Rebuttals came from such writers as the Anglicans Bishop Joseph Butler (1692–1752) and Samuel Clarke (1675–1729), the Protestant Jacques Abbadie (around 1654–1727; his 1684 *Traite de la verité de la religion chretienne* was frequently reprinted and translated into several languages), and the Roman Catholic Luke Joseph Hooke (1716–96). Butler, who was to influence considerably the thinking and apologetics of John Henry Newman (1801–90), led those eighteenth-century Christians who replied to the rationalism of the Enlightenment.[5]

Their apologetics fostered proximately the rise of fundamental theology and its reasoned defence of basic Christian beliefs. But the practice of apologetics formed a long-standing prehistory of

[3] H. Stirnimann, 'Erwägungen für Fundamentaltheologie: Problematik, Grundfragen, Konzept', *Freiburgerzeitschrift für Philosophie und Theologie*, 24 (1977), 291–365, at 293–301.
[4] See 'Deism', *Oxford Dictionary*, 468; 'Enlightenment, the', ibid. 550; C. Taylor, *A Secular Age* (Cambridge, Mass.: Harvard University Press, 2007).
[5] See 'Butler, Joseph', *Oxford Dictionary*, 258–9; and M. J. Buckley, *At the Origins of Modern Atheism* (New Haven: Yale University Press, 1987); id., *Denying and Disclosing God: The Ambiguous Progress of Modern Atheism* (New Haven: Yale University Press, 2004).

fundamental theology. 'Apologies' for the Christian religion stretch back to innumerable authors, like St Thomas Aquinas (*c.*1225–74) in his *Summa contra Gentiles* and St Augustine of Hippo (354–430) in his *City of God*, through Tertullian (before he lapsed into Montanism and died, *c.*225), St Justin Martyr (d. *c.*165), and other second- and third-century apologists (who rebutted objections and offered educated outsiders a case for the Christian faith), as far as New Testament 'apologies', like St Paul's speeches in Athens to Jews, Epicurean philosophers, Stoics, and others (Acts 17: 16–34).[6]

The twentieth century saw a flowering of Christian apologists, who often deployed world-class skills as writers: in the English-speaking world, for instance, one thinks of C. S. Lewis (1898–1963), G. K. Chesterton (1874–1936), and Dorothy Sayers (1893–1957). Among professional theologians, such figures as Paul Tillich (1886–1965), Wolfhart Pannenberg (b. 1928), and Alistair McGrath (b. 1953) have, in their different ways, been considered outstanding apologists for Christian faith.

Apologetics and fundamental theology

If Christian apologetics developed from New Testament times and, historically speaking, provided the proximate background for the emergence of fundamental theology in the eighteenth century, what difference(s) exist between apologetics and fundamental theology? They both come from those who personally share Christian faith and operate within the believing community and at its service. They both aim to respond to objections raised by critics and to offer a credible account of central beliefs about such matters as the existence of a personal God, the divine self-revelation in Jesus Christ, and the nature of faith.

Yet apologetics and fundamental theology differ on at least three scores. First, a Christian apologist may deal simply with one question: does the existence of horrendous evil in our world rule out the existence of an all-powerful, all-loving God? Or has science made belief in God something to be relegated to the past? Or what can we

---

[6] On the history of Christian apologetics, see A. Dulles, *A History of Apologetics* (orig. edn. 1971; San Francisco: Ignatius Press, 2005).

know about the history of Jesus? Can we show that belief in his resurrection from the dead is also reasonable and not merely a matter of blind faith? Fundamental theology, however, must deal not only with these but also with many other questions. Its agenda, as we shall see later in this chapter and in subsequent chapters, constitutes a whole theological discipline in its own right. As a branch of theology, it is an exercise of 'faith seeking understanding' over a coherent and cohesive range of topics. Along with its apologetic function, fundamental theology embodies the study of various central Christian doctrines, like divine revelation and human faith.

Second, good apologetics characteristically has a sharply defined audience: apologists can seek, for example, to alert non-believers to the weakness of the case currently being made against God and religion. But fundamental theology frequently has a wider range of readers in mind: believers who wish to grasp the reasons for and the implications of their religious beliefs and so deal with difficulties they encounter about their faith; students and teachers of theology and religious studies; and interested outsiders who want to examine in depth the truth of basic Christian beliefs.

Third, polemics (in the good sense of that word and not as mindless ranting) belong to the exercise of apologetics. With their telling phrases and brilliant language, C. S. Lewis and G. K. Chesterton exemplified such polemics at their best. Some recent works, like the responses by John Lennox and Tina Beattie to the new atheists, illustrate how Christian polemics continue in good shape.[7] The tone of fundamental theologians, even when rebutting objections to Christian faith, is or should be more expository and less polemically inclined to illustrate defects in opposing positions.

Terms and boundaries

To bring the identity of fundamental theology into sharper focus, let me compare and contrast it with (1) the philosophy of religion, (2)

---

[7] T. Beattie, *The New Atheists: The Twilight of Reason and the War on Religion* (London: Darton, Longman & Todd, 2007); J. C. Lennox, *God's Undertaker: Has Science Buried God?* (Oxford: Liam Hudson, 2007).

philosophical theology, (3) systematic (and dogmatic) theology, and (4) natural theology. In all four cases there are connections to be made and comparisons to be drawn.

The philosophy of religion

Some classical and more recent collections of essays do not go out of their way to distinguish the philosophy of religion from philosophical theology. A book edited by Antony Flew and Alastair MacIntyre over fifty years ago, *New Essays in Philosophical Theology*, aimed to 'apply the latest philosophical techniques and insights' to theological issues and helped to launch the term 'philosophical theology' into wider circulation—in particular, among philosophers of the analytic school. They acknowledged borrowing the term from Paul Tillich,[8] but did not provide any precise reference to his already published works.[9] Very recently T. P. Flint and M. C. Rea recall that earlier choice of title and see *The Oxford Handbook of Philosophical Theology* as standing in some continuity with the agenda set by Flew and MacIntyre. Neither Flew and MacIntyre nor Flint and Rea clearly distinguish philosophical theology from the philosophy of religion. In fact, Flint and Rea announce that 'the target audience' of their handbook of philosophical theology comprises 'philosophers of religion'.[10] Like Flint and Rea, William Wainwright in *The Oxford Handbook of Philosophy of Religion* seems to use 'philosophical theology' (which goes back to Aquinas, Maimonides, some classic Arab thinkers, Augustine, and even earlier writers) and 'philosophy of religion' (which as a name and a distinct discipline came into general usage in the nineteenth century) as largely equivalent terms. He

---

[8] A. Flew and A. MacIntyre (eds.), *New Essays in Philosophical Theology* (London: SCM Press, 1955), p. x.

[9] With all due respect to these two notable thinkers, I wonder whether 'philosophical theology' came into their mind when they read such statements from vol. i of Tillich's *Systematic Theology* (Chicago: Chicago University Press, 1951) as 'every creative philosopher is a hidden theologian' (25), and 'systematic theology includes philosophical discussion' (29). I have not been able to find Tillich using the phrase 'philosophical theology' prior to 1955 (when Flew and MacIntyre published their collection of essays under that title).

[10] T. P. Flint and M. C. Rea (eds.), *The Oxford Handbook of Philosophical Theology* (New York: Oxford University Press, 2009), 5.

makes no studied distinction between philosophy of religion and philosophical theology.[11]

I would propose, however, joining such authors as John Macquarrie and Stephen Davis (see below) in drawing a firm distinction between the philosophy of religion and philosophical theology. In the five chapters that comprise part one ('Philosophical Theology') of his *Principles of Christian Theology*, Macquarrie addressed 'The Tasks of Philosophical Theology': 'Human Existence', 'Revelation', 'Being and God', 'The Language of Theology', and 'Religion and Religions'.[12] He set out two central functions of philosophical theology: first, in the cause of establishing that theology is 'reasonable', it 'lays bare the fundamental concepts of theology and investigates the conditions that make any theology possible'. Second, philosophical theology also has 'an apologetic function', in that it shows how 'theology can claim to have foundations in the universal structures of human existence and experience'. In this context Macquarrie also clarified the 'difference between philosophical theology and the philosophy of religion'. The latter studies religion from a 'disinterested' point of view, whereas 'philosophical theology belongs *within* the theological enterprise'.[13]

In parenthesis let me note that by treating such a theme as revelation and by recognizing an 'apologetic function' that also belongs to philosophical theology, Macquarrie, even if he did not realize this, attended to themes and issues that others deal with under the rubric of 'fundamental theology'. But my central concern here is to endorse his position about the philosophy of religion differing from philosophical theology.

[11] W. J. Wainwright (ed.), *The Oxford Handbook of Philosophy of Religion* (New York: Oxford University Press, 2005), 3–10. Not surprisingly, we read in the index: 'theology, philosophical, *see* philosophy of religion' (549). Apropos of the emergence of the philosophy of religion, one should note that its central topics (the existence and nature of God and the relationship of human beings to the divine Being) have been discussed since philosophy began. See also B. Davies (ed.), *Philosophy of Religion: A Guide and an Anthology* (Oxford: Oxford University Press, 2000); W. L. Rowe and W. J. Wainwright (eds.), *Philosophy of Religion: Selected Readings* (3rd edn. New York: Oxford University Press, 2002).

[12] J. Macquarrie, *Principles of Christian Theology* (orig. edn. 1966; London: SCM Press, 1977), 43–173.

[13] Ibid. 39–40; italics mine.

Forty years after Macquarrie brought out *Principles of Christian Theology*, Stephen Davis published *Christian Philosophical Theology*. Without using the term 'foundational theology'[14] or 'fundamental theology' (Ebeling, Fisichella, Joest, Latourelle, O'Collins, and many others), he set himself to produce 'a coherent statement and defence of certain central claims of the Christian world-view'. They include such basic claims as that God exists and 'reveals himself to human beings, and does so preeminently in his Son Jesus Christ'. Significantly, Davis, while recognizing that '"philosophical theology" is sometimes used as a synonym for "philosophy of religion"', states that he will use 'philosophical theology' 'to mean the kind of approach that a *believing* philosopher would make to Christian theological topics'.[15]

Like or even more than Macquarrie and Davis, I want to draw a clear distinction between philosophical *theology* and the philosophy of religion. The former, inasmuch as it is an exercise of theology, entails personally sharing in faith and seeking to understand it—just as fundamental (or foundational) *theology* does. Exponents of the philosophy of religion know *about* faith and theology, but do not necessarily share the vision of faith. In some sense philosophy of religion seems analogous to the philosophy of history and the philosophy of science. Those engaged in these latter disciplines know *about* the thought and practice of working historians and scientists, but need not be themselves professional historians and scientists.

Philosophical theology

A more sensitive task concerns the overlap and distinction between fundamental theology and philosophical theology (or what, in the

---

[14] Francis Schüssler Fiorenza used this term as a title for his *Foundational Theology: Jesus and the Church* (New York: Crossroad, 1984). Where some forms of traditional fundamental theology focused on three large issues (the existence of God, the divine identity of Christ, and the foundation/mission of the Church), Fiorenza attended to the second and third issues. He aimed to move beyond any search for unshakeable foundations ('foundationalism') and establish a 'reflective equilibrium' between 'hermeneutical reconstruction', 'retroductive warrants', and 'background theories'.

[15] S. T. Davis, *Christian Philosophical Theology* (Oxford: Oxford University Press, 2006), 1–2; italics mine.

subtitle to their *Analytic Theology*, Oliver Crisp and Michael Rea call 'the philosophy of theology')[16]. Even though the editors of and contributors to both *The Oxford Handbook of Philosophical Theology* and *Analytic Theology* never mention fundamental theologians, they also approach their task as believers and in the spirit of *credo ut intelligam* (I believe in order that I might understand), and they often deal with topics that belong to fundamental theology. The first part of *The Oxford Handbook* examines themes such as revelation, tradition, and the inspiration of the Scriptures that have long belonged to the agenda of fundamental theology. *Analytic Theology* likewise includes such mainstream topics of fundamental theology as faith (which responds to revelation) and biblical inspiration, as well as human experience, a theme which some fundamental theologians (e.g. Karl Rahner) have developed and to which we return in Chapter 3 below.

This overlap between the interests of philosophical theologians and fundamental theologians should have long ago led to a fruitful dialogue between the two groups. Through their *Analytic Theology*, Crisp and Rea aim at overcoming a current 'divide' that they correctly observe to exist: namely, the divide between many *systematic* theologians and those (already numerous) analytic philosophers who are fascinated by theological issues. One should welcome this invitation to a more widespread 'interdisciplinary conversation'.[17] But there is also a conversation that should be promoted between *philosophical* theologians and *fundamental* theologians. As we have just seen, the two groups share an interest in clarifying and expounding some central beliefs. Here it is not only philosophical theologians but also fundamental theologians who should be alerted to the need to recognize and interact with those 'other' scholars who also work on some of the major topics of their discipline. The *Dictionary of Fundamental Theology*, edited by René Latourelle and Rino Fisichella, included an entry on the 'Philosophy of Religion' by Salvatore Spera.[18] But neither Spera nor any other contributor to this major dictionary discussed philosophical theology as such or even seemed to be

---

[16] O. D. Crisp and M. C. Rea (eds.), *Analytic Theology: New Essays in the Philosophy of Theology* (Oxford: Oxford University Press, 2009).
[17] Ibid. 2.
[18] *DFTh* 852–68.

aware of its continued existence and growing strength.[19] Fundamental theologians and philosophical theologians need to discover each other. They share much common ground and should be accepted and even welcome partners.

Along with the overlap between philosophical theology and fundamental theology, one should also observe some differences. The former discipline tends to be speculative and not empirical. The latter discipline often deals with questions of fact: for instance, the evidence for the life and activity of Jesus, as well as for his resurrection from the dead. Philosophical theology *also* takes up topics that do not belong to the agenda of fundamental theology. For example, philosophical theologians have recently dedicated much attention to the precise nature of divine omnipotence, to God's foreknowledge of what human beings will freely do, and to the relationship between the divine and human minds of Christ—topics that fundamental theologians do not treat. *The Oxford Handbook of Philosophical Theology* includes chapters on themes that likewise lie outside the scope of fundamental theology such as: morality and divine authority, the Trinity, original sin, atonement, and the Eucharist.

This contemporary work by philosophical theologians (or theological philosophers) illustrates splendidly the conviction of Karl Rahner, a conviction that goes back to Aquinas, Anselm of Canterbury (*c.* 1033–1109), and even to Justin Martyr (a second-century philosopher turned theologian and Christian apologist), that philosophy 'is an inner moment of theology'.[20] In recent times theologically minded philosophers have been drawn to some of the central beliefs studied by systematic or dogmatic theology. These philosophers have set themselves not only (a) to show how these beliefs are not logically incoherent and can be supported by various evidential considerations, but also (b) to

---

[19] In an essay 'How Philosophical Theology Became Possible within the Analytic Tradition of Philosophy', in Crisp and Rea (eds.), *Analytic Theology*, Nicholas Wolterstorff remarks: 'never since the Middle Ages has philosophical theology so flourished as it has during the past thirty years' (155–68, at 165).

[20] K. Rahner, 'Philosophy and Theology', *Theological Investigations*, vi, trans. K.-H. Kruger and B. Kruger (London: Darton, Longman & Todd, 1969), 71–81, at 80. Rahner anticipates here what the suggestive subtitle (*The Philosophy of Theology*) chosen by Crisp and Rea conveys: philosophy belongs to theological reflection and enjoys its proper place *within* theology.

explore intellectually, with due respect to the ineffable mystery of God, some aspects of these beliefs.

A spectacular example of (b) comes from the revival of interest in 'middle knowledge' (*scientia media*), a theory first developed by Luis de Molina (1535–1600) to reconcile authentic human freedom with the gifts of divine grace and God's foreknowledge of everything that will happen. He proposed that God knows and takes into account decisions that rational creatures would freely make in any situation in which they might be placed. Molina called it 'middle knowledge', because it is more than knowing mere possibilities but less than a vision of actual future events. Since the 1970s, Alvin Plantinga (b. 1932) and other analytic philosophers have revived interest in and stirred up fresh debate about Molina's theory.[21] It was through studying and teaching the doctrine of divine grace, a central theme for dogmatic or systematic theology, that Molina himself came to develop his (philosophical) views about God's foreknowledge.

Dogmatic/systematic theology

This last example brings us to dogmatic theology and systematic theology and the distinction to be drawn between them and fundamental theology. *Dogmatic* theology, often seen to be the chief branch of theology, draws on Scripture and tradition to examine and present coherently all the major doctrines of Christian faith. In that sense it comes across as a fully deployed expansion of the creeds confessed at worship. In modern times, it was Karl Barth (1886–1968) who stood out for his vast work in dogmatic theology: *The Church Dogmatics*. The first volume appeared in 1932, but this monumental treatment of Christian dogmas was still incomplete at his death.[22]

Since it also aims to present the main Christian doctrines in a coherent and scholarly fashion, *systematic theology often coincides in practice with dogmatic theology. But it may differ by including a treatment of moral issues. It may also differ by paying more attention to methodology, the use of philosophical principles, and other such

---

[21] See e.g. T. P. Flint, *Divine Providence: The Molinist Account* (Ithaca, NY: Cornell University Press, 1998).

[22] K. Barth, *Church Dogmatics*, 13 vols., trans. G. T. Thompson et al. (Edinburgh: T. & T. Clark, 1936–69).

fundamental issues as revelation and the human condition that shape the conditions for the possibility of receiving revelation. Paul Tillich included such fundamental issues in his *Systematic Theology*.[23]

Some years later Wolfhart Pannenberg published the three volumes of his *Systematic Theology* (German original 1988–93).[24] This outstanding work differs from normal systematic or dogmatic theology through its persistent appeal to critical rationality. Pannenberg does not want to distinguish between fundamental theology and systematic theology, as if 'the former has to confirm the credibility of the Christian revelation, the latter to unfold its content'. He finds this 'division of labour' unjustified, and asks: 'does not an unfolding of the content of Christian teaching inevitably involve the question of its truth and true significance?' 'Dogmatics' as systematic theology should 'also argue on behalf of the doctrinal content that it unfolds and confirm its truth'.[25]

Pannenberg, who has always defended theology's role in the general marketplace of human ideas, repeatedly argues for doctrines on philosophical and anthropological grounds as well as defending and expounding them as reasonable conclusions from 'historical facts' construed in revelatory terms. In his *Systematic Theology* and other writings, he has frequently tackled questions of fundamental theology (e.g. the nature of the human condition, the historical character of God's self-revelation, and the truth of Christ's resurrection). The tone and manner of Pannenberg's arguments often align him with fundamental theologians and apologists, who are bent on showing that Christian faith and its basic beliefs are publicly reasonable and credible. Thus, at times the way in which Pannenberg, like Tillich, has done his systematic theology illustrates an overlap with fundamental theology.

Natural theology

One should complete this 'mapping' exercise by introducing a further term, *natural theology*. In passing, Wainwright uses it synonymously

[23] P. Tillich, *Systematic Theology*, 3 vols. (Chicago: Chicago University Press, 1951–63).

[24] W. Pannenberg, *Systematic Theology*, trans. G. W. Bromiley, 3 vols. (Grand Rapids, Mich.: Eerdmans, 1991–8).

[25] Ibid. i. 20; see further 48–61.

with the philosophy of religion.[26] But can it be simply understood that way?

As contrasted with 'revealed theology' (which accepts and examines the witness to revelation that warrants such beliefs as those in the Trinity and the incarnation), natural theology deals with the knowledge of God's existence and nature available through the light of human reason. Reflecting on human beings (and, in particular, their higher faculties of intellect and will) and on the whole created universe in its beauty and order, those who practise natural theology aim to establish truths about the being of God and about human beings in their relationship to God. In doing this, they appeal to ordinary 'sources' (the generally available data of the world) and employ ordinary 'means' (the power of the human intellect).

Encouraged by such biblical passages as Wisdom 13: 1–9, Romans 1: 18–23, and Psalm 19: 1 ('the heavens declare the glory of God; the heavens proclaim the work of God's hands'), Christian thinkers elaborated natural theology long before the term itself came into wide use. Thus Thomas Aquinas held that some truths about God could be established on the basis of unaided reason. Following Francis Bacon and his *Advancement of Learning* (1603), exponents of natural theology, especially in England, developed the 'two books' tradition: the book of God's word (the Bible) and the book of God's works. They understood the Scriptures and nature to be distinct but complementary sources for our knowledge of God.

From the time of the Enlightenment, when the validity of traditional arguments for God's existence came under fire, non-believers challenged natural theology. Much later, Karl Barth and some other Christian theologians, retrieving positions developed by Protestant Reformers in the sixteenth century, vigorously excluded any kind of natural theology, arguing that sin had made unaided human reason simply incapable of knowing God. Mostly natural theology has been practised by such Christian believers as William Paley (1743–1805), who shaped natural theology in the English-speaking world. Even if they set to one side what they knew through revelation, nevertheless, they raised questions about God only because they were already familiar with the answers. Apropos of the human relationship to

---

[26] Wainwright (ed.), *Oxford Handbook of Philosophy of Religion*, 4.

God, an approach shaped by 'purely natural' theology presents an abstract, philosophical view of humanity—quite different from the concrete view of sinful humanity found in the biblical history of salvation and the theologies that draw on that history.

In his *Christian Theology: An Introduction*, Alister McGrath dedicates some pages to the scope and limits of natural theology.[27] Arguing that only Christians have the 'right' way of seeing nature, he subsequently published *The Open Secret: A New Vision for Natural Theology*.[28] His Gifford Lectures for 2009[29] took up the origins of life, the 'directionality of evolution', and an updated form of 'natural theology'. For his 2009–10 Hulsean Lectures at the University of Cambridge, he chose the general theme of 'Darwinism and the Divine Evolutionary Thought and Natural Theology', and dedicated his sixth and final lecture to 'Darwinism and the Future of Natural Theology'.

While McGrath and others[30] continue to endorse the practice of natural theology, it remains, like the philosophy of religion, distinct from fundamental theology. The latter does not set faith aside (as natural theology, despite being called natural *theology*, has normally been understood to do), but remains an exercise of 'faith seeking understanding' (in the spirit of Anselm, Aquinas, Barth, and many others).[31] Moreover, as we shall see in a moment, fundamental theology takes up a much wider agenda than simply truths about God, the world, and the human condition that may be available through the 'natural' powers of thought.

---

[27] (4th edn. Oxford: Blackwell, 2007), 159–70.

[28] Oxford: Blackwell, 2008.

[29] A. McGrath, *A Fine-Tuned Universe: The Quest for God in Science and Theology* (Louisville, Ky.: Westminster John Knox, 2009); see also N. Ormerod, 'Charles Taylor and Bernard Lonergan on Natural Theology', *Irish Theological Quarterly*, 74 (2009), 419–33; A. Padgett, '"Theologia Naturalis"; Philosophy of Religion or Doctrine of Creation?', *Faith and Philosophy*, 21 (2004), 493–502; Pannenberg, 'Natural Theology', in *Systematic Theology*, i. 73–118.

[30] Michael Sudduth has much to say about natural theology in 'The Contribution of Religious Experience to Dogmatic Theology', in Crisp and Rea (eds.), *Analytic Theology*, 214–32; Sandra Menssen and Thomas D. Sullivan push the claims of natural theology in *The Agnostic Inquirer: Revelation from a Philosophical Standpoint* (Grand Rapids, Mich.: Eerdmans, 2007), 22–30, 44–61.

[31] In the expression 'natural theology', the term 'theo-logy' usually means 'thinking/talking about God', and this 'neutral' stance brings it close to the philosophy of religion.

My main misgiving about natural theology is that the term could readily suggest that drawing conclusions about the existence and nature of God from the created universe is a merely natural exercise of unaided human reason. Beyond question, the active presence of the risen Christ and his Holy Spirit need not be consciously felt, but in a wide variety of ways this presence *is extended to everyone*.[32] Right from the beginning, God has freely called all men and women to the supernatural destiny of eternal life; that call affects every human act, including the activity of reflecting on the knowledge of God available through created reality. In that sense, while they may not be aware of this, those who practise 'natural theology' are always engaged with 'supernatural theology'.

Themes for fundamental theology

As its name suggests, fundamental theology studies foundational or basic issues. These have frequently included: (1) the revelation of God in the history of Israel and Jesus Christ; (2) the conditions that open human beings (in particular, their experience in its deepest aspects) to accepting in faith the self-communication of God; (3) the testimony that puts us into contact with the ministry, death, and resurrection of Christ and that makes faith in and through him a credible option; (4) the transmission (through tradition and the inspired Scriptures) of the experience of God's self-communication; (5) the founding and mission of the Christian Church; (6) questions about theological knowledge and methods, including issues arising from the interpretation of texts. Some exponents of fundamental theology have also (7) rightly attended to world religions, their claims, the reasonable credentials that commend them to their followers, and the impact on them of the risen Christ and his Holy Spirit.

Obviously issue (1) presupposes some (limited) knowledge of God. Otherwise how could anyone have reacted to certain events by accepting in faith that it was God who had spoken and acted—for instance, through the Old Testament prophets and pre-eminently through Jesus Christ? Traditionally, however, theological reflection

---

[32] See G. O'Collins, *Salvation for All: God's Other Peoples* (Oxford: Oxford University Press, 2008), 206–29.

on God preceded fundamental theology and was dealt with under the rubric of the 'preambles of faith'.[33] But was this satisfactory?

Reading *The Oxford Handbook of Philosophical Theology* has raised for me some questions about expanding further the programme for fundamental theology: does some study of the divine existence and attributes and of God's activity in creation belong to the curriculum of fundamental theology? Before reflecting on the historical revelation of God, should those who engage in fundamental theology take up such questions as: how might the eternal God be revealed in time? What might one say in reply to those for whom the existence of horrendous evil rules out the very existence of God?

Such reflections on 'God-questions' could well follow the lead of the *Oxford Handbook* and also pay some attention to the science and religion debate that Richard Dawkins and other contemporary atheists have kept vigorously alive. Chapters by Del Ratzsch ('Science and Religion') and Robin Collins ('Divine Action and Evolution') offer guidelines for a contemporary programme of fundamental theology.[34] In short, practitioners of philosophical theology might be pleased to find one valuable consequence of their discipline being heard and appropriated by fundamental theologians: the question of God should take its place on the agenda for fundamental theology.

This chapter has sorted out differences between fundamental theology and five related disciplines (apologetics, philosophy of religion, philosophical theology, dogmatic/systematic theology, and natural theology). It has also listed eight major themes that should find their place on programmes for fundamental theology. We move now to questions about God, the first major theme for fundamental theologians.

A coda: the contribution of Bernard Lonergan

In sorting out the distinctive character of fundamental theology and the themes that shape or should shape its proper identity, one should

---

[33] See J. P. Whalen and T. Horvath, 'Preambles of Faith', in *New Catholic Encyclopedia*, xi (2nd edn. Farmington Hills, Mich.: Gale, 2003), 635–6.

[34] Flint and Rea (eds.), *The Oxford Handbook of Philosophical Theology*, 54–77, 241–61, respectively.

also recall the contribution of Bernard Lonergan (1904–84). Rightly dissatisfied with the 'old [nineteenth-century] fundamental theology', he developed what he called a 'fifth functional specialty, foundations', which followed four other specialities (research, interpretation, history, and dialectic). Instead of reflecting on a set of doctrines, Lonergan's 'foundations' present 'the horizon within which the meaning of doctrines' can be apprehended. His foundations promise to elucidate 'conflicts revealed' in 'dialectic' and provide a principle to 'guide the remaining specialties', concerned, respectively, with doctrines, systematics, and communications.[35] When dealing with theological styles and methods, the final chapter of my book will appropriate some of Lonergan's thought on historical consciousness and conversion.

---

[35] B. J. F. Lonergan, *Method in Theology* (orig. edn. 1972; Minneapolis: Winston Press, 1979), 131–2; see further on 'foundations', 267–93. For what Lonergan understands by 'horizons' and 'dialectic', see ibid. 235–7 ('horizons') and 235–66 ('dialectic').

2

Faith in a Personal God

Before moving to examine what it means to say that God is revealed, above all in Jesus Christ, and that, through experiencing the self-disclosed God, human beings can come to faith, one needs to pause and reflect on the existence and attributes of God. By definition, Christian, Jewish, and Muslim believers accept the existence of a personal God who has entered into a relationship with them and with the communities to which they belong. Many of them would add that their faith does not lack rational support; there are good reasons for thinking that God exists. But many of them are also aware of the challenges to their faith. Where was God in Auschwitz? Where was God in the Tsunami of Christmas 2004? Has modern science made belief in God obsolete? Or worse, are faith in God and religious practice not only irrational but also socially and morally destructive? Is the very concept of an all-powerful, all-good, and all-knowing God coherent in itself?[1]

The God-question raises a vast repertoire of issues. Let me set myself the modest task of sketching some of the issues that fundamental theologians may have to tackle before they reflect on

---

[1] For an initial account of such difficulties against faith in God, see John Cottingham, *Why Believe?* (London: Continuum, 2009); and David Ferguson, *Faith and its Critics: A Conversation* (Oxford: Oxford University Press, 2009); E. Reitan, *Is God a Delusion? A Reply to Religion's Cultural Despisers* (Chichester: Wiley-Blackwell, 2009).

the human condition and the divine self-communication in the history of Israel and Jesus Christ. The context and country in which they work can make one or more of these issues an important priority. In any case they should use all the philosophical expertise available. Once they have built long-term relationships with philosophers, fundamental theologians will be in a position to capitalize on growth in philosophical theology. It can prove one of their greatest assets towards articulating a vision of God.

Five questions shape this chapter. What account do believers give of the essential attributes of God? Does the existence of horrendous evil provide a decisive reason for doubting or simply denying the existence of God? What account might believers give of God's activity in the world? How do believers describe or even explain the grounds for their faith in God? In what contexts do they approach the God-question?

The divine attributes

In the light of biblical faith and the Christian tradition, leading thinkers like Thomas Aquinas elaborated an orderly account of the divine attributes: in particular, God is eternal, totally spiritual (or non-material), truly and fully personal, and possessed of unlimited power (omnipotent), perfect goodness, and unlimited knowledge (omniscient).[2] Such a divine Being must be considered worthy of unconditional admiration, praise, and worship on the part of human beings.

Some believers highlight two characteristics of God, as being 'beyond' (transcendent) and 'within' (immanent). A friend of mine, Peter Steele, speaks of a 'strangeness beyond description' and a 'nearness beyond denying'. God is the Stranger 'beyond strangeness'

[2] On the attributes of God, see W. L. Rowe, 'Divine Power, Goodness and Knowledge', in W. J. Wainwright (ed.), *The Oxford Handbook of Philosophy of Religion* (New York: Oxford University Press, 2005), 15–34; W. L. Rowe and W. J. Wainwright (eds.), *Philosophy of Religion* (3rd edn. New York: Oxford University Press, 2002); and J. E. Brower et al., 'The Divine Attributes', in T. P. Flint and M. C. Rea (eds.), *The Oxford Handbook of Philosophical Theology* (Oxford: Oxford University Press, 2009), 105–238.

but also the very air we breathe, and the fountain of all life. The closing section of Chapter 4 below will retrieve something of the Old Testament's sense of God as being mysteriously other and, simultaneously, intimately close: in other words, of the 'coincidence' of the divine transcendence and immanence.

The attributes of God raise numerous questions and difficulties that deserve attention, especially from those with a philosophical cast of mind. Take, for instance, issues raised by space and time and the creation of a spatial, temporal universe. How can a totally spiritual, non-spatial Being who cannot be measured create—that is to say, make out of nothing—a material, spatial universe that we measure in many ways? Then, if God is eternal and has no beginning and no end (or, if one likes, has a 'past' without beginning and a 'future' without end), how can such a Being produce a world that exists 'in time'? Here some philosophers maintain that, while being eternal or ever-lasting, God does not exist 'outside time'. Whatever particular position they adopt, the 'gap' between the space-time universe and a Creator by nature non-spatial and eternal continues to attract the attention of philosophers. This gap may require attention also from fundamental theologians, when they write about a spiritual and eternal God revealed within a world of space and time.

The omniscient attribute of God throws up at least one persistent puzzle, and this too may need to figure on the agenda for fundamental theology. If the omniscient God knows 'in advance' what human beings will freely do—for instance, in deciding to accept in faith or decline in disbelief the divine self-revelation—does this 'foreknowledge' rule out genuine human freedom? Do we have to choose between (1) human freedom and (2) a divine 'foreknowledge' that directs God's providential ordering of the world's affairs? Some Christians and other believers hold that God determines 'in advance' what human beings will decide and do; hence the divine knowledge about their actions is simply based on 'predetermining decrees'. But for those who decline this conclusion as incompatible with a human freedom that is genuinely self-determining, what position presents the best credentials and the most convincing solution?[3]

---

[3] See T. P. Flint, 'Divine Providence', in Flint and Rea (eds.), *The Oxford Handbook of Philosophical Theology*, 262–85; Flint outlines skilfully the advantages and disadvantages of three main positions, while personally endorsing one

Lastly, those who believe in God as being all-good, all-powerful, and all-knowing must reckon with these three divine attributes appearing to be incompatible with the presence of horrendous evil in our world. Does such evil rule out the very existence of God? Can we reconcile faith in God with the terrible evils that afflict human beings—in particular, innocent human beings? Many writers point out, of course, how much of this evil comes from the misuse of created freedom. Yet human beings, even when they commit the most monstrous acts of evil, depend on God from moment to moment for their continued existence. Nevertheless, if God constantly overrode their evil decisions or miraculously prevented such decisions from having the desired effect, this would make a travesty of these agents enjoying authentic freedom. If God equips them with freedom, he should respect their relative autonomy, even when used in a thoroughly evil way.

Apologists have frequently argued that God (for mysterious, 'higher' reasons) allows such evil to happen but does not directly commit it. In cases where innocent people suffer atrociously for seemingly no good reason, apologists have pressed the argument that, whereas non-believers cannot point to any positive reasons for such suffering and leave us to face 'absurd' evil, believers can hope that in their future life with God they will be provided with an explanation. Here and now, Christian believers can point to the passion and death of Christ, which do not solve intellectually the problem of evil but provide a powerful motive and a model for accepting unmerited suffering.[4] (Chapter 6 below will attend in detail to 'the Crucified Revealer', or the identity of God revealed in the crucifixion of Jesus.) In any case, those who want to 'explain' such painful mysteries as the dreadful suffering of innocent persons may be like Job's friends in arrogantly claiming to enjoy a 'God's eye' view of things.[5]

---

solution, that of God's 'middle knowledge' (which was briefly described in Ch. 1 above).

[4] See M. McCord Adams, *Horrendous Evil and the Goodness of God* (Ithaca, NY: Cornell University Press, 1999); id., *Christ and Horrors: The Coherence of Christology* (Cambridge: Cambridge University Press, 2006).

[5] See D. H. Burrell, *Deconstructing Theodicy: Why Job has Nothing to Say to the Problem of Suffering* (Grand Rapids, Mich.: Brazos, 2008).

Here it would be too much to expect fundamental theologians to master all the arguments and counter-arguments. But whenever and wherever the problem of evil and issues of theodicy (or the vindication of God's loving providence in view of the existence of evil) come up, they can invoke the help of various philosophers. Once they have built strong ties with philosophical theologians, they can work closely and cooperatively with them.[6]

Special divine activity

Chapters 4, 5, and 6 of this book will focus on God's self-revelation in biblical history. Claims about the special revealing activity of God obviously require some account of how such activity is possible or at least not blatantly incoherent. How might God cause certain self-disclosing things to happen in our world: e.g. by speaking through a prophet, providentially guiding some events, bringing about a miracle (or something that cannot be explained through the working of ordinary causality), being present in Christ in a qualitatively unique way, bringing about his resurrection from the dead, and inspiring the writing of Sacred Scriptures? (What is developed here under the heading of 'Special divine activity' will be taken further when discussing 'special acts of God' in the section on 'Word and Event' in Chapter 4 below.)

Western thinking about divine causality, or the active relations between God and the world, have been deeply affected for several centuries by the deist worldview, which—expressed in terms of the modern Big Bang theory—would mean that God created the universe and put it on automatic pilot about 13.7 billion years ago. That would mean that no specific divine action lies behind any particular occurrence. There would be only one (initial and ongoing) divine act and

---

[6] See M. Bergmann, 'Skeptical Theism and the Problem of Evil', in Flint and Rea (eds.), *The Oxford Handbook of Philosophical Theology*, 374–99; P. Draper, 'The Problem of Evil', ibid. 332–51; P. van Inwagen, 'The Problem of Evil', in Wainwright (ed.), *Oxford Handbook of Philosophy of Religion*, 188–219; S. Menssen and T. D. Sullivan, *The Agnostic Enquirer: Revelation from a Philosophical Standpoint* (Grand Rapids, Mich.: Eerdmans, 2007), 123–70; K. J. Murray, 'Theodicy', in Flint and Rea (eds.), *The Oxford Handbook of Philosophical Theology*, 353–73.

no divine sub-acts, whether miraculous or providential. What if we reject this reduction of divine causality to one initial act and insist on maintaining infinitely many, divine sub-acts, which would include both 'extraordinary' sub-acts like the call of the Jewish people, the incarnation, Jesus' miracles, and his resurrection, and the 'ordinary' sub-acts that constitute the exercise of God's providence, according to the normal laws of the universe, in the lives of every individual? How might we conceive the divine interaction, whether ordinary or extraordinary, with all the physical objects, living beings, and human beings that make up the created realm?[7]

First things first: since the time of David Hume (1711–76), the difficulty of establishing causal connections and offering causal explanations has at times been exaggerated.[8] Even if it can be hard to trace many effects back to their causes and to analyse successfully the nature of causation itself, nevertheless, we can demonstrate some causal ties and say something about causation.

How then might we conceive divine causality in general? This question must be considered once we name Christ's incarnation and resurrection as the supremely self-revealing divine acts. To begin with, we should part company with those who would present God simply as a cause or even 'the' cause among other causes. God's action is not an action alongside other (created) actions. Events caused by God are not simply events alongside other (created) events. Between the divine first cause (and the way it produces effects) and secondary causes there is far more difference than likeness. Let me name three differences.

1. Unlike created, secondary causes, God is neither spatial nor temporal. Nevertheless, while being timeless, or eternal and non-

---

[7] See P. Gwynne, *Special Divine Action: Key Issues in the Contemporary Debate (1965–1995)* (Rome: Gregorian University Press, 1996); S. W. Holtzer, 'The Possibility of Incorporeal Agency', in W. J. Abraham and S. W. Holtzer (eds.), *The Rationality of Religious Belief: Essays in Honour of Basil Mitchell* (Oxford: Clarendon Press, 1987), 189–209; N. Murphy, 'Natural Science', in J. Webster, K. Tanner, and I. Torrance (eds.), *The Oxford Handbook of Systematic Theology* (Oxford: Oxford University Press, 2007), 543–60; T. F. Tracy, 'Theologies of Divine Action', in P. Clayton and Z. Simpson (eds.), *The Oxford Handbook of Religion and Science* (Oxford: Oxford University Press, 2006), 596–611.
[8] See R. J. Read and K. A. Richman (eds.), *The New Hume Debate* (London: Routledge, 2000).

spatial, God is intimately related to time and present to space as the inmost ground of all being.[9]

2. After its creation, the world remains radically dependent on God. At every moment, God is responsible for the world's persistence and continually active in sustaining in existence the things that have been created. Neither the entire universe not anything within it is or can be fundamentally self-sustaining. Unsupported by God, things cannot continue in existence, just as they could not in the first place bring themselves into existence.

3. What follows then for created, secondary causes, if from moment to moment they all fundamentally depend upon God's active support for their continued existence? They have only a relative autonomy, and can operate only if directly supported by God. Even if they possess and exercise causal powers proper to them, God is necessarily and intimately involved in their activity. Hence, every effect and every phenomenon in the world has God as its primary and first cause. We would be wildly astray, then, if we pictured uncreated and created activity as the operation of two quite separate agents.

All of this means that the self-revealing God must be conceived of as a radically different kind of agent from created agents. At times the Bible puts together God and human beings as co-responsible for some decision and/or action (e.g. Acts 1: 15–26; 15: 28). In the practice of their religious faith, believers think of themselves as being in personal interaction with God: in their prayer, in the enlightening and life-giving thoughts that come to them, and in the providential ordering of their lives. But, just as divine causality is radically unlike any created causality, so God is a very different kind of agent from ourselves.

Above, we noted how God is timeless (or beyond any temporal succession) and non-spatial, that is to say, incorporeal and immaterial. When we add further divine attributes and recognize God as being all-powerful, all-knowing, and all-perfect, we may well ask ourselves: what kind of action concepts apply to such an agent? How many of our notions about personal, human actions and their

---

[9] For some of the issues connected with these claims, see W. L. Craig, 'Divine Eternity', in Flint and Rea (eds.), *The Oxford Handbook of Philosophical Theology*, 145–66; and H. Hudson, 'Omnipresence', ibid. 199–216.

mechanism can we transfer to God? When, for example, we do something in the external world (as opposed to doing something in our minds), bodily movements come into play. Such activity outside ourselves does not promise to be very enlightening about the actions of God, who is incorporeal.

We may find more help from two analogies, the first at the intra-personal level—from the way our mind or conscious centre controls our bodily actions. To observe how 'the mental' affects and guides the material need not mean lapsing into the dualistic explanation of the mind–body relationship offered by Descartes, as if the human soul were an immaterial substance controlling a machine-like body. Our analogy simply suggests that divine action could be seen to be something like human action within a human agent, something like the interaction of mind–brain or mind–body within a human person. We experience ourselves as agents when our thoughts affect our bodies—an experience that offers an 'intimate' analogy to God's action on us and our world.

The other analogy that promises to throw light on the divine action can be drawn from the interpersonal sphere: from the way human beings, often unconsciously and even very mysteriously, have influences on one another. The various impacts of human persons on other human persons, especially those of a loving and life-giving kind, could offer some images of action that might be transferred, in a cautious and qualified way, to God and the divine actions.

A further general issue concerns the great variety of divine actions in human history to which the Bible bears witness. How is it possible for the supreme Being (who is both beyond time and space and is the intimate ground of all being) to be 'more' or differently engaged 'here' rather than 'there'? In any case, how could we tell that this supreme Being is 'more' engaged in this or that particular slice of space and time? The chance of answering both questions positively opens up once we admit that love and freedom radically characterize God's exercise of causality. The personal spontaneity of love allows for endless variation in the God–world relationship and, in particu-lar, for effects that are qualitatively distinct from God's 'ordinary' work in creating and then sustaining creation. We can know God to have acted in special ways, when the events or effects (e.g. Jesus' new life after death) differ from what would normally have happened otherwise (e.g. Jesus' remaining dead and his body corrupting in the tomb). The quality and nature of the effects point to God's special activity.

Thus far I have been stating, rather than offering any detailed argument for, positions I hold on divine causality. What, then, of the divine acts in biblical history? Here *three principles* may help to clarify matters a little.

First, both in biblical history and in general it is easier to grasp and talk about effects rather than causes. The effects are usually obvious; causes and their precise nature can remain shadowy and to a degree mysterious. The Jewish people, for example, understood and lived their call, the deliverance from Egypt, the Sinai covenant, the Mosaic law, the Sabbath rest, the institution of kingship, various religious feasts, their holy Scriptures, the challenges of the prophets, the return from Babylonian exile, and much else besides, as all coming from God. When they experienced these realities, they took them to be effects of God's activity on their behalf. From the effects, including their very existence as the chosen people, they knew in faith the divine cause. Their early creeds show how the Israelites gave a causal explanation to specific features of their history, naming God as the agent, even if the precise way God brought these things about remained mysterious (e.g. Josh. 24: 2–13; Deut. 26: 5–11).

For us today the question clearly arises: do we correctly explain the history of the chosen people if we name God's special activity on their behalf as the major cause of that history? However, my point here is not to mount arguments to bolster the plausibility of this reading of Israel's story. Rather, it is simply to use examples from biblical history to illustrate how effects are clearer than causes, especially when it is a matter of claiming the presence of special divine activity.

An even more basic example than those from biblical history is creation itself. We see innumerable kinds of created reality every day. But we never directly observe the cause of this effect, the very act of creation and conservation. At best, we see God's creative action only in and though the effects. The Book of Genesis beautifully symbolizes this point by speaking of Adam being plunged into 'a deep sleep', so that he would not observe the creation of Eve (Gen. 2: 21–2).

Second, the traditional adage that 'every agent brings about something similar to itself' (*omne agens agit sibi simile*) reminds us that efficient causes are also 'exemplary' causes. Effects reflect the characteristics or properties of their causes, and these characteristics can serve to identify causes. Children resemble parents, not only through their common humanity but also genetically and in other ways. In their colour, shape, and scent, new roses will take after the bushes from which they have been grown. Causes leave their 'impression' on their effects. They are present in their effects, which 'participate' in them. Hence, the observer can recognize the imprint and image of the cause in its effect(s).

Applied to God, this means that whatever is brought about will resemble and reflect its divine cause. God leaves a divine impression on all creation and, above all, on created human beings (see Gen. 1: 27). God is always and necessarily present in whatever is created. All the divine effects, albeit in varying ways and degrees, participate in God and share the divine life.

Israelite history illustrates a third principle or characteristic of divine activity. God's different acts on behalf of the chosen people took place with a view to a future completion. Together they formed a dynamic movement towards a final goal, a progressive assimilation to God, which aimed at the fullest possible participation in the divine life. To be sure, God often had to write straight with crooked lines. Human freedom and human dissidents saw to that. Nevertheless, God's acts were/are never disconnected, still less arbitrary. Paul can read a final unity in God's ceaseless activity for the salvation of Jews and Gentiles (Rom. 9–11), even if the apostle must admit deep mystery in the unfolding story (Rom. 11: 33–5). Israel's special history wrote large what spiritually sensitive and committed people continue to experience. God's providential activity for each one moves progressively towards a final goal: the fullest possible assimilation to God and participation in the divine presence.

These three principles set the stage for what Chapters 4, 5, and 6 will present about the special, self-revealing activity of God in biblical history. Here I speak of 'activity' (special or otherwise) and wish to avoid the language of divine 'interventions', a terminology still used by many theologians and philosophers alike.[10] For those who recall military 'interventions' in various parts of the world, that language

---

[10] See e.g. how R. Collins can take for granted the terminology of 'interventionist' and 'non-interventionist' accounts of divine action: 'Divine Action and Evolution', in Flint and Rea (eds.), *The Oxford Handbook of Philosophical Theology*, 241–2.

can too easily suggest a kind of 'meddlesome' God, who prior to the intervention was an 'outsider' and now comes actively on the scene for the first time. But, as we stated above, God is always intimately present everywhere and in every situation, from moment to moment sustaining in being everything that is and standing behind/under every effect as its primary or first cause.

The climax of the special history of divine self-revelation came with the resurrection of the crucified Jesus. It served pre-eminently to illustrate the three principles of God's activity enunciated above. (What is said here will be taken further in Chapter 6 below, 'The Crucified and Resurrected Revealer'.)

First of all, Mary Magdalene, Peter, and the other Easter witnesses saw the primary and immediate 'effect of the resurrection' appearing to them, the living Jesus himself. They gave their causal explanation, 'he has been raised', but never claimed either to have witnessed the divine cause in action (the very event of the resurrection) or to understand how it worked in itself. In faith, they knew the cause, the resurrecting power of God, but unlike the effect that cause remained shrouded in mystery.

Second, in the resurrection, the divine agent brought about something *sibi simile*. God's resurrecting power left its impression on the effect, Jesus' raised and glorified humanity. In his transformed human existence Jesus became even more like unto God, as the Son in whom one can recognize even more fully the image of his Father (see Rom. 1: 3–4; Col. 1: 15). His risen humanity reflects and resembles to the ultimate extent possible its divine cause. In the highest degree imaginable, through his risen life he participates in God (see Rom. 6: 10).

Finally, the third principle we detected in divine activity toward human beings is realized par excellence in the case of Jesus' resurrection. From the incarnation on, God's action formed a dynamic movement towards its future completion: Christ's full participation in the divine presence when he sits at God's 'right hand' (e.g. Rom. 8: 34) and subjects all things to God (1 Cor. 15: 20–8).

When dealing with the attributes of God and the account of them given by believers, I threw a spotlight on divine causality. I did this because of the negligible role that reflection on God's activity has played in recent fundamental theology. Yet such reflection needs to engage the attention of fundamental theologians who want to think through the implications of their claims that certain events and words reveal God in a special way. But what of the very existence of God?

The existence of God

Reflection on reasons for accepting the existence of a personal God normally come from those who already believe in God. In this sense, they exemplify the statement put in the mouth of God by Blaise Pascal: 'you would not seek me if you had not found me.'[11] Gifted already with faith in God, believers consider why such faith is credible. Far from replacing belief, their arguments for the reasonableness of belief in God arise from a prior faith in and experience of God. Centuries before Pascal, Augustine, who echoed Isaiah 65: 1 (also cited in Rom. 10: 20), said of God: 'He has searched for you before you search for him; and he has found you so that you will find him' (*quaesivit vos antequam quaereretis eum; et invenit vos ut inveniretis eum*) (*Enarrationes in Psalmos*, 138. 14).[12]

What we read in Pascal and Augustine lends plausibility to the 'ontological argument', a way of 'demonstrating' the existence of God developed by Anselm of Canterbury (*c*.1033–1109). Since what we mean by God is 'that which nothing greater can be conceived' (*id quo nihil majus cogitari possit*), the very idea of God requires that God really exists. Otherwise we would be involved in a contradiction, being able to imagine 'something greater than God'—namely, a God who exists. Thomas Aquinas, Immanuel Kant, and others have rejected the argument for moving fallaciously from the level of mere thought to that of actual existence. Other philosophers, however, in various ways have defended the argument. More recently some have claimed that, instead of being a 'proof', the ontological argument simply explicates the (implicit) knowledge of God we already possess.[13]

---

[11] *Pascal Pensées*, trans. A. J. Krailsheimer (Harmondsworth: Penguin, 1966), 314; numbered 919 in this edition, this *Pensée* is numbered 553 in some other editions.
[12] See also Augustine, *Confessions*, 10. 18 and 20.
[13] See W. Abraham, 'Systematic Theology as Analytic Theology', in O. D. Crisp and M. C. Rea (eds.), *Analytic Theology: New Essays in the Philosophy of Theology*

In the 'Five Ways', set out in his *Summa Theologiae*, Thomas Aquinas produced the most famous set of arguments for God's existence. From the fact of motion (change) in the world, the First Way infers the existence of a first Unmoved Mover. The Second Way argues from our experience of causes producing effects to an ultimate Uncaused Cause. The Third Way moves from the observed contingency of our world—neither the universe as a whole nor anything within it had to exist—to a first Necessary Cause. The Fourth Way begins with the limited grades of perfection found in the universe to arrive at a First Unlimited Cause. The Fifth Way observes our world's orderly design, which can be explained only through the purposeful activity of a divine Designer.[14]

The Five Ways were subsequently radically challenged by the work of David Hume, Immanuel Kant, and other philosophers. But in the late twentieth century many philosophers became convinced that 'Hume's and Kant's allegedly devastating criticisms of philosophical theology [including approaches to the existence of God] did not withstand careful scrutiny'.[15] (1) The cosmological arguments (First to Fourth Way) and (2) the teleological argument (Fifth Way) still offer valuable perspectives on our (limited) knowledge of God.[16]

As regards the cosmological argument (1), the Principle of Sufficient Reason requires some adequate explanation for the existence and nature of the universe. Why is there a universe in the first place? Why is there something rather than nothing?[17] Is it convincing to answer: 'it's simply there'? Does the universe bring about its own

(Oxford: Oxford University Press, 2009), 54–69, at 62–3; B. Leftow, 'The Ontological Argument', in Wainwright (ed.), *Oxford Handbook of Philosophy of Religion*, 80–115.

[14] *Summa Theologiae* I. 2. 3. See A. R. Pruss and R. M. Gale, 'Cosmological and Design Arguments', in Wainwright (ed.), *Oxford Handbook of Philosophy of Religion*, 116–37, at 118–21; J. F. Wippel, 'The Five Ways', in B. Davies (ed.), *Thomas Aquinas: Contemporary Philosophical Perspectives* (Oxford: Oxford University Press, 2002), 159–225.

[15] Wainwright, *Oxford Handbook of Philosophy of Religion*, 6; see e.g. the assessment of Kant's criticisms made by Menssen and Sullivan, *The Agnostic Inquirer*, 22–30.

[16] On both cosmological and teleological argument, see Pruss and Gale, 'Cosmological and Design Arguments'.

[17] See J. C. Lennox, *God's Undertaker: Has Science Buried God?* (Oxford: Lion Hudson, 2007), 62–4.

existence, simply popping into existence, as a massive exception to the Principle of Sufficient Reason (and any universal causal principle)? It is widely agreed that whatever comes to be has a cause distinct from itself, or—in brief—that there are no uncaused events and no self-causation. If so, can the universe be the big exception to this principle. If it is such a uniquely exceptional case, how did/does it cause itself?[18]

(2) The teleological argument moves from the orderly character of the world to claim the existence of God as the Designer and Final Cause of everything. In their different ways, Aristotle in the fourth century BC, Thomas Aquinas, and others understood the universe to reveal intelligent purposes and point to God as the final cause of all things.

After the more general challenges from Hume and Kant, the teleological argument had to face further objections when Charles Darwin (1809–92) explained biological design through the survival of the fittest and a natural selection through which present living beings developed gradually from less complex forms. Mechanistic explanations of order in the world as simply resulting from the random operations of natural forces dominated for years. For many, Darwin's alternative explanation of order as a non-designed, natural process replaced faith in God as the Designer and Final Cause of everything. Darwin or, at least, Darwinism seemed to have 'killed God'.[19] However, recent advances in astronomy, physics, and biology have shown just how massive and far-reaching is the order in a universe that has apparently existed for only a relatively brief time (since the Big Bang). The universal law of gravitation and the other laws of nature seem precisely tuned to allow for the production of life and intelligent life. Many sophisticated people have been impressed by the fine-tuning of the universe that has developed human life. The odds against such an

---

[18] See D. H. Mellor, *The Facts of Causation* (London: Routledge, 1995).

[19] On Darwin and Darwinism, see W. A. Dembski, 'In Defence of Intelligent Design', in Clayton and Simpson (eds.), *Oxford Handbook of Religion and Science*, 667–80; A. E. McGrath, 'Darwinism', ibid. 681–96; N. A. Manson (ed.), *God and Design: The Teleological Argument and Modern Science* (New York: Routledge, 2003); W. B. Provine, 'Evolution, Religion, and Science', in Clayton and Simpson (eds.), *Oxford Handbook of Religion and Science*, 557–80; J. P. Schloss, 'Evolutionary Theory and Religious Belief', ibid. 187–206.

astonishing order emerging by mere chance give a new plausibility to the argument for a rational Designer.[20]

This is not to exclude a theory of biological evolution in some form; doing that would help perpetuate the false idea of a widespread, long-standing, and inevitable conflict between science and religion.[21] In fact an evolutionary model offers a more admirable picture of God. Instead of constantly tinkering with things 'from the outside', God works in an evolving world 'from the inside', and with wisdom and power brings about life, higher forms of life, and eventually the emergence of human beings.[22]

In any case, a comprehensive Darwinian theory does not seem able to account for two qualitative leaps, those involved in the emergence of life and of mind. The theory supposes the existence of life, but is not able to answer the question: why do living organisms exist on the planet earth in the first place? Evolution begins to function only when the first, self-reproducing beings come on the scene; it does not explain the origin of such beings. Pruss and Gale show how 'we still do not have a reasonably probable [exclusively] scientific explanation for the origin of life'. Add to this that some scientists doubt that 'Darwinian evolution can account for all biological mechanisms... on the microscopic level we find biochemical complexity of such a degree that it could not be expected to come about through natural selection.' Moreover, how could it explain such a dramatic novelty or 'qualitatively new thing' as human intelligence?[23] How consciousness arose and why it has the particular qualities it has remain cloaked in mystery.[24]

Various interactions between the natural sciences and philosophy (and theology) characterize the legacy of Aquinas' Five Ways and any function they might enjoy today. In place of debates about the origin

---

[20] On the origins of life and the 'directionality of evolution', see the Gifford Lectures for 2009 by A. McGrath, *A Fine-Tuned Universe: The Quest for God in Science and Theology* (Louisville, Ky.: Westminster John Knox, 2009).

[21] For a brilliant rebuttal of this untruth, see R. Numbers (ed.), *Galileo Goes to Jail and Other Myths about Science and Religion* (Cambridge, Mass.: Harvard University Press, 2009).

[22] See R. Collins, 'Divine Action and Evolution', in Flint and Rea (eds.), *The Oxford Handbook of Philosophical Theology*, 241–61; T. Kelly, *Stars, Life, and Intelligence: Being a Darwinian and a Believer* (Adelaide: ATF Press, 2009).

[23] Pruss and Gale, 'Cosmological and Design Arguments', 130, 135.

[24] See Menssen and Sullivan, *The Agnostic Enquirer*, 38–40.

of the visible universe and its fine-tuned character, some point to the inner religious life of the heart as underpinning their faith. Experiences of God's closeness and even a sense of mystical union with God serve to justify and illuminate belief in an all-loving and ever present divine Being. In this context Jerome Gellman and others continue to pay particular attention to the work that Rudolf Otto (1869–1937) encouraged.[25] He set himself to describe religious impulses and feelings as they appear to those who experience them. Otto argued that religious faith originates with the numinous experience of the 'mysterium tremendum et fascinans' (the awe-inspiring and fascinating mystery).[26]

The rediscovery of Søren Kierkegaard (1813–55), the religious existentialism of Martin Buber (1878–1965) and Gabriel Marcel (1889–1973), the ethics of responsibility of Emmanuel Levinas (1906–95), a wider knowledge of Christian, Jewish, and Muslim mysticism, and the influence of Buddhist and Hindu spirituality have made such an experiential approach to faith in God an attractive option for many. Instead of reflecting on the visible world and its orderly character, they move to the inner 'country' of prayer and the heart, where they experience themselves as embraced by an intimate Presence. They know God to be closely present to them and connected with them.[27]

Gellman's chapter ends with a bibliography of works on mysticism and religious experience coming from a wide range of scholars: both classical, like Henri Bergson, William James, Evelyn Underhill, and R. C. Zaehner, and contemporary, like William Alston, Caroline Franks Davis, Bernard McGinn, and William Wainwright.[28] To these we should add the work of Sir Alister Hardy (1896–1985), the Linacre Professor of Zoology at the University of Oxford, who in 1969 founded the Religious Experience and Research Centre, now housed at the University of Wales, Lampeter. Through his Gifford Lectures on the evolution of religion delivered at the University of Aberdeen

[25] See J. L. Gellman, 'Mysticism and Religious Experience', in Wainwright (ed.), *Oxford Handbook of Philosophy of Religion*, 138–67; P. H. Wiebe, 'Religious Experience, Cognitive Science, and the Future of Religion', in Clayton and Simpson (eds.), *Oxford Handbook of Religion and Science*, 503–22.

[26] R. Otto, *The Idea of the Holy*, German orig. 1917, trans. J. W. Harvey (Harmondsworth: Penguin, 1959).

[27] See M. Sudduth, 'The Contribution of Religious Experience to Dogmatic Theology', in Crisp and Rea (eds.), *Analytic Theology*, 214–32.

[28] Gellman, 'Mysticism and Religious Experience', 163–7.

(1963–4 and 1964–5),[29] he signalled his interests and intentions. His centre put together a vast database of personal reports of spiritual experiences. Hardy published a preliminary account of the findings,[30] arguing that religious awareness has an objective counterpart and responds to the divine Reality. Hardy and his colleagues aimed to investigate and delineate the nature and functions of religious experiences. For those who approach the question of God through such experiences, his centre remains a valuable resource.[31] (The closing pages of our next chapter will take up again the theme of religious experience.)

Approaches to the God-question

The God-question assumes so many different forms around the world. Challenges and interests differ from continent to continent, from country to country, and from department to department. This chapter does not purport to summarize all the possibilities that we might find in the vast, global matrix of reflection on the existence and nature of God. But, in general, one might risk distinguishing three approaches.

First, many writers privilege meaning, evidence, and truth (understanding truth in terms of what we can justifiably claim to know and conclude from the evidence). What this chapter has so far sketched follows this way of raising the God-question. Are there evidential considerations that lend support to faith in God, whether the public evidence of a philosophical and scientific nature or the personal testimony derived from religious experience? In the case of the latter,

---

[29] The lectures were published as *The Living Stream: A Restatement of Evolution Theory and its Relation to the Spirit of Man* (London: Collins, 1965), and *The Divine Flame: An Essay towards a Natural History of Religion* (London: Collins, 1966).

[30] A. Hardy, *The Spiritual Nature of Man: A Study of Contemporary Religious Experience* (Oxford: Clarendon Press, 1983); he summarizes his study as showing a widespread, deep awareness of 'a benevolent, non-physical power which appears to be partly or wholly beyond, and far greater than the individual self' (1).

[31] On the work of Hardy, see D. Hay, *Something There: The Biology of the Human Spirit* (London: Darton, Longman & Todd, 2006).

many bring up the question: does religious experience have evidential value? If so, what is it?

Personal prayer and public worship provide a second, widespread setting and source for developing an account of God. Here one asks: how do prayer and worship bear witness to the experience of God and prompt it? What do we learn if we consult worshippers in matters of faith in God? Texts for worship, sacred scriptures, visual images, and religious music show us how God is experienced, rather than dispassionately described, in prayer and worship of all kinds.

A third approach to the God-question typically asks: what does faith lead believers to do, or leave undone, in the world? Does it bring something special, even unique, to the struggle for promoting the common good and relieving the massive injustice of human society? What does and could faith in God mean for the poor and suffering victims of our world? This third approach will develop its account of God with an eye on and for the sake of the millions of victimized non-persons who surround us.

Belief in God and reflection on that faith express themselves, then, as knowledge, worship, and action. Hence, apropos of faith, we can distinguish (1) faith seeking 'scientific' understanding, (2) faith seeking worship, and (3) faith seeking social justice. In all three accounts, the word 'seeking' has a significant function for believers. Faith in God seeks a knowledge and understanding that in this life will never be conclusive and exhaustive. It seeks to worship God with an adoration that will be fully realized only in the afterlife. It seeks a just society that can never completely come in this world. A proper attention to the force of 'seeking' will thus ensure that we respect the future implications for all three ways of approaching the God-question.[32]

Conclusion

The witness of the Sacred Scriptures to God's self-revelation (Chapters 4, 5, and 6 below) divulges a remarkable ensemble of religious experiences, both individual and collective. The leading protagonists

---

[32] When presenting 'three styles of theology', the final chapters of this book will develop further the three ways of approaching the God-question.

of biblical history experienced many presences, some silences, and no absences of God. They told their story of God out of what they had lived through, understood, and interpreted. Before moving to the story of the divine self-communication, this study of fundamental theology should offer some reflections on the condition of those to whom God wished and wishes to communicate. In any case, since I will persistently appeal to 'experience', I should first offer some account of what I mean by that language.

3

The Human Condition

Having reflected, provisionally, on some aspects of the doctrine of God, we need to say something about the human subject who in faith accepts the self-revealing God. Before moving to God's self-disclosure in the biblical history that climaxed with the story of Jesus, what account should we give of human beings? Some reflections on the human condition will set the stage for what follows in this account of fundamental theology. Let us look initially at four possibilities.

Four possible visions

First, we might identify the human condition by speaking of _homo dolens_ (the human being who suffers). Human beings suffer through all that they have lost and continue to lose, as well as through what they fear about the present and the future. Loss, sometimes terrible loss, and fear, sometimes paralysing fear, constantly characterize the lives of men and women. In a remarkable poem written during the Second World War, 'Ecce homo', David Gascoyne (1916–2001) pictured the awful story of human pain and linked it to the passion of Christ. 'He is in agony till the world's end, | And we must never sleep during that time!'[1] Everywhere suffering characterizes the human condition.

---

[1] D. Gascoyne, _Collected Poems_ (Oxford: Oxford University Press, 1965). He quotes here Blaise Pascal, _Pensée_ 919 in A. J. Krailsheimer's trans. (Harmondsworth: Penguin, 1966); numbered 553 in some other editions.

In a particular way, Christ drew near to all human beings in pain. His body on the cross expressed his presence to those who suffer anywhere and at any time. His death on Calvary between two criminals symbolized forever his solidarity with those who suffer and die, an identification with human pain expressed also by the criteria for the last judgement (Matt. 25: 31–46). The final blessings of the kingdom will come to those who, without recognizing Christ, have met his needs in the people who suffer by being hungry, thirsty, strangers, naked, sick, or imprisoned. To articulate the worldwide presence of Christ in all who suffer, we might say: *ubi dolor, ibi Christus* (wherever there is suffering, there is Christ). A *homo dolens* version of the human condition would display this radical need met by the redemption revealed and embodied in Christ.

Second, we might be attracted to the theme of *homo interrogans* (the human being who asks questions). With their many questions, children express in their own way the ceaseless drive towards meaning and truth that human beings are born with.[2] Sooner or later, we question ourselves: where do we come from? Who are we? What does our existence mean—in its sinful failures, apparent successes, and future destiny? Is there a supreme Being in whose presence we play out our lives? Do we go to meet that Being beyond death? The psychiatrist Viktor Frankl (1905–97), the founder of logotherapy, understood the struggle to find meaning to be the principal driving force in human beings.[3]

Philosophers and theologians, like Joseph Maréchal (1878–1944) and Karl Rahner (1904–84), have unfolded the dynamic thrust of the human intellect that constantly presses beyond the immediate data of sense experience towards the fullness of meaning and truth in the Absolute. In Rahner's vision of the human condition, human beings put everything in question and do so within an infinite horizon of questioning. Every answer prompts a new question. Human beings

---

[2] Robert Coles, in *The Spiritual Life of Children* (Boston: Houghton Mifflin, 1990), shows how, with surprising feeling and subtlety, children ponder the great questions about the human predicament: our origin, our nature, and our final destiny. On Coles's work, see G. O'Collins, *Jesus our Redeemer: A Christian Approach to Salvation* (Oxford: Oxford University Press, 2007), 77–80.

[3] See V. Frankl, *Man's Search for Meaning: An Introduction to Logotherapy*, trans. I. Lasch (London: Hodder & Stoughton, 1964).

are the question that they can never adequately settle and answer by themselves.[4]

Artists and writers find their place among those who have expressed strikingly the questing and questioning spirit of *homo interrogans*. Shortly before his death in Tahiti, the post-impressionist painter Paul Gauguin (1848–1903) wrote out three questions on a large triptych he had completed: 'Where do we come from? What are we? Where are we going?' Great writers, like Leo Tolstoy (1828–1910), have constantly raised these eternal questions in their novels and dramas. A *homo interrogans* anthropology or vision of humanity aligns itself with a tradition that goes back to Paul and his radical questions (Rom. 7: 13–25). Without using the term, the Second Vatican Council in *Gaudium et Spes* (the pastoral constitution on the Church in the modern world) took over a method of correlation practised by Paul Tillich: 'Man will be ever anxious to know, if only in a vague way, what is the meaning of his life, his activity, and his death' (*Gaudium et Spes*, 41; see 10). The divine revelation correlates with our most serious questions: 'The most perfect answer to these questionings is to be found in God alone, who created human beings in his own image and redeemed them from sin; and this answer is given in the revelation in Christ his Son who became man' (*Gaudium et Spes*, 41).[5] Revelation matches the reality and need of human beings as those who are essentially questioners.

A third possibility would be to follow Wolfhart Pannenberg and present humanity as *homo historicus* (my expression, not his), as the being embedded in history, which is still incomplete but moving towards its final consummation. In a tour de force, Pannenberg brought together the religious implications of (human) biology, cultural anthropology, psychology, sociology, and history to construct a religious account of human beings as both created in the image of God and marred by sin that breaks and distorts their true identity. Part of the natural world, human persons are social beings, whose subjective

---

[4] K. Rahner, *Foundations of Christian Faith: An Introduction to the Idea of Christianity*, trans. W. V. Dych (New York: Seabury Press, 1978), 31–3.

[5] As it does elsewhere, *Gaudium et Spes* holds together here the orders of creation and redemption (God who 'created' and 'redeemed' us). The 'perfect' answer to our radical questioning (as opposed to imperfect, partial, or inadequate answers) is found in Christ, the final and universal mediator of revelation and redemption.

identity is shaped by society, with its institutions, political order, and culture that is expressed and developed in a particular way by language. Pannenberg understands history to embrace all these realities and to embody the concrete reality of human life.[6] Such a vision of the human person as *homo storicus* would coordinate well with the divine self-revelation in biblical history that looks for its consummation at the end of time.

Homo symbolicus (the human being as symbolic) is a fourth attractive option for the fundamental theologians fashioning a vision of the human condition. The human person is essentially symbolic, a being that is both material and spiritual and hence constantly expresses itself in symbolic acts. Human beings reveal themselves to others and to themselves when they perform properly human acts which are always symbolic: speaking, working, dressing, eating, love-making, travelling, worshipping, falling ill, and dying. Symbolism ranges right across everything that human beings do and endure. Such cultural anthropologists as Clifford Geertz (1926–2006) and Claude Lévi-Strauss (1908–2009) and such philosophers as Ernst Cassirer (1874–1945) and Susanne Langer (1895–1985) have highlighted the symbol-creating activity of human beings.

A brief account of a symbol could run as follows: (1) something or someone perceptible that (2) represents dynamically something or someone else, especially something invisible or abstract. The 'something perceptible' could be a story we hear, a group of people we see united for prayer, a body we touch, the perfume we smell, or the wine we taste. Our five senses constantly take in the symbolic reality that surrounds us. Whatever they may be, symbols always reveal, represent, or—even better—'re-present' (in the sense of somehow actually making present) what is symbolized. A letter, a portrait, or the tombstone of my deceased mother symbolizes her, mediating and realizing for me her presence. These symbols re-present a person whom death has made invisible. The incarnate and visible Word of God symbolized and re-presented the invisible Father. In John's language, 'he who has seen me has seen the Father' (John 14: 9). Symbolic language can also express such 'abstractions' as the qualities of prudence and simplicity: 'I send you out as sheep in the midst of

---

[6] W. Pannenberg, *Anthropology in Theological Perspective*, trans. M. J. O'Connell (Philadelphia: Westminster Press, 1985).

wolves; so be wise as serpents and innocent as doves' (Matt. 10: 16). The symbols of defilement, unfolded in Leviticus and other biblical books, represent the invisible, inner reality of human sin and guilt.[7]

A *homo symbolicus* vision of humanity can appeal to the way in which the divine self-communication 'corresponds' to our symbolic nature. If God wishes to communicate with *homo symbolicus*, this revelation must take a symbolic form or road. God the revealer is necessarily God the symbolizer. The symbols of revelation take such (1) linguistic forms as oracles, parables, and formulas of self-presentation ('I am the bread of life', 'I am the good shepherd', 'I am the vine and you are the branches', and so forth—from John's Gospel). (2) Symbolic actions and events run from the Babylonian captivity and the liturgical feasts of the Israelites, through the miraculous deeds of Jesus and his crucifixion, down to the use of water in baptism by missionaries and ministers from the beginning of Christianity. (3) Persons find their place in this summary of symbols: prophets with their symbolic actions and words (see Jer. 16: 1–21; Ezek. 24: 15–25; Hos. 1: 1–8), Jesus himself, Pilate and the other persons immediately responsible for his death, the apostles—not least Paul who recognized the deeply symbolic nature of his ministry as being led captive by God the victor in a triumphal procession (2 Cor. 2: 14) or as being a mother in the pain of childbirth until Christ is formed in his converts (Gal. 4: 19)—and countless other persons down the centuries. Through what they do and suffer, all men and women (and not least the sick and the old) present themselves as symbolic beings who can mediate to others something of the divine truth or sinful resistance to that truth. (4) Finally, all created things are potentially or actually symbols appropriate to the revealing activity of God: for example, fountains bubbling with water (see John 4: 13–14), olive trees (Rom. 11: 17–24), lumps of clay moulded by potters (Rom. 9: 19–21), and other human artefacts like icons and printed copies of the Bible. As is the case with human beings themselves, all other created things can symbolize and make present what is invisible—in particular, the invisible things of God.

---

[7] See P. Ricœur, *The Symbolism of Evil*, trans. E. Buchanan (Boston: Beacon Press, 1967); id., *Evil: A Challenge to Philosophy and Theology*, trans. J. Bowden (London: Continuum, 2007).

An anthropology of *homo symbolicus* can also deliver much. Human life is nothing if not symbolic. Both among ourselves and before God, all that we do and experience begins and ends in symbols. Yet it is human experience, whether special experiences or common human experiences of pain (*homo dolens*), of questioning (*homo interrogans*), of multi-faceted and incomplete history (*homo storicus*), and of symbol-creating (*homo symbolicus*), that discloses and conveys God's revealing and saving activity. Our experience is the *medium* through which we encounter the self-communication of God. This holds both for the foundational recipients of revelation in Old and New Testament times, for later Christian and Jewish believers, and, as we shall see in a chapter below, for all people anywhere who respond in faith to God. God's self-manifestation either meets us in our experience or it does not meet us at all. Given the essentially personal and interpersonal character of revelation, non-experienced revelation would be a simple contradiction in terms.

Hence I prefer to offer an account of the human person as *homo experiens* (the human being who experiences), a theme which we find vividly deployed in the Yahwist account of creation and its astonishingly subtle picture of the universal human condition. Creation and sin put their mark on all history, right from the beginning. In experiencing their created and then sinful condition, the primal couple form a prototype of humanity as a whole, an image of what human beings experience always and everywhere.[8] Encouraged by this example, I will bring together fourteen points to illuminate the reality of human experience in general and then add some items on religious experience in particular.

Homo experiens

1. From the outset one must observe how polyvalent the notion and reality of experience are; they defy reduction to a simple formula. Ours may be 'the age of experience', when many people put aside their inherited traditions and search experientially for insight and

---

[8] See A. LaCoque, *The Trial of Innocence: Adam, Eve and the Yahwist* (Eugene, Ore.: Cascade Books, 2006).

explanation. Faced with the major questions of life, they look for answers in and though their experience, and appeal to their experience to justify their beliefs and behaviour. Nevertheless, the concept of experience remains 'many-levelled and ambiguous'.[9] Despite its popularity, it resists precise definition.[10]

2. In contemporary Indo-European languages we speak about experience in two related ways. It is a *process*, made up of a series of sub-experiences. Any tourist's experience of a new country or a new city would be a typical example. So too would be the Israelites' experience of God, recorded and interpreted in the Old Testament. We also apply 'experience' to the *condition* that results. Some observant, well-read, and adventurous tourists like Patrick Leigh Fermor or William Dalrymple reach the point of becoming genuine experts. Whatever the field, be it teaching, tourism, management, surgery, or anything else, an expert is someone who has learned much through his or her experiences, and who now 'has' the experience to cope well with new, surprising, and difficult circumstances. Such people are thoroughly 'experienced'.

3. My third point is also, at least initially, a linguistic one. Unlike English, French, Italian, Spanish, and some other modern languages, German enjoys not one but two nouns to express experience: *Erfahrung* (with its corresponding verb *erfahren*) and *Erlebnis* (with its corresponding verb *erleben*). *Erfahrung* suggests travelling, exploring, and learning things through time and trouble. *Ein erfahrener Mensch* is a person who has learned much through a series of experiences. Often enough the language of *Erfahrung* highlights either the realities we encounter and come to know or the condition that objectively results from many experiences: in brief, the objective pole. *Er-leben* points to life (*Leben*), which reveals itself in experiences. It suggests the feelings and emotions our experiences can arouse—in short, the subjective pole.

All that said, any distinction between *erfahren* and *erleben* should be based on and supplemented by further examples. Usage and context are decisive, rather than any artificial attempts to exploit

---

[9] W. Kasper, *The God of Jesus Christ*, trans. M. J. O'Connell (New York: Crossroad, 1989), 79.

[10] On experience, see H. Wissman et al., 'Erfahrung', *TRE* x. 83–141. Years ago a German friend of mine set himself to write a comprehensive account of 'experience'; after completing over a thousand pages, he abandoned the project; there was and is simply too much to say.

the fact that German offers a choice of terms not found in other languages. At the same time, we need some distinction between the objective and subjective poles of experience, irrespective of whether or not we explicate this distinction with reference to the German *Erfahrung* and *Erlebnis*.

4. The fourth observation follows closely on the third. Experience necessarily involves some direct contact between the subject experiencing and the object experienced. Somehow the object is or becomes present, so as to be immediately encountered. An indirect or second-hand experience by proxy would be a contradiction in terms. Experiences are either first-hand and in some sense immediate or they do not exist at all. One cannot experience marriage without actually getting married oneself. A prophet cannot experience God by proxy and at second hand.

This immediacy should not be misconstrued as if I meant to deny the presuppositions and prior conditioning involved in all experiences. Every experience has its presuppositions. Social, cultural, and religious conditioning makes our experiences possible and intelligible. Acknowledging the immediate nature of experience in no way implies the assertion that we bring a clean, presuppositionless state, a kind of *tabula rasa*, to our experiences. When the prophets experienced God and later when the disciples experienced Jesus in his ministry, they all brought with them their prior conditioning, presuppositions, questions, and expectations.

Nor should the immediacy of experience be misunderstood in the religious sphere as if we could encounter God alone rather than 'in, with, and under' other experiences. God deals immediately with human beings.[11] We can and do experience God, and that means that we immediately experience God. Yet it is always 'in, with, and under' other experiences that God communicates with us.

---

[11] Like other teachers of the spiritual life, St Ignatius Loyola (1491–1556) insisted on this in his *Spiritual Exercises* no. 330: 'Only God Our Lord gives consolation to the soul without preceding cause; for it is the Creator's prerogative to enter the soul, and to leave her, and to arouse movements which draw her entirely into love of His Divine Majesty. When I say "without cause" I mean without any previous perception or understanding of some object due to which consolation could come about through the mediation of the person's own acts of understanding and will'; in J. A. Munitiz and P. Endean (eds. and trans.), *Saint Ignatius of Loyola: Personal Writings* (London: Penguin Books, 1996), 351.

Affirming the immediacy of experience reminds us that every experience has its objective and subjective pole. In all experiences a subject somehow comes into contact with an object. In given experiences the subject may be more prominent, in others the object. On some or even many occasions the subject may misinterpret the object, or at least remain deeply puzzled by what has been experienced. But we never have a 'purely subjective' experience nor, for that matter, a 'purely objective' one. In any experience a subject directly encounters an object. We must resist the temptation to speak of 'purely subjective' experiences. That would be a contradiction in terms.

5. Particularity characterizes all experiences. They are always concrete and specific, never general and universal. An experience means *this* specific reality experienced at *this* particular time and in *this* particular place. Amos, who inaugurated the era of classical prophecy, specifies where he was ('among the shepherds of Tekoa') and when it was ('in the days of King Uzziah of Judah and in the days of King Jeroboam son of Joash of Israel, two years before the earthquake') that he experienced visions and oracles from the Lord (Amos 1: 1). Later prophets (or those who compiled their messages) followed Amos in placing and/or dating precisely their visions and experiences of God's word (e.g. Isa. 1: 1; Jer. 1: 1–3; Ezek. 1: 1–3).

6. All experiences show an *active* and a *passive* component. The subject not only acts but also undergoes something. The symbolic language of Jesus' parables invites their hearers not only to receive them but also to reflect and respond actively to their experience. (a) Admittedly some experiences put the subject in a much more active role. Laboratory experiments, in which research scientists carefully set up the conditions for what will be experienced, provide a classic instance of such 'active' experiences. (b) The experience of dying and death (*Todeserfahrung* in German) serves to exemplify dramatically the more 'passive' experiences. Yet passive elements turn up in cases of (a): after all, a scientific experiment may turn out quite differently from what was planned. Cases of (b) do not exclude active involvement in what the subject experiences. John's Gospel goes out of its way to show how Jesus actively participated in his own death (John 19: 30).

Before leaving this sixth point, it could be worth noting two opposite tendencies in philosophy which, respectively, emphasize unilaterally the active and passive dimensions of experience. On the one hand, idealism in its various forms highlights the activity of the human spirit. On the other hand, empirical strains of philosophy tend to underline one-sidedly the passive aspects of human experience. Any balanced approach should refuse to follow either trend and absolutize either the active or the passive side of experience.

7. Unlike the logical conclusions of deductive argumentation, the evidence of experience simply imposes itself directly. What we experience is undeniable. The immediate 'authority' of what we experience when we read reverently biblical texts or participate in the sacramental actions of the Church will not go away. These experienced symbols (words and actions), precisely as experienced, present themselves directly.

Here, however, I am not claiming that we always read off correctly the immediate evidence of experience. Notoriously people have misinterpreted great biblical symbols, turning the creation story into a 'scientific' account of the universe's origins or the sign of the cross into a guarantee of worldly domination by Christians. We may also get things wrong by forgetting that our experience is only partial. In fact, before the end of the world, all experience remains partial and provisional. We can rush toward error when we absolutize some experience and refuse to remain open to the evidence of new experiences which may modify what we have already learned. In the biblical story, people are repeatedly summoned not only to remember their foundational experiences but also to open themselves to new experiences: in the end, the experience of the incarnate Symbol of God who came to live among them. Hence, C. S. Lewis, while showing how experience yields direct evidence and does not 'try' to deceive, also indicates the need to discern carefully what is experienced—a lesson inculcated by the very first Christian letter (1 Thess. 5: 19–21).[12] In particular, the multi-levelled nature of the central religious symbols that we experience individually and collectively could lead us to misread what we see and misinterpret what we hear.

8. Experiences easily invite categorization into good/bad, pleasant/ painful, enlightening/puzzling, or, more simply, positive/negative experiences. Obviously we are threatened here with a facile reductionism that assesses experiences according to a calculus of pleasure. In those terms sickness, physical disabilities, and pain of all kinds

---

[12] See C. S. Lewis, *Surprised by Joy: The Shape of my Early Life* (London: Collins, 1959).

would be dismissed as 'merely' negative experiences to be avoided as far as possible. However, viewed in their full context and for their long-term consequences, such experiences can turn out to be beneficial, humanly and spiritually. Not only the ancient Greeks but also early Christians realized that we can learn much through the things we suffer (e.g. Heb. 5: 8). So-called 'bad' experiences may prove to be enlightening and redemptive—a point that repeatedly emerges also from many of the world's greatest dramas and novels. In saying this, I shrink from alleging that 'learning through painful experience' solves the problem of evil. Short of the final vision of God, this problem or rather mystery has no adequate solution. Nevertheless, the experience of learning through suffering, including unmerited suffering, should not be ignored.

9. In a way my next observation picks up on an aspect of the third point above: with varying degrees of intensity, the whole person is involved in and revealed by his or her experiences. Every experience, even the most trivial one, enjoys at least a minimal 'totality' by affecting the entire person. Any experience whatsoever is 'my' experience and not simply that of my arm, my eye, or my imagination alone. Of course, the more profound the experience, the greater its impact on the totality of my being, for good or evil.

On the objective side, even though as limited beings we experience only partial fragments of reality, our experiences somehow point to all reality. Objectively as well as subjectively, the whole of reality is involved in every experience. In and through experiencing parts of reality, as whole persons we stand in contact with the whole.

10. Human beings come across as those who suffer, question, are radically historical, create symbols, and *experience*, but also as rational, *thinking* animals. How then does experience relate to and differ from thought?

Obviously thinking about joy differs from a joyful experience; thinking about the risen Christ differs from experiencing the risen Christ. Experiences display a concrete particularity that differentiates them from universal concepts, dictionary definitions, discursive thought, and general judgements. We use concepts and judgements to communicate our experiences. But they do not simply coincide with those experiences.

Here we might adapt a dictum from Immanuel Kant and say, 'Thought without experience is empty; experience without thought is blind.'[13] On the one hand, experiences make us think and prompt us to understand. Consciously religious experiences lead us to think about God and understand at least a little the divine–human relationship. Experiencing for the first time the symbolic drama of the Christian sacraments brings some people to a new and real knowledge of themselves, humanity, and God. Without any personal contact with the Christian liturgy, at best they would enjoy only an abstract, 'empty' appreciation of the sacraments—a merely notional knowledge acquired through study rather than a real knowledge by acquaintance. On the other hand, thought may help to explain some experiences and to prepare us for new experiences. Thinking about what we witness in the sacramental life of the Church can help us to participate more fully, intelligently, and experientially in that life. Thought can clarify what we have experienced, as well as prepare us to understand and interpret what we going to experience. There is a constant interplay between experience and thought; while distinguishable, they remain always inseparable.

Here we should fashion and add a further, related dictum: 'Language without experience is empty; experience without language is mute.' As well as plotting the inseparable relationship between thought and experience, we should do the same for language and experience. Without experience, language remains abstract and lifeless. Without language, experience remains confused and largely unintelligible. We can put this positively by citing early Christian preaching about Jesus. From the very beginning, in the pre-Pauline formulations of faith (e.g. 1 Cor. 15: 3–5), Christians enjoyed a language that clarified what they experienced of the risen Lord through the gift of the Holy Spirit. There never was a time when they lacked the language of faith that not only stated and accompanied but even constituted their experience: for instance, the experience of the Spirit prompting them to acclaim the risen Jesus as Lord (1 Cor. 12: 3).

In short, experience, thought, and language form a distinguishable but inseparable unity. Thought without experience is empty;

---

[13] Apropos of our empirical knowledge of the world, Kant observed: 'Thoughts without content are empty; intuitions without concepts are blind': *Critique of Pure Reason*, trans. P. Guyer and A. W. Wood (Cambridge: Cambridge University Press, 1998), 193–4.

experience without thought is blind. To that we add: language without experience is empty; experience without language is mute.

11. Thought and language suggest a further observation that relates closely to the seventh and eighth points above and prepares for the twelfth point below: experience is always *interpreted* experience. 'Experience' without interpretation would be, at best, a mere sensation. We should banish the delusion that there could be non-interpreted experiences. It is curious how this fond delusion lingers on, as if, for instance, Peter, Mary Magdalene, and other early disciples first met Jesus and only later began to interpret him for themselves and others. In reality there never was a non-interpreted Jesus. Right from and even right in their initial encounters with him, the first disciples began to interpret him. It is impossible for us as thinking and speaking beings to have non-interpreted experiences. In every experience the process of interpretation begins, a process that may not continue very long in the case of trivial experiences, but that may last a lifetime for such life-transforming experiences as Paul's encounter with the risen Christ on the road to Damascus. Anyone who experiences at depth the biblical and liturgical realities at the heart of Christianity knows how we never come to an end in the struggle to interpret and understand them.

Many of the victims of modern media saturation may simply glance at their experiences, without being willing or able to go very far toward interpreting and understanding them. But those who bring a rich and informed judgement to their experiences can grasp them in a much more profound way. Paul's experience outside Damascus was a one-off event; he had not enjoyed the ongoing grace of being closely associated with Jesus during his ministry. Yet the wealth of Paul's religious formation and commitment, while radically turned around by his encounter with the risen Christ, helped to set him exploring and elucidating that experience for his whole lifetime.

This observation hearkens back to my second point. Very 'experienced' persons will often be led by their condition to discern and appreciate their new experiences in a more effective way than others do. However, we should also recognize that such 'experienced' persons may 'bring so much' to fresh experiences that they are unable to open themselves to these experiences and be challenged by them. They may believe that they already know it all. Being an expert has its risks as well as its advantages.

12. Interpreting our experiences coincides largely with discovering their meaning. A meaningless experience—an experience that lacks all meaning and is literally 'absurd'—seems as impossible to conceive as a totally negative experience. Every experience has some meaning. Nevertheless, the meaning or at least the full meaning of an experience may call for years of exploring before we find (and in a sense also create) its meaning. In particular, this holds true for painful episodes; it can seem that some wounds will never heal and some experiences will never make sense. Yet time can not only heal all but also make sense of all.

The journeys that I examined in *The Second Journey* exemplify over and over again how it may take years of patient travelling before the painful experiences that initiated a midlife quest fall into place and yield their meaning.[14] The journey to discover meaning may prove a long one. Paul acknowledged how the central symbol of the Christian message, the crucified Jesus, came across to many as scandalous nonsense (1 Cor. 1: 23) rather than meaningful and life-giving truth. But he gave himself wholeheartedly to his ministry of preaching in the hope that as many Jews and Gentiles as possible would eventually come to find a supreme meaning in the death and resurrection of Christ. In his own case it took a word from the risen Lord to make sense of some mysterious affliction that he had been enduring (2 Cor. 12: 7–9).[15]

13. Paul's highly personal letters (at least the seven clearly authentic ones: Romans, 1 and 2 Corinthians, Galatians, Philippians, 1 Thessalonians, and Philemon) guide us to a penultimate characteristic of experience: the struggle for its *communicability*. If all experience is immediately personal (see point (4) above), how can we communicate it to others? When we 'codify' our experiences in the attempt to express them to others, do we really get anywhere? Some people write autobiographies in the hope of expressing to others what they have been through. But in our desolate moments it can seem that we are nothing but solitaries living within our own skins and incapable of communicating with each other, or at least incapable of communicating to others the things that really matter. Yet we also know how the flesh of our experience can become a word for/to others. Despite

---

[14] G. O'Collins, *The Second Journey: Spiritual Awareness and the Midlife Crisis* (3rd edn. Leominster: Gracewing, 1995).
[15] See M. J. Harris, *The Second Epistle to the Corinthians* (Grand Rapids, Mich.: Eerdmans, 2005), 852–66.

the element, sometimes painful element, of incommunicability that qualifies our personal experiences, the miracle of dialogue can take place and we can communicate something of what we have experienced.

In communicating our experiences we enjoy the benefit of many symbols. We can tell our story and use further symbolic 'language'. Our style of life and body language (in the broadest sense of that term) can effectively symbolize what we experience. At the same time, symbolic self-communication always involves something 'kenotic'. Even though our symbols make present what is symbolized (in this case, our experience), the symbols never perfectly coincide with what they symbolize. A gap opens up and a 'kenotic' hiddenness remains to qualify whatever self-revelation we succeed in communicating. This observation, in a cautious and reverent way, raises a question about Jesus himself: was there and to what extent was there a 'kenotic' gap between his experience of God and what he could communicate to others in a self-revealing way?

14. Lastly, a word about *tradition*, which may be understood as the transmission of a group's experiences. A wide range of symbols mediate socially the collective experience of a whole people, of a particular culture (which may not coincide with a given nation), and of the Church herself. Various strands of tradition (e.g. their inherited language, shared values, and cultural achievements) symbolize and express a group's identity.

As human beings and believers we live through the tension between inherited traditions and contemporary experiences. On the one hand, tradition enables us to evaluate, understand, and articulate our new experiences. On the other hand, new experiences can challenge and modify past experiences, in that way altering the shape of the tradition we transmit to the coming generation. Ideally, we should be at ease with the tension, neither misusing tradition to protect ourselves against new experiences nor ignoring tradition as if our human and Christian experience began yesterday.

Talking about tradition in the singular should not be taken to imply that we inherit a monolithic block. The traditions we receive vary in value and may be in tension with each other. There can likewise be a tension between contemporary experiences, which in any case also vary in value. Both our traditions and our experiences invite choice and discernment. It would be a delusion to imagine that either our inherited tradition or our contemporary experience constituted a clearly unified and self-justified whole. We return to these issues in a subsequent chapter on tradition.

Thus far this chapter has sketched some major characteristics of experience. The notion, language, and reality of experience are notoriously polyvalent. Nevertheless, I had to offer at least an interim report on experience to clarify what I mean by saying that human beings experience in faith the self-revelation of God. This chapter would remain patently incomplete, however, if it lacked some reflections on religious experience. Without being separate from 'ordinary' human experience or, to put matters positively, while remaining within human experience, religious and mystical experiences relate consciously and explicitly to the divine Being.[16]

Religious experience

Saintly persons who are truly contemplatives in action and find God in all things let their lives become a constant religious experience. They live in the presence of God. They see all created reality for what, with varying degrees of intensity, it all truly symbolizes and reveals: the divine reality. For those whose faith is magnificently alive, every moment is or can be a sign and sacrament of God's presence.

The Gospels record for us the final years of one whose life shows itself to have been a constant religious experience. From what we can glimpse of his 'interior' existence, Jesus lived in the presence of the God whom he called 'Abba' (Father dear), completely given over to the service of the divine kingdom that was breaking into the world.[17]

How frequent are religious experiences for rank and file believers? Or for those who are not (yet) believers but cling to the hope that one day things will open up and they will spot the pattern of it all? I could

---

[16] See C. F. Davis, *The Evidential Force of Religious Experience* (Oxford: Clarendon Press, 1989); J. L. Gellman, 'Mysticism and Religious Experience', in W. J. Wainwright (ed.), *The Oxford Handbook of Philosophy of Religion* (New York: Oxford University Press, 2005), 138–67: P. Gerlitz et al., 'Mystik', *TRE* xxiii. 533–92; K. Hoheisel and H.-G. Heimbrock, 'Religionspsychologie', ibid. xxix. 1–19. Mystical experiences of union with God, coming as 'flashes' during prayer or in the ordinary activities of daily life, awaken a new awareness of God.

[17] See G. O'Collins, *Jesus: A Portrait* (London: Darton, Longman & Todd, 2008), 16–37.

not claim to possess full and detailed answers to these questions. But what believers testify about their experiences at common worship, in personal prayer, and in the 'ordinary' occasions of life suggests some degree of frequency in their consciously explicit experience of God. Add too the kind of data collected by Sir Alister Hardy and his collaborators in the Religious Experience Research Unit (see Chapter 2 above) from a wide range of 'ordinary' people. Many situations, from painful and even tragic events through to 'moments of glad grace' (W. B. Yeats, 'When you are old') in personal relationships, can trigger a vivid sense of God's loving presence.

Explicitly religious experiences have often been named in *spatial* terms as occurring in 'boundary situations' (Karl Jaspers), as being 'limit experiences' (David Tracy) or 'peak experiences' (Abraham Maslow), or as associated with 'the ground of being and meaning' (Paul Tillich). This spatial language allows us to glimpse two inseparable aspects of religious experience. (a) It puts us in conscious touch with the totality of things, that is to say, with God as the ground of everything and the all-determining reality. (b) In experiencing God, we also know that it is we who know God. We experience ourselves in our radical dependence and contingency. We meet God not only in our profound need but also with a fundamental trust that, at its heart, the world holds together and our existence finally has its worth. Explicitly religious experience means, then, co-experiencing God and ourselves. I cannot imagine a religious experience in which we would encounter God without any sense whatsoever of ourselves. Here, as elsewhere, the principle enunciated in point (4) above holds good. All experience necessarily exposes the subject as well as the object. The Old Testament narratives of prophetic experiences repeatedly display the two poles. The scenario of Isaiah's vision of the divine throne room, for instance, displays both 'the Lord sitting on a throne' and also the prophet's sense of being 'a man of unclean lips' (Isa. 6: 1–13). On the occasion of a great catch of fish, Peter experiences Jesus as 'Lord' and himself as a 'sinful man' (Luke 5: 1–11).

Besides reflecting on the frequency and nature of religious experience, let me add a word about its very possibility. Here I wish to align myself with those like Karl Rahner, who expound the basic dynamism of the human spirit as creating the conditions for the possibility of religious experience. We can explicitly experience God because *every* human experience reveals its openness to the infinite.[18] When we consciously experience God, what was hitherto dim and implicit becomes illuminated and explicit. We are able to encounter God because all human experiences are already primordially religious. In any experience whatsoever we experience at least minimally ourselves and God.

In recent times and earlier, various authors have explored the dynamism of the human spirit, interpreting its openness to the infinite in terms of our intellect and will.[19] One might put new heart into this approach by altering the terms and highlighting our drive toward the fullness of life, meaning/truth, and love. Spontaneously we seek to escape from death, absurdity, and isolation. We long to live, to see the basic meaning and truth of things, and to love and be loved.[20]

We may misinterpret our partial and provisional experiences of life, meaning, and love (see point (7) above). We may dismiss as merely 'negative' those experiences of death, absurdity, and isolation which will eventually turn out to be quite the opposite (see points (8) and (12) above). But our primordial drive toward life, meaning, and love will never disappear. The parable of the prodigal son (Luke 15: 11–32) can be interpreted in this threefold way. The young runaway faces death by starvation, experiences the absurdity of his situation, and finds himself abandoned by his good-time 'friends'. His follies have obscured his vision of where life, meaning, and love are truly to be found. In deciding to return home, he goes back to where he will once again experience those three realities.

---

[18] See Rahner, *Foundations of Christian Faith*, 19–23, 31–5, 51–71. W. Pannenberg concurs: 'we experience simultaneously the Infinite [upper case] that lies within finite things and the finite that is its manifestation'; 'the confused intuition of the Infinite, which lies, prethematically, at the basis of all human consciousness, is already in truth a mode of the presence of God' (*Metaphysics and the Idea of God*, trans. P. Clayton (Grand Rapids, Mich.: Eerdmans, 1990), 25, 29).

[19] See e.g. Kasper, *The God of Jesus Christ*, 104–6.

[20] See the transcendental therapy of Karlfried Graf Dürckheim (1896–1988), who studied situations in which human beings felt threatened by death in its various forms, became overwhelmed by a sense of injustice and meaningless absurdity, and were abandoned, cruelly treated, and hated. Then they could be given life, experience a deeper order and meaning in things, and know themselves to be the object of generous love. These experiences made people long even more for some experience of life, meaning, and love that would change everything.

The story of the two disciples on the road to Emmaus (Luke 24: 15–35) also suggests how religious experiences, especially any profound ones, yield life, meaning, and love. The disciples 'know' Jesus in 'the breaking of the bread'. His scripture lesson has illuminated the sense of what they had been through and had taken to be a meaningless, deadly tragedy. His words, actions, and presence set their hearts 'burning' within them. The quest for life, meaning, and love constitutes the innate drive of all human beings. This quest has its centre and climax in our primordial search for God as the fullness of life, meaning, and love. It is a process that achieves its definitive consummation in the world to come. Without intending to say all that, Luke in fact illustrates our triple quest through the magnificent Emmaus story, which sooner or later gives us the 'I was there' feeling.

With some account in place of what human experience and, in particular, explicitly religious experience entails, we can turn now to the heart of fundamental theology: the divine self-revelation as experienced and interpreted in the biblical record of the Old and New Testament.[21]

---

[21] As a Christian I use the terminology of Old Testament and New Testament. Here 'old' is understood as good and does not imply any 'supersessionism', or the view that the New Testament has rendered obsolete, replaced, and so 'superseded' the Old Testament.

4

General and Special Revelation

On any showing, the self-revelation of God belongs to the heart of fundamental theology's agenda. This chapter aims to articulate a Christian vision of divine revelation. Here a coherent account may go at least a little way towards justifying theological claims about revelation, while not purporting to offer something that seems ruled out: a full rational defence of divine revelation. Yet, even if the faith that responds to revelation cannot be fully justified, to a degree its reasonableness can be established.

From the outset, distinctions must be drawn between revelation, on the one hand, and biblical inspiration and the canonical Scriptures, on the other. Unquestionably, they were and remain closely related realities. Yet we must shun the endemic tendency to collapse divine revelation into inspiration and its result, the Sacred Scriptures. A later chapter will examine biblical inspiration and the scriptural canon. Here let me say in advance that, as such, the Scriptures are written testimonies which, after the history of special divine revelation had begun, came gradually into existence under the inspiration of the Holy Spirit at various stages of the foundational history of God's people. Thus the Scriptures differ from revelation in the way that written texts differ from living, interpersonal events. It makes perfectly good sense to say with exasperation, 'I left my copy of the Bible behind in the London Underground.' But I would have a good deal of explaining to do if I were to say to a friend, 'I left revelation behind in the Underground.'

Let me turn to revelation, its nature, its link with salvation, its means, and its mediators, and the faith with which human beings respond to God's self-disclosure. This chapter will draw on the Scriptures to lay the groundwork for later questions: for instance, about the distinction between past, present, and future revelation; about the nature of faith with which human beings respond to God's self-disclosure; and the divine revelation that reaches human beings in general and the followers of world religions in particular.[1]

General revelation

Ordinary speech and theological usage more or less coincide in understanding 'reveal' to mean 'allow to appear', 'disclose', 'display', 'divulge', 'make known', 'manifest', 'show', or 'unveil' (suggested by the Latin re-velare or 'remove the veil (velum)'). 'Revelation' is, primarily, the act (sometimes startling act) of revealing and, secondarily, the new knowledge made available through this act.

---

[1] On revelation, see W. J. Abraham, *Crossing the Threshold of Divine Revelation* (Grand Rapids, Mich.: Eerdmans, 2006), 58–111; D. Brown, *Tradition and Imagination: Revelation and Change* (Oxford: Clarendon, 1999); R. Bultmann, 'The Concept of Revelation in the New Testament', *Existence and Faith: Shorter Writings of Rudolf Bultmann*, trans. S. M. Ogden (London: Hodder & Stoughton, 1961), 58–91; A. Dulles, *Models of Revelation* (New York: Doubleday,1983); G. Mavrodes, *Revelation in Religious Belief* (Philadelphia: Temple University Press, 1988); S. L. Menssen and T. D. Sullivan, *The Agnostic Inquirer: Revelation from a Philosophical Standpoint* (Grand Rapids, Mich.: Eerdmans, 2007); H. R. Niebuhr, *The Meaning of Revelation* (New York; Macmillan, 1941); W. Pannenberg, 'The Revelation of God', in *Systematic Theology*, trans. G. W. Bromiley, i (Grand Rapids, Mich.: Eerdmans, 1991), 189–257; K. Rahner and J. Ratzinger, *Revelation and Tradition*, trans. W. J. O'Hara (London: Burns & Oates, 1966); P. Ricœur, 'Toward a Hermeneutic of the Idea of Revelation', *Harvard Theological Review*, 70 (1977, 1–37); M. Seckler, 'Der Begriff der Offenbarung', *HFTh* ii. 60–83; R. Swinburne, *Revelation: From Analogy to Metaphor* (Oxford: Clarendon Press, 1992); G. Wiesner et al., 'Offenbarung', *TRE* xxv. 109–210; N. Wolterstorff, *Divine Discourse: Philosophical Reflections on Claims that God Speaks* (Cambridge: Cambridge University Press, 1995). Commentaries on Vatican II's Constitution on Divine Revelation, *Dei Verbum* (the Word of God), have much to say about revelation; for a bibliography on *Dei Verbum*, see G. O'Collins, *Retrieving Fundamental Theology* (Mahwah, NJ: Paulist Press, 1993), 178–217.

Immanuel Kant famously remarked that two things make human beings think of God: the 'starry skies' above and the 'moral law' within their hearts.[2] Without using the term 'general revelation', he pointed to (1) the way in which the natural order and beauty of the created world display the divine wisdom and power and so manifest God to human beings everywhere. Kant, somewhat like John Henry Newman a century later, also (2) recognized how the moral law written on human hearts (see Rom. 2: 14–15) makes known the will and character of God. Thus two basic features of the universe, 'out there' in visible, created reality and 'in here' within the moral conscience of human beings, disclose something of God and the divine nature, character, and purposes.

All human beings have access to this general revelation of God mediated through the beautiful and orderly works of creation and through their own, inner spiritual reality. The author of the Book of Wisdom concentrated on the former, when criticizing any nature worship that took 'the luminaries of heaven' or other natural forces to be 'the gods that rule the world'. Delighting 'in the beauty of these things, people assumed them to be gods'. They should have known 'how much better than these is their Lord, for the author of beauty created them'. 'If the people were amazed at their power and working', Wisdom goes on to say, 'let them perceive from them how much more powerful is the One who formed them'. The argument reaches its climax with the statement: 'from the greatness and beauty of created things comes a corresponding perception of their Creator' (Wisd. 13: 1–9). We do not detect here a natural theology that argues from the world to the existence and attributes of God. Wisdom envisages no such argument, but rather an experience of the created world through which human beings should acknowledge the divine presence and enjoy a living contact with God.

Centuries before the Book of Wisdom was written, the order and beauty in the world which God has created and continues to sustain inspired the vivid hymn that is Psalm 104. Other psalms also praised creation's beauty and harmony (e.g. Ps. 19: 1–6; see Job 38–9) and

---

[2] I. Kant, *Critique of Practical Reason*, trans. Mary Gregor (Cambridge: Cambridge University Press, 1997), 133: 'Two things fill the mind with ever new and increasing admiration and reverence, the more often and steadily one reflects on them, *the starry heaven above me and the moral law within me*' (italics his).

poetically celebrated the Creator's power and intelligence that can be experienced and recognized in the natural world.

Before leaving the Old Testament, we should note that the Israelite experience of nature was subordinate to their experience of history. An ancient confession of faith summarized the saving history through which the people had experienced YHWH's concern and favour (Deut. 26: 5–9). What had happened historically counted for more than any divine self-manifestation in nature. Even the 'account of origins' supplied by the opening chapters of Genesis fits into the larger context of Israel's salvation history. Those chapters show us how the Israelites, in the light of specific experiences of God in their own history, pictured poetically the origins of the world and the human race. The stories found there responded to the question: what must the beginning have been like for our past and present historical experience to be what they were/are? The subordination of everything to the experience of salvation history went so far that even the *feasts* that dealt with creation and nature were tied to Israel's history. The feast of the unleavened bread (originally an agricultural festival which took place at the barley harvest in the spring) was converted into a celebration of the exodus from Egypt (Exod. 12: 14–20; 13: 3–10; 23: 15; 34: 18). A harvest feast at the end of the year, the festival of the booths, commemorated the time of wandering in the desert (Lev. 23: 42–3). The Passover feast itself, which seemed to have begun as a spring festival of nomadic herders, was drawn into the story of the exodus from Egypt (Exod. 12: 1–28) and eventually combined with the feast of unleavened bread. For the Israelites the experience of God through history took precedence over any divine self-manifestation through the seasonal events of nature as such.

Like other peoples, the Israelites associated clouds, thunder, lightning, smoke, and earthquakes with the presence of God. They 'historicized' these phenomena of nature by linking them with the presence of God during their wandering in the wilderness (e.g. Exod. 19: 16–19). Such natural phenomena accompany a theophany inserted into the story of the exodus from Egypt.

When we turn to the New Testament, we find Paul reflecting on what we can call general revelation. He observes about human beings in general: 'what can be known about God is plain to them, for God has shown it to them. Ever since the creation of the world his eternal power and divine nature, invisible though they are, have been understood and seen through the things he has made'

(Rom. 1: 19–20).[3] In the next chapter the apostle moves to the inner witness of the conscience, exemplified by some who do not possess the law of Moses, morally sensitive and responsible Gentiles: 'When Gentiles, who do not have the law, do by nature (instinctively) what the law requires, these, while not having the law, are a law for themselves (behave as the law commands)' (Rom. 2: 14). The honourable and praiseworthy conduct of some Gentiles prompts Paul to draw the conclusion: 'they show that what the law requires is written on their hearts, to which their own conscience bears witness' (Rom. 2: 15). Their conscience, or 'natural' moral sensibility, lets them know what is right or wrong. Hence the apostle expects that such Gentiles will not be condemned in God's final judgement. They have lived responsibly and avoided actions that went against their conscience (Rom. 2: 15–16).[4] The obedience of the heart shown by such admirable Gentiles has existed and even flourished. They will be justified by 'the law' which has been 'written on their hearts'—with 'heart' understood biblically as the personal centre that receives knowledge and divine revelation and is the seat of the emotions and will.

Whether or not he consciously intended to do so, the language of Paul in Romans 2 extends to Gentiles the promises made to the Israelites about the law 'written on their hearts' and the 'new heart' and 'new spirit' that will enable them to observe the divine ordinances (Jer. 31: 33; Ezek. 11: 19–20; 36: 26–7). The divine law, written on their hearts, enables the Gentiles also to know, instinctively and without being taught, what they should do.

The metaphor of writing implies a writer. This observation does not extend falsely the metaphor in question, but attends to what we find earlier in Jeremiah (who includes a writer in his metaphorical talk of writing) and elsewhere in Paul. In the passages we have just cited, Jeremiah envisages YHWH not only as the present 'Speaker' but also as the future 'Writer' on human hearts, just as Ezekiel envisages God as the 'Implanter' of new, responsive 'hearts of flesh'. In Romans 2, Paul presumably has in mind a divine 'Writer' as the one who writes on the hearts of Gentiles; the writing does not involve any human agent. Although the apostle does not here precisely identify the divine Writer,

[3] See J. D. G. Dunn, *Romans 1–8* (Dallas: Word Books, 1988), 56–8; J. A. Fitzmyer, *Romans* (New York: Doubleday, 1993), 273–4, 278–81.
[4] On Rom. 2: 14–16, see Fitzmyer, *Romans*, 306–7.

his use of a similar metaphor, which involves 'writing' on the hearts of Christians through 'the Spirit of the living God' (2 Cor. 3: 2–3),[5] could encourage us to interpret Romans 2: 15 in terms of the Holy Spirit working in the hearts of Gentiles to support them 'in the witness of their conscience' and empower them to put into practice the essential requirements of the law. Whether or not we link the passage in Romans 2 (about Gentiles) with that in 2 Corinthians 3 (about Christians), the former passage indicates that the praiseworthy conduct of Gentiles witnesses to the divine activity at work in their moral conscience. Thus Paul's teaching in the opening two chapters of Romans yields support for Kant's observation about the created universe and the moral conscience operating in human hearts to manifest the work of God in the world.

General revelation and faith

Through revelation, including the general revelation that we have just outlined, God calls and enables human beings to enter into the new personal relationship of faith. Accepting the revelation mediated through the created universe and the voice of conscience involves men and women with God as One worthy of unconditional praise, worship, and obedience. While Paul himself does not use the term 'faith' in this context, he does indicate what knowing or experiencing God through such general revelation entails: it should lead human beings to 'honour' God as God and 'give thanks to him' (Rom. 1: 21).[6] The Letter to the Hebrews, however, speaks more fully of faith in ways that fit the case of those who believe in God in response to a general revelation coming through visible, created reality (rather than the inner voice of conscience witnessing to the moral order). The heroes

---

[5] See V. P. Furnish, *II Corinthians* (New York: Doubleday, 1984), 181–3, 192–6; M. J. Harris, *The Second Epistle to the Corinthians* (Grand Rapids, Mich.: Eerdmans, 2005), 261–6.

[6] See Fitzmyer, *Romans*, 282. As Dunn puts it, Paul thinks of 'thankful dependence', 'of thanksgiving as characteristic of a whole life, as the appropriate response of one whose daily experience is shaped by the recognition that he stands in debt to God, that his very life and experience of living is a gift from God' (*Romans 1–8*, 59).

and heroines of faith, featured in a classic passage (Heb. 11: 1–12: 27), begin with Abel, Enoch, and Noah, who precede the call and special history of the people of God that opens with Abraham and Sarah. They represent humanity in general and the general (not special) history of revelation. Hebrews shapes its version of faith to fit also their case.

The passage from Hebrews starts by declaring: 'Now faith is the substance/assurance of things hoped for, the proof of things not seen. By this [faith] the elders [our ancestors] received approval. By faith we understand that the universe was fashioned by the word of God, so that from what cannot be seen that which is seen has come into being' (11: 1–3). A further verse closely concerns our enquiry: 'without faith it is impossible to please God; for whoever would approach him must believe that he exists and that he rewards those who seek him' (11: 6).[7]

The opening three verses of Hebrews 11 describe the content of faith and do so in a way that matches general revelation. The passage hints at the future. Divine promises (presumably of some eternal inheritance) have aroused the hope of human beings and their trust that God will keep those promises, which concern future 'things which are not seen'. Faith also involves a view of the past. We understand by faith the unseen origin of the world: it 'was fashioned by the word of God'. Just as people of faith rely on the word of God about the genesis of the universe, so too do they rely on the word of God's promise when considering the *goal* of the world and their existence in the future.

Both in their view of the past and their hope for the future, the lives of those who have faith (triggered by general revelation) are entwined with the life of the invisible God. Faith cannot prove the 'unseen things' of God; rather faith itself is 'the proof' of these things. As C. R. Koester comments, 'the unseen realities of God give proof of their existence by their power to evoke faith'. It is the divine reality that evokes faith, not faith that 'creates' the divine reality. The divine 'object' of faith and hope 'can be known by its effects on human beings'.[8] The invisible power of God evokes faith and hope, and

---

[7] On these and other relevant verses on faith, see C. R. Koester, *Hebrews* (New York: Doubleday, 2001), 468–553.
[8] Ibid. 480.

directs men and women toward invisible ends. One cannot see God and the word of God, but one can know them from their results. Both faith and the created universe witness to the invisible power of God and the reality of the unseen world of God.

Even though it does not explicitly do so, the account of faith provided by Hebrews allows us to glimpse the human questions to which faith, triggered by the general revelation of God, supplies the answer. (1) Is there anything beyond the visible world? Are we bonded with things unseen or, rather, with the unseen God? (2) Where do we and our universe come from? Has 'that which is seen' come 'into being from that which cannot be seen': that is to say, from God and his creative word? We are born into a world that is not of our making. Do we nourish faith in the invisible Creator from whom all things have come? Such faith is close to gratitude toward the unseen Giver, a gratitude for the past from which we have emerged and for the future to which we have been summoned. (3) Does it matter how we behave? Should we imitate our 'ancestors', approved by God for their persevering faith? Should we live as pilgrims afflicted by various sufferings but always hoping for 'a better country' (Heb. 11: 16) and yearning for a God-given life to come? In short, may we and should we trust God as the One who 'rewards those who seek him'?

Such questions are not limited to Christians but apply to every human being in the face of the general revelation of God. Does Hebrews 11: 6 let us glimpse something further about the shape that faith stirred by such general revelation can take? Let us analyse five key elements in that verse.

1. First, it is a faith that 'pleases' God. Subsequent exhortations in Hebrews fill out what such 'pleasing God' entails: 'let us give thanks, by which we offer God worship in a *pleasing* way with reverence and awe' (Heb. 12: 28). Such grateful worship of God issues in acts of kindness that build up community: 'do not neglect to do good and to share what you have; for such sacrifices are *pleasing* to God' (Heb. 13: 16). A further verse summarizes such 'pleasing God' in terms of doing the divine will: 'May the God of peace... make you complete in everything good so that you may do his will, working among us that which is *pleasing* in his sight' (Heb. 13: 20–1). We could sum up what this view of 'pleasing God' entails: it envisages a faith that gratefully offers to God a reverent worship and does his will through acts of

kindness and service of others. Obviously explicit faith in Christ will vigorously empower this life of faith. Yet a vertical relationship with God (through grateful worship) and horizontal relationship with other human beings (through self-sacrificing kindness) does not as such depend on a conscious relationship with Christ. A faith that pleases God, triggered by general revelation, is a possibility open to all.

2. What 'drawing near to God' involves is also illustrated by various other passages in Hebrews. It means approaching God in prayer and worshipping God. Thus the anonymous author writes of 'drawing near to the throne of grace' (Heb. 4: 16). Christians will be conscious of doing this through Jesus, 'since he always lives to make intercession for them' (Heb. 7: 25). But approaching God in prayer and worship does not demand an awareness that such 'drawing near' depends on the priestly intercession of the risen and actively present Christ. That intercession functions, whether or not the worshippers are conscious of Christ when they approach God in prayer.

3. Obviously those who approach God in prayer display faith that he *exists*. They answer the question 'is there anything beyond the visible world?' by bonding with the invisible God. Their faith involves accepting that the world is made by God, whom they worship as the unseen Creator from whom all things have come and toward whom all things are directed. God is both the origin and the goal of the world (Heb. 2: 10).

4. In the faith sparked by general revelation, God is accepted not only as the origin of the universe but also as the One who 'rewards those who seek him'. This means letting God be the future goal of our existence. God is accepted as just and faithful to his promises, however they are construed. In some way those with faith live as pilgrims who hope for 'a better country'. Obviously those who embrace faith do not always enjoy the 'normal' (material) blessings in this life. It is precisely that challenge which prompts the author of Hebrews into appealing elsewhere for perseverance: 'do not abandon that confidence of yours; it brings a great reward' (Heb. 10: 35). At least here in 11: 6, the author does not specify what shape this reward will take, nor does he distinguish between 'rewards' for his Christian readers and for all those others 'who seek' God. He summons all 'God-seekers' alike to put their future in the hands of the just and faithful God (see Heb. 10: 23).

5. Finally, 'seeking' God brings out an attitude that a sincere 'drawing near to God' in worship and prayer presupposes. One approaches God in prayer, because one hopes to receive a favourable response, whatever form it may take. 'Drawing near to the throne of grace' calls for a confidence that one's prayers will be heard. The author of Hebrews leaves matters quite open—as regards the when, the where, and the how of the reward of those who 'seek' God in prayer. Nothing is indicated about when, where, and how prayer will be answered. Everything is concentrated in the assurance that it will be answered.

The five major themes contained in Hebrews 11: 6 allow us to appreciate something of the shape taken by faith triggered by the general revelation of God. While Paul in the opening chapters of Romans indicates, albeit concisely, how and where this revelation takes place,[9] Hebrews 11 lets us spot some key aspects of the faith with which human beings respond to general revelation. In a later chapter we will take up the response of faith to God's special revelation.

Special revelation

Christian faith holds that in a special way (which goes beyond general revelation) God has spoken and acted in the history of Israel and of Jesus Christ, or—to put this more fully—that, in the history of the Old and New Testament, the Father, Son, and Holy Spirit are disclosed as the God who cares for all human beings with an infinitely merciful love. 'Revelation' is the most general term available to designate comprehensively the process or set of events in which God is manifested, the object of faith (the self-revealing God), and the central content of Christian theology (what the tripersonal God has made known to us).

---

[9] Luke's account of Paul's ministry in Acts also opens up further reflection on general revelation, not only through the apostle's longer speech in Athens (Acts 17: 16–34) but also in a much shorter speech made by Paul and Barnabas in Lystra: 'the living God . . . made the heaven, the earth, the sea, and all that is in them . . . he has not left himself without witness in doing good, giving you rains from heaven and fruitful seasons, and filling you with food and your hearts with joy' (Acts 14: 15, 17). On these two speeches, see G. O'Collins, *Salvation for All: God's Other Peoples* (Oxford: Oxford University Press, 2008), 152–60.

Models of revelation

Well into the twentieth century much theology and official teaching more or less identified revelation with content: that is to say, with a set of divinely authenticated truths otherwise inaccessible to human reason and now accepted on God's authority. This 'propositional' view represented revelation as primarily the supernatural disclosure of new truths which significantly enriched our knowledge about God. The First Vatican Council (1869–70), for instance, although it did speak of God as being 'pleased to *reveal himself* and his eternal decrees' (DzH 3004; ND 113; italics mine), placed its emphasis on a propositional approach and closely associated revelation with doctrine and creed. Thus it explained the act of faith as assent to truths or believing 'the things' to be true that God had revealed (DzH 3008; ND 118).

This propositional version of divine revelation has its partial counterpart in the language of the media. Every now and then headlines may announce: 'Startling Revelations Shock Prime Minister.' Two investigative journalists have uncovered a sordid episode involving the bribing of a cabinet minister. Their newspaper dramatically unveils for the public some new and important items of information that may significantly change the prevailing attitude toward the government in power. We are asked to accept as accurate what the journalists report about facts that would have remained unknown to us unless the journalists had discovered them.

During the twentieth century more and more theologians and such official documents as the 1965 Constitution on Divine Revelation *Dei Verbum* (the Word of God) of the Second Vatican Council developed the model of interpersonal encounter or dialogue. Instead of highlighting revelation as God revealing hitherto unknown truths (lower case and in the plural), they understood it to be primarily the self-revelation of God who is Truth (upper case and in the singular) itself. They expounded revelation as first and foremost the gratuitous and redemptive self-manifestation of God who calls and empowers human beings to enter by faith into a new personal relationship. Over and over again the Scriptures witness to such revelatory events, in which God dramatically encountered such figures as Abraham, Moses, Isaiah, Peter, Mary Magdalene, and Paul, and in unexpected ways called them to rethink their worldview and religious commitments and turn to a new faith commitment.

When noting the shift that has taken place from a propositional to a personal model of revelation, I do not want to represent the two models as mutually exclusive. In fact, they imply each other. The experience of a revealing and redemptive dialogue with God does not remain private, incommunicable, and locked away within an inarticulate subjectivity. The faith that responds to the self-revealing God announces what it now knows of God. As Paul put matters: 'Since we have the same spirit of faith as he had who wrote, "I believed, and so I spoke", so we too believe, and so we speak' (2 Cor. 4: 13). In addressing human beings, God says something that they can formulate and pass on. We may call revelation 'propositionable', since it can be expressed in true propositions derived from the divine dialogue with human beings.

Moreover, revelation as a person-to-person, I–Thou encounter between God and human beings does not merely give rise subsequently to true propositions, as if the role of language were only to put into words what had already taken place. Divine revelation also (and, indeed, very often) comes about when human beings are addressed by the words of Scriptures, preaching (supremely Jesus' proclamation of the kingdom), the classic creeds and other doctrinal statements, the words and actions which constitute the sacraments, icons and further works of sacred art, and other accounts drawn from previous revelatory encounters with God. Thus the formulations of faith not only issue from such encounters but also provoke them. A narrative or other version of prior revelatory encounters and 'the things' disclosed through them can bring about fresh revelatory situations and initiate the faith of later believers.

To sum up: even if the personal question (*Who* is revealed?) remains the primary one, the propositional content of revelation (the answer to the question '*What* is revealed?') has its proper place. The personal model emphasizes the *knowledge of* God (a knowledge by acquaintance) which the event of revelation embodies. But this implies that the believer enjoys a *knowledge about* God. The communication of truth *about* God belongs essentially to revelation, even if always at the service of the personal experience *of God* or encounter *with God.*

Both models of revelation, and not merely the propositional one, remain strongly cognitive. The personal model may attend primarily to our 'experienced knowledge of' God, but it continues to speak of knowledge. This model speaks of God's self-disclosure and the divine–human dialogue, but such disclosure involves emerging from a mysterious hiddenness to make oneself 'known'. 'Dia-logue' (*dia-logos*) implies a 'word' (*logos*) communicated or a meaning to be understood. The language of revelation retains a firmly cognitive sense. Church teaching and much theology have shifted from talking about the manifestation of meanings, truths, and mysteries (in the plural) to talking about the divine revelation in Christ, who is *the* Meaning, *the* Truth, and *the* Mystery (in the singular).[10] Yet cognitive overtones still hang around this updated language. There is meaning to be understood, a truth to be known, and a mystery to be disclosed. Cognitive concerns inevitably attend the term 'revelation' and its normal synonyms. This raises an issue when we recall the full scope of biblical and liturgical language.

Biblical witness

In both the Old and the New Testament words expressing God's saving activity normally enjoy a clear priority over such 'communicating' words as 'reveal' and 'make known'. (This observation holds true also of the language of Christian liturgy, which is deeply shaped by biblical language.) Here John's Gospel proves a major exception (perhaps the only biblical exception) to this judgement. Many years ago Rudolf Bultmann highlighted the strong emphasis on revelation found in the Fourth Gospel.[11] Even if that Gospel never formally gives Christ the title of 'Revealer', a rich and variegated language of revelation is applied to him: 'glory' (and 'glorify'), 'light', 'signs', 'truth', 'witness' (as both noun and verb), the 'I am' sayings, 'disclose',

---

[10] Thus the sixteen documents of the Second Vatican Council (1962–5) speak of 'mystery' in the singular 106 times but in the plural only 22 times.

[11] When expounding 'the Theology of the Gospel of John and the Johannine Epistles', Bultmann presented Christ as 'the Revealer whom God has sent', whose 'distinguishing characteristic is the "I am..." of the Revealer' (*Theology of the New Testament*, ii, trans. K. Grobel (London: SCM Press, 1955), 4). In *The Gospel of John: A Commentary*, trans. G. R. Beasley-Murray (Oxford: Basil Blackwell, 1971), Bultmann made the theme of revelation central to his two major divisions of the Gospel: 'The Revelation of the Doxa to the World' (chs. 2–12), which contained subsections ('The Encounter with the Revealer', 'The Revelation as Krisis', 'The Revealer's Struggle with the World', and 'The Revealer's Secret Victory over the World'); and 'The Revelation of the Doxa before the Community' (chs. 13–20). While some major themes of this commentary (e.g. its stress on Gnosticism and speculations about sources) have been generally and rightly questioned, Bultmann correctly read the Fourth Gospel in the key of revelation.

and so forth. The Johannine vocabulary concerned with Christ's identity and activity is heavily revelatory.

Key words constantly recur for expressing the revelation that Christ has brought in his own person. Through the incarnation, believers contemplate the divine 'glory' (*doxa*) of the Word of God (1: 14). His 'sign' at the marriage feast in Cana discloses 'his glory' (2: 11); at the end he prays that the Father would 'glorify' (*doxazein*) him (17: 5: see 17: 22, 24). He is the 'light (*phōs*) of the world' (8: 12; see 3: 19–21; 12: 35, 46), the light that 'shines in the darkness' (1: 5; see 1: 7). He is 'the truth' (*alētheia*) (14: 6; see 1: 17). He bears 'witness' (*marturia*) (8: 13–14, 18) to what he has seen (3: 11).

Where the other Gospels call Jesus' miracles 'acts of power' (*dunameis*), John turns toward their revealing function and speaks of 'signs' (*sēmeia*). Right from their first occurrence these signs 'disclose' (*phaneroun*) the 'glory' of Jesus (2: 1), which is not something reserved for his future (eschatological) condition.[12] According to John, Jesus will enter into his definitive glorification by dying and rising (17: 1, 4–5). But that glory has been disclosed in advance through the earthly ministry, and this theme of his glory already manifested serves to sum up the whole ministry (12: 37–43).

The 'I am' sayings, which reveal various aspects of Jesus' person and work ('I am the true bread, I am the light of the world, I am the good shepherd, I am the way, the truth, and the life', and so forth), culminate in the absolute 'I am' (8: 58) that recalls the divine self-presentation of Exodus 3: 14. Jesus is the epiphany of God.

From its opening verses, John's Gospel makes it clear that the coming of Christ reveals One who was eternally 'with God' (the Father). Very quickly the Holy Spirit enters the divine 'equation'. While not directly recounting the baptism of Jesus, the evangelist implies it and twice adds the detail that the Spirit not only descended on Jesus but also 'remained on him' (1: 32–3). What of the revelation of the Holy Spirit in the Johannine testimony?

---

[12] See Mark 13: 26 about 'the Son of Man coming with great power and glory'; Matt. 25: 31 about the Son of Man at the future judgement 'sitting on the throne of his glory'; and Luke 24: 26 about the risen Christ 'entering into his glory'. By way of exception, Luke applies the language of glory (9: 31–2) to the episode of the Transfiguration which, like Mark and Matthew, he situates in the earthly ministry of Jesus.

According to John, the Spirit comes from Jesus, is sent by Jesus, or is bestowed by Jesus (7: 39; 15: 26; 19: 30, 34; 20: 22). At the same time, the sending of the Spirit, so it is disclosed, does not involve merely Jesus; this sending depends on the Father as does the inner-trinitarian 'proceeding': 'When the Spirit comes whom I will send you from (*para*) from the Father, the Spirit of truth who proceeds (*ekporeutai*) from (*para*) the Father, that One will bear witness to me' (15: 26). John also talks about the Father 'giving' the Spirit (14: 16–17) or 'sending' the Spirit (14: 26), albeit in response to Jesus' prayer and in the name of Jesus.

John's witness to the revelation of the tripersonal God is located firmly in the immediate context of Jesus' death and resurrection (13: 1–21: 25). The evangelist also witnesses to that revelation being communicated through the incarnation (1: 1–18) and the public ministry (1: 19–12: 50). As the Revealer right from the start (1: 14), Jesus has manifested the glory of God the Father (17: 4). But the account of the Last Supper, the passion, and the resurrection articulates the trinitarian revelation even more clearly, above all as regards the manifestation of the Holy Spirit.

Revelation and salvation

It is not that John's Gospel lacks the language of salvation. The revelation that this Gospel attests goes beyond any 'mere' matter of information. It sets believers free from sin, judgement, hunger, and thirst, and communicates to them saving life. 'Life' (*zōē*) turns up constantly in John, and highlights the salvific force of revelation. Jesus is 'the bread of life' (6: 48), who 'gives life to the world' (6: 37) and gives it 'abundantly' (10: 10; see 10: 28). He is the 'light of life' (8: 12), even life itself (14: 6; see 11: 25). The light of revelation is inseparable from the life of salvation, and vice versa.

If we look beyond John's Gospel, salvation language predominates over revelation language when the Bible and Christian liturgy witness to what God does for human beings faced with sin and evil. The Nicene Creed confesses the motive for the incarnation to be 'for the sake of our salvation' (*propter nostram salutem*), rather than 'for the sake of revealing himself to us' (*propter revelationem sui ipsius nobis*). Almost inevitably the terminology of revelation does not cover the full scope of what God does for us, and seems to narrow things down to the divine answer to our quest for meaning and enlightenment.

But here we should recall that revelation proves both informative *and* effective. The very fact that God speaks to human beings is a saving and transforming gift. Far from being a mere presupposition *prior* to salvation, the divine self-manifestation redeems and saves us. As the Scriptures often affirm, the word of God shows itself to be powerful, 'living and active' (Heb. 4: 12). When it signifies and communicates something, it also effects what it signifies and brings about a saving communion between God and human beings. Thus Paul understands his apostolic preaching to communicate the realities he proclaims. As the word of God, this preaching creates the faith and reconciliation it announces (2 Cor. 5: 18–20). Far from being merely the 'disinterested' telling of past events, it brings the revealing and saving action of God to bear on its hearers (Rom. 10: 14–17). Such a dynamic view of revelation enjoys its counterpart in passages from the Old Testament, like God's communication to the prophet Isaiah: 'as the rain and snow come down from heaven and do not return there until they have watered the earth, making it bring forth and sprout, giving seed to the sower and bread to the eater, so shall *my word* be that goes out from my mouth. It shall not return to me empty, but it shall accomplish that which I purpose, and succeed in the thing for which I sent it' (Isa. 55: 10–11; italics mine). Modern speech-theory also appreciates the power of the word. Sincere sharing and self-disclosure affect the partners in dialogue. They do much more than reveal facts about themselves. Through self-revelation and mutual acceptance they change each other.

In short, the divine self-revelation is ever so much more than the mere communication of information. God's word always brings with it healing and transforming power. When it calls its hearers to faith, it powerfully enables them to respond. If it is a word, it is 'the word of life' (1 John 1: 1), the truth that sets free (John 8: 32) and transforms.

'Revelation' and 'salvation' merge so closely that the Second Vatican Council employed the terms almost interchangeably in *Dei Verbum*. The opening chapter shuttled back and forth between the two terms. Take this passage from article 2:

This economy of *revelation* takes place through deeds and words, which are intrinsically connected with each other. Thus the works performed by

God in the history of *salvation* manifest and bear out the doctrine and realities signified by the words; the words, for their part, proclaim the works and elucidate the mystery they contain. The intimate truth, which this *revelation* gives us about God and the *salvation* of human beings, shines forth in Christ, who is both the mediator and the fullness of all *revelation*.

(italics and trans. mine)

As far as the council was concerned, the history of revelation is the history of salvation and vice versa. Here we could integrate the way in which the special activity of God in biblical history involves both revelation and salvation and speak of the divine *self-communication*. Together, revelation and salvation constitute the history of God's self-communication to human beings.

This revealing and saving history takes place within human experience. Revelation involves the divine Revealer, acts of revelation, and those who in faith receive the revelation. Likewise salvation involves the Saviour, acts of salvation, and the saved. Revelation and salvation cannot, as it were, hang in the air without reaching their 'object' and being accepted (or rejected) by their addressees. When God is revealed and salvation takes place, revelation comes to individuals and the community, and people experience salvation. Revelation and salvation simply cannot happen *outside* the experience of human beings. Understood in terms of the analysis offered in Chapter 3, experience provides the context where God's revelation and salvation have occurred and will continue to occur.

Hence I propose speaking of revelation as an essential part of the total process of *experiencing the divine self-communication*. 'Experience' points to the place where human beings meet God. 'Self-communication' indicates that revelation always involves the offer of saving grace, that active presence of the tripersonal God who delivers human beings from evil and comes to share with them the divine life.

No other Christian writers have expressed more beautifully the human experience of the divine self-communication than John (in the First Letter of John) and Augustine. (I speak here of 'John' as the author of that letter, however we precisely identify him.) The First Letter of John opens by testifying to that revelation which was *heard*, *seen*, and *touched* in Jesus Christ, and proclaims the apostolic experience of God's self-manifestation in his Son:

That which was from the beginning,
which we have heard, which we have seen with our eyes,
which we have looked upon and touched with our hands,
concerning the word of life—the life was made manifest,
and we saw it and testify to it, and proclaim to you the eternal life,
which was with the Father and was made manifest to us—
that which we have seen and heard we proclaim also to you,
so that you may have fellowship with us;
and our fellowship is with the Father and with his Son Jesus Christ.

(1 John 1: 1–3)

In his turn, Augustine fastens upon the five senses to portray his conversion. He heard, saw, smelled, tasted, and touched God. Or rather God took the initiative and spoke to him, shone upon him, shed fragrance about him, touched him, and let him taste the divine goodness:

You called to me; you cried aloud to me; you broke my barrier of deafness. You shone upon me; your radiance enveloped me; you put my blindness to flight. You shed your fragrance about me; I drew breath and I gasp for your sweet odour. I tasted you, and now I hunger and thirst for you. You touched me, and I am inflamed with love for your peace.

(*Confessions*, 10. 27)

In this powerful and poetic way, Augustine expresses his total experience of God—that is to say, the saving revelation that broke in and changed Augustine's life forever.

Both John and Augustine invoke the immediacy of their experience. John's statement gives considerable space to the active aspect of the apostolic experience: 'What we have heard, seen, looked upon, and touched we testify to and proclaim.' Augustine's language highlights his own initial receptivity in the face of the divine activity: God called to him, cried alone to him, and so forth. Then comes Augustine's response which puts matter much more intensely than John: 'I gasp, I hunger and thirst, I am inflamed with love for your peace.' The degree of intensity and activity/passivity can vary, and (in terms of a distinction that I will explain in the next chapter) John deals with the experience of apostolic, 'foundational' revelation and Augustine with that of later, 'dependent' revelation. Nevertheless, in both cases human beings encounter God directly and not from a distance.

Furthermore, both John and Augustine write about events in which they are personally and deeply involved, not about pieces of information they have picked up from some authority nor about conclusions they have reached through argumentation. They were very much alive when the experiences of God happened to them and also disclosed what their life was and was to be. Their entire existence was affected; we can spot a multi-levelled structure in what they went through. Their accounts show us how—in different degrees—the human senses, intellect, feelings, will, memory, and other powers were involved. If in Augustine's case an individual person was the subject of the experience, John proclaims the collective experience of the apostolic community. What 'we have seen and heard' has called that community into existence and shaped its destiny. Where Augustine's individual concerns come through strongly, John's proclamation summarizes a collective experience that founds and supports a common life and mission.

I have been applying to the passages from John and Augustine some items in my analysis of experience. One might continue to do this, by remarking on the concrete nature of the apostolic experience ('what have heard, seen, looked upon, and touched'). Likewise the experiences of John and Augustine carry meaning, reveal novelty, and can be classified as positive. Both writers remember, discern, interpret, and communicate what they have undergone.

The account offered in the last few pages about revelation provides the means for reflecting on the religious experiences which John and Augustine record and which are nothing if not experiences of God's revealing and saving self-communication to human beings. For those who want a brief answer to the question 'What is special revelation?' (or revelation in the special history of divine self-communication) we can hardly do better than point to the experiences which, in their different ways, these two writers evoke and describe.

Means of revelation

How was/is revelation experienced? By what means did/does it take place? Years ago at a wedding breakfast in Oxford, a guest seated next to me enquired what I was doing: 'At the moment', I replied, 'I am writing a book on revelation.'[13] Excitedly he asked: 'Have you had any revelations yourself?' Obviously he supposed that revelation always implied dramatic, intense experiences in which one sees a vision or in an ecstasy hears a heavenly voice. This was to forget 'the many and various ways' (Heb. 1: 1) in which God has spoken and continues to speak. Any human experience can convey a self-communication of God. The means of revelation can encompass both common and uncommon experiences and all manner of positive and negative experiences.

The Old Testament records an innumerable variety of experiences which proved the means for conveying some divine self-communication.[14] An extraordinary vision of the heavenly throne room mediates the call of the prophet Isaiah or perhaps, more specifically, his call to intervene in Judean politics (Isa. 6: 1–13). Ezekiel's ecstasies, the patriarch Joseph's dreams (Gen. 37: 5–10) and his interpretation of dreams (Gen. 40: 1–23), and the theophanies experienced by Moses convey God's revealing and saving purposes. But God also speaks through ordinary, inner states of anxiety and joy, through current events, and through everyday sights. Thus the psalms of individual lamentation and thanksgiving repeatedly express such all-pervasive human troubles as sickness, false accusation, loneliness, and persecution. Various sufferers picture these situations and their experience of God's activity on their behalf (e.g. Pss. 3, 6–7, 12, and 22). The coming birth of a child (its mother was probably either the wife of Isaiah or the mother of Hezekiah) becomes a sign that witnesses to the truth of the prophet's prediction (Isa. 7: 10–14). Jeremiah sees an almond branch (1: 11–12), a pot on the boil (1: 13–14), and a potter at work (18: 1–12), and these sights all bring him God's revealing word. The fall of Jerusalem in 587 BC, while in one sense a relatively minor political catastrophe of the kind that has happened over and over again in human history, also manifested the purposes of God. The Israelites came to know God and the meaning of life more profoundly both through exceptional moments and dramatic events like the return from their Babylonian captivity and through quietly

---

[13] G. O'Collins, *Theology and Revelation* (Cork: Mercier Press, 1968).
[14] On God's self-revelation in the Old Testament, see H.-D. Preuss, *Old Testament Theology*, trans. L. G. Perdue, i (Edinburgh: T. & T. Clark, 1995), 200–26.

pondering the everyday experience of death that says so much about the vanity of human wishes (Ecclesiastes).

The psalms testify to the way the Israelites experienced God's presence and power in situations that regularly recurred or through activities in which they repeatedly engaged—like pilgrimages to Jerusalem and worship in the temple. Yet prophets called on the same people to be open to new and extraordinary divine acts. Thus Hosea proclaimed a renewal in which the people would experience a fresh start (2: 6–7, 14–15; 3: 4–5). Isaiah announced a new Davidic king (9: 1–7; 11: 1–10), Jeremiah a new covenant (31: 31–4), Ezekiel (in his vision of the valley of the dry bones) a new life for the people (37: 1–14), and Second Isaiah a new exodus (40: 1–11). Nothing expressed more vividly the need to reckon with new, surprising experiences than the divine command in Second Isaiah: 'Remember not the former things, nor consider the things of old. Behold I am doing a new thing' (Isa. 43: 18–19). H. W. Wolff sums up the way in which the prophets called the people to face new events in which God's revealing and saving activity would be experienced: 'The breakthrough to what lies in the *future* is the heart of their mission and the essential element in their prophetic office. To be sure, they are concerned with Israel's *traditions* and *history*, and even more with its *present*, but the accounts of their calls and of the missions entrusted to them make it clear that the absolutely decisive factor is the announcing and bringing in of what is *radically new*.'[15]

It seems incontestable. The experiences that carry divine revelation into human history can stretch from what is utterly common to what is stunningly new and even unique. That conclusion emerges easily from the Old Testament with its rich variety of historical, sapiential, and prophetic books. The record of Israel's experience is almost four times as long as the New Testament and took something like a thousand (as opposed to less than one hundred) years to come into existence.

At the same time, however, the briefer New Testament record establishes the same thesis: all manner of ordinary and extraordinary experiences mediated God's saving revelation. In his preaching Jesus introduced a wide range of everyday events which point to the divine

---

[15] H. W. Wolff, *The Old Testament: A Guide to its Writings*, trans. K. R. Crim (London: SPCK, 1974), 62; italics mine.

mercy, presence, and power: a woman hunting through her house for some mislaid money, a boy who leaves home to see the world, the growth of crops, sheep that stray, and many other items that belonged to daily life in ancient Galilee. The ministry of Jesus took place in the violent setting of a divided country occupied by a foreign power—a tragic situation that turns up repeatedly in human history. In such a context the killing of a religious reformer like John the Baptist and the slaughter of those Galileans 'whose blood Pilate mingled with their sacrifices' (Luke 13: 1) came easily. At the end Jesus himself was executed as one of a batch, outside the walls of Jerusalem—a normal enough affair under the Roman administration. In that sense the crucifixion belonged among the 'ordinary' experiences which conveyed saving revelation of God. Nevertheless, among the means by which that revelation came, one must also remember the miracles performed by Jesus and the unique event of the resurrection. Nothing could be more 'extraordinary' or 'uncommon' than his victory over death, the beginning of the new creation.

All in all, in the history of the Old and New Testament and in our situation today, God communicates his saving self-revelation through an indefinitely wide range of experiences: from the most dramatic and unusual to the most ordinary and commonplace. God's purposes can be served by all kinds of means—from the remarkable language of Second Isaiah to the dull words of some preacher in the twenty-first century. Family life, political episodes, religious worship, aesthetic experiences, and other human realities can all shape the medium through which God's saving word comes to us. An endless variety of experiences convey the divine revelation.

We must reckon also with 'primitive' means that can bear and bring revelation: such as (1) dreams and (2) the casting of lots. (1) We noted above the dreams of the patriarch Joseph and his role as an interpreter of dreams. The New Testament follows suit with the dreams of Joseph (Matt. 1: 20–4; 2: 13–15, 19–23), dreams that played a crucial part in guiding his actions at the birth of Jesus and in the face of threats from Herod the Great. Carl Jung and other psychologists would encourage us to assign more importance to our dreamlife; it need not be a mere concession to some 'primitive' instinct of human beings if God were also to use dreams as means for communicating revelation. (2) But what of the casting of lots? In a key episode that involved his son Jonathan and the war against the

Philistines, Saul used the *Urim* and *Thummim* to decide between two alternative courses of action (1 Sam. 14: 36–46). We find something similar in the Acts of the Apostles, when Peter presided at the choice between two possible candidates to replace Judas Iscariot. Lots were cast to let Jesus the 'Lord' show his choice of the one who should complete the ranks of the twelve apostles (Acts 1: 15–26). Both the Old and the New Testament shared the belief that God's will could be shown through the casting of lots (e.g. Lev. 16: 8; 1 Chron. 25: 8–31). Chosen by lot for the once-in-a-lifetime privilege of offering incense in the Temple, Zachariah was 'in place' to receive from an angel a message announcing the birth of John the Baptist (Luke 1: 8–20). The casting of lots, no less than dreams, could feature among the means for indicating God's purposes and for bringing about the divine will.

More serious doubts can flare up when we move beyond positive and 'peak' experiences of individuals and groups (e.g. visions, deliverance from death, and prophetic calls) and 'neutral' means like dreams and the casting of lots, and begin including such 'negative' experiences as episodes of suffering, sin, and further evil among the means through which God communicates saving revelation. Yet the witness of the Bible proves clear. If the Israelites knew their God through the peak experiences of liberation from Egypt and entry into the promised land, God also spoke to them through the trough experience of their deportation to Babylon. The passage we quoted above from 1 John builds itself around 'the word of life' that has been 'heard', 'seen', 'looked upon', and 'touched'. But the Johannine literature testifies as well to the experience of Christ's death and invites its readers to 'look on him whom they have pierced' (John 19: 35–7). Paul recalls the dramatic meeting on the road to Damascus that turned his life around (1 Cor. 9: 1: 15: 8; Gal. 1: 11–15). Yet he also recognizes the divine power of salvation manifested in the 'weakness' or utter vulnerability he constantly experiences on his apostolic mission (2 Cor. 4: 7–12; 6: 4–10; 11: 23–9; 12: 7–10).

In theory and even more in practice, many Christians are slow to admit that episodes of ugliness rather than beauty, of hatred rather than love, and of sin rather than virtue can become the channels of God's saving revelation. Such experiences appear destructive rather than redemptive, confusing and threatening rather than illuminating. Nevertheless, the Scriptures and repeated Christian experience agree:

evil, including sin, can become means by which divine revelation is communicated. When King David committed adultery and murder, his sin occasioned some profound moments of truth about his state before God and future destiny (2 Sam. 11–12).

In this case the courageous intervention of the prophet Nathan prompted David into discerning and interpreting the situation very quickly. Frequently, however, episodes of sin and evil do not reveal any meaning so readily. It may take years, even a lifetime, before some disorders and seemingly pointless atrocities are understood for what they say about revelation and salvation and the human need for God's initiatives. Sinful and tragic situations can leave us lastingly appalled and puzzled. If the first Christians rapidly appreciated and interpreted the unique and positive experience of Jesus' resurrection, his shameful death on a cross did not quickly yield up its meaning and purpose. Initially they could only say that the crucifixion happened 'according to the definite plan and foreknowledge of God' (Acts 2: 23), which is about as minimal an interpretation a believer might offer. However quickly or slowly the divine message comes through, negative episodes of suffering, sin, and other evil can convey the divine self-manifestation, no less than happier 'moments of glad grace' (W. B. Yeats, 'When you are old').

Word and event

Let me begin by explaining the heading. A key maxim in workshops on contemporary writing cautions: 'Show, don't tell.' For all its value, however, this maxim does not apply to the means adopted for communicating the divine self-revelation. God both shows (in events of great symbolic power) and tells (through the words of prophets, Jesus, apostles, and others). Revelation displays a kind of sacramental principle. Like the sacraments where actions (e.g. in baptism the use of water) and words (the baptismal formula) work together to effect the sacrament, revelation comes about, above all, by means of *words* that proclaim and illuminate *events*.

The Israelites remembered and interpreted the exodus and other crucial events as YHWH's deeds which disclosed the divine intentions in their regard. Words glossed such events. After their deliverance from the Egyptians, Miriam and other women did not celebrate the courage of the Israelites or the leadership of Moses. Their song highlighted YHWH's act of salvation: 'Sing to the Lord, for he has triumphed gloriously; the horse and his rider he has thrown into the sea' (Exod. 15: 21). They acknowledged God as the real agent of their victory: 'I am the Lord your God, who brought you out of the land of Egypt, out of the house of bondage' (Exod. 20: 2).

Christians inherited such convictions about God's saving deeds, and added what they themselves had experienced in Jesus' life, death, and resurrection, along with the coming of the Holy Spirit. They added their word when discerning and interpreting these events as the climax in the divine activity on behalf of the human race. Thus the discourse of Peter on the day of Pentecost elucidated the deeds of God: 'People of Israel, listen to what I have to say. Jesus of Nazareth, a man attested to you by God with mighty works, wonders, and signs which God did through him in your midst, as you yourselves know—this Jesus, delivered up according to the definite plan and foreknowledge of God, you crucified and killed by the hands of lawless men. But God raised him up, having freed him from death, because it was impossible for him to be held in its power' (Acts 2: 22–4).

The words of the Nicene Creed and other early professions of faith would embody the same conviction: the preaching of the apostles had shown how certain historical events, centred on Jesus of Nazareth, manifested God and carried a decisive meaning for human salvation.

Having said all that, we need to scrutinize further 'event' and 'word', which summarize the means used for divine revelation. The series of collective experiences, in which God acts and which together make up the history of revelation and salvation, include events that undoubtedly took place (like the reign of King David, deportation to Babylon, the preaching of John the Baptist, the ministry of Jesus, and the fall of Jerusalem) and things like the creation and fall of Adam and Eve that have a mythical rather than an historical character. The dissimilarities between the known factual status of, let us say, the departure of Abraham and Sarah from Ur and Haran into Canaan and the crucifixion of Jesus are startling. Nevertheless, revelation and salvation encompass events which on any showing belong to human history. In the Roman Forum the images of Jewish captives and the seven-branch candlestick from the temple carved inside the Arch of Titus still vividly assure viewers about the factuality of what, in their very different ways, the Romans, the Christians, and the Jews experienced at the fall of Jerusalem in AD 70. At the heart of the biblical history of revelation and salvation lies a set of events which certainly occurred—to be experienced then by believers and non-believers alike and accessible now to common historical investigation, even if the Christian discernment and interpretation of these events embodies a specifically theological understanding shared only by believers.

The *word* lights up the revealing and saving values of events, which in some cases might otherwise seem merely anonymous and meaningless blows of fate. Thus the message of Second Isaiah, Jeremiah, and Ezekiel discerns and interprets the Babylonian captivity—something that without their prophetic word could look like just another dreary case of a small nation overrun and deported by a major power. The divinely authorized word of interpretation shows such events of secular history to be acts of God in the special history of revelation and salvation. That word also authorized the message prompted by such simple, everyday sights in the life of Jeremiah as those of an almond branch, a pot on the boil, and a potter at his work (see above). Whether the events were major or seemingly only minor, the revealing word opened up their revelatory meaning.

When then is the more significant means for the divine self-revelation to human beings: the experienced event or the interpreting word? Many theologians continue to put fuller weight on the word of God (the *locutio Dei*) rather than on the events to be interpreted. They can appeal, of course, to the creedal phrase about the Holy Spirit 'speaking through the prophets'. They stress the role of reflection, discernment, perspective, and interpretation—in short, the place of the word—as the key to the history of revelation and salvation. The presence of the interpreting word makes a particular stretch of secular history in the ancient Middle East a window through which we can glimpse God's saving intentions.

Such a stress on the perspective supplied by the revealing word leaves unanswered the question: why was this special prophetic and apostolic interpretation available for *these* historical experiences and events and not for *those*? Was there something about *these* historical experiences that prompted and even required that theological reflection? A one-sided stress on the word may rob of any special significance the events that it interprets. But the truth about the history of revelation and salvation is surely the opposite. Ultimately the word remains subordinate to the events and, specifically, to those events concerned with the person who stands at the centre of that history. God's supreme act in the history of Israel was to raise Jesus from the dead. Here action has priority over word, the effected reality over any interpretation of it.

Puzzlement over the meaning of 'acts of God' may lead theologians to press the role of word over the event. Some scholars have followed George Ernest Wright (1909–74) in labelling biblical events as '(mighty) acts of God' but without explaining in depth what such special acts of God mean. In the light of what was expounded in Chapter 2 above, I suggest briefly characterizing such acts as follows.

First, to describe some event in that way is to recognize a special presence and a particular activity of God, who is doing something qualitatively different from the 'ordinary' divine work of creating and sustaining the universe. There are various degrees of engagement on the part of God. Some events or series of events, as well as some persons, reveal more of the divine concerns and interests than others. To deny such different degrees of divine engagement with the world and its multiform history logically leads to deism.

Second, the particular divine activity qualified as 'a special act of God' remains in some measure recognizably independent of the world and created causality. Thus the resurrection of Jesus manifests in a unique way an autonomous divine causality. Other happenings designated 'special acts of God' may also be 'acts of human beings' and entail an array of human causes and agents. Thus the events which brought about the Babylonian captivity or the execution of Jesus involve fairly elaborate interactions from different human agents. Yet even in such cases a certain degree of independent divine causality remains, and allows Paul, for example, to say of what God allowed to happen, 'he gave up his only Son for all of us' (Rom. 8: 32).

Third, special acts of God imply a religious claim and convey moral messages. Thus the ministry, death, and resurrection of Jesus challenged and continues to challenge men and women to rethink their worldview and way of life. On the day of Pentecost, Peter's proclamation of God's special activity in the history of Jesus concluded with the call to repent and be baptized (Acts 2: 38).

Fourth, the freedom, unpredictability, and novelty of a special act of God involves an element of mystery. Such acts are never unambiguously so. They remain concealed to the extent that people may see or fail to see these events as acts of God. Recognition remains uncompelled. The factor of relative concealment allows cognitive freedom to persist. There are signs to be perceived but no overwhelming evidence; we have enough light to make us responsible but not enough to take away our freedom.[16]

Mediators of special revelation

Like the means for the divine self-communication, the mediators and messengers of that saving revelation have been and remain indefinitely various. In the whole history of God's self-communication, both inside and outside the Jewish-Christian story, certain individuals enjoy uncommon (religious) experiences or else display an uncommon capacity to discern, interpret, and express the experiences they share with others. Either way they play a special role in communicating the divine revelation and salvation. Whether institutionalized (e.g. as kings and priests) or non-institutionalized (e.g. as prophets), these individuals prove themselves to be chosen channels through which people at large experience God's self-communication. In this sense there is no absolute equality in the human experience of God. Hence part of our answer to the question 'How did/does the divine self-communication occur?' must consist in pointing to the role and variety of mediators and messengers.

Such mediators people the pages of the Old and New Testament: Abraham and Sarah, Moses, the prophets, Mary of Nazareth, the apostles, and the supreme case, Jesus himself (see 1 Tim. 2: 5). The history of Christianity (and of other religions) shows a constant line of men and women whose special gifts enabled them to convey God's saving words to others: saints, founders of religious movements, prophetic figures, outstanding church leaders, and the rest. Nor should we pass over the innumerable lesser mediators: from Christian parents in Korea to catechists in Africa, from parish priests in California to the Little Sisters of Jesus in Papua New Guinea. Later

---

[16] This theme of sufficient but not overwhelming light characterizes the *Pensées* of Pascal; see the trans. by A. J. Krailsheimer (Harmondsworth: Penguin, 1988), nos. 394, 427, 429, and 461.

I will examine the roles of some of these mediators: in particular, Jesus and his apostles. Here let me dwell on one group, the Old Testament prophets, who served as intermediaries between God and the people.

Even a cursory glance at Old Testament prophecy reveals its rich diversity: from the early prophets like Deborah (Judg. 4: 4–16; 5: 1, 12),[17] Elisha, and Elijah, through such classic prophets as Amos, Hosea, and Isaiah, down to the post-exilic prophets like Haggai, Zechariah, and Malachi. On occasion Abraham (Gen. 20: 7; see Ps. 105: 15) and David (Acts 2: 29–31) were called prophets. Moses was deemed to be the founder of Israelite prophecy and even its pinnacle (Deut. 18: 15–20; 34: 10–12). The name of prophet belonged also to the non-Israelite Balaam (Num. 22–4) and to bands who used music and dancing to enter into a state of ecstatic exaltation and induce divine utterances (1 Sam. 10: 5–7; 19: 20–4; 1 Kgs. 22: 10, 12). Prophetic elements also showed up in the life and work of Nazirites like Samuel. The Old Testament record of prophets and prophetic experiences exhibits a remarkable diversity.

In one way or another, prophets were called to interpret and make known the divine mind and will. God was specially present to the point of even identifying with what they said or did. Their personal judgement and human words became endowed with divine authority. In the Old Testament the expression 'the word of God' occurs 247 times, and in 225 of those cases we deal with a prophetic word.[18]

The story of the prophets matches point after point from the account of experience provided in Chapter 3 above. Let us dwell on five such points. First, Amos records the *intense immediacy* of his call; it was something that suddenly and directly came to him, even though he lacked any expected training and preparation. God abruptly acted and swept Amos into a new existence. The shepherd-turned-prophet explained to the priest of Bethel: 'I am no prophet nor a prophet's son; but I am a herdsman and a dresser of sycamore trees, and the Lord took me from following the flock. The

[17] The Hebrew Bible names three other women as prophetesses: Miriam (Exod. 15: 20), Huldah (2 Kgs. 22: 14), and Noadiah (Neh. 6: 14).

[18] On prophecy, see R. E. Clements, *Old Testament Prophecy: From Oracles to Canon* (Louisville, Ky.: Westminster John Knox, 1996); H. B. Huffmon et al. 'Prophecy', *ABD* v. 477–502; W. Klein et al., *TRE* xxvii. 473–517; Preuss, *Old Testament Theology*, ii. 67–9; E. Zenger et al., *Einleitung in das Alte Testament* (Stuttgart: Kohlhammer Verlag, 1995), 293–436.

Lord said to me, "Go, prophesy to my people Israel"' (Amos 7: 14–15; see 3: 8). Amos and other classical prophets did not take the initiative in actively seeking a prophetic career. They experienced a call coming to them from God, who unexpectedly overwhelmed them. As Jeremiah's complaints vividly illustrate, at times prophets followed their call with deep reluctance (see e.g. Jer. 20: 7–9). If the prophetic experiences exemplified the immediacy of a direct and deep encounter with God, the role of the prophets, at least initially, was passive rather than active. They reacted only after God had acted upon them.

Second, the life of the prophets was revealed in their initial experience. It disclosed what their life was and was to be. If God's call took Amos' life in a new direction, this proved even more startlingly true of Jeremiah. His whole life, and not just some months of it, coincided with his prophetic vocation and experience.

Third, the prophetic experience comes across as a multi-levelled affair affecting *the entire existence of the subject* and involving a broad range of spiritual and physical powers. While frenzy characterized the early bands of prophets and admittedly could be, in principle, a medium for communicating genuine revelation, it is not a fully human form for conveying God's saving message and becomes less prominent as time went by. To be sure, we meet an unusual psychological intensity, even abnormality, in Ezekiel's visions, ecstasy, shaking, dumbness, and possible temporary paralysis (e.g. 3: 22–7; 4: 4–8; 24: 27; 33: 22). However, the classical prophets normally do not mediate the divine message through ecstasy, dreams, or other such states, but by consciously using their various powers. They look, listen, answer, and deliver a message. Thus Isaiah's vision in the temple ends: 'I heard the voice of the Lord saying, "Whom shall I send, and who will go for me?" Then I said: "Here am I! Send me." And he said, "Go, and say to this people: 'Hear and hear, but do not understand'" (Isa. 6: 8–9). Jeremiah provides another such case, when the Lord first questions him about the things he sees before communicating the divine intentions (Jer. 1: 11, 13; see Amos 8: 1–2). Here and elsewhere, prophecy presents itself as a complex experience involving the whole person and a full range of human powers.

Fourth, like other experiences, the prophetic experience does not exist in general. Usually the prophetic writings, even if these introductions or 'superscriptions' come from later editing, make this point by specifying the *particular* date and place of their origin. The last chapter cited the opening words of Amos and the vision in the temple recounted by Isaiah; both passages highlight the particularity of their experiences. Jeremiah likewise indicates the specific setting in which the word of the Lord came to him: 'in the days of Josiah the son of Amon, king of Judah, in the thirteenth year of his reign. It came also in the days of Jehoiakim the son of Josiah, king of Judah, and until the end of the eleventh year of Zedekiah, the son of Josiah, king of Judah, until the captivity of Jerusalem in the fifth month' (Jer. 1: 2–3). For all his abnormality, Ezekiel also provides details as to the date and place of his prophetic experience (1: 1–3). Such experience is nothing if not concrete. It happens at particular times, in particular places, and to particular persons who must convey this or that message to specific audiences.

Fifth, the previous chapter's analysis of human experience observed how it is discerned, interpreted, and *communicated*. The Nicene Creed ('the Holy Spirit spoke through the prophets') reminds us that the prophets were primarily speakers. Jeremiah seems to have used Baruch as his secretary (Jer. 36: 1–32). Normally it was left to followers of the prophets and others to collect, edit, arrange, and expand the prophetic oracles before publishing them in written form. The prophets themselves proclaimed the divine word, announcing God's saving intentions and denouncing human failure. They also expressed their prophetic message through symbolic gestures. Thus Isaiah acted out a threatening future by going around naked and barefoot for three years like a prisoner-of-war (Isa. 20: 2–4). Jeremiah carried a yoke on his shoulders (Jer. 27: 1–2) as a sign of the yoke of Babylon imposed by God on Judah and her neighbours (Jer. 21: 1–10; 32: 3–5). Jeremiah also remained unmarried and childless to suggest the grim prospects that awaited Jewish parents and their children (Jer. 16: 1–9). Hosea may have entered an unhappy marriage as a means for communicating his word from the Lord (Hos. 1: 2–9). As well as expressing some message, these symbolic gestures also mysteriously helped to bring about what they represented. The prophets shared in the dynamic role of God's revealing word, which effects what it signifies.

A later chapter will take up the theme of inspiration. To anticipate matters, we can state that the special divine self-communication to the prophets meant that they were inspired to speak and act, but not—in general—to write. The inspiration to write down their prophetic utterances belonged rather to those who came after them. The same conclusion emerges from the picturesque descriptions that Isaiah, Jeremiah, and Ezekiel gave of their vocations: they were all called to speak. The lips of Isaiah were consecrated for that mission (Isa. 6: 6–7), while Jeremiah received the word of the Lord in his mouth (Jer. 1: 9). Ezekiel, admittedly, had to eat a scroll that was to fill his stomach (Ezek. 2: 8–3: 3). This detail suggests writing. Yet even in his case the predominant theme remained speaking (e.g. Ezek. 2: 4, 7; 3: 1, 4).

Much of what I have drawn from the prophets and other material that has appeared in this chapter may well have raised for many readers the bothersome question: do we really know that these things happened? Can we be sure, for instance, that the experiences of the prophets, now well over two thousand years ago, authentically derived from God and that they did inwardly hear communications from God? Reflection on the prophetic experience offers at least seven reasons for being positive but cautious about our conclusions.

Discerning the prophetic experience

1. For the Old Testament the prophetic message, conveyed through words and symbolic actions, remains primary. From the message we may be able to infer something about the personal experiences that lie behind it, but precise and assured evaluations will be hard to come by.

2. We also have to reckon with the chronological gap between the actual events in the lives of the prophets and the final form of the biblical text. Oral and written traditions stretching over many years normally intervened before that text became settled. That complex process reduces any hopes about reaching easy certainties.

3. Third, the prophets repeatedly affirm the divine origin of their message. They do so frequently by means of such traditional formulas as 'Thus says the Lord'. But they themselves normally show little interest in reflecting on and analysing their inner experiences as such.

4. Fourth, such formulas remain so brief and stereotyped that they hardly describe in any real sense the nature of the experiences

that may lie behind them. Traditional expressions for introducing authoritative messages, they rarely seem autobiographical statements about experiences of the prophets. 'The word of the Lord' and 'Thus says the Lord' do not necessarily involve the claim that the prophets literally heard an inner or an outer voice speaking to them. Such conventional categories of announcement may be just that, conventional and no more. Likewise 'to receive a vision' can serve as a technical term for a prophetic revelation, and by no means should always be taken literally.

5. Another, fifth aspect of the problem is this. On the one hand, we cannot expect a given prophet to deliver a message that in form and content strikingly diverges from earlier prophetic messages. It would be unreasonable to demand that level of originality as a test of authentic prophetic experience. On the other hand, however, the fact that later prophets draw on earlier messages and expressions, even if they introduce their own modifications, obviously leaves us with the questions: to what extent are they continuing a tradition rather than witnessing to their personal experience? Where do the traditional elements end and where does their own experience begin? To demand massive originality from the prophets would be to slide over the fact that they are human beings born into a society with its religious traditions and language. Yet the more their message resembles what has gone before, the less sure we will be about identifying the shape of their own personal experience.

6. Further questions arise when we notice how the frontier between what a prophet sees and what a prophet hears often gets blurred. Take the case of Balaam. With 'open eyes' and seeing 'the vision of the Almighty', he delivers 'the oracle' of one 'who hears the words of God' (Num. 24: 15–16; see 24: 3–4). What we meet here is properly speaking no vision but a message, words that the Lord puts into Balaam's mouth (Num. 23: 5, 12, 16). The biblical text calls Samuel's experience as a boy at the sanctuary in Shiloh a 'vision' (1 Sam. 3: 15), but the vision consists in his hearing God's call. At times the Scriptures speak about prophets or others having 'visions' and 'seeing' something or about God 'appearing' or 'showing' this or that, when the reality of some visual experience is not the issue. Talk about a vision or an appearance may simply mean that a communication from God has taken place; a promise or some other message has been received. It

would, for example, be a mistake to insist on the visionary nature of the experience in Genesis 12: 7. Even if it speaks of an 'appearance', the text focuses rather on the promise understood to have been communicated to Abraham: 'The Lord appeared to Abram and said, "To your descendants I will give this land"'. Isaiah reports a 'stern vision', but it is a vision that has been 'told' to him, an 'oracle', something that he has 'heard from the Lord of hosts' (Isa. 21: 1–2, 10). This blurring of the frontier between what is seen and what is heard by the prophets belongs to a general tendency to play down the visual phenomena. What is heard predominates over what is seen.

7. Finally, the *call* of the prophets not only essentially shapes their stories but also highlights the difficulty of discerning what happened. The prophets know themselves to be specially chosen and called by God. Amos simply states his call as a fact (7: 14–15), without elaborating on how it came about. But with others, like Isaiah, Jeremiah, and Ezekiel, we have call-narratives that use common motifs to express the individual experience of the prophet and the personal authority they possess from God.

Ronald Clements classifies the prophetic call-narratives into two groups.[19] The first group, which includes Jeremiah, evokes also the call-experiences of Moses (Exod. 3: 1–4: 17), Gideon (Judg. 6: 11–32), and Saul (1 Sam. 9: 1–10: 16). Here God overcomes an inadequacy and reluctance on the part of the person called. Members of the second group, through some vision of God, are summoned to join the deliberations of the heavenly council (e.g. Isaiah, Ezekiel, and Micaiah-ben-Imlah (1 Kgs. 22: 5–28)). God may be represented as specially equipping the prophet for the task, as in the case of Isaiah where we find the cultic motif of ritual cleansing (Isa. 6: 6–8).[20]

Now in both groups the prophet is often warned that his message will be rejected and that he must endure opposition. But does such a warning truly belong to the original call-experience? Or has a subsequent experience of rejection been projected back into the story of the original call-experience? Such a prior warning, narrated as part of the call-experience, also happily meets the objection: if the

---

[19] R. E. Clements, *Prophecy and Tradition* (Oxford: Basil Blackwell, 1975), 33–9.
[20] Some scholars interpret Isa. 6: 1–13 not so much as the prophet being called but rather as introducing his intervention in Judean politics.

prophetic message were from God, the people would have accepted it. With such a warning inserted into the call-narrative, the people's refusal to listen confirms the authenticity of a given prophet. Or has the warning about the opposition and hostility to be faced become simply a traditional way of speaking about a prophetic call? New prophets, while aware of being authentically called by God, stand in a tradition that prompts them to use traditional motifs to describe the experience of their call.

While not intended to cast doubt on the whole reality of prophets' experiencing the revealing word of God, these seven considerations aim at raising questions and encouraging an appropriate caution when interpreting the prophetic texts. They heard the voice of God, but we need to be modest and careful about our interpretation of the details. The questions I have just raised are not typically raised in the Old Testament itself. What we do find is a persistent awareness of the need to discriminate true prophets from false ones. Both in the history of Israel and elsewhere the possibility of falsehood looms over all prophecy. Has God spoken through *this* prophet? Does the divine authority and a genuine (and genuinely interpreted) experience of God stand behind his or her message?

True and false prophets

Sometimes the Old Testament simply labels certain men as false prophets (e.g. Jer. 27: 12–22) and as those who preach false messages of hope, but does not go into detail about their 'prophetic' lies. Ezekiel finds a major problem with false prophets who advocate nationalistic hope (Ezek. 13: 1–23). Where Old Testament texts go into detail, they identify true and false prophets by appealing in a clear-eyed way to three criteria: past tradition, present behaviour, and future fulfilment.

1. Loyalty to the inherited faith and, in particular, to the Torah provided a major criterion for sorting out prophets. Working signs and wonders might establish a prophet's legitimacy (e.g. 1 Kgs. 18: 20–40). While the power to produce 'omens or portents' could legitimize prophetic proclamations (Deut. 13: 2), this test remained subordinate to fidelity to the covenant effected through Moses. A

heterodox message would not only unmask false prophets but should also carry drastic consequences for them. Prophets who flouted the Mosaic law were to be executed (Deut. 13: 2–5; 18: 19–22).

Jeremiah urged one major lesson from the nation's religious past. Normally the true prophets pronounced words of judgement and predicted disaster. Speaking to the prophet Hananiah, Jeremiah said: 'The prophets who preceded you and me from ancient times prophesied war, famine, and pestilence against many countries and great kingdoms' (28: 8; see 26: 16–19). The bearer of bad news was more likely to be a true prophet. Bearers of good news could easily be false prophets, dominated by their audience and ready to make pleasing announcements. Jeremiah did not, however, propose the word of woe as an absolute criterion; he recognized that a true prophet might bring good tidings of great joy. Yet such joyful prophecies would have to be established by their fulfilment: 'As for the prophet who prophesies peace, when the word of the prophet comes to pass, then it will be known that the Lord has truly sent the prophet' (Jer. 28: 9).

2. Present lifestyle also serves to test prophetic authenticity. False prophets will lead lives stained by moral evil (Jer. 23: 9–40). Hence one knows that 'they speak visions of their own minds, and not from the mouth of the Lord' (Jer. 23: 16). Through Jeremiah God names two false prophets, Ahab and Zedekiah, who have 'committed adultery with their neighbours' wives' and 'have spoken in my name lying words which I did not command them' (Jer. 29: 21–3). Schooled by experience, Isaiah points to some prophets whose vision is blurred by drunkenness; these will 'stumble in giving judgment' (28: 7). In this way prophetic authenticity can be verified or falsified by the test of present moral conduct, rather than by attempts to investigate the historical origins of a prophetic career and assess the experiences that gave rise to it. As William James put this approach, 'by their fruits ye shall know them, not by their roots'.[21]

Where immoral conduct unmasks the false prophet, obedience to the divine will leads true prophets into a life of suffering. This suffering comes as part of the prophetic vocation and is not simply the suffering that virtuous people might expect. Just as the prophets afflict the people with words of judgement, so they themselves will

[21] W. James, *Varieties of Religious Experience* (London: Fontana, 1974), 41.

suffer hostility and endure persecution (Amos 7: 10–17). Loyalty to his prophetic mission brings Jeremiah deep suffering at the hands of the people, the king, the princes, the priests, and the 'prophets' (Jer. 20: 1–26; 26: 1–24). He is known as a genuine prophet by the 'fruits' of persecution. Nevertheless, the mark of suffering does not prove an absolute criterion. False prophets do not always prosper; they may even have to endure a violent death (Jer. 29: 21).

3. Lastly, the future and the fulfilment of predictions feature among the tests of prophecy. True and false prophets will be revealed in retrospect. The death of Hananiah, for example, establishes the falsity of his message and the truth of Jeremiah's (Jer. 28: 15–17). The death in battle of Israel's king vindicates Micaiah-ben-Imlah's prophecy (1 Kgs. 22: 8–40). It is along these lines that Deuteronomy offers a rule for determining whether a prophetic message comes from the Lord or not: 'when a prophet speaks in the name of the Lord, if the word does not come to pass or come true, that is a word which the Lord has not spoken; the prophet has spoken it presumptuously; do not be frightened by it' (Deut 18: 22).

The Old Testament took the 'fulfilment' of prophecy in a broader sense, and not necessarily as some precise prediction being realized exactly.[22] Ezekiel witnesses to his God-given confidence that in the long run authentic prophecy will be acknowledged as such. The Lord encourages him: 'The people are impudent and stubborn. I am sending you to them, and you shall say to them, "Thus says the Lord God." And whether they hear or refuse to hear (for they are a rebellious house), they will know that there has been a prophet among them' (Ezek. 2: 4–5).

All in all, the Old Testament yields a range of tests by which to evaluate the authenticity of prophets. Past, present, and future factors combine to discern and interpret the prophetic experiences.

Conclusion

We will turn next to the saving revelation mediated through the experience of Jesus Christ and the apostolic generation. He entered the history of a people who had been prepared by a divine call and a

---

[22] See Clements, *Prophecy and Tradition*, 53–4.

divine self-communication over many centuries. The experiences of the prophets and the prophetic books that followed formed a major part of the religious context in which Christ played his normative role. It is not possible to ignore or even reject the prophetic experience and still keep one's Christian faith whole.

Such considerations, as well as the power and beauty of the prophetic texts, can prompt us to accept *in general* that the Holy Spirit 'spoke through the prophets'. Yet it remains difficult to settle specifics and confidently affirm just how, when, and where prophets received those personal experiences of God that constitute historical revelation. Some episodes in the life of Jeremiah and Isaiah's vision in the temple might count among such specific instances. In these cases we would like to put the questions: did the prophets perceive an external object or hear an external voice? Or were their experiences rather a matter of objective but interior voices and images? And for that matter, what did Moses perceive when he saw God 'face to face' (Exod. 33: 11)? We might press analogies from the experience of Christian and other mystics. Whatever answer we propose, we need to remember that these are our questions and our distinctions. People in the Old Testament never thought in such terms. We may finish up looking for exact answers when the data cannot support such precision. Ultimately, it seems enough to maintain in general the experience of a special divine self-communication mediated through the prophets, while allowing that particulars may be hard to discern and interpret.

One remarkable result from the religious experience of the prophets, the psalmists, and others should, however, engage our attention: their *image of God*.[23] Israelite experience bred an image of God that set Judaism quite apart from other peoples. At first the Israelites made room for the gods of other peoples. But with increasing clarity they came to acknowledge the exclusive nature and identity of their God. The gap between YHWH and the other 'gods' opened up the point that the Israelites denied the reality of other gods. Yet the difference between Judaism and other religions was more than just

---

[23] See J. J. Scullion, 'God in the Old Testament', *ABD* ii. 1041–8; M. S. Smith, *The Early History of God* (2nd edn. Grand Rapids, Mich.: Eerdmans, 2002); id., *The Memoirs of God: History, Memory, and the Experience of the Divine in Ancient Israel* (Minneapolis: Fortress Press, 2004).

monotheism. Echn Aton's *Song of the Sun* clearly acknowledged only one God. And the Greek philosophers reached the notion of the Absolute or Unmoved Mover. We spot some fundamental differences when we recall that Echn Aton's one god was the sun god. And over against the conclusions of Greek thought, YHWH, if utterly transcendent, was experienced not as a remote Unmoved Mover but as a tender, loving God who called for exclusive love and loyalty from human beings and, especially, from Israel.

The Old Testament image of God combined in an extraordinary way two elements: *majestic transcendence* and a *loving closeness*. If initially and partly associated with sanctuaries and other such places, YHWH was experienced as transcending the normally accepted limits of *space* and went beyond the usual 'frontiers', bringing Israel on its exodus 'from the land of Egypt, and the Philistines from Caphtor and the Syrians from Kir' (Amos 9: 7). Unlike gods of other Middle Eastern nations, Israel's deity was not identified in space as the sun or another heavenly body. The sun, the moon, and the stars were among the things created by God (Gen. 1: 14–18). YHWH also passed beyond the limits of *time*. Other Middle Eastern deities issued from chaos and various myths proclaimed their genesis. Israel's God, however, was known to be simply and always there, 'the first and the last' (Isa. 44: 6), the God who 'in the beginning created the heavens and the earth' (Gen. 1: 1). The Israelites admitted neither a theogony nor an ageing process for their God.

Despite this transcendence of space and time, however, Israel did not shrink from mythical language when speaking of the divine deeds. God crushed 'the heads of Leviathan', 'cut Rahab into pieces' (Ps. 74: 13–14; 89: 10; Isa. 51: 9), and came riding on a storm in a spectacular scenario: 'Smoke went up from his nostrils, | and devouring fire from his mouth; | glowing coals flamed forth from him. | He bowed the heavens, and came down; | thick darkness was under his feet. | He rode on a cherub, and flew: | he came swiftly upon the wings of the wind' (Ps. 18: 7–10; see 29: 3–10; 77: 17–20). Aristotle would have valued the transcendence of Israel's God, but he could not have accepted the lively, mythical imagery of the psalmists. Israel's neighbours accepted such mythical language, but did not recognize a God who transcended space and time.

As regards sexuality, we likewise find a striking blend of elements in Israel's attitude toward God. On the one hand, YHWH had no spouse and offspring, and remained beyond the sexual activities typical of ancient deities. But, on the other hand, Hosea and other prophets talked of God as a husband who revealed a wounded and tender love when his people acted like a harlot: 'Behold, I will allure her, and bring her into the wilderness, and speak tenderly to her' (Hos. 3: 14). Second Isaiah pictured God as 'crying out like a woman in travail' (Isa. 42: 14; see 46: 3–4; 49: 15). YHWH was known to transcend sexuality, and yet the prophets felt free to introduce masculine and feminine imagery in describing God as spouse, mother, and father.[24]

To sum up: the Israelites experienced YHWH as a loving and tenderly devoted God. At the same time, they treasured an elevated notion of their deity. Being so utterly transcendent, YHWH was not to be represented in any carved, moulded, or painted form. Such divine images were strictly forbidden (Exod. 20: 4–5; Lev. 19: 4; Deut. 4: 15–20). This highly elevated and yet intensely personal notion of God was the highest product coming from prophets and others in the Old Testament who experienced the divine self-communication. To talk apologetic language: one could call this notion a moral miracle. It could have arisen only from authentic experiences of God and was not to be explained through the 'merely' human powers of a tiny nation which enjoyed no special philosophical or other intellectual talents.

---

[24] See G. O'Collins, *The Tripersonal God* (Mahwah, NJ: Paulist Press, 1999), 12–23. When expounding above 'Special Revelation', I began at once to speak of the 'tripersonal God' rather than the 'triune God'. The latter (more widely used) expression safeguards the oneness of God but could be misunderstood to indicate an impersonal reality, like a 'triune' flag with three distinct bands of colour or a 'triune' plant (such as the Irish shamrock) with trifoliate leaves. 'Tripersonal', while it could be misunderstood as espousing 'tritheism' or belief in three (intimately related) gods, upholds the personal reality of God and the personal distinctions within God. But it must be understood in analogous terms. When we speak of three persons within God, they are radically unlike human persons we experience.

5

Jesus the Fullness of Revelation

In his *Ascent of Mount Carmel*, St John of the Cross (1542–91) said this about the full revelation communicated by God: 'In giving us his Son, his one Word (for he possesses no other), he spoke everything to us at once and in this sole Word—and he has nothing more to say.'[1] The great Spanish mystic comments here, of course, on John's Gospel.

From its first chapter this Gospel develops the theme of Jesus as the Son who reveals the Father. In responding to Philip, Jesus declares: 'Whoever has seen me has seen the Father' (John 14: 9). Philip has so far failed to grasp that Jesus in his person and activity is totally taken up with revealing the Father (John 1: 18). The disciples and others have 'never seen the form' of the Father, but the One whom the Father has sent has completely represented and disclosed him (John 5: 37–8). From the beginning, Jesus has been mediating his vision and knowledge of the Father (e.g. John 6: 46; 8: 19, 38). Hence Philip is rebuked for not recognizing that Jesus is the very revelation of the Father.[2]

[1] John of the Cross, *The Ascent of Mount Carmel*, 2. 22. 3; *The Collected Works of Saint John of the Cross*, trans. K. Kavanaugh and O. Rodriguez (rev. edn. Washington, DC: ICS Publications, 1991), 230.

[2] See A. T. Lincoln, *The Gospel According to John* (London: Continuum, 2005), 206–7, 391–2.

But in its prologue John's Gospel writes of the Word of God, 'the Word that was with God, the Word that was God', and 'the Word that became flesh and lived among us' (John 1: 1, 14). John of the Cross, biblical scholar and mystic, brings out the implications of what the evangelist has written. In his one and only Word, God has once and for all said everything to us, and now has nothing more to say. Jesus is not merely *a* revelation of God but is *the* full revelation of God.

Fundamental theology has the task of justifying or at least making a reasonable presentation in support of what John's Gospel proposes. We saw in the last chapter how this Gospel strongly emphasizes the revelation that Christ has brought in his own person. He is the very epiphany of God. In Chapter 7 we will draw on John's Gospel for paradigmatic cases which illustrate different journeys to accepting in faith the revelation that Jesus has brought and that he himself is. But what kind of case can be made to establish the historical reasons and inner coherence that support the Johannine vision of Jesus as the Revealer and the Revelation of God? We begin with the historical witness to what happened when the Word became flesh and lived among us. What can be reasonably argued about the major source of that witness, the four Gospels?[3]

The fourfold witness to the historical Jesus

The Gospels, it has been convincingly argued, came from one eyewitness (John) and from three other evangelists who took much of their material from eyewitnesses. Mark drew especially on Simon Peter. Luke (as well as drawing on Mark's Gospel and Q or *Quelle* (source), a collection of Jesus' sayings also used by Matthew) relied on a number of eyewitnesses (Luke 1: 2), who included women (Luke 8: 1–3). Matthew drew on eyewitnesses, as well as on Mark and

---

[3] For details on other (minor) sources for the life of Jesus (e.g. the letters of the apostle Paul and the work of Flavius Josephus) see G. O'Collins, *Christology: A Biblical, Historical, and Systematic Study of Jesus* (2nd edn. Oxford: Oxford University Press, 2009), 2–4. On the non-canonical or 'apocryphal' Gospels, which add little or no reliable data and none of which is an authentic, first-century work, see C. S. Keener, *The Historical Jesus of the Gospels* (Grand Rapids, Mich.: Eerdmans, 2009), 47–69.

Q. Eyewitness testimony played a major role in the formation of all three Synoptic Gospels (Mark, Matthew, and Luke).[4]

The four Gospel portraits of Jesus can be classified as more representational and historical (Mark, Matthew, and Luke), or more theological, impressionistic, and concerned to develop characteristic effects produced by Jesus (John). The first three evangelists here and there modify the traditions derived from eyewitness testimony to Jesus (e.g. the longer form of the Lord's Prayer found in Matt. 6: 9–13), occasionally project back into the lifetime of Jesus traditions which come from the post-Easter period (e.g. Matt. 18: 20), and are largely responsible for the contexts in which they place the sayings and doings of Jesus. Yet their testimony provides reliable access to the history of what Jesus said, did, and suffered. At the same time, these evangelists have their particular spiritual and theological messages; they are not to be reduced to mere compilers of traditions that they have drawn from eyewitnesses or otherwise inherited.

One of them, Luke, presses on to write a second volume, the Acts of the Apostles, in which he presents the presence and power of the risen Christ and the Holy Spirit in the mission and life of the early Church. Yet the Christians' ongoing experience of the exalted Christ and his Spirit continued to depend upon the past history of Jesus and did not dissolve it. From the opening chapters of his Gospel to the end of Acts, Luke makes it clear that the history of Jesus was decisively important for the life and preaching of the Church. In his life, death, and resurrection, Jesus proved the source of salvation for the world and the basis of Christian identity (Acts 4: 10–12; 28: 31).

John's Gospel emerged from decades of prayerful, theological contemplation, which took Luke's work a stage further by merging two horizons: the *memory* of Jesus that the author recalled from a past which ended with Good Friday, Easter Sunday, and the appearances of the Risen One, and his continuing *experience* of the exalted Lord through to the closing years of the first century. In a lifelong process of understanding and interpretation, the author of the Fourth Gospel gained deeper insights into the meaning of the events

---

[4] See R. Bauckham, *Jesus and the Eyewitnesses: The Gospels as Eyewitness Testimony* (Grand Rapids, Mich.: Eerdmans, 2006). Mark, Matthew, and Luke are called 'Synoptic Gospels', because, when they are printed in parallel columns, one can see at a glance how they frequently match each other.

in which he had participated, which had deeply formed him, and which he reflectively remembered. Like some wonderful modern paintings, his portrait of Jesus plays down some features in Jesus' activity (e.g. the preaching of the kingdom, his parables, and the exorcisms) and develops other features (e.g. Jesus' encounters with individuals, his questions, and his self-presentation). The master-piece which is the Fourth Gospel brings out what was to some extent implicit in the life of Jesus and displays for readers the deep truth about him.[5]

According to the standards of the ancient world, the four Gospels counted as biographies.[6] Even so, obvious limits should be recalled. Unlike his near contemporary Marcus Tullius Cicero (106–43 BC), Jesus left no letters or personal documents that biographers could quote. The only time he was recalled as writing anything came when he 'wrote with his finger on the ground' (John 8: 6–8). This was in response to some scribes and Pharisees who had caught a woman in the act of adultery and wanted Jesus to agree to her being stoned. According to several later manuscripts, Jesus wrote on the ground nothing about himself but 'the sins of each of them'.[7] Jesus did not bequeath to his followers any written instructions, and he lived in almost total obscurity, except for the brief period of his public ministry. According to the testimony provided by the Synoptic Gospels, that ministry could have lasted as little as a year or eighteen months. John implies a period of at least three years. Even for the short span of the ministry, much of the chronological sequence of events (except for the baptism of Jesus at the start and his passion at the end) is, by and large, irretrievably lost. Moreover, the fact that explicitly and, for the most part, Jesus did not proclaim himself

[5] The terminology of 'explicit' (John) and 'implicit' (the Synoptic Gospels) Christology distinguishes between a clearly stated version of Christ's divine identity and one that, for the most part, remains implicit. This distinction, which merely addresses the manner of saying something, is not equivalent to the distinction between high and low Christologies (which recognize or fail to recognize Christ's divinity, respectively). A truly high Christology may remain (largely) implicit.

[6] See R. A. Burridge, *What are the Gospels? A Comparison with Graeco-Roman Biography* (2nd edn. Grand Rapids, Mich.: Eerdmans, 2004); and Keener, *The Historical Jesus of the Gospels*, 73–84.

[7] On the controversy over the woman caught in adultery, see Lincoln, *Gospel According to John*, 524–36.

but the kingdom of God makes access to his interior life difficult. In any case the Gospels rarely mention his motives or deal with his states of mind. These sources make it difficult (yet not impossible) to penetrate his inner life. But they do allow us to reconstruct much of the message, activity, claims, and impact of Jesus in the final years of his life, as well as glimpsing every now and then his feelings and intentions (e.g. Mark 3: 3; 6: 6; Luke 19: 41–4).[8]

In drawing on the Gospels, I use the widely accepted scheme of three stages in the transmission of testimony to Jesus' words and deeds: the initial stage in his earthly life when his disciples and others listened to him, saw him in action, spoke about him, repeated to others his teaching, and began interpreting his identity and mission; the handing on by word of mouth or in writing (including the use of notebooks) of testimony about him after his death and resurrection; and the authorial work of the four evangelists later in the first century.

In sifting through the relevant texts in search of authentic sayings and doings of Jesus (stage one), we use at least five primary criteria developed by twentieth-century scholars: (1) embarrassment (what created difficulty for the early Church), (2) multiple attestation (material found in several *independent* traditions), (3) discontinuity (items that are not characteristic either of Judaism or early Christianity, or even of both), (4) coherence (what corresponds to items already established as authentic through other criteria), and (5) deadly opposition (that led to Jesus' crucifixion). Secondary criteria include traces of Aramaic (especially in Mark's Gospel) and details about the Palestinian environment and Jerusalem that we know from other sources and turn up in the Gospels (e.g. the pool with five porticoes in John 5: 2). Let us see how the primary criteria apply.

---

[8] On the history of Jesus, see K. Bailey, *The Middle-Eastern Jesus* (London: SPCK, 2008); J. H. Charlesworth, *The Historical Jesus: An Essential Guide* (Nashville: Abingdon Press, 2008); J. D. G. Dunn, *Christianity in the Making*, i: *Jesus Remembered* (Grand Rapids, Mich.: Eerdmans, 2003); P. R. Eddy and G. A. Boyd, *The Jesus Legend: A Case for the Historical Reliability of the Synoptic Jesus Tradition* (Grand Rapids, Mich.: Baker Academic, 2007); M. Hengel and A. M. Schwemmer, *Geschichte der frühen Christentums*, i: *Jesus und das Judentum* (Tübingen: Mohr Siebeck, 2007); Keener, *The Historical Jesus of the Gospels*; J. P. Meier, *A Marginal Jew: Rethinking the Historical Jesus*, 3 vols. (New York: Doubleday, 1991–2001), 4th vol. (New Haven: Yale University Press, 2009).

As regards (1), some embarrassment was felt over the fact that Jesus submitted to baptism at the hands of John the Baptist. Along with its positive aspects, this act clashes with the Church's tendency to keep John subordinated to Jesus and would have embarrassed early Christians in any debates with those who remained disciples of John and did not move quickly to faith in Jesus (see Acts 19: 2–3, and the history of the Mandeans, a group faithful to John right down to the twenty-first century[9]). Moreover, different traditions in the New Testament (e.g. John 8: 46; Heb. 4: 15) witness to the conviction that Jesus led an utterly sinless life. How then could he have accepted 'a baptism of repentance for the forgiveness of sins' (Mark 1: 4)? His baptism by John was a doubly embarrassing matter (e.g. Matt. 3: 14). This embarrassment suggests that the followers of Jesus did not make up this episode: at the start of his ministry Jesus was baptized by John. (2) There is multiple witness for the conclusion that during his ministry Jesus, from the wider ranks of his disciples, called a core group of twelve and gave them some kind of authoritative office and leadership role. Mark attests the original call (3: 13–19) and subsequent trial mission of the Twelve (6: 7–13); Q reflects the existence of this core group (Matt. 19: 28 = Luke 22: 30). Then they are 'in place' as the key group to receive a foundational appearance of the risen Christ, a fact first attested by a preaching formula quoted by Paul (1 Cor. 15: 3–5), and subsequently narrated in various ways by the Easter chapters of the Gospels. In its own different and less than enthusiastic way, John's Gospel confirms the existence of the Twelve (John 6: 71).[10]

(3) In his preaching Jesus persistently presented himself as the Son of Man, a title with a striking range of meanings. There was some Jewish background to Jesus' Son of Man sayings (e.g. the Book of Ezekiel and Dan. 7: 13–14), but scarcely any follow-up in the emerging Church. The designation was not useful in preaching the good news, and does not appear in creedal or liturgical formulas (which preferred the titles of 'Christ', 'Lord', and 'Son (of God)'. It was too flexible and even vague, ranging from the mysterious, heavenly being in Daniel 7 to simply serving as a circumlocution for 'I' (e.g. Matt. 8: 20 = Luke 9: 58). The discontinuity between Jesus' frequent

[9] On the Mandeans, K. Rudolph, 'Mandaeism', *ABD* iv. 500–2.
[10] See Lincoln, *Gospel According to John*, 239.

use of this designation and its almost total absence in the language of the early Church encourages us to conclude that the Son of Man sayings derive from 'stage one' and Jesus himself. (4) We find the parables of the lost coin and of the lost (prodigal) son in only one source, the Gospel of Luke (15: 8–32), but they correspond extremely well with Jesus' special concern for sinners. That is attested by accounts of his eating with such people and by sayings criticizing him for doing so (e.g. Matt. 11: 19 = Luke 7: 34).[11] Hence we may confidently accept these parables as coming from Jesus himself. (5) The fifth criterion aims at excluding versions of Jesus which portray him simply as a teacher of Gnostic wisdom or as a wandering holy man. Such portraits cannot account for the deadly opposition on the part of religious authorities that led to his death. Why would anyone, whether Jewish priests or Roman prefect, want to do away with such a harmless character? One accounts for the opposition that built up against Jesus and led to his execution by recognizing that there was a historical core to the charges brought against him: of violating the Sabbath, working wonders through diabolic power, challenging purity regulations, acting as a false prophet, and even making blasphemous pretensions of being on a par with God and sharing the divine authority to forgive sins.

The five primary criteria help us to establish particular sayings and doings as authentically derived from Jesus. When I draw on the Gospels, I will indicate whether I judge that some passage testifies to what Jesus said or did at stage one, or whether the passage seems to reflect what a particular evangelist at stage three (and/or the tradition at stage two) understood about Jesus' work and identity. Only occasionally will I stop to justify why I hold some saying or deed to have its historical origin in what Jesus said or did. But I will attribute to him only examples where such justification in possible.

Eyewitness testimony offers a more general argument for historical authenticity. Richard Bauckham (see n. 4 above) has argued persuasively that the four Gospels provide a credible means of access to the historical Jesus, since they derive from the testimony of eyewitnesses (both major ones like Peter, the Twelve, Martha, and Mary of Bethany, and minor ones like Bartimaeus in Mark 10). For decades

[11] On this verse, see J. A. Fitzmyer, *The Gospel According to Luke 1–X* (New York: Doubleday, 1981), 680–1; J. Nolland, *Luke 1–9: 20* (Dallas: Word Books, 1989), 345–6.

some or even many scholars imagined stage two to be a long process of anonymous, collective, and mainly oral transmission that separated the original witnesses from those who wrote the Gospels. Bauckham points out that the period between Jesus and the final composition of the Gospels (stage three) was spanned by the continuing presence and testimony of those who had participated in the story of Jesus: namely, the original eyewitnesses. Until the final years of the first century, those authoritative, living sources continued to provide first-hand witness to Jesus.

Bauckham proposes that many of the named characters in the Gospels were eyewitnesses and were known in the circles in which the traditions about Jesus began to be transmitted. They included Mary Magdalene, Joanna (one of the particular sources for Luke), and Cleopas (of the Emmaus story in Luke 24). Some, like Jairus (Mark 5: 21–43) and Simon of Cyrene (Mark 15: 21), could well have remained eyewitness sources for specific stories. The Twelve were especially qualified to testify to the public history of Jesus, since they had participated in it from its early stages to the end and beyond (in the Easter appearances).

Bauckham produces plausible (internal and external) evidence to rehabilitate the case for Simon Peter being the major eyewitness source behind the Gospel of Mark. The naming of Peter creates an 'inclusion' which holds that Gospel together from 1: 16–18 right through to 16: 7. Readers can share the eyewitness perspective which the testimony of Peter embodied. Bauckham identifies the anonymous disciple of John 1: 35–40 with the beloved disciple of John 21: 24, the ideal witness to Jesus who was with him 'from the beginning' (John 15: 27). This establishes the major 'inclusion' in the Fourth Gospel, even though an 'inclusion' involving Peter is not abandoned. He is present from Chapter 1 to Chapter 21, yet within the wider involvement of the beloved disciple. That disciple spent hours with Jesus before Peter ever set eyes on Jesus (John 1: 35–42). Bauckham makes a strong case for the author of the Fourth Gospel being the beloved disciple, who is not to be identified with John the son of Zebedee or any other member of the Twelve. He was an individual disciple, a close follower of Jesus, and not to be dissolved into a merely representative figure.

Bauckham defends all four Gospels as being close to eyewitness reports of the words and deeds of Jesus. Between the earthly story of Jesus (stage one) and the writing of the Gospels (stage three), the original eyewitnesses played a central and authoritative role in guiding the transmission of the traditions about Jesus (stage two). Bauckham's book should help put an end to the unfounded impression that a long period of creative, collective development of the Jesus traditions preceded the work of the evangelists.

For many years one objection to the notion of a community 'creatively' making up Jesus traditions has struck me as persuasive. Paul's letters and the Acts of the Apostles indicate a vigorous controversy in early Christianity about the possible obligation of Gentile converts to practise the Jewish law. In particular, did male converts need to be circumcised? It would have been tempting to credit the earthly Jesus with some precise instructions in this area. Mark's Gospel reports some pronouncements from Jesus about food laws and washing (Mark 7: 1–23) but simply nothing for or against the obligation of circumcision. Despite pressing interests in this matter, neither Mark nor the traditions on which he drew felt free to invent and attribute to Jesus some clear statement that circumcision was no longer obligatory.

Besides supporting the conclusion that the Gospels prove to be substantially reliable guides to the history of Jesus, or at least to the final years of that history, Bauckham's landmark volume illuminates the obvious differences between the Synoptic Gospels and John. Not having been eyewitnesses themselves, the first three evangelists remained close to what the original eyewitnesses told them of the sayings and doings of Jesus. Mark, Matthew, and Luke allowed themselves only a small degree of creative interpretation. The Fourth Gospel, however, offered an extensively interpreted version of the story of Jesus. Through a more delineated plot, greater selectivity of the events recorded, and the fashioning of lengthy discourses and debates, this Gospel became a strongly reflective interpretation of Jesus' mission and identity. That was the way in which one central eyewitness understood what he and others had personally experienced. When testifying to the history of Jesus in which he had participated so closely, the beloved disciple allowed himself a greater degree of interpretative appropriation precisely because he himself had been an eyewitness.

Finally, in putting the case for some reliable access to the historical Jesus through the Gospels, we should not neglect what has already been indicated about experience and interpretation (Chapter 3 above). The pursuit of the historical Jesus (stage one) should not lead us to foster the illusion that our research could yield some nuggets of original 'facts' about Jesus, historical data that somehow preceded all later beliefs, doctrinal interpretations, and affirmations about him. Human experience and, indeed, all personal knowledge are never like that. No one (and no instrument, not even the most sophisticated camera) can ever record and communicate the non-interpreted, unmediated 'hard' reality of somebody (or, for that matter, of something). Historically there never was a non-interpreted, 'non-theological' Jesus. Here, as elsewhere, there never was a 'view from nowhere', a 'given' that had not yet been interpreted. 'Fact' and interpretation are inseparable.

Right from their first encounters with him, the beloved disciple, Peter, Mary Magdalene, Joanna, and others among the first followers necessarily interpreted Jesus and their experience of him. When the evangelists came, decades later, to put the testimony and traditions into Gospel shape, they handled material in which, so to speak, the input from Jesus himself and various responses to him were inextricably intertwined. It cannot be otherwise with our human experience of a historical figure. Not even the most detailed oral reports from the very first meetings with someone can ever give us the 'pure' story of that person, free from any significance that becomes attached to him or her.

Mark, Matthew, and Luke manifested their personal attitude toward and personal relationship with Jesus, now risen and exalted in glory. There are no good grounds for holding that any of these three evangelists enjoyed contact with Jesus during his earthly existence. They were and remain, however, central figures in transmitting the story of Jesus, the response he immediately evoked, and the further response he continued to evoke. That further response leads us into the Christian tradition in all its diversity: forms of worship; preaching, creeds, and other doctrinal texts; and millions of lives that have taken their inspiration from Jesus. That faith response which Jesus continues to evoke in the living tradition will be taken up in later chapters.

Those who wish to investigate further the historical Jesus will find extensive further reading in the work of Bauckham, Dunn, Keener, Meier, and other contemporary scholars. Once we accept the general reliability of the four Gospels, do we find in them witness to the self-revelation of God—in particular, to the divine self-manifestation that led to the specifically Christian belief in God as tripersonal? John's Gospel, as we saw in the last chapter, testifies clearly and explicitly to the revelation of God as Father, Son, and Holy Spirit. But what of the other three Gospels, which, in what they report about the words and deeds of Jesus, often tend to leave matters implicit? In their (generally implicit) account, what and whom did people experience when they experienced Jesus in his life, death, and resurrection?

The preaching of the kingdom: parables and miracles

Many of his contemporaries perceived Jesus as a religious teacher[12] and a prophet (e.g. Mark 6: 15; 8: 28; Luke 7: 16, 39; John 6: 14; 7: 20). Inasmuch as this teaching and prophetic role implied proclaiming, interpreting, and applying the word of God, these contemporaries attributed to Jesus some function in mediating revelation. But what of Jesus himself? At times he expressed his mission in prophetic terms (e.g. Mark 6: 4; Luke 13: 33). What sense did he reveal of his own particular commission and authority? We begin with his proclamation of the kingdom.

Few claims are historically more certain about Jesus than that he proclaimed a theme that was rare in Judaism and would be rare in the New Testament outside the Synoptic Gospels: the kingdom or royal reign of God.[13] Jesus spoke frequently of the divine kingdom, whether as already *present* (e.g. Matt. 12: 28 = Luke 11: 20; Luke 17: 20–1) or as to come in the *future* (e.g. Mark 9: 1; Matt. 6: 10 = Luke 11: 2). 'The kingdom' was more or less a way of talking about God as Lord of the world and God's decisive, climactic action to liberate sinful men and women from the grip of evil and bless them with a new and final age of salvation.

---

[12] In the Gospels, 'teacher' is applied to Jesus 43 times as *didaskolos*, 16 times as *rabbi* or *rabbouni*, 6 times (all in Luke) as *epistata*, and once as *kathēgētēs* (Matt. 23: 10).

[13] For an extensive discussion of the divine kingdom, see Meier, *A Marginal Jew*, ii. 289–506.

The telling of *parables* was one of the distinctive characteristics of Jesus' work for the present and coming kingdom. They were not merely *about* the kingdom; they revealed the kingdom with its challenge and grace. As speaker of the parables, Jesus identified with the kingdom and effected its powerful presence. These stories called their hearers to repentance, enacted the divine forgiveness, and mediated religious transformation. The parables have prompted scholarly comment from a long line of writers: R. Bultmann, J. D. Crossan, C. H. Dodd, J. R. Donahue, R. W. Funk, J. Jeremias, A. Jülicher, J. Lambrecht, B. Scott, M. A. Tolbert, D. O. Via, A. Wilder, and others. John Meier will take up the parables in the fifth and final volume of his *A Marginal Jew*.[14]

All three Synoptic Gospels recall not only that Jesus worked *miracles* but also that his miraculous deeds powerfully symbolized the kingdom, and were inextricably bound up with his proclamation of the kingdom. His healings and exorcisms showed themselves to be compassionate gestures, the first fruits of God's merciful rule already operative in and through the person of Jesus. Matthew edited Q material to present Jesus as saying: 'If it is by the Spirit of God that I cast out demons, then the kingdom of God has come upon you' (Matt. 12: 28; see Luke 11: 20). His exorcisms, in particular, manifested the strength of the Spirit (Mark 3: 22–30), which, according to the Synoptics, empowered Jesus' ministry for the kingdom, right from his baptism.[15]

How much attention should fundamental theologians give to the parables and the miracles? From the start, Jesus' parables have clearly played their part in opening people up to the revelation of God and the divine will. Evidence remains partial and elusive for the precise impact on Jesus' audience when they first heard his stories of the prodigal son, the good Samaritan, the rich man and Lazarus, and other vivid parables. But his parables offered his contemporaries and

---

[14] On the parables, see G. O'Collins, *Following the Way* (London: HarperCollins, 1999); id., *Jesus: A Portrait* (London: Darton, Longman & Todd, 2008), 81–126, 233–5.

[15] On the miraculous activity of Jesus, see Eddy and Boyd, *The Jesus Legend*, 39–90; Eric Eve, *The Healer from Nazareth: Jesus' Miracles in Historical Context* (London: SPCK, 2009); H. C. Kee, *Medicine, Miracle and Magic in New Testament Times* (Cambridge: Cambridge University Press, 1986); R. Latourelle, *The Miracles of Jesus and the Theology of Miracles*, trans. M. J. O'Connell (Mahwah, NJ: Paulist Press, 1988); Meier, *A Marginal Jew*, ii. 509–1038; H. E. Remus, 'Miracle, New Testament', *ABD* iv. 856–69.

innumerable later human beings a wealth of wisdom and hinted at Jesus being, in fact, divine Wisdom come among us in person. His parables continue to question their audience, challenge the 'normal' standards and securities of life, and call for the whole-hearted response of faith. These stories answer the central questions: what is God like? And how is God dealing with human beings in these last times? The parables invite their hearers (and readers) to acknowledge God's sovereign power and Jesus as the Lord of the kingdom already present in their midst. Fundamental theologians, when they deal with faith's response to the divine self-manifestation, may not bypass the parables. Not only at the time of Jesus' ministry but also now his parables have their place in authenticating the divine self-revelation that he communicated and embodied and that continues to call people to commit themselves to him in faith.

Apropos of Jesus' *miracles*, they should feature in courses taught by fundamental theologians, who need to face various challenges.

1. First, such theologians should clarify what they mean by miracles as special acts of God, who, occasionally and for good reasons, suspends or overrides 'normal' causality to bring about an event that stunningly conveys the divine love and mercy and invites an appropriate human response. Theologians need to watch their language here, avoiding, for instance, that unpleasant and inaccurate word 'violating' used even by some who defend miracles but speak of God working miracles by 'violating the laws of nature'.[16] My description of miracles also attends to their religious context and message, something ignored by those who reduce miracles to unusual events for which we have (so far) no satisfactory explanation. We return to this point below.

2. Second, theologians may need to enter into debate with their contemporaries who simply exclude miracles in principle, either because they deny or doubt the existence of an all-powerful, all-loving God or because they believe that God operates and is revealed *only through*

---

[16] Any of the four meanings given for 'violate' by the *Oxford Dictionary of English* (2005) would be used inappropriately of God: (1) fail to comply with (e.g. an oath, treaty, or law); (2) treat with disrespect; (3) disturb (e.g. a person's privacy); and (4) assault sexually. Presumably those who write of God 'violating' the laws of nature have the first meaning in mind. Yet God continues faithfully to 'comply with' the range of laws of nature introduced with creation itself; a miracle involves a very rare exception (made for good reasons) to God's general practice of 'compliance'. The very rare occurrence of exceptions does not mean that God *fails to comply* with the laws he established.

normal, everyday events (general revelation). Some, like David Hume, have argued that 'the usual course of nature' always trumps the evidence put forward on behalf of a miraculous exception. In other words, even if there is a God who might occasionally and for good reasons work miracles, under no circumstances could God produce enough evidence to justify our believing that a miracle has taken place. Many commentators find such a position breathtaking in its arrogance.[17]

Another objection to the miracles of Jesus (and later miracles) argues that they suggest a capricious God who miraculously cures a few people but leaves the rest to suffer and die. Even if Jesus cured several hundred sick and disabled people, what about the millions of other sick and disabled sufferers in his world? This objection ignores the situation of human beings as highly complex organisms, exposed to all kinds of bodily disorders and moving toward biological death. After God created such beings (through the long process of evolution), it would then seem capricious to override constantly the breakdowns in their organic systems and cure them all miraculously. Very occasional miraculous acts that carry a powerful religious message (to which we return below) are not incompatible with God normally supporting the operations and breakdowns of highly complex organisms. If God continuously interferes with the working of what has been created, that would be acting in a capricious and arbitrary way.

Others again flatly exclude the miracles of Jesus (and other miracles) in the name of their trust in the 'hard-nosed' evidence of *science*. Answering this objection appropriately would involve an enormous digression into the philosophy of science to establish the truth status of evidence and conclusions coming from scientists. It is worth remarking that some hard-nosed scientists accept the occurrence of miracles. They recognize that the *instantaneous* cure of a seriously ill or disabled person, for example, will never be explained on merely scientific grounds. Which scientists prove themselves to be truly hard-nosed: those who join teams investigating alleged miracles or those who reject out of hand the possibility of miracles as incompatible with science?

---

[17] For trenchant criticisms of Hume's argument, see J. Earman, *Hume's Abject Failure: The Argument against Miracles* (Oxford: Oxford University Press, 2000); and D. Johnson, *Hume, Holism, and Miracles* (Ithaca, NY: Cornell University Press, 1999). But see also R. J. Fogelin, *A Defense of Hume on Miracles* (Princeton: Princeton University Press, 2003).

3. Third, fundamental theology should enter debate with those who dismiss the miracle stories of Jesus as secondary accretions, an unfortunate product of the fervid imagination of the first Christians. Those early believers worshipped Jesus as their risen Lord. What could be more natural and inevitable than their looking back through the golden haze of Easter and glorifying his human life by attributing to him all kinds of wonderful deeds? Was this not, after all, standard practice in ancient times? Legends of healing and other miracles gathered quickly around the names of great religious leaders. In any case, some of the alleged miracles have magical overtones: the healing of the deaf-mute in the Decapolis (Mark 7: 31–7) and the healing of the blind man at Bethsaida (Mark 8: 22–6).[18] In both cases the saliva of Jesus functions to heal an infirmity. Then what of Jesus' psychological powers? Can we attribute some of his alleged miracles to his powers of suggestion, which had strikingly visible effects on people who were physically disabled or mentally disturbed?

This part of the record of Jesus' ministry cannot, however, be repudiated as easily as that. To begin with, in Mark's Gospel almost half of the treatment given to Jesus' public life concerns miracles. Many of the miracles are inextricably bound up with other elements in the narrative. These deeds of power revealed in advance the full divine rule and integral salvation of God's coming kingdom. If the miracle stories were removed from Mark's account of Jesus' ministry, a great deal would have to be ripped away with them. It would be very difficult to cut all the miracle stories out of Mark and still recognize that Gospel as a substantially reliable guide to the ministry of Jesus. Either we accept Mark and his miracle stories or we dismiss his Gospel as an unreliable source for the history of Jesus' activity.

Moreover, here if anywhere, the criterion of *multiple (independent) witness* applies. Besides the actual miracle stories themselves, Mark also records sayings connected with one class of extraordinary deeds, the exorcisms (Mark 3: 14–15, 22–7; 6: 7). Then Matthew and Luke add material from Q (their common source for many sayings of Jesus), which attests that the earthly Jesus worked miracles (Matt. 11: 5 = Luke 7: 22). An interesting pointer supplied by Q concerns the 'woes' Jesus

---

[18] On these two miracles, see J. Marcus, *Mark 1–8* (New York: Doubleday, 2000), 471–81; id., *Mark 8–16* (New Haven: Yale University Press, 2009), 592–602; and Meier, *A Marginal Jew*, ii. 690–4, 711–14.

pronounced against certain Galilean towns: 'Woe to you, Chorazin! Woe to you, Bethsaida! For if the mighty works done in you had been done in Tyre and Sidon, they would have repented long ago in sackcloth and ashes' (Matt. 11: 21 = Luke 10: 13).[19] Here Jesus speaks of miracles done in two towns, but while the Gospels report his miraculous activity in Bethsaida (Mark 8: 22–6; Luke 9: 10–11), they have nothing to report from Chorazin. Thus we have a Q *saying* about miracles in Chorazin but *no matching story* or *stories*. It appears that this saying came from the earthly Jesus, and that the Gospels and/or their sources did not feel free to invent accounts of miracles worked in Chorazin or to locate in that town 'unattached' miracles found in the tradition. Further, Luke includes a warning against Herod Antipas which is generally agreed to come from Jesus and which indicates that he worked miracles: 'Go and tell that fox for me, "Listen, I am casting out demons and performing cures today and tomorrow, and on the third day [meaning 'in a short time'] I finish my work"' (Luke 13: 32).[20] Jesus insists that no threats from 'that fox' will cut short his miraculous activity. Finally, summary accounts of Jesus' activity include his miracles (e.g. Matt. 4: 23; 11: 5 = Luke 7: 22). Thus at least six different sources witness to the miraculous activity of Jesus. If we wish to widen the application of the criterion of multiple witness, we could also point to ancient Jewish sources. They accepted the fact that Jesus worked miracles but explained it all as sorcery.[21]

As regards the view that first-century believers were prone to make up miracles and attribute them to religious heroes, we should remind ourselves of John the Baptist. The four Gospels have much to say about the forerunner of Jesus. This great prophet played a pre-eminent role in preparing people for the ministry of Jesus, and later he was remembered with honour in the emerging Church. The Baptist had been 'there' as *the* trailblazer when the Christian movement began. And yet no miracles were attributed to him—a

---

[19] On this saying, see J. A. Fitzmyer, *The Gospel According to Luke X–XXIV* (New York: Doubleday, 1985), 850–4; U. Luz, *Matthew 8–20*, trans. J. E. Crouch (Minneapolis: Fortress, 2001), 151–4; J. Nolland, *Luke 9: 21–18: 34* (Dallas: Word Books, 1993), 555–6; id., *The Gospel of Matthew* (Grand Rapids, Mich.: Eerdmans, 2005), 467.

[20] On this verse, see Fitzmyer, *Gospel According to Luke X–XXIV*, 1027–33; Nolland, *Luke 9: 21–18: 34*, 740–1.

[21] See Babylonian Talmud's tractate *Sanhedrin*, 43a; see J. P. Meier, *A Marginal Jew: Rethinking the Historical Jesus*, i (New York: Doubleday, 1991), 96–7, 107.

point that John's Gospel explicitly notes (John 10: 41).[22] The case of
the Baptist establishes that, at least in first-century Palestine, it was by
no means inevitable that, as a way of enhancing their memory,
traditions of supposed miracles would gather around John, Jesus,
or any other religious leader.

To sum up: there exists no convincing evidence that Jesus was
remembered first as a preacher, and only later had a miracle tradition
attached to his name. Here we might remember the historical
conclusion of Rudolf Bultmann (1884–1976) about the miracles of
Jesus: 'undoubtedly he healed the sick and cast out demons'.[23] Later
on, Bultmann was to argue that miracles are offensive and inconceivable to 'modern' persons.[24] But that is another question. In any case,
disparaging remarks about first-century people often suggest or imply
that they were more or less uniformly gullible and credulous, and
persistently ignore all the elements of sophisticated (and sceptical)
culture that had built up for centuries around the ancient Mediterranean
world—not to mention elsewhere. Moreover, Bultmann's claim about
'modern' persons ignores, of course, those millions among his and our
contemporaries who do not find miracles offensive and inconceivable.

4. Fourth, apropos of the record of Jesus' miracles, I suspect that it
is the significance rather than the fact of his miracles which poses
a problem for many people. Hence I suggest that not only their
historical status but also their *significance* should find its place in
the agenda for fundamental theology. The evangelists and also Jesus
himself shunned any exhibitionism. As a saying preserved by
Q shows, Jesus understood the preaching of the good news to the
poor as the climax of his miraculous deeds (Matt. 11: 5 = Luke 7: 22).
When pressed to do so, Jesus refused to legitimize his claims by some
spectacular 'sign from heaven' (Mark 8: 11–12). Although the words
are found only in Luke, what he reports Jesus saying to 'the seventy'
disciples (when they returned from their mission rejoicing that in his
name 'even the demons' submitted to them) coheres perfectly with
his reluctance attested elsewhere to exaggerate the importance of

---

[22] See Lincoln, *Gospel According to John*, 312–13.
[23] R. Bultmann, *Jesus and the Word*, trans. L. P. Smith and E. Huntress
(London: Collins Fontana, 1958), 173.
[24] R. Bultmann, 'New Testament and Mythology', in H. W. Bartsch (ed.),
Kerygma and Myth: A Theological Debate, trans. R. H. Fuller (London: SPCK,
1972), 5.

miraculous deeds: 'I have given you authority to tread upon serpents and scorpions, and over all the power of the enemy, and nothing shall hurt you. Nevertheless, do not rejoice in this, that the spirits are subject to you. But rejoice that your names are written in heaven' (Luke 10: 17–20).

For Jesus and the evangelists, his miracles were not overwhelming arguments that should *force* people to believe that he was the Messiah and the Son of God. His audience could disqualify the witness of these deeds by attributing them to demonic influence (Mark 3: 22). Those who refused to be touched to the depths of their existence by Jesus' parables were not going to be persuaded by his miraculous deeds.

Positively, Jesus seems to have understood his miracles as revealing the way in which anti-God forces were being overcome. The divine power was finally and effectively saving human beings in their whole physical and spiritual reality: 'If it is by the finger of God that I cast out demons, then the kingdom of God has come upon you' (Luke 11: 20).[25] Over and over again Jesus associated his miraculous deeds with his call to a faith that would believe in his authority to forgive sins and save people from the forces that afflicted them (e.g. Mark 2: 1–12).[26] No less than his preaching, his miracles revealed the reign of God and the divine promise to deliver sick and sinful human beings from the grip of evil.

Interestingly, many of Jesus' miracles embodied that blending of action and word (or the sacramental principle) which we noted in the last chapter (in the section on 'Word and Event') to be characteristic of the revelatory events. When healing a leper with the words 'be thou made clean', Jesus also stretched out his hand and touched him (presumably on the face) (Mark 1: 40–5).[27] In bringing back to life the little daughter of Jairus, Jesus took the dead child by the hand, as well as saying, 'Little girl, get up' (Mark 5: 41). The healing of a crippled woman involved words, 'woman, you are set free from your ailment', and a gesture in that Jesus 'laid hands upon her' (Luke 13: 10–17). In giving sight to a man born blind, Jesus combined word

---

[25] On this verse, see Fitzmyer, *Gospel According to Luke X–XXIV*, 916–23; Nolland, *Luke 9: 21–18: 34*, 639–41.

[26] On this passage, see Marcus, *Mark 1–8*, 215–24.

[27] For more information on the verses that will now be quoted from the Gospels, see Marcus (on Mark), Luz and Nolland (on Matthew), Fitzmyer and Nolland (on Luke), and Lincoln (on John).

with action: 'he spat on the ground and made mud with his saliva and spread the mud on the man's eyes, saying to him, "Go, wash in the pool of Siloam"' (John 9: 6–7). Thus many of the miracles worked by Jesus that disclosed his mission and identity involved a sacramental combining of word and action. Perhaps the pre-eminent example of this feature occurs in a miracle reported by all four Gospels, the feeding of the five thousand (Mark 6: 30–44; Matt. 14: 13–21; Luke 9: 10–17; John 6: 1–13). Mark, as do the other evangelists, tells the story with 'eucharistic' language that anticipates the words and gestures of Jesus at the Last Supper: '*taking* the five loaves and two fishes, he *looked up* to heaven, and *blessed* [element of word] and *broke* the loaves, and *gave* them to his disciples to set before the people, and he *divided* the two fish among them' (6: 41). John, of course, will add to the story of this miracle the discourse on the bread of life, one of the great passages in his Gospel about the saving revelation of Christ. But the other three evangelists also convey a sense of the revelation mediated through Jesus' sacramental blending of word and gesture in the multiplication of the loaves and fishes.

The kingdom in person

Origen packed a lot into a comment about Jesus being 'the kingdom in person, *autobasileia*' (*In Mattheum*, 24. 7).[28] Both in his preaching and miraculous deeds Jesus was inseparably connected with the arrival of the divine kingdom. Through his person and presence, God's rule had come and was coming. Mark, followed by Matthew and Luke, clearly saw Jesus and his activity that way. A saying about God's kingdom coming with power (Mark 9: 1) could then be applied to Jesus himself as the Son of Man coming in his kingdom (Matt. 16: 28). High implications about Jesus' saving function and personal identity emerge from the ways in which the Synoptic Gospels portray his role for the kingdom. But how did Jesus think of himself and reveal himself and his mission?

---

[28] 'Jesus is wisdom itself, justice itself, truth itself, the kingdom itself.' Origen said this when commenting on Matt. 24: 7, but did so when recalling Matt. 18: 23–35 (the parable of the debtors).

At the very least, he seems to have conceived of his mission as that of one who had been sent by God (Mark 9: 37; 12: 6) to break Satan's power (Luke 10: 17–18) and to realize the final rule of God (Matt. 12: 28). Despite evidence that Jesus distanced himself from talk of being 'the Messiah' or an anointed and promised deliverer sent by God (e.g. Mark 8: 27–31; 15: 2), it is quite implausible to argue that Jesus was oblivious of performing a messianic mission. He gave some grounds for being perceived to have made such a claim (e.g. Mark 11: 1–11). Otherwise it is very difficult to account both for the charge against him of being a messianic pretender (Mark 14: 51; 15: 2, 9, 18, 26, 32) and for the ease with which his follows began calling him 'the Christ' immediately after his death and resurrection. He had also disclosed messianic consciousness by a key saying about his miraculous activity (Matt. 11: 2–6 = Luke 7: 18–23), and implied something about himself when contrasting 'mere' Davidic descent with the higher status of being the Messiah (Mark 12: 35–7).

But there was more to his self-disclosure than that. At times he went beyond a prophetic 'I was sent' to say 'I came' or 'I have come'. He was remembered as having taken a small child in his arms and saying: 'Whoever receives one such child in my name receives me, and whoever receives me receives not me but him who sent me' (Mark 9: 36–7). In a parable about the wicked tenants of a vineyard, Jesus obliquely referred to himself as 'the Son' who had finally been 'sent' (Mark 12: 6). Yet on other occasions he went beyond the normal prophetic 'I was sent' to affirm, 'I came': 'I came not to call the righteous but sinners' (Mark 2: 17); 'I came to cast fire upon the earth. Would that it were already kindled!' (Luke 12: 49; see Matt. 10: 34–6).

This 'coming' language is also connected with a major self-designation used by Jesus: 'The Son of Man came not to be served but to serve' (Mark 10: 45). Occasionally the language of 'coming' and 'sending' is combined (e.g. Luke 13: 34–5). Without insisting that every 'sending' and 'coming' saying derives from the historical Jesus, they are numerous enough to support the conclusion that he understood and revealed his mission both as one who came and as one who had been sent by the Father. The Old Testament prophets disclosed their sense of having been sent by God, but never purported to come in their own name. Furthermore, they never presented themselves as 'sons of God', nor were they ever called that. In short, none of them ever explained his mission as a personal initiative, 'I have come'.[29]

Over and above any such sayings, Jesus showed that he so identified himself with the message of God's kingdom that those who responded positively to this message *committed themselves to him* as disciples. To accept the coming rule of God was to become a follower of Jesus. To be saved through the kingdom was to be saved through Jesus. With authority Jesus encouraged men and women to break normal family ties and join him in the service of the kingdom (Mark 10: 28–31; Luke 8: 1–3). By relativizing in his own name family roles and relationships, Jesus was scandalously at odds with the expectations of his and other societies. All of this raises the question: who did Jesus think he was and who did he reveal himself to be if he made such personal claims?

The personal authority with which Jesus taught and performed miracles was blatant. Unlike the normal miracle workers in Judaism, he did not first invoke the divine intervention, but simply went ahead in his own name to heal people or deliver them from diabolic possession. He likewise spoke with his own authority, prefacing his teaching with 'I say to you' (Matt. 5: 21–44) and not with such prophetic rubrics as 'thus says the Lord' or 'oracle of the Lord'. It was above all the 'objects' over which he asserted authority that made such claims startling, Either by what he said or by what he did (or both), Jesus claimed authority (a) over the observance of the Sabbath (e.g. Mark 2: 23–8; 3: 1–5), (b) over various regulations of the Torah, and (c) over the Temple (e.g. Mark 11: 15–17)—three divinely authorized channels of salvation. A unique sacredness attached to that day, that code, and that place.

(a) John Meier deals at length with Jesus' actions and sayings about the Sabbath.[30] He portrays Jesus as taking a humane, commonsense attitude towards Sabbath observance out of a 'desire to shield ordinary pious Jews from the attraction of sectarian rigorism'. He sought 'to instill a proper sense of priorities',[31] summed up in one saying commonly agreed to go back to the historical Jesus: 'the Sabbath was made

---

[29] John's prologue twice writes of John the Baptist as having 'come'. But the Baptist does not say this of himself, and the prologue says this after having described him as being 'sent'. Furthermore, John 'comes' to 'testify to the Light', and not to pursue an autonomous mission (John 1: 6–8).

[30] *A Marginal Jew: Law and Love,* iv (New Haven: Yale University Press, 2009), 252–97.

[31] Ibid. 296.

for human beings, not human beings for the Sabbath' (Mark 2: 27). Some or even many scholars may agree with Meier in interpreting the next verse ('the Son of Man is lord of the Sabbath') as a 'creation either of Mark himself or of a pre-Markan redactor'.[32] Whatever one's conclusions about Mark 2: 28, Jesus clearly taught on his own authority and not out of traditional sources of authority when setting priorities for Sabbath observance.

(b) While Jesus never aimed at abrogating or annulling the Mosaic Law as a whole, he took it upon himself not only to criticize the *oral law* for running counter to basic human obligations (Mark 7: 10–12) but also to set aside the *written law* on such matters as retribution, divorce, and food (Matt. 5: 21–48; Mark 7: 15, 19; 10: 2–12). Apropos of Jesus' teaching on divorce, Meier concludes: he 'absolutely forbade divorce and branded divorce and remarriage as the sin of adultery'. Here Jesus rejected 'an institution accepted and regulated by the Torah'.[33] This was to make a startling claim to personal authority that put him on a par with the divine Lord who had prescribed these matters through Moses. We might put what was at stake as follows: 'Of old it was said to you by God speaking through Moses, but I say to you.'

Meier discusses at length and with truly impressive learning what can be said about Jesus' attitude towards purity laws that affected, among other things, what might or might not be eaten.[34] While recognizing a certain 'indifference' to purity rules on the part of Jesus, Meier doubts that a key verse about food laws derives from the historical Jesus: 'there is nothing outside of a man that, by entering into him, can defile him, but those things that come out of man are the things that defile him' (Mark 7: 15). Meier puts vividly what is at stake here: 'it hardly seems credible... that Jesus should have rejected or annulled in a single logion all the laws on prohibited foods enshrined in Leviticus and Deuteronomy.'[35] Such a revocation in the Torah would have swept away a major barrier between Jews and Gentiles, one that set Jews religiously and ethnically apart from others.

---

[32] At the end of a closely knit argument, Meier judges this saying to make a 'mind-boggling claim' that is 'perfectly intelligible within the context of the 1st-century Christian faith in Jesus' (ibid. 291–2). But cannot some mind-boggling claims be intelligible also within the context of Jesus' ministry?

[33] Ibid. 74–181, at 126, 128.

[34] Ibid. 342–477.

[35] Ibid. 342–477, at 385.

Meier's objection to the authenticity of this logion is complex but appeals, above all, to two arguments from silence: one from the ministry of Jesus and the other from the situation of early Christianity. First, if Jesus had clearly revoked food laws, why do the Gospels never report Jesus and his disciples eating forbidden food? Why did this abrogation of the food laws fail to emerge as a charge made against Jesus in his passion? Second, the Acts of the Apostles and Paul's letters let us glimpse the fierce arguments over regulations from the Torah: did they apply to Gentile converts, not to mention Jewish Christians? But neither side in the argument appealed to any teaching from Jesus on the subject.[36]

On the particular issue of food laws, much depends on how far one is disposed to admit such arguments from silence. Do we need a new criterion for excluding as inauthentic some logia of Jesus: 'a logion that could be expected to be quoted elsewhere (either in the Gospels and/or in Paul and/or in Acts) cannot be deemed authentic if these texts do not cite it'? The key issue, of course, centres here on the words 'could be expected' and on the grounds supporting such an expectation. But, in general, Meier's conclusions are clear and to be endorsed. After examining teaching concerned with the Sabbath, divorce, and food laws (along with other such matters as Jesus' abolition of oath-taking), Meier states about Jesus' claims: 'he and he alone' could 'tell Israel how to interpret God's law as befits members of the kingdom'. Jesus taught on his own authority, claiming to 'know directly and intuitively what God's will is'.[37]

(c) Apropos of the Temple saying, it is admittedly hard to establish its original form (Mark 14: 57–9; Acts 6: 13–14). But it involved some claim that his mission was to introduce a new relationship between God and the chosen people, which would supplant the central place of their current relationship, the Temple in Jerusalem.[38]

Seemingly on a level with Jesus' astonishing assertion of personal authority over the sacred day, central place, and God-given law for guiding Jewish life was his willingness to dispense with the divinely established channels for the forgiveness of sins (sacrificial offerings in

---

[36] Ibid. 393–7. We do read (Mark 7: 20) of a charge made against 'some' of Jesus' disciples for eating with 'defiled hands, that is, without washing them'— a detail repeated in another Gospel (Matt, 15: 2). But neither they nor Jesus are accused of eating forbidden food.

[37] Ibid. 415; on Jesus' charismatic sense of his own authority, see further 659–60.

[38] N. T. Wright, *Christian Origins and the Question of God*, ii: *Jesus and the Victory of God* (London: SPCK, 1996), 489–519.

the Temple and the mediation of priestly authorities) and to take on God's role by forgiving sins in his own name. He did this by word (e.g. Mark 2: 1–11; Luke 7: 47–9) and by table fellowship with sinners (e.g. Luke 15: 1–2).[39]

All in all, Jesus claimed or at least implied a personal authority that should be described as putting himself on a par with God. Since he gave such an impression during his ministry, one can understand members of the Sanhedrin charging Jesus with blasphemy. They feared that he was not merely a false prophet but was even usurping divine prerogatives (Mark 14: 64).[40]

What did Jesus disclose about himself and the *final* reign of God? Apparently he saw his ministry not only as embodying the climax of God's purposes for Israel (Mark 12: 2–6), but also as involving his own uniquely authoritative role for bringing others to share the final kingdom. He said to the core group of twelve disciples: 'I assign to you, as my Father assigned to me, a kingdom that you may eat and drink at my table in my kingdom' (Luke 22: 39–40). Here Jesus testified to himself as critically significant for entry into the life of the final kingdom. He expressed other such claims in terms of his self-designation, 'the Son of Man': 'I tell you, every one who acknowledges me before human beings, the Son of Man will acknowledge before the angels of God. But those who deny me before human beings will be denied before the angels of God' (Luke 12: 8–9). Jesus disclosed here that the full and final salvation of human beings depended on their present relationship to him.

Jesus' revelation of his decisive role for human salvation hereafter emerges as even more startling when we recall how he identified himself with the Son of Man who was to come 'with the clouds of heaven' (Mark 14: 62) and 'with great power and glory' (Mark 13: 26), who would 'send out the angels and gather his elect' (Mark 13: 27), and who, sitting upon 'his throne of glory' (Matt. 19: 28; 25: 31), was to judge the nations (Matt. 25: 31–46). This language about the coming Son of Man portrays Jesus acting in a final scenario of human salvation as supremely authoritative—in fact, as divine judge.[41]

---

[39] See G. S. Shogren, 'Forgiveness: New Testament', *ABD* ii. 835–8.
[40] On some aspects of Jesus' claim to authority, see B. Chilton, 'Amen', ibid. i. 184–6; G. E. Hasel, 'Sabbath', ibid. v. 859–6; H. Weder, 'Disciple, Discipleship', ibid. ii. 207–10.
[41] On the Son of Man sayings, see Meier, *A Marginal Jew*, iv. 285–93, 334–5; O'Collins, *Christology*, 63–5.

Here and now Jesus aimed at mediating the life of the kingdom by establishing a new family of God. Becoming the brothers and sisters of Jesus, men and women could enjoy a new relationship with God, even to the point of addressing God as their loving and merciful 'Abba' (Father dear or even Daddy) (Mark 3: 31–5; Matt. 6: 9; Luke 11: 2). Jesus himself showed that he was conscious of a unique divine sonship (Matt. 11: 25–7), an intimate filial relationship with 'Abba' that gave him the right to invite others to share in the life-giving fatherhood of God.[42] This relationship underpinned his role as the Revealer and the Saviour in creating the new family.

Knowing and naming God in a new way formed a striking feature of Jesus' message of the kingdom. In the Hebrew Bible, God was known by many names, above all the personal name of YHWH. This, the most sacred of names, appears about 6,800 times both by itself or in compounds. In *God is King: Understanding an Israelite Metaphor*, Marc Zvi Brettler points to 'God is King' as the 'predominant metaphor for God in the Old Testament, appearing much more frequently than metaphors such as "God is lover/husband" (e.g. Jeremiah 3, Ezekiel 16 and Hosea 2) or "God is father" (Deuteronomy 32: 6; Isaiah 63: 16; Jeremiah 3: 19)'.[43] This latter metaphor is certainly rare; in the whole of the Old Testament God is named (or addressed) as 'Father' hardly twenty times. Through the preaching of Jesus, this name moved to centre stage. 'King' dropped out entirely (except for Matt. 5: 35, which echoes Ps. 48: 1). Jesus preached the kingdom of God, but at the heart of the kingdom was the divine Father, not the King. Prompting Jesus' self-revelation was his intimate experience of God as the loving, trustworthy 'Abba'.

The Trinity revealed?

From all that has been said so far about what Jesus intended and disclosed when preaching the kingdom, we have seen hints of how this story bore a trinitarian face. In a human way he lived his personal identity of being the Son in constant relationship to the Father and empowered by the Holy Spirit. Beyond question, we should not

---

[42] On Jesus as Son of God, see O' Collins, *Christology*, 119–40.
[43] (Sheffield: JSOT Press, 1989), 160.

expect to find anything like a fully deployed revelation of the Trinity in what the Synoptic Gospels recall about Jesus. It would be wildly anachronistic to look for such a clear doctrine in the story of Jesus' ministry. Nevertheless, there were hints of God's tripersonal reality in that ministry, hints that (with other sources—e.g. John's Gospel and the whole experience of the resurrection and Pentecost) provided the starting point for belief in the Trinity which would be elaborated fully in the Nicene-Constantinopolitan Creed of 381 that all Christians use when celebrating the Eucharist.

We begin with the baptism of Jesus, related by Mark 1: 9–11 and, with some variations, by Matthew 3: 13–17 and Luke 3: 21–2. John 1: 29–34 refers to the baptism but does not tell the story as such.

The baptism

Mark (followed by Matthew and Luke) recalls some kind of a disclosure of the Trinity at Jesus' baptism: in the voice of the Father, the obedience of the Son, and the descent of (and anointing by) the Holy Spirit.[44] The Spirit descended on him 'like a dove', and 'a voice came from heaven: "You are my Son, the Beloved, with you I am well pleased"' (Mark 1: 10–11). Even if, according to Mark and—somewhat less emphatically—Luke (3: 22), but not according to Matthew (Matt. 3: 17), the voice from heaven was directed to Jesus, these evangelists (and still less Matthew[45]) do not seem to be thinking of a divine call accompanied by visionary elements. The Gospels do not support the conclusion that the voice from heaven conveyed to Jesus for the first time his divine commission.

The story of the baptism, in particular the earliest version from Mark, functioned (1) to reveal the identity of Jesus (as approved from heaven in his state of being God's beloved Son), (2) to tell of his consecration for his mission, (3) to introduce his public activity, and (4) to indicate the form that activity would take (as witnessing to the

[44] On the baptism of Jesus, see Meier, *A Marginal Jew*, ii. 100–16, 182–91. On Mark's version of the baptism, see Marcus, *Mark 1–9*, 158–67; on Matthew's version, see Nolland, *The Gospel of Matthew*, 150–8; on Luke's version, see Fitzmyer, *The Gospel According to Luke I–IX*, 479–87; and Nolland, *Luke 1–9:20*, 157–65; on John's version, see Lincoln, *Gospel According to John*, 113–15.
[45] Matthew depicts Jesus' baptism as a public manifestation for others, even if it is only Jesus who sees or experiences the descent of the Spirit (Matt. 3: 16).

Father and being empowered by the Spirit). The revelatory opening of heaven, the sound of the Father's voice, and the descent of the (creative and prophetic) Spirit disclosed that with Jesus, the bearer of God's Spirit, the final time of salvation was being inaugurated. Mark 1: 10 writes of 'the heavens being torn apart'. The evangelist will use the same verb (schizō) about the curtain of the Temple being 'torn in two'—symbolizing, among other things, the revelation of Jesus' identity to the centurion and through him to others (Mark 15: 38). The episode of the baptism assures Mark's readers that Jesus was related to God in a special, filial way and would initiate a heaven-blessed ministry.

In Mark's narrative, John the Baptist says of the 'mightier one' coming after him: 'He will baptize you with the Holy Spirit' (1: 8). When following Mark at this point, Matthew and Luke add a significant phrase: 'He will baptize you with the Holy Spirit *and with fire*' (Matt. 3: 11; Luke 3: 16).[46] In the event, neither Mark nor Matthew reports any coming of the Holy Spirit, as does Luke (Luke 24: 49; Acts 1: 8; 2: 1–4), who also portrays the Spirit as 'fiery' (Acts 2: 3, 19). Matthew will include a mandate from the risen Jesus to baptize 'in the name of the Father, and of the Son, *and of the Holy Spirit*' (Matt. 28: 19). Where Luke clearly refers the being 'baptized with fire' to the fire of the Spirit at Pentecost, Matthew may understand this fire to be the judgement (Matt. 25: 41) facing those who fail to respond appropriately to the call to repentance (Matt. 7: 19; 13: 40, 42, 50; 18: 9). In any case, the three Synoptic Gospels all envision Jesus being baptized with the Holy Spirit and engaging in his ministry as one empowered by the Spirit. His baptism signifies the arrival of the final age and the fulfilment of God's promise to pour out the divine Spirit (Isa. 44: 3; Ezek. 39: 29; Joel 2: 28–9).

According to Mark, the Spirit who had come down on Jesus 'drove' him at once into the wilderness (Mark 1: 12). Like Matthew 4: 1, Luke puts this more gently: Jesus 'was led by the Spirit' into the desert (Luke 4: 1). For Luke, the earthly Jesus showed himself in his ministry of preaching and healing to be the paradigmatic Spirit-bearer (Luke 4: 14, 18–21; 6: 19). Here Luke approaches the conviction of John 1: 32–3, that Jesus possessed the Spirit permanently and was the source of the

---

[46] On baptism with 'Spirit and fire', see Nolland, *Luke 1–9: 20*, 152–3; id., *The Gospel of Matthew*, 145–8.

Spirit. Unlike Matthew 11: 25, Luke introduces Jesus' prayer of thanksgiving to the 'Father, Lord of heaven and earth' by representing Jesus as 'rejoicing in the Holy Spirit' (Luke 10: 21–4). He depicts Jesus as delighting, under the influence of the Spirit, in his relationship to God experienced as his Father.

It is, then, in trinitarian terms that the evangelists depict the start of Jesus' ministry. But what of Jesus himself and, in particular, his consciousness of sonship and awareness of the Holy Spirit? The Gospel stories of Jesus' baptism, while based on a historical episode, may not be readily used as sources of information about some deep experience that Jesus himself underwent on that occasion. As John Meier convincingly argues, Jesus' consciousness of his sonship and of the Spirit could have 'crystallised' before, during, or even after the baptism. Although this consciousness may have been developed and confirmed by what he experienced at the Jordan, we cannot be 'more specific' about 'when and how this happened'.[47] What can we say about Jesus' experience of the Spirit and consciousness of sonship *during his ministry* for the kingdom?

The Holy Spirit

Apparently Jesus was aware of being empowered by the Spirit, and deplored the attitude of some hostile critics. So far from acknowledging the divine Spirit as being at work in his ministry, they attributed Jesus' redeeming activity to Satan and so sinned against the Spirit (Mark 3: 22–30). But Jesus never unambiguously pointed to his deeds as signs of the Spirit's power. Matthew has Jesus say, 'if by the Spirit of God I cast out demons, the kingdom of God has come upon you' (Matt. 12: 28; see 12: 16). But we find here an editorial modification introduced by the evangelist. Luke seems to provide the original version of the saying: 'if by the finger of God I cast out demons...' (Luke 11: 20).[48]

The Synoptic Gospels never credit Jesus with an awareness of the Spirit that had the intensity of his consciousness of 'Abba', his loving Father. He never, for instance, prayed to the Spirit: 'Holy Spirit, all things are possible to you, but not my will but yours be done.' Rather

---

[47] Meier, *A Marginal Jew*, ii. 108–9.
[48] Ibid. 407–23; see also J. Nolland, *The Gospel of Matthew*, (Grand Rapids, Mich.: Eerdmans, 2005), 499–501.

he prayed in the Spirit or with the Spirit in him. Jesus seems to have described and thought of the divine Spirit in a fairly normal prophetic way: the dynamic power of God reaching out to have its impact on Jesus and through him on others. It took Jesus' resurrection and exaltation to disclose a clearer and fuller picture of the Spirit and the relationship of Jesus to the Spirit.

The sonship of Jesus

It was Jesus' sonship rather than any theme connected with the Spirit that Mark and Matthew exploit to structure a 'christological inclusion' into their Gospels. Mark begins with a double announcement of Jesus as the Son of God in the context of his baptism (1: 1, 11), and via the metaphorical sense of baptism as suffering (10: 38) has the revelation of Jesus' sonship peak immediately after the crucifixion with the confession of the centurion: 'indeed this man was Son of God' (15: 39). Matthew uses a double Christological frame: the theme of 'God with us' (1: 23; 28: 20), and that of the obedient Son of God who is tried and tested at the beginning (3: 13–17; 4: 1–11) and at the end (27: 39–54).

The witness from the ministry makes it clear that Jesus himself understood and disclosed his relationship to God as sonship. Because it was/is a relationship with God, this means that we deal with some kind of divine sonship. But what kind of divine sonship did Jesus imply or even lay claim to? Merely a somewhat distinctive one, or a divine sonship intimate to the point of being qualitatively different and radically unique?

First, in an important passage, Jesus referred to the Father, identified as 'Lord of heaven and earth', and claimed a unique and exclusive knowledge of 'the Father' possessed by 'the Son', who was tacitly identified with 'me': 'all things have been delivered to me by my Father and no one knows the Son except the Father, and no one knows the Father except the Son and anyone to whom the Son chooses to reveal him' (Matt. 11: 25–30 = Luke 10: 22). This was to affirm a unique mutual knowledge and relationship of Jesus precisely as Son to the Father, a mutual relationship out of which Jesus revealed the God whom he alone knew fully.[49]

---

[49] See Nolland, *The Gospel of Matthew*, 468–78; Fitzmyer, *The Gospel According to Luke X–XXIV*, 864–70.

Second, Mark 13: 32 (followed probably by Matt. 24: 36) has Jesus referring in an unqualified way to 'the Son' and, with respect to the end of the age, (implicitly) acknowledging the limits of his (human) knowledge over against 'the Father': 'of that day and of that hour no one knows, not even the angels in heaven, nor the Son, but only the Father'.

Third, the Parable of the Vineyard and the Wicked Tenants reaches its climax with the owner sending to the tenants 'my son' and their killing this 'beloved/only son' (Mark 12: 1–12). Mark or the pre-Markan tradition has apparently added 'beloved/only' and almost certainly the tacit reference to the resurrection at the end. But the substance of the parable, with its allegorical allusion to his own violent death, seems to derive from Jesus himself. A son could act as his father's legal representative in a way that slaves or servants could not; in the parable this differentiates the son from the previous messengers. Apparently Jesus intends his audience to identify him with the son in the story—the only parable in which he gives himself a more or less clear part.[50] But neither here nor elsewhere in the Synoptic Gospels does Jesus ever come out in the open and say: 'I am the Son of God.' (See, however, Matt. 27: 43, where those who taunt him during the crucifixion recall: 'He said, "I am the Son of God"', even though Matthew's Gospel, despite 26: 63–4, has never previously represented Jesus as saying just that.)

Three times the Synoptic Gospels report Jesus as referring to the divine sonship enjoyed by others here and hereafter (Matt. 5: 9; Luke 6: 35; 20: 36). All in all, even if every one of the references to his own unique sonship and the participated sonship of others comes from the earthly Jesus himself, we are faced with much less use of this theme than we find in the Old Testament. In a fairly widespread way those Scriptures name the whole people (e.g. Hos. 11: 1), the Davidic king (e.g. Ps. 2: 7), and righteous individuals (e.g. Wisd. 2: 13, 18) as children/sons/daughters of God. The situation is the opposite with God as Father. The Old Testament rarely calls God 'Father' and hardly ever does so in any prayers addressed to God.[51] Jesus changed that

---

[50] On this parable see G. O'Collins, *Salvation for All: God's Other Peoples* (Oxford: Oxford University Press, 2008), 101–3.

[51] For details, see G. O'Collins, *The Tripersonal God* (Mahwah, NJ: Paulist Press), 12–23.

situation, revealing through his public ministry his dialogue with 'Abba' and disclosing how he was humanly aware of his oneness-in-distinction with the Father.

Mark's Gospel at least five times calls God 'Father'—most strikingly in Jesus' prayer in Gethsemane: 'Abba, Father, all things are possible to you; take this cup from me. Yet not my will but yours be done' (14: 36). Even if 'Abba' was not a child's address to its male parent,[52] Jesus evidently spoke of and with God as his Father in a direct, familial way that was highly unusual or even unique in Palestinian Judaism. 'Abba' was a characteristic and distinctive feature of Jesus' prayer life. In several passages in Matthew (e.g. 6: 9; 11: 25–6; 16: 17), in one passage at least in Luke (11: 2), and perhaps in other passages in these two Gospels, 'Father' (in Greek) stands for the original 'Abba' (in Aramaic).[53] The example of Jesus, at least in the early days of Christianity, led his followers to pray to God in that familiar way—even as far away as Rome (Rom. 8: 15; Gal. 4: 6). As James Dunn points out, 'the clear implication of these passages is that Paul regarded the "Abba" prayer as something distinctive to those who had received the eschatological Spirit': in other words, 'as a distinguishing mark of those who shared the Spirit of Jesus' sonship, of an inheritance shared with Christ'.[54]

Altogether in the Synoptic Gospels (excluding merely parallel cases), Jesus speaks of God as 'Father', 'my heavenly Father' 'your (heavenly) Father', or 'our Father' fifty-one times. Sometimes we deal with a Father-saying that has been drawn from Q (e.g. Matt. 11: 23–7 = Luke 10: 21–2). Or else we find a Father-saying which, while attested by Matthew alone (e.g. Matt. 16: 17) or by Luke alone (e.g. Luke 22: 29), seems to go back to Jesus himself. Matthew shows a liking for 'heavenly' and may at various points have added the adjective to sayings that originally spoke only of 'your Father' or 'my Father' (e.g. Matt. 6: 32). The same evangelist may at times have inserted

---

[52] See G. D. Fee, *God's Empowering Presence: The Holy Spirit in the Letters of St Paul* (Peabody, Mass.: Hendrickson, 1994), 410–12; Meier, *A Marginal Jew*, ii. 358–9.

[53] When reporting Jesus' prayer in Gethsemane, Matthew and Luke do not reproduce the Markan 'Abba', just as they drop other Aramaic expressions that Mark records (Mark 3: 17; 5: 41; 7: 11, 34; 15: 34). The only Markan Aramaisms that survive in either Matthew and Luke are 'Hosanna' (Mark 11: 9–10 = Matt. 21: 9) and 'Golgotha' (Mark 15: 22 = Matt. 27: 33).

[54] J. D. G. Dunn, *Christology in the Making* (2nd edn. London: SCM Press, 1989), 27.

'Father' into his sources (e.g. Matt. 6: 26; 10: 29, 32–3). Even discounting a number of such cases as not directly derived from Jesus himself, we can be sure that he spoke fairly frequently of God as 'Father' or 'Abba'.

Further, Jesus called those who did God's will 'my brother and sister, and mother', but not 'my father' (Mark 3: 31–5). He invited his hearers to recognize God as their loving, merciful Father. However, being his brothers and sisters did not put others on the same level with him as sons and daughters of God. Jesus distinguished between 'my' Father and 'your' Father. He did not invite his disciples to share with him an identical relationship of sonship. If Jesus did say 'Our Father' (Matt. 6: 9, unlike Luke 11: 2 where there is no 'our'), it was in a prayer he proposed for others ('pray then like this'—Matt. 6: 9). When he invited his hearers to accept a new relationship with God as Father, it was a relationship that depended on his (Luke 22: 29–30) and differed from his. Was he aware that his sonship differed so much that it was quite distinctive and even unique?

At least we can say this: when Jesus applied the language of divine sonship to himself, he filled it with meaning that went beyond the level of his merely being a man like Adam made in the divine image (Luke 3: 38), or someone perfectly sensitive to the Holy Spirit (Luke 4: 1, 14, 18), or someone bringing God's peace (Luke 2: 14; 10: 5–6), albeit in his own way (Matt. 10: 34), or even a/the Davidic king (Luke 1: 32) who would in some way restore the kingdom of Israel. He not only spoke like 'the Son' but also acted like 'the Son' in knowing and revealing the truth of God, in changing the divine law, in forgiving sins (outside the normal channels of sacrifices in the Temple and the ministry of the levitical priesthood), in disclosing himself as the one through whom others could become children of God and who would at the end act as divine judge for all people. All of this clarifies, as we saw above, the charge of blasphemy brought against Jesus at the end (Mark 14: 64); he had given the impression of claiming to stand on a level with God and to enjoy a unique filial relationship with God.

Inasmuch as Jesus experienced and expressed himself as the Son, this means that YHWH of the Old Testament was now revealed to be the Father. The revelation of the Son necessarily implied the revelation of the Father.

The highpoint of this chapter has been establishing the trinitarian face of the kingdom that Jesus preached and inaugurated. Once again

I should warn against being anachronistic and reading the revelation of the Trinity too clearly and too fully into the story of Jesus' ministry. Nevertheless, that ministry exhibits him living out in a human way his filial relationship and mission as One sent/coming from the Father and acting in the power of the Holy Spirit.

We must complete our account of the self-manifestation of the tripersonal God in Christ, by reflecting on his crucifixion, resurrection, exaltation, and sending of the Holy Spirit. But before doing that, we need to reflect on the appropriate language to use about the fullness of revelation in Christ.

Revelation past, present, and future

In the quotation that opened this chapter, John of the Cross declared that, with his Son, God, 'spoke everything to us' and did so 'once and for all'. Jesus, of course, did not act alone but gathered around him disciples and then chose the core group of the Twelve. We return below to the founding fathers and mothers of the Church in their once-and-for-all role in mediating normatively to all later generations the self-manifestation of God in Jesus Christ. In that sense we need to modify the statement of John of the Cross and say: in his Son *and in the founding figures* Jesus gathered around him, God 'spoke everything to us'.

Apropos of this revelation being unsurpassable and (in some sense perfect and complete), rather than provisional and fragmentary, the prologue of Hebrews announces: 'Long ago God spoke to our ancestors in many and various ways by the prophets, but in these last days he has spoken to us by the Son' (1: 1–2). Where, in the logic of John's prologue, the divine revelation communicated through Jesus is full because he is *the Word* of God, Hebrews attributes the fullness of revelation to his identity as *the Son of God*. Both John and Hebrews highlight the divine identity of the One who has come 'from above' into the world. Paul, however, typically thinks more 'horizontally' and historically: Christ's resurrection from the dead, located within the whole sweep of history since Adam, has initiated and really anticipated the fullness of saving revelation to come when God will be all in all (1 Cor. 15: 20–8).

Whether we follow the language of John, Hebrews, or Paul, should we then describe this revelation as 'definitive'—in the sense of its being not merely decisive but even final, totally complete, and something simply over and done with? The use of 'definitive' risks, however, playing down the way in which the New Testament when using the language of revelation is heavily slanted towards the *future divine manifestation* that will be the second coming of Christ.[55] Thus Hebrews announces that Christ 'will appear a second time' to 'save those who are eagerly waiting for him' (9: 28). Paul proclaims that 'the revealing of the Lord' will be on 'the day of his final coming' (1 Cor. 1: 7–8), and reckons 'the sufferings of the present time' not 'worth comparing with the glory that will be revealed to us' (Rom. 8: 18). First John, while opening with the witness of the Johannine community to 'the life' that 'was revealed' in Christ (1: 1–4), proceeds to comfort its readers with the promise, 'when he [God] is revealed, we will be like him for we shall see him as he is' (3: 2). First Peter, even though it recognizes that Christ 'was revealed at the end of the ages' (1: 20), repeatedly refers to the 'salvation ready to be revealed in the last time' (1: 3) and 'the grace that Jesus Christ will bring you when he is revealed' (1: 13; see 1: 7). We find a similar tension between past and future revelation in the Letter to Titus. On the one hand, it rejoices that 'the grace of God has appeared, bringing salvation to all' (2: 11). Yet, on the other hand, two verses later it looks toward the future revelation: 'we wait for the blessed hope and the manifestation of the glory of our great God and Saviour, Jesus Christ' (2: 13).

Add too passages in the New Testament that represent revelation as happening *here and now*: for instance, the messages that the exalted Christ addresses through the Holy Spirit to seven churches in Asia Minor. The faithful should hear in faith 'what the Spirit is saying' to them right now (Rev. 2: 1–3: 22). In Revelation and elsewhere divine revelation comes across as being a living event and reality. The First Letter of John 'testifies to' and 'declares' here and now what has been revealed (1: 1–3). Paul expounds faith as the 'obedience of faith' given to God as he communicates himself through the apostolic preaching (Rom. 16: 26). Through the proclamation of the good news, God's 'righteousness is revealed' to elicit the faith of human beings and

---

[55] See A. Dulles, *Models of Revelation* (New York: Doubleday, 1983), 228–9.

bring them into a right relationship with God (Rom. 10: 16–17). In a lyrical passage the apostle portrays faith as responding to what is heard, 'the word of Christ' (Rom. 10: 14–17). The good news Paul preaches is nothing less than 'the [revealing] word of God' working to bring about faith and keep it alive (1 Thess. 2: 13). The sufferings that characterize Paul's ministry made the life of Christ 'visible' in the 'mortal flesh' of the apostle (2 Cor. 4: 11).[56] The heart of the apostolic preaching was the message of the crucified Christ's resurrection, the climax of divine revelation to which believers responded and continue to respond in faith (1 Cor. 15: 3–11).

To sum up: the New Testament presents the divine self-revelation as something that has happened (past), that is happening (present), and that will happen (future). How can we relate these three sets of affirmation that at first sight seem mutually exclusive? If revelation has been completed in the past, how can it happen today and reach its final fullness in the future? If revelation is also a present event, how can we speak of it as having reached its perfect culmination two thousand years ago?

One frequent false move (1) flatly ignores what the New Testament says about the revelation to come, and (2) alleges that present revelation is not revelation in the proper sense but only a growth in the collective understanding of that revelation completed and closed once and for all with Christ and his apostles (see Jude 3). Undoubtedly such a growth in understanding does take place. How could I say otherwise at a time when an interest in John Henry Newman (1801–90) and his writings flourishes as much as ever? His *Essay on the Development of Christian Doctrine* of 1845 espouses the growth in collective understanding and interpretation that tradition has brought. Nevertheless, we would not do justice to tradition if, while accepting the development it has effected toward understanding a past revelation, we denied that it produces an actual revelation of God. In a later chapter we will reflect on the role of the Holy Spirit as the 'soul' of living Christian tradition. The witness of the Spirit brings it about that the divine self-revelation recorded in the Scriptures is not only more fully understood but also actualized as God's living revelation to the Church and through her to the world.

---

[56] On this verse, see M. J. Harris, *The Second Epistle to the Corinthians* (Grand Rapids, Mich.: Eerdmans, 2005), 347–9.

To deny present revelation is to doubt the active power here and now of the Holy Spirit in guiding tradition and mediating the living presence of the risen Christ. This also means reducing faith to accepting some revealed truths inherited from the past, rather than taking faith in its integral sense, as full obedience given to God revealed here and now through the living voice of the good news. In short, to deny such present revelation of God involves selling short its human correlative, faith.

Of course, if one persists in holding that revelation entails *primarily* the communication of revealed truths (rather than the personal disclosure of God), it becomes easier to relegate revelation to the past. As soon as the whole set of revealed doctrines was complete, revelation ended or was 'closed'. For this way of thinking, later believers cannot immediately and directly experience revelation. All they can do is remember, interpret, and apply truths revealed long ago to the apostolic church.

Those who think this way should learn to appreciate how present revelation (effected through the reading and proclaiming of the Scriptures,[57] the Church's worship ('announcing the death of the Lord until he comes'—1 Cor. 11: 26), and innumerable other means) *actualizes* the living event of the divine self-manifestation and continues to do so in innumerable contexts and for innumerable people who respond in faith. God is not silent but continues to speak to us. This ongoing revelation does *not add* to the essential 'content' of what was fully revealed through Christ's life, death, resurrection, and the sending of the Holy Spirit. As a living encounter with Christ through his Spirit, this divine self-manifestation never stops; yet this encounter adds nothing essentially new to what the apostolic generation came to know through their experience of Christ and his Spirit.

What we need here is a terminology that distinguishes between revelation, (1) inasmuch as it reached an unsurpassable, once and for all climax with Christ and his apostles, (2) inasmuch as it continues and calls people to faith in a living encounter with God, and (3) inasmuch as it will be gloriously consummated in the life to come. In one sense revelation is past (as 'foundational'), in another it is present (as 'dependent'), and in a further sense it is a reality to come (as 'future' or 'eschatological'). The first and second senses call for comment.

---

[57] See how the Scriptures serve to 'instruct for salvation through faith in Christ Jesus' (2 Tim. 3: 15).

Some speak of (1) as 'original' revelation,[58] but I prefer to name it 'foundational', a term that echoes New Testament language. According to the Letter to the Ephesians, 'the household of God' is 'built upon the foundation of the apostles and prophets, Christ himself being the cornerstone' (2: 19–20). The vision of the new Jerusalem in the Book of Revelation includes a similar image to describe the foundational role of the Twelve in the service of Christ: 'the wall of the city had twelve foundations, and on them the twelve names of the twelve apostles of the Lamb' (21: 14). Where 'original', as meaning 'existing from/at the beginning', seems purely factual, 'foundational' adds a sense of the revelation in question being somehow 'constructive', normative, and sustaining.

Others speak of (2) as 'participatory' revelation.[59] Yet we should recall that the apostolic generation participated in the events that climactically embodied God's self-revelation: Christ's life, death, and resurrection, together with the outpouring of the Holy Spirit. Hence one could talk of the participatory revelation involving the apostles. In these terms later believers would participate in a participation. Or should we say that, as regards God's self-communication in Christ, the apostolic generation participated in a foundational way; later believers participate in a dependent way—that is to say, in dependence upon these apostolic witnesses? Or perhaps it is simpler and clearer if we distinguish between the foundational revelation communicated to the apostolic Church and the dependent revelation available to all later believers.

The foundational role of the apostles and the apostolic generation included four functions. (1) The summary formulas of preaching recorded in Paul's letters (e.g. 1 Cor. 15: 3–5), the Acts of the Apostles (e.g. 2: 22–4, 32–3, 36; 3: 13–15; 4: 10–12; 5: 30–2),[60] and elsewhere in the New Testament (e.g. Luke 24: 34) reflect a primary function of Peter, Paul, and other apostolic witnesses. Their basic message

---

[58] Paul Tillich speaks of 'original' and 'dependent' revelation (rather than 'foundational' and 'dependent' revelation) and gives that language his own nuances: *Systematic Theology*, i (Chicago: Chicago University Press, 1951), 126–8.

[59] Aylward Shorter has proposed the terminology of 'foundational' and 'participant' revelation: *Revelation and its Interpretation* (London: Geoffrey Chapman, 1983), 139–43.

[60] On these verses, see J. A. Fitzmyer, *The Acts of the Apostles* (New York: Doubleday, 1998), 254–6, 258–61, 284–6, 300–2, 336–8.

('the crucified Jesus has been raised from the dead and of that we are witnesses') gathered the first Christians. Those who had not seen and yet believed (John 20: 29) depended upon the testimony of the Easter witnesses for their coming, through the power of the Holy Spirit, to faith in and experience of the risen Jesus.[61] (2) Believers entered the community through being baptized 'into' Christ's death and resurrection (Rom. 6: 3–11). Together they celebrated eucharistically the death of the risen Lord in expectation of his final coming (1 Cor. 11: 26). Thus the post-Easter proclamation initiated the liturgical life of the Church.

(3) The apostolic leaders made the normative decision not to impose on Gentile converts the observance of the Mosaic law (Acts 15: 1–30; Gal. 2: 1–21). The resurrection of the crucified Jesus brought the new/second covenant which both confirmed God's promises to the chosen people (Rom. 9: 4; 11: 29; 2 Cor. 1: 20) and liberated Gentile believers from the obligation of circumcision and other burdens of the law (Gal. 5: 1). (4) Finally, the apostles and other Christians of the apostolic age wrote the Gospels and other New Testament writings, inspired books that perpetually witness to the climax of divine revelation in Christ and to the origins of the Church.

In short, the apostles and their associates shaped once and for all the essential (2) sacramental and (3) moral life of the Church. Through (4) the books of the New Testament, they left for all subsequent ages of believers a divinely inspired record of the unsurpassable revelation in Christ and its reception in the first decades of church life. Right from the birth of Christianity, through (1) their Easter preaching the apostles witnessed to the climax of God's self-manifestation which they had experienced in the crucifixion and resurrection of Christ, along with the outpouring of the Holy Spirit.

I sum up these once and for all apostolic functions by speaking of those who witnessed to that 'foundational' revelation which took place normatively through a specific set of events and the experiences of a specific set of people. God's saving word came through the history of Israel, the prophets, and then—in a full and perfect fashion—through Jesus of Nazareth and the experiences in which

[61] On this dependence from the apostolic witnesses, see K. Rahner, *Foundations of Christian Faith: An Introduction to the Idea of Christianity*, trans. W. V. Dych (New York: Seabury Press, 1978), 274–6.

he and his first followers were immediately involved. Christians experience now God's self-communication reaching them through the Scriptures, preaching, sacraments, and other means that recall and re-enact the past events and experiences which affected the chosen people, the prophets, Jesus himself, his apostles, and other founding fathers and founding mothers. Thus the mediation of revelation (and salvation) through the Scriptures, the preached word, the sacraments, and other means depends essentially upon accepting the foundational and authoritative testimony about certain past acts of God. Revelation, as believers experience it and accept it now, remains 'dependent' revelation. The adjective 'dependent' expresses a permanent relationship to the apostolic witness, whose faith and proclamation of the gospel sprang from their special, immediate experience of Jesus during his lifetime and as risen from the dead. The apostolic witness to foundational revelation continues to be determinative and normative for the post-apostolic history of Christians and their experience of God in Christ.

To complete this reflection on past (foundational) revelation and ongoing (dependent) revelation, we need to ask: when did foundational revelation end and the period of dependent revelation begin? The traditional answer refers to the end of the apostolic age. Rightly understood, this response allows for the full reception of revelation by recognizing that the apostolic experience of Christ *also* included the phase of discernment, interpretation, and expression of that experience. Peter, Paul, and other founding fathers and mothers of the Church spent a lifetime reflecting on and proclaiming their experience of the crucified and risen Jesus and his Holy Spirit. Collectively and personally they gave themselves to interpreting and applying the meaning, truth, and value of their total experience of Jesus. That experience lodged itself profoundly in their memories to live on powerfully and productively until the end of their lives.

Understood that way, the period of foundational revelation covered not merely the climactic events (the life, death, and resurrection of Jesus, together with the outpouring of the Spirit) but also the decades when the apostles and their associates assimilated these events, fully founded the Church for all peoples, and wrote the inspired books of the New Testament. During those years the apostles were not receiving new truths from Christ, as if he had failed to reveal to them everything he wanted to through his ministry, death, and post-resurrection appearances. Rather they were led by the Holy Spirit to express, interpret normatively, and apply what they had experienced of the fullness of revelation in Christ (John 15: 26; 16: 13).[62] In these terms the activity of the Spirit through the apostolic age also entered into foundational revelation and its phase of immediate assimilation. That age belonged to the revealing and redemptive Christ-event, and did so in a way that would not be true of any later stage of Christian history.

When the apostolic age closed—roughly speaking at the end of the first century—there would be no more founding of the Church and writing of inspired Scriptures. The last period of foundational revelation, in which the original witnesses brought into being the visible Church and completed the written word of God, was ended. Through the apostolic Church and its Scriptures, later generations could share dependently in the saving self-communication of God mediated through unrepeatable events surrounding Jesus and his first followers. All later believers would be invited to accept the witness of those who announced what they had personally experienced of the full divine revelation in Christ: 'we proclaim to you the eternal life which was with the Father and was made manifest to us' (1 John 1: 2).[63]

By speaking of faith, tradition, biblical inspiration, the founding of the Church, this chapter has anticipated themes that later chapters will treat. Before moving to such themes, however, we need to complete our account of God's revelation in Christ by examining the crucifixion, resurrection, and outpouring of the Spirit.

---

[62] On these verses, see Lincoln, *Gospel According to John*, 411–12, 421.

[63] As this verse shows, the period of dependent revelation was already inaugurated in the experience of those who accepted in faith the proclamation of the original witnesses in the Johannine community—not to mention those who responded in faith to the preaching of Paul (see above).

6

The Crucified and Resurrected Revealer

The history of the divine self-manifestation reached its peak with the events of Good Friday, Easter Sunday, and the outpouring of the Holy Spirit. Those events, often summarized as the Paschal Mystery,[1] revealed God to be the Giver, the Given, and the Self-Giving. For all human beings and for their salvation, the Father gave up the Son (Rom. 8: 32). The Son was given up (1 Cor. 11: 23) or gave himself up (Gal. 2: 20). The Spirit, who is the process of Self-Giving, gave Christ the new life of the resurrection in which all human beings can share (Rom. 8: 11). Putting things this way retrieves a sense of how the original Christians' belief in the tripersonal God emerged from their experiencing the resurrection of the crucified Jesus. Later believers have followed suit.

At public worship and in private prayer, many Christians make the sign of the cross 'in the name of the Father, and of the Son, and of the Holy Spirit'—a practice that goes back to the fourth century and even earlier. This gesture and the invocation that accompanies it associate belief in the triune God with the Paschal Mystery. Even without clearly realizing it, they derive their faith in the Trinity from what was revealed at the first Good Friday, Easter Sunday, and Pentecost.

---

[1] W. Kern and G. O'Collins, 'Paschal Mystery', *DFTh* 758–76.

In Western iconography, the 'throne of grace' (*Gnadenstuhl*) is undoubtedly the most significant representation of the Trinity. Created for centuries in a painted or carved form, it shows the Father holding the cross that bears the dead Son (or the Father simply holding the body of the Son), with the Holy Spirit as a dove hovering between them or above them. One cross links the three figures: this unity is also expressed by their being turned toward each other. Frequently, as in the version by El Greco exhibited in the Prado, the dead body of the Son already hints at the luminosity of his coming resurrection.

The classical Eastern icon of the Trinity, created by St Andrew Roublev and to be found at the Tretiakov Gallery in Moscow, presents the three 'angels' who visited Abraham and Sarah (Gen. 18: 1–15). A divine harmony pervades the composition, in which the three figures sit around one table and are entirely referred to each other in mutual self-gift. The Roublev icon, along with the sacred tradition behind it, is one of the few representations of the Trinity in which the Holy Spirit has a human face, albeit in angelic style. The presence of a chalice on the table suggests the cup of the passion (see Mark 10: 38–9), and the table itself brings to mind the Last Supper, celebrated just before Christ's death and resurrection. Despite the obvious differences between the Roublev icon and the 'throne of grace', they converge in representing the Trinity in the light of Good Friday and Easter Sunday—something that also characterizes the earliest Christian witness.

The doctrine of the Trinity was grounded in God's self-disclosure through the whole Easter mystery. The crucifixion revealed the utter sinfulness and lostness of the world. In their archetypal representatives (Judas, Caiaphas, and Pilate), the desire of men and women to run their own affairs and distance themselves from God seemed to have its own way and even enjoy its triumph. The apparent collapse of Jesus' mission could lead one to despair and even cynicism about God, or at least about human creatures who are supposedly made in the divine image and likeness. But it was precisely and supremely in the crucifixion and resurrection that the tripersonal God was experienced as powerfully engaged against sin and for human deliverance. Jesus' message about the coming of the divine reign and the infinite mercy of Abba was vindicated when Jesus received radically new, indestructible life from God and with God (e.g. Rom. 6: 9–10; Acts 13: 14). The resurrection revealed that the tripersonal God was/is present in suffering and on/around the cross—a dramatic truth valued by artists who painted or carved the 'throne of grace'. Named by Paul as an 'offence' and 'folly' to others (1 Cor. 1: 23), the cross was experienced and accepted by Christians as *the* mysterious way of divine self-communication.

In short, the Trinity was revealed in the death and resurrection of Christ, along with the coming of the Holy Spirit. Hence the cross and resurrection should inseparably shape Christian language about God, but have failed to attract regular interest from those who practise fundamental theology (and its partial equivalent, philosophical theology). The cross will be the subject of this chapter's first major section.

Revelation through the cross

Only a lunatic fringe will deny that Christ died by crucifixion (probably in the spring of AD 30). When defining Christian faith in terms of the resurrection, St Augustine of Hippo (354–430) remarked: 'everyone believes that he died.'[2] But, obviously, not everyone believes that Christ's death on the cross pre-eminently mediated God's self-revelation. What might fundamental theologians highlight about the divine revelation on Calvary which the first Christians experienced and to which they responded with faith? To answer this question, we need to join Richard Bauckham and set it within a broader context.[3]

Early Christians included Jesus unambiguously within the identity of the God of Israel, recognizing in Jesus the characteristics by which Jewish monotheism identified the one, true God. Jesus was believed to be intrinsic to who God is. His life and ministry in the cause of the present and coming kingdom of God helped believers answer more completely the question: what is God like? He was understood to share in God's creative activity and sovereignty over all things (e.g. 1 Cor. 8: 6; Col. 1: 15–17), and was identified with the divine name, 'the name that is above every name' (e.g. Phil. 2: 9). Unlike the angels, he

[2] *Enarrationes in Psalmos*, 120. 6; see 101. 7.
[3] R. Bauckham, *Jesus and the God of Israel: 'God Crucified' and Other Studies on the New Testament's Christology of Divine Identity* (Milton Keynes: Paternoster, 2008), 1–59.

reigned from the divine throne in heaven—a belief reflected in the twenty-one quotations from or allusions to Psalm 110: 1 to be found scattered across most of the New Testament writings: 'The LORD said to my Lord, "Sit at my right hand until I make your enemies my footstool".' Jews of the Second Temple period showed little interest in this text, whereas for the first Christians it was supremely significant. They believed that Jesus participated in the unique divine sovereignty over all things (e.g. Eph. 1: 21–2). Hence worship was understood to be the only proper response to Jesus (e.g. Matt. 28: 17; Phil. 2: 9–11; Rev. 5: 11–14).

Here, Bauckham insists, we find no break with Jewish monotheism but rather the development of a Christological monotheism, a consistency along with genuine novelty. The controlling image of God had been that of the Emperor of the universe, seated high on his heavenly throne. In the light of Second Isaiah, the hymn in Philippians 2: 5–11 presented the image of God as slave and included the cross within the identity of God. When Christians read Isaiah's servant passages (in particular, Isa. 52: 13–53: 12) in the light of the crucifixion, they realized that God was revealed not only as the 'lofty' One who reigns from his high and holy throne, but also as the One who abases himself to the condition of the crushed and oppressed. Terrible humiliation was understood to belong to the image of God as truly as glorious exaltation did. In a supreme act of self-giving, God had defined himself for the world. By 'pouring himself out' (Phil. 2: 7), God revealed his identity on the cross. Henceforth Christians would point to the cross when responding to the questions: where is God? Who is God?

In this context Bauckham helpfully appeals to John 8: 28 as referring to God revealed in the crucifixion: 'Jesus said, "When you have lifted up the Son of Man, then you will realize that I am [he], and that I do nothing on my own, but speak these things as the Father instructed me".' Commentators on this verse have often been distracted by the unity between Father and Son, manifested in the latter's obedience (see John 5: 30), an obedience finally embodied in his death on the cross (see John 12: 32). Yet, if we recall other 'I am' statements (e.g. Exod. 3: 14; John 6: 20; 8: 58; 18: 6, 8), we appreciate the full force of this 'I am' statement: it is God who has been revealed when lifted up on the cross.[4]

---

[4] Bauckham, *Jesus and the God of Israel*, 46–8; on John 8: 28, see further A. T. Lincoln, *The Gospel According to St John* (London: Continuum, 2005), 269.

Decades before the writing of John's Gospel, Paul was among the first (or perhaps the first) to grasp the startling nature of what the crucifixion disclosed, when he wrote of 'the Lord of glory' being crucified by 'the rulers of this age' (1 Cor. 2: 8).[5] Now exalted in glory and installed in heaven, the crucified Christ has been revealed as the true ruler of the world (see 1 Cor. 15: 25). The last place human beings would be inclined to look for God would be in the dreadfully painful and humiliating death on a cross. But it was paradoxically in that very show of 'weakness' and apparent 'folly' that the 'power' and 'wisdom' of God were revealed, or—as we might say—that the powerful and wise God was manifested (1 Cor. 1: 17–25). Here the messages of Paul and the 'throne of grace' coincide. The artistic representation displays the dead Jesus (often still on the cross) in his Father's arms and announces to onlookers: 'This is the identity of God.'

Only a few years after the final composition of the Fourth Gospel, St Ignatius of Antioch (d. *c.* 107) wrote of the Son of God being truly born and crucified (*Epistle to the Smyrnaeans*, 1–2). In the late second century, in his homily 'On the Pasch', St Melito of Sardis spoke of Christ's crucifixion as revealing the divine Creator in a shameful human death: 'He who hung up the earth is himself hung up; he who fixed the heavens is himself fixed [on the cross]; he who fastened everything is himself fastened on the wood; the Master is reviled' (96). The way was open for Tertullian a few years later to identify the figure on the cross as 'the crucified God' (*Adversus Marcionem*, 2. 27; *De Carne Christi*, 5. 4).

Bauckham's work shows how Christ revealed the divine identity and did so not least on the cross. Christ redefined the divine identity in which the Father and the Son are inseparably united but in differentiation from each other, since the crucified Jesus did not and does not compete with nor replace God the Father. What Bauckham writes has its pictorial counterpart in the Roublev icon and various versions of the 'throne of grace'. Here the work of exegetes and artists converges.

In tracking the progressive way in which the original witnesses appropriated the divine self-manifestation on the cross, we might

---

[5] On this verse see J. A. Fitzmyer, *First Corinthians* (New Haven: Yale University Press, 2008), 176–7 and also 126–7; A. C. Thiselton, *The First Epistle to the Corinthians* (Grand Rapids, Mich.: Eerdmans, 2000), 245–8.

trace a movement from Paul, to Mark, to Luke, and, finally, to John. First of all, after he has named the extreme limit of Christ's self-emptying as 'death on a cross', Paul signals the cosmic confession that has responded to the manifestation of Christ's exalted status. All this has happened 'to the glory of God the Father'—a phrase which points to an (obedient) identity-in-relationship as Son of the Father, revealed in the utter humiliation of the crucifixion which issued in 'high' exaltation (Phil. 2: 6–11).

At the beginning of his Gospel, Mark calls Jesus 'the Son of God' (1: 1) and reports the heavenly voice revealing just that (1: 11; see also 9: 7). The evangelist and his readers accept the divine identity of Jesus, but it is only at Jesus' death that this identity was revealed to someone in Mark's story. When the Roman centurion who was in charge of the crucifixion saw how Jesus died, he declared: 'Truly this man was Son of God' (15: 39). Even before the body of Jesus was taken down from the cross, a soldier who presided over the execution recognized Jesus' identity-in-relationship as Son of the Father. The centurion was 'an unexpected character to enunciate the radical inversion of values that sees a dying criminal as God's true Son'.[6]

In the last chapter we noted how Luke has John the Baptist announce a coming baptism 'with the Holy Spirit and with fire' (3: 16) and presented the earthly Jesus as the paradigmatic bearer of the Holy Spirit. After picturing Jesus at death 'committing his spirit' into 'the hands' of the Father (23: 46), Luke presses beyond the resurrection narrative to Pentecost when 'the rush of a violent wind' and 'the tongues of fire' perceptibly manifested the coming of the Holy Spirit. Jesus, the bearer of the Spirit, had become the Co-Sender of the Spirit (Acts 2: 1–3, 33). In Luke's scheme, the self-revelation of God as Father, Son, and Holy Spirit involves both death and resurrection.

The Fourth Gospel acknowledges a 'trinitarian' face in the event of the crucifixion. That gospel calls Jesus 'Son' seventeen times and 'Son of God' nine times. In his work and personal identity, Jesus is the divine Revealer of God the Father. As the unimprovable Revealer right from the start (1: 14), Jesus has manifested the glory of God the Father (17: 4). In a final, high priestly prayer, Jesus addresses his Father and accepts 'the hour' of his death that has come and will glorify both the

---

[6] J. Marcus, *Mark 8–16* (New Haven: Yale University Press, 2009), 1057–9, 1066–8, at 1057.

Father and the Son (17: 1–26). But immediately before that prayer, during his last discourse to his disciples Jesus has repeatedly promised the sending/coming of the Holy Spirit (14: 26; 15: 26; 16: 7, 12–15). Thus the final discourse and prayer of Jesus fill his imminent death on the cross with 'trinitarian' meaning. At the end, Jesus declares that he has accomplished all that the Father sent him to do (19: 30; see 17: 4). Then he 'gives up his spirit', or—more accurately—'hands over the Spirit'. His death manifests itself in the gift of the Holy Spirit, imparted to the little group gathered around the cross.

When a soldier pierces his side, blood and water come out (19: 14). The attentive reader should recall, among other things, a previous reference to the gift of the Holy Spirit when Jesus attended the Feast of Tabernacles. For seven days water was carried in a golden jug from the Pool of Siloam to the Temple, recalling the water that gushed from a rock in the desert (Num. 20: 2–13) and symbolizing a hope for the coming messianic deliverance (Isa. 12: 3). Jesus, understood to be replacing this festival, on its last day announced the 'living water' that would stream from him: 'Let those who are thirsty come to me; let those who believe in me drink. As the Scripture has said, "streams of living water will flow out of his heart".' The evangelist adds: 'Now he said this about the Spirit which those who believed in him were to receive; for as yet there was no Spirit, since Jesus was not yet glorified' (John 7: 37–9).[7] This gift and glorification were to come on the hill of Calvary. To be sure, the Gospel of John will tell of the gift of the Holy Spirit when Jesus met a group of disciples on the first Easter Sunday (20: 22–3). But the evangelist has already twice signalled the revelation and imparting of the Spirit as taking place at the cross.

We would not do justice to the manifestation of the Trinity made through the cross in the period of foundational revelation, if we failed to mention a theme precious to Paul and John: the disclosure of the *divine love*. Faced with discord among the Corinthian Christians who were divided in their loyalty to different leaders (including Paul himself), the apostle challenged them bluntly: 'was Paul crucified for you?' (1 Cor. 1: 13). The love which led Christ to accept death (and so deliver human beings from the power of sin and cleanse them from the results of sin) never failed to astonish Paul: 'he loved me and gave

---

[7] On these verses see Lincoln, *Gospel According to John*, 253–8.

himself up for me' (Gal. 2: 20; see 1: 4).[8] In his Letter to the Romans, Paul assured his audience of the love of Father, Son, and Holy Spirit manifested in the work of redemption (5: 1–11), and then returned to this theme in a lyrical passage. Nothing, Paul assured his addressees, can 'separate us from the love of God [revealed] in Christ Jesus our Lord' (8: 31–9). From start to finish, love characterizes God's self-communication.

The Johannine epistles sum up what the divine self-disclosure has finally made clear by saying: 'God [the Father] is love' (1 John 4: 8, 16). Love is not only the way God acts in the world or the way human beings should relate to each other. It reveals the very nature of God. In John's Gospel five chapters of discourse and prayer (13–17) introduce the three chapters that tell the story of Jesus' passion, death, and resurrection (18–20). Love forms the leitmotiv of those five chapters of discourse and prayer. They begin by emphasizing the revelation of Jesus' love (13: 1), and end with the prayer that the love with which the Father has loved him may be communicated to his disciples (17: 26). John's Gospel expects its readers to ponder the story of the first Good Friday and Easter Sunday in the key of love. Years ago, as we saw in Chapter 4, Rudolf Bultmann rightly identified John as the Gospel of revelation. The climax of this Gospel of revelation comes with Christ's death and resurrection, and it is a climax to be understood primarily in terms of love—that love between Jesus and his Father in which the disciples participate. In the aftermath of Easter, Peter can become pastor to Christ's flock only after he has three times testified to his love (21: 15–19).[9]

We should not move forward from cross to resurrection without recalling how the story of revelation through the cross has unfolded in the period of dependent revelation: that is to say, in the aftermath of the apostolic age. The body of Christ on the cross has disclosed for all time how the Son of God drew near to human beings in their suffering. He is mysteriously but truly present to those who suffer anywhere and at any time. His death on Calvary between two criminals symbolizes forever his close solidarity with all men and women who

---

[8] On Gal. 1: 4 and 2: 20, see J. L. Martyn, *Galatians* (New York: Doubleday, 1997), 88–91, 259.

[9] See further G. O'Collins, 'The Revelation of Love', in *Retrieving Fundamental Theology* (Mahwah, NJ: Paulist Press, 1993), 120–8.

undergo suffering. This identification with human pain was also revealed by the criteria for the final judgement (Matt. 25: 31–46). The final blessing of the kingdom will come to those who, even without recognizing Christ, meet his needs in the people who suffer by being hungry, thirsty, strangers, naked, sick, or imprisoned. Blaise Pascal's reflection ('He will be in agony to the end of the world') has classically articulated the crucified Christ's enduring presence in the mystery of all human suffering.[10] To express the worldwide presence of Christ manifested (and to be experienced through faith) in those who suffer, we could well say, 'where there is suffering, there is Christ' (*ubi dolor, ibi Christus*). It is Christ who is constantly revealed on the cross of human suffering: 'where there is a cross, there is Christ' (*ubi crux, ibi Christus*).

Revelation through the resurrection

Where the challenge of the crucifixion concerns its revelatory significance rather than its factual status in human history, the challenge of the resurrection covers all that the Easter message points to, reveals, and elicits in believers. Augustine repeatedly highlighted the acceptance of Jesus' resurrection and what it discloses as the praiseworthy faith that sets Christians apart from Jews and adherents of other religions: 'The praise (*laus*) of the faith of Christians does not consist in their believing that Christ died but in believing that Christ is risen. Even the pagans believe that he died...In what does your praise consist? It consists in believing that Christ is risen and in hoping that you will rise through Christ. This is the praise of faith' (*Enarrationes in Psalmos*, 101. 7). Having said that, Augustine at once quoted Paul on the response to what Easter revealed: 'if you confess with your lips that Jesus is Lord and believe in your heart that God raised him from the dead, you will be saved' (Rom. 10: 9).

---

[10] Listed *Pensée* 552 in such editions as W. F. Trotter's translation (New York: E. P. Dutton, 1958), which follow the standard Brunschvicg edition, this *Pensée* is numbered 919 in A. J. Krailsheimer's translation (Harmondsworth: Penguin, 1966), which adopts the order of the *Pensées* as Pascal left them at his death in 1662.

One could enlist further passages from Augustine to illustrate his conviction that accepting Christ's resurrection and what it disclosed forms and fashions the distinctive faith of Christians, and sets them apart from others. At the beginning of an Easter sermon, for example, he declares: 'in the resurrection of Christ our faith finds its stability (*constabilita est*). Even pagans, non-believers (*impii*), and Jews believe in the suffering of Christ, only Christians in his resurrection' (*Sermo*, 233. 1). Against Faustus the Manichean, Augustine writes: 'even the pagans believe that Christ died; that Christ rose is the particular faith of Christians.' Augustine goes straight on to quote Romans 10: 9 in support of his claim (*Contra Faustum Manicheum*, 16. 29).

One of the most interesting biblical and theological debates in the twentieth century took place between Karl Barth (1886–1968) and Rudolf Bultmann (1884–1976): it was a debate on Christ's resurrection and what it revealed. With his mildly critical review of Barth's 1924 book *The Resurrection of the Dead*, Bultmann initiated this debate which lasted into the 1950s. Whatever their disagreements over interpreting the resurrection, Barth remained satisfied that he and Bultmann agreed on its central significance for understanding God's revelation through Christ. In his *Church Dogmatics* Barth wrote: 'we must at least give him [Bultmann] credit for emphasizing the central and indispensable function of the event of Easter for all that is thought and said in the New Testament.' Barth went on to praise Bultmann for not having neglected the resurrection as some others did.[11] Barth's complaint could still be directed against numerous theologians (including some fundamental theologians and philosophical theologians) for failing to pay sufficient attention to the resurrection.

What is perhaps more serious has been the failure of some Christian theologians to explain the resurrection, when interpreting their faith in Jesus (and response to the revelation he embodied), to the adherents of the great religions of Asia. In this interreligious dialogue some Christians accentuate the incarnation, the Jesus of history, and the cosmic Christ, but omit or largely omit the resurrection of the crucified Christ. Augustine and, for that matter, Barth would find this

---

[11] K. Barth, *Church Dogmatics* III/2, trans. H. Knight et al. (Edinburgh: T. & T. Clark, 1960), 443.

astonishing; for them faith in the resurrection and the revelation it brought identify and distinguish Christians.

What should fundamental theologians (and philosophical theologians) do in this context? Their task is twofold: first, the apologetic task or putting a reasonable case for accepting the resurrection of Jesus, and, second, the doctrinal task or showing how it embodies the fullness of revelation.[12]

A case for the resurrection

Any 'apology' for the resurrection should cover at least three areas. (1) First, it needs to clarify and establish the *meaning* of the Easter claim: that the crucified Jesus was personally delivered from death and the grave to live a new, transformed, bodily existence, in which he manifested himself to certain key witnesses (in particular, to individuals like Peter, Paul, and Mary Magdalene, and to 'the eleven'). (2) Second, such an 'apology' should explore the grounds for this claim that originated with leading New Testament witnesses. What new experiences, received and interpreted in the light of prior factors (their Jewish faith, the Scriptures, and their memories of the earthly Jesus), led to these claims? Here fundamental theologians need to scrutinize the original disciples' new experiences (the appearances of the risen Christ and the discovery of his empty tomb, as well as the gift of the Holy Spirit and the success of their ministry that confirmed their Easter faith). (3) Third, in putting his case for the truth of Christ's resurrection, Augustine followed Origen, St Athanasius of Alexandria, and others in arguing from visible effects which his audience could see for themselves (almost the whole of contemporary Roman society believing in the resurrection) to the only adequate

---

[12] About these two tasks I have published many articles, chapters in works in collaboration, and six books: e.g. *Jesus Risen: An Historical, Fundamental, and Systematic Examination of Christ's Resurrection* (New York: Paulist Press, 1987); and *Easter Faith: Believing in the Risen Jesus* (London: Darton, Longman & Todd, 2002). See also S. T. Davis, D. Kendall, and G. O'Collins (eds.), *The Resurrection: An Interdisciplinary Symposium* (Oxford: Oxford University Press, 1997); C. S. Keener, *The Historical Jesus of the Gospels* (Grand Rapids, Mich.: Eerdmans, 2009), 330–48, 379–88, 579–90, 680–1.

cause for this historical phenomenon. Right down to our own day, writers have proposed various forms of this effect–cause argument— or, as we might also describe it, a 'novelties-to-explain' argument. Fundamental theology, when dealing 'apologetically' with the case for the resurrection, should also attend to such arguments.[13]

The meaning of the claim

As regards (1), in *Jesus Risen* I took issue with some of those who alter the essential Easter claim and re-imagine it as this: the relevant New Testament texts may appear to be speaking about Jesus and his personal resurrection, yet 'really' the early Christians were not talking about Jesus himself but merely referring to some change in their own existence, their new life in the Spirit. Their language about the 'resurrection' should be decoded that way, and in fact made no claim whatsoever about the post-mortem existence and destiny of Jesus.

Such 're-imagining' the New Testament claim about the resurrection of Jesus, whether it comes in a more sophisticated form or in more popular forms (e.g. 'Jesus only rose in the minds and hearts of his disciples'), may enjoy the attractive plausibility of many revisionist views but crumbles on several counts. Repeatedly it fails to face the richly complex way the claim about Jesus' personal resurrection is conveyed through a variety of idioms: pre-Pauline preaching and confessional formulas (e.g. Rom. 4: 25; 10: 9; 1 Cor. 15: 3–5); a new (Christian) attribute for God (e.g. Gal. 1: 1);[14] the Easter narratives of the four Gospels; a long, reflective argument developed by Paul (1 Cor. 15: 12–58); and missionary speeches in the Acts of the Apostles which centre on Jesus' resurrection (e.g. Acts 2: 31–2; 3: 15; 4: 10; 13: 30, 37). The New Testament complements these claims about Jesus' personal resurrection by also speaking of his being 'alive' (e.g. Luke 24: 5, 23; Rom. 14: 9), 'exalted' (e.g. Phil. 2: 9) to God's 'right hand'

---

[13] On much of this 'apology' for the resurrection, see N. T. Wright, *The Resurrection of the Son of God* (London: SPCK, 2003).

[14] God was now defined not simply as the Raiser of the dead (as in the Eighteen Benedictions) but specifically as the Raiser of the dead Jesus; see R. Martin-Achard, 'Resurrection (Old Testament)', *ABD* v. 680–4; G. W. E. Nickelsburg, 'Resurrection (Early Judaism and Christianity)', ibid. 684–91.

(e.g. Acts 2: 33; Rom. 8: 34; Col. 3: 1; Heb. 8: 1; 10: 12; 12: 2; 1 Pet. 3: 22), or of his 'entering' or being 'assumed into glory' (e.g. Luke 24: 26; 1 Tim. 3: 16).

Whether it uses resurrection or exaltation language, it is obvious that the New Testament's primary claim concerns Jesus' own life and glorious destiny after death. Take, for instance, the formula cited by Paul in 1 Corinthians 15: 3–5. Christ is the subject of all four verbs: he 'died', 'was buried', 'has been raised',[15] and 'appeared'. The last two verbs ('has been raised' and 'appeared') are just as informative as the first two ('died' and 'was buried'); the one who died and was buried is the one who has been raised and appeared. In the case of both pairs of verbs, the second verb supports what the first claims. We know that Christ died because he was buried; burial is a sure pointer to death. We know that Christ has been raised because he appeared bodily alive (in glory) to a number of individuals and groups; dead persons do not appear like that. To be sure, the dying, being buried, being raised from the dead, and appearing to key witnesses carried and continues to carry enormous implications for the lives of those who follow Jesus. But, in the first instance, the event of the resurrection (or so it was claimed) affected Jesus himself. Secondarily, it affected others—a point nicely summarized in another formula cited by Paul: 'he was raised for our justification' (Rom. 4: 25). But there would have been no 'justification' unless he had already been raised.[16]

A further major problem for those who re-imagine and reduce the New Testament claim about the resurrection of Jesus is that they 'know' better than the biblical authors what they meant when they wrote what they did. The reductionists are sure that the New Testament authors cannot possibly mean what they are apparently saying about Jesus' own resurrection but must mean something else (e.g. the rise of new consciousness in the disciples). But this 'method' of interpretation is self-destructive. In a 'tu quoque' spirit it can be applied to what the reductionists themselves write. They cannot

---

[15] The perfect tense of *egēgertai* indicates the abiding results of the event of the resurrection which took place on 'the third day'.

[16] On 1 Cor. 15: 3–5, see Fitzmyer, *First Corinthians*, 539–50; G. O'Collins, *Christology: A Biblical, Historical, and Systematic Study of Jesus* (2nd edn. Oxford: Oxford University Press, 2009), 84–6; Thiselton, *The First Epistle to the Corinthians*, 1186–205. On Rom. 4: 25, see J. A. Fitzmyer, *Romans* (New York: Doubleday, 1993), 389–90.

mean what they say about the primary significance of 'resurrection' language in the New Testament. Their 'method' gives readers the licence to set aside what is clearly intended and find whatever they want in the language of the reductionists.

Here an interesting difference emerges between modern reductionists and traditional sceptics like David Hume. This philosopher recognized the meaning of the New Testament assertions but in the name of a general principle (no evidence could ever establish a 'violation' of the laws of nature that are based on 'firm and unalterable experience') rejected the truth of the resurrection. Since he did not think that the dead could rise in any circumstances, then he could not accept the resurrection of Jesus as a fact (1 Cor. 15: 13), no matter how strong the supporting evidence might be.[17] The argument with Hume concerns his background theories: they do not make room for an omnipotent and all-loving God who for good reasons could override the laws of nature (which he himself created) and raise some dead person to new life. It was such presuppositions that led Hume, while recognizing the *meaning* of the Easter message, to reject its *truth*. The reductionists, however, tamper with the *meaning* of this message and then accept the *truth* of some proposition that they have fashioned for themselves.

The Easter appearances

The second area in which fundamental theologians need to reflect and enter 'apologetic' debate concerns the Easter appearances and the discovery of the empty tomb. As regards the first item, the New Testament records appearances to individuals and to groups (e.g. 1 Cor. 15: 5–8; Luke 24: 34; Acts 10: 40–1; 13: 3–4; John 20: 11–18). (a) These encounters depended upon the initiative of Jesus himself (he 'appeared' or 'let himself be seen'). (b) There is a reticent 'ordinariness' about the Easter appearances as reported very briefly by Paul and narrated by the Gospels. Unlike other communications from God, they do not take place during ecstasy (e.g. Acts 10: 9–10;

---

[17] D. Hume, 'Of Miracles', in *Enquiry Concerning Human Understanding*, ed. L. A. Selby-Bigge (3rd edn. Oxford: Clarendon Press, 1975), Section X, 109–31, at 114.

2 Cor. 12: 2–4), nor in a dream (e.g. Matt. 1: 20; 2: 12–13, 19–20, 22), nor—with the seeming exception of John 20: 19—by night (e.g. Acts 16: 9; 18: 18; 23: 11; 27: 23–4). The appearances take place under 'normal' circumstances and without the traits of apocalyptic glory which we find elsewhere (e.g. Mark 9: 2–8; Matt. 28: 3–4). The one exception comes when Acts describes Paul's experience on the Damascus road when he faces 'a light from heaven, brighter than the sun' (Acts 26: 13; see 9: 3; 22: 6, 9). But there is no mention of this phenomenon when Paul himself refers to his encounter with the risen Christ (1 Cor. 9: 1; 15: 8: Gal. 1: 12, 16). (c) The appearances were episodes of revelation (e.g. Gal. 1: 12, 16), which called the recipients to faith (e.g. John 20: 29) in (d) a special experience that (e) corresponded to their non-transferable mission and role in being, with Christ, founders of the Church, and which (f) had something visually perceptible about it.

As regards (d) and (e), those disciples who had been with him during his ministry recognized the risen Christ as being identical with the master whom they had known and followed: 'It is the Lord' (John 21: 7). No later group or individual believer, not even Paul, could duplicate this aspect of those post-resurrection meetings with Christ. Peter, Mary Magdalene, and other disciples are presented as bridge persons who linked the period of Jesus' ministry with the post-Easter situation. In that sense also, their experience of the risen Lord was unique and unrepeatable. Yet more should be added about the 'once only' experience and its aftermath, the foundation of the Church (which will be the theme of Chapter 11 below).

Peter, Paul, and the other apostolic witnesses who meet the risen Christ are understood to have the mission of testifying to that experience and founding the Church. These witnesses have seen for themselves and believed. In proclaiming the good news and gathering together those who have not seen and yet are ready to believe, these original witnesses do not depend upon the experience and testimony of others. Their function for Christianity differs from that of any subsequent believers, inasmuch as they alone have the once-and-for-all task of inaugurating the mission and founding the Church. Others will bear the responsibility for continuing that mission and keeping the Church in existence. But the coming into being of the Church and its mission cannot be duplicated. The way in which that unique function (e) implies some difference between the experience of the founding generation and all subsequent believers is expressed in John's classic distinction between those who have seen and believed, the persons covered by (d), and all those who are 'blessed' because they 'have not seen and yet believe' (John 20: 29).

As regards point (f), in referring to the encounters with the risen Christ, the New Testament privileges the language of sight. He 'appeared' to some people (e.g. 1 Cor. 15: 5–8; Luke 24: 34) and they 'saw' him (e.g. 1 Cor. 9: 1; Matt. 28: 17; John 20: 18, 20). Occasionally in the New Testament, the Greek 'see' (*horaō*) can be used of intellectual perception, just as blindness is a metaphor for incomprehension. Thus 'for those outside everything is in parables, so that they may indeed see but not perceive, and may indeed hear but not understand' (Mark 4: 11–12). But, normally, 'seeing' and 'appearing' include some visible component (e.g. Mark 9: 4; Luke 5: 12; John 1: 29; Acts 2: 3). Passages like Mark 4: 11–12 deal with the intellectual perception of some truth or the failure to comprehend some truth. One can 'see' truth in a purely interior, non-corporeal way. But with the Easter encounters we deal with a claim about a bodily resurrected person appearing to other persons who exist within the space-time world and see him. In that case it is difficult to imagine how a purely spiritual, interior seeing could be reconciled with the New Testament terminology of the appearances. This is not to suggest that when the risen Jesus appeared he was an exterior object to be perceived and recognized by anyone who happened to be present, irrespective of their personal dispositions. Further, one must admit that Paul and the evangelists show little interest in describing and explaining in detail the nature of the appearances. In any case their (partly) unique and unrepeatable nature rule out the possibility of fully conceptualizing these experiences and expressing them according to the canons of ordinary, fact-stating discourse. Here I wish simply to point out that some visual component seems implied by the New Testament language for the encounters with the risen Jesus. Unlike the Old Testament prophets, who characteristically heard the word of the Lord (see Chapter 4 above), the apostolic witnesses typically saw the risen Lord rather than heard his word.

Before leaving this summary account of the Easter appearances, let me alert readers to a widespread conviction that it is possible to account 'scientifically' for any occurrences, no matter how extraordinary they seem, by finding some close analogies. There can be nothing genuinely new under the sun; allegedly unique events can always be explained by relating them to our existing body of knowledge. Thus the appearances of the risen Christ to Mary Magdalene, Peter, Paul, the eleven, and the other witnesses can be subsumed under general 'laws' about hallucinations, mystical experiences, near death experiences, bereavement experiences, and so forth. This is to blunt anything special, let alone once-and-for-all, about the appearances and the event they allegedly revealed, Christ's resurrection from the dead.

Those who value analogies look for significant likenesses between events, objects, and persons. They may detect many similarities or perhaps only a few; the similarities they observe may be close or only remote. On the scale of 'like–unlike', the analogy between events or objects may come anywhere between two extremes. A merely remote analogy will hardly help our understanding and interpretation. Yet, even in the case of close analogies, we may not use the existence of some close similarities to conclude that the two events or objects must therefore be similar in other respects, let alone in all other respects.

Given the way some misuse the principle of analogy, it is important to remark that analogies should not encourage a one-sided orientation toward typical events at the expense of unusual or even unique claims. By dealing with what is similar but not identical, analogy allows for what is dissimilar or even different, even strikingly different, and does not unilaterally suppress the new. Analogy, by looking for some measure of likeness but not straight identity, makes plenty of room for novelty, and allows us to appreciate what is new by relating it to the old and familiar. Hence appeal to analogies does not justify denying or simply excluding in principle the possibility of the dramatically unfamiliar or even of the genuinely new.[18]

What never fails to surprise me is that those who propose some analogy to the Easter appearances do not stop and list the points of similarity *and* dissimilarity between the alleged analogy and the appearances. If they were to do that, they might become aware of striking differences that blunt the force of the analogy they propose. Take, for instance, the case of bereavement experiences that have been regularly studied since the pioneering work about 227 widows and 66

---

[18] See C. A. J. Coady, 'Astonishing Reports', in *Testimony: A Philosophical Study* (Oxford: Clarendon Press, 1992), 179–98.

widowers done by Dewi Rees forty years ago.[19] Some comparison can be drawn between the experiences of Rees's bereaved persons and those of the first disciples after the death of Jesus. Both cases feature deep grief, guilt about circumstances that preceded the death, contact with the beloved dead, and a lasting sense of presence. Beyond that, detailed comparison turns up serious differences. To begin with, the disciples of Jesus remembered him as having made extraordinary claims to personal authority (see Chapter 5 above) and then as having died an utterly shameful death in a place for public executions. Rees reports no examples of anything like that among his 293 widows and widowers. Apropos of the place of their spouses' death, 270 out of the 293 either died at home (161 cases) or in hospital (109 cases). The cases examined by Rees and later by others (e.g. Colin Murray Parkes in a series of studies) do not parallel what the New Testament reports about the terrible death of Jesus and the situation of his disciples.

Further differences show that the suggested analogy fails to be close and illuminating. First, the widows and widowers studied by Rees were all *individuals*. He did not report any cases of two or more people (e.g. a widow and her daughter) simultaneously experiencing their deceased husband/father. This moves the bereavement analogy away from the situation of the disciples of Jesus. In their case, groups such as the eleven and more than 500 followers of Jesus—and not just individuals—saw the risen One. Second, about 40 per cent of the cases studied by Rees reported that they continued to experience their dead spouses for *many years*. Here they differed from the witnesses to the risen Christ, who testify to having seen him only once or at most only several times.[20] Apart from Paul, whose Damascus road encounter with Christ took place several years later, the Easter witnesses met the risen Jesus only over a short period (of days or possibly weeks) and not over many years.

Third, only 27 per cent of the widows and widowers studied by Rees had ever mentioned their bereavement experiences to anybody

---

[19] For the work of Rees (and others) and those who have pressed the analogy between bereavement experiences and the Easter appearances, see O'Collins, *Christology*, 93–100; id., *Easter Faith*, 5–24.

[20] In John's Easter narrative, the seven disciples to whom Jesus appeared in Galilee (21: 1–23) include some who were present at two earlier appearances (John 20: 19–29) and one (Thomas) to whom the Lord had appeared once before (20: 26–9).

else (not even to close friends and relatives) before they were asked to take part in Rees's enquiry. This fact also undermines the usefulness of the bereavement analogy. Those to whom the risen Christ appeared quickly passed on the good news to others. They did not keep their experience to themselves. Fourth, even if they looked at life differently, those whose bereavement experiences were reported by Rees did not dramatically change their lifestyle. They did not publicly proclaim their experience. Such disciples as Peter and Paul told the world of their Easter experience, becoming missionary witnesses to the crucified and risen Lord and creating a new religious community. Fifth, this testimony to Christ also included claims about his empty tomb—something not found in the modern literature about bereavement.

Thus, serious differences exist between the case of the bereaved (studied by Dewi Rees, Colin Murray Parkes, and others) and that of the Easter witnesses to Jesus risen from the dead. We may not allege anything like a close analogy. Appeal to bereavement experiences, like other suggested analogies, fails to prove an illuminating comparison that would explain (or explain away) the Easter experiences which pointed to the resurrection of Jesus.

The discovery of the empty tomb

A second 'apologetic' task for fundamental theologians listed above concerns the case for the empty tomb of Jesus. The discovery of his empty tomb served as a secondary sign, which was ambiguous in itself but which, when taken with the appearances, served to confirm the reality of the resurrection. The Gospel stories of one or more woman finding Jesus' tomb to be mysteriously open and empty contain a reliable historical core. The arguments I have over the years mounted to support that conclusion convince me as much as ever.[21]

---

[21] See in chronological order, G. O'Collins, *The Easter Jesus* (new edn. London: Darton, Longman & Todd, 1980), 38–45; id., *Jesus Risen*, 121–6; id., 'The Resurrection: The State of the Questions', in Davis, Kendall, and O'Collins (eds.), *The Resurrection*, 13–17; id., 'The Resurrection Revisited', *Gregorianum*, 79 (1998), 171–2; id., *Easter Faith*, 45–9, 66–71.

Two traditions report the empty tomb story: the Markan tradition (paralleled to some extent by Matthew and Luke) and the somewhat different traditions which entered John's Gospel. Early polemic against the message of the resurrection supposed that the tomb was known to be empty. Naturally the opponents of the Christian movement explained away the missing body as a plain case of theft (Matt. 28: 11–15). What was in dispute was not whether the tomb was empty but why it was empty. We have no early evidence that anyone, either Christian or non-Christian, ever alleged that Jesus' tomb still contained his remains.

Furthermore, the place of women in the empty tomb stories speaks for their historical reliability. Women were central: Mary Magdalene (John 20: 1–2) and other women with her (Mark 16: 1–8) found to their astonishment Jesus' tomb to be open and empty on the first Easter Sunday. If these stories had simply been legends created by early Christians, they would have attributed the discovery of the empty tomb to male disciples, given that in first-century Palestine women were, for all intents and purposes, disqualified as valid witnesses. Legend-makers do not normally invent positively unhelpful material.

One could add fresh items and refinements to the case for the empty tomb. Paul, for instance, quotes a kerygmatic tradition about Christ's burial and resurrection (1 Cor. 15: 4) and goes on to repeat six times the same verb (in precisely the same perfect, passive form, *egēgertai*), twice speaking of Christ being raised 'from the dead' (1 Cor. 15: 12–20). Several times elsewhere the apostle uses the same verb (*egeirō*) and predicate ('from the dead') in what many scholars hold to be formulaic traditions that he has taken over (Rom. 10: 9; Gal. 1: 1; 1 Thess. 1: 10). That, for Paul and for the tradition, the addition 'from the dead' points to a resurrection from the grave is suggested by Paul's citing the kerygmatic announcement of Christ's burial (1 Cor. 15: 4). The resurrection 'from the dead' entails a rising from the tomb.

Furthermore, Matthew, Luke, and John employ the same verb (*egeirō*) and predicate ('from the dead') with reference to Jesus' own resurrection (Matt. 27: 64; 28: 7; Acts 3: 15; 13: 30; John 2: 22) and to the case of Lazarus (John 12: 1, 9, 17). In both cases, the three evangelists join Paul in pointing to a rising from the grave and an empty tomb, just as John 20: 9 and Acts 10: 41 do when they use *anistēmi ek nekrōn* (rise from the dead).

In any case, as many have remarked, for a Pharisaic Jew like Paul a resurrection which did not involve an empty tomb would have been inconceivable. No one expected a resurrection in which bodies that had been buried were not involved. No empty tomb meant no resurrection. Wolfhart Pannenberg rightly remarks: 'for Paul the empty tomb was a self-evident implication of what was said about the resurrection of Jesus.'[22]

Novelties to explain

In putting the case for the resurrection of Jesus, many apologists centuries ago and some fundamental theologians in modern times have argued from visible effects to the only adequate cause, the resurrection. Augustine, for instance, did this in his *City of God*: given the fact that the apostolic witnesses were 'of no social standing, the dregs of society, very few in number and unlearned', the success of their message about the resurrection cannot be explained through mere human resources. God must have been working in these people and attesting the truth of their message. Unless one accepts the resurrection, one cannot account for the 'incredible' historical truth that 'a handful of men, untrained in the liberal arts and thoroughly uneducated in philosophy, without any knowledge of literature, with no training in dialectics, without any high-sounding rhetoric, were sent by Christ as fishermen into the sea of this world with nets of faith only—and still more wonderful because rarer—[these fishermen] caught many fish of every kind, even in fact some philosophers'. Augustine called it an extraordinary 'miracle' that 'the whole world' believed the Easter message proclaimed by a small band of poor, unlearned men. This miracle cannot be explained unless Jesus truly rose from the dead (22. 5).

Where Augustine argued that the meagre resources of the disciples cannot account for the success of their mission, other apologists focus more on Jesus himself. Thus Hans Küng compares Jesus with three others who founded religious movements: the Siddhartha

---

[22] W. Pannenberg, *Systematic Theology*, trans. G. W. Bromiley, ii (Edinburgh: T. & T. Clark, 1994), 359.

Gautama, Confucius, and Muhammad. In the case of all three founders, time was on their side. Buddhism originated with Gautama, who spent most of his long life teaching the way of enlightenment. The Chinese sage Confucius also passed many years spreading his wisdom and attracting disciples, until he died and was buried with great pomp outside Kufow. A wealthy wife and then military victories helped Muhammad to propagate his teaching. As the recognized prophet of Arabia, he died in Medina and was buried there. In these three instances we can point to publicly verifiable causes that furthered the spread, respectively, of Buddhism, Confucianism, and Islam: the long careers of the founders, financial resources, and success in battle. In the case of Christianity the founder had none of these advantages: his public career was extremely short (three or four years at the most); he lacked military and financial support. Add too the way Jesus' life ended in humiliating and 'shameful death' on a cross. After all this, the subsequent 'almost explosive propagation' of his 'message and community' remains a 'historical enigma', unless we admit a proportionate cause, his resurrection from the dead.[23]

Nowadays an Augustine-style argument from publicly observable effects to the only adequate cause (Christ's resurrection) takes at times the form of an appeal to novelties found at the very origin of Christianity. First, some like myself have constructed an argument that begins by asking: what options were available for the first disciples when Christ was crucified as a messianic pretender and even a blasphemer? Could they have modified their messianic belief in him (Mark 8: 29; 11: 1–10) and proposed him to be another martyred prophet like John the Baptist and others before him? Hardly, it seems to me. To be crucified was not only to suffer an utterly cruel and humiliating form of execution but also to die under a religious curse (Gal. 3: 13)[24] and 'outside the camp' of God's covenanted people (Heb. 13: 12–13). In other words, crucifixion was seen as the death of a criminal and godless person who perished away from God's presence in the place and company of irreligious men. To honour anyone put to death in such a way was an awful and profound offence (1 Cor. 1: 23). Given that the crucifixion was such a disgrace, could Jesus' disciples have proclaimed him *even* as a *martyred prophet*?

---

[23] H. Küng, *On Being a Christian*, trans. E. Quinn (London: Collins, 1977), 345.
[24] On Gal. 3: 13, see Martyn, *Galatians*, 316–21.

In fact, they began preaching the crucified Jesus as the divinely endorsed Messiah risen from the dead to bring salvation for all. The notion of a Messiah who failed, suffered, was crucified, and then rose from the grave was simply foreign to pre-Christian Judaism. Since their previous religious beliefs could not have led Jesus' disciples to make such startlingly new claims about him, what triggered this religious novelty? Where did it come from, if not from the resurrection of Jesus himself?

Second, some scholars when elaborating the effect–cause argument have stressed the centrality of the theme of resurrection in early Christian preaching. Forty years ago C. F. Evans showed how 'the central place of the resurrection faith in the New Testament' could not be expected or explained 'either from contemporary Judaism or from the preaching' of Jesus.[25] A theme which at best had been on the religious periphery moved to centre stage. Neither the Jewish background nor the teaching of Jesus himself sufficiently accounts for the given effect: the central importance which the New Testament attributes to the resurrection. Unless Jesus had been raised from the dead, we have no cause adequate to explain the centrality of the resurrection in the faith, preaching, and theology of the first Christians.

In a lecture delivered in 2002, N. T. Wright developed a similar argument. An examination of first-century Judaism and the surrounding world shows a variety of beliefs about the existence (or absence) of life after death. But we find nothing which closely resembles what the first Christians began proclaiming about Jesus and the nature of his resurrection. Since that preaching could hardly have come from prior beliefs, the historian must look for another explanation: the event of Jesus' resurrection itself.[26]

Wolfhart Pannenberg has mounted a similar effect–cause argument on the basis of an observable shift in religious expectations. In late Judaism some cherished a hope that the resurrection of *all the dead* and a general judgement would terminate human history. Then the followers of Jesus began announcing that this one individual had already been raised to a glorious existence that anticipated the end of all history. What caused such a new element in religious history—the

---

[25] C. F. Evans, *Resurrection and the New Testament* (London: SCM Press, 1970), 132.
[26] N. T. Wright, 'Jesus' Resurrection and Christian Origins', *Gregorianum*, 83 (2002), 615–35.

shift from an expectation of general resurrection at the end of history to the proclamation of something no one expected, the glorious, final resurrection of one individual that has already initiated the end? What prompted this radical change in expectations held by a significant group of first-century Jews about the fulfilment of human life through resurrection? Historians of Christianity have documented the effect, a remarkable change in expectations. A plausible cause is available: the actual resurrection of Jesus from the dead.[27]

Where Evans, Wright, Pannenberg, and others have fashioned effect–cause arguments out of demonstrable changes in the beliefs of Jesus' first disciples after his death and burial, Richard Swinburne has named the new celebration of Sunday as the effect to be accounted for.[28] Why did these Jewish disciples no longer give priority to Saturday and turn 'the first day of the week' into *the* day for meeting and worshipping together? What made them hold this day so special that they not only changed their day but also their manner of worship (1 Cor. 11: 23–6)? An obvious reason is close at hand: Sunday was the day when Jesus' tomb was discovered to be open and empty, and the day when they first encountered the risen Lord.

Without being a strict proof, this argument also enjoys a certain plausibility. Those who reject it need to produce an alternate explanation as to why the disciples of Jesus changed their special day of worship from the Jewish Sabbath to the Christian Sunday.

The resurrection as revealing: Jesus, God, human beings and their world

After completing the 'apologetic' task of making a reasonable case for accepting the resurrection of Jesus, fundamental theologians should press on and illustrate how that resurrection embodied the fullness of the divine self-revelation. What did and does the resurrection of the crucified Jesus reveal about him, God, human beings, and their world?

---

[27] W. Pannenberg, *Jesus: God and Man*, trans. L. L. Wilkins and D. A. Priebe (London: SCM Press, 1968), 96.

[28] R. Swinburne, 'Evidence for the Resurrection', in Davis, Kendall , and O'Collins (eds.), *The Resurrection*, 191–212, at 207–12.

1. We begin with Jesus. His rising from the dead vindicated his certainty in the powerful future of God's kingdom (Mark 14: 25). The presence of the kingdom, manifested in Jesus' preaching and miracles, had suffered an apparent defeat through his condemnation and crucifixion. Now its power was reasserted and revealed in a much more striking way through the resurrection and gift of the Holy Spirit. This denouement fully justified the personal authority with which Jesus had spoken of the kingdom and which he had claimed over the Sabbath, the Temple, the law, forgiveness of sins, final judgement, and human salvation. The resurrection showed that, so far from being cursed by the God whom he called 'Abba' (see Gal. 3: 13), Jesus had been divinely vindicated in himself, in his teaching, and in that utter fidelity to his vocation for which he sacrificed everything, even life itself. The resurrection disclosed that his self-sacrifice had been accepted by God and that, so far from being a messianic pretender as the title on the cross asserted, he was/is the divinely appointed Messiah. In short, the resurrection fully and finally revealed the meaning and truth of Jesus' life, person, work, and death. It set the divine seal on Jesus and his ministry.

To say all this is not to lapse back into a discredited apologetic about the resurrection being the miracle proving Christ's claim to divinity. First, instead of anachronistic talk about 'proof', I wish to associate myself with the themes of vindication (Acts 2: 36; 3: 14–15; 4: 10) and revelation (Gal. 1: 12, 16)[29] which Luke and Paul, respectively, develop in their interpretation of the resurrection. Second, far from being reduced to a great miracle, even 'the greatest of miracles', the resurrection is presented as something qualitatively different and superior—the beginning of the end of all things (e.g. Rom. 8: 29; 1 Cor. 15: 20). Calling the resurrection 'the Paschal Mystery' at the start of this chapter aimed at studiously avoiding miracle language. Third, some past apologetics misrepresented the (largely implicit) claims made by Jesus during his ministry, taking them in individual isolation as if he were simply and boldly asserting 'I am God'. The modern respect for his 'Abba-consciousness' recognizes that Jesus' claims were claims-in-relation. By much of what he said and did (see the last chapter) he made claims to stand in a unique relationship to the God

---

[29] On Gal. 1: 16, see Martyn, *Galatians*, 157–9.

whom he called 'Abba' and with whom he shared authority over the Sabbath, the Temple, the law, forgiveness of sins, the final judgement, and human salvation. Jesus' assertion of divinity is distorted if it is plucked out of its historical context and not respected as a claim-in-relationship.

Besides its revelatory importance for Jesus' person and historical activity, his resurrection also manifested the transformed being that the glorified humanity of Jesus now enjoyed (and enjoys). His human life, or total embodied history, rose with him and was transfigured into a final mode of existence.[30] This revelation of Jesus' new and definitive way of existing radically changed the value of what was remembered and recounted from his earthly history. The early traditions and then the Gospels offered much more than a mere record from the past. They challenged their readers and hearers with words and deeds, the value and truth of which were now fully disclosed. These were/are the words and deeds of the risen Son of God, their divine Lord.

We saw above how the New Testament weaves the wider language of exaltation into its account of Jesus' new life. Even more than the language of resurrection, 'exaltation' bespeaks the post-death revelation of Jesus' status and dignity. A royal psalm which came up for debate during Jesus' ministry (Mark 12: 35–7 parr.) opens as follows: 'The LORD says to my Lord: "Sit at my right hand, until I make your enemies my footstool"' (Ps. 110: 1). Finding here an Old Testament prophecy of Jesus' exaltation, the first Christians also saw fulfilled in the resurrection a promise that Jesus apparently made at his trial before the Sanhedrin: 'You will see the Son of Man seated at the right hand of the Power and coming with the clouds of heaven' (Mark 14: 62).[31] We noted above how frequently the New Testament draws on Psalm 110 for the image of the exalted Jesus being seated not near the divine throne but at the very right hand of God.

Nothing illustrates more clearly than one hymn how the first Christians used the language of exaltation to express the revelation of Jesus' divine status that calls for the worship of the whole world.

---

[30] See G. O'Collins, *Jesus Risen*, 182–7; id., *Jesus our Redeemer: A Christian Approach to Salvation* (Oxford: Oxford University Press, 2007), 250–62.
[31] See R. E. Brown, *The Death of the Messiah: From Gethsemane to the Grave*, i (New York: Doubleday, 1994), 494–500; Marcus, *Mark 8–16*, 1005–8, 1015–17.

Publicly exalted to the glory which he already possessed in his pre-existent divine state of 'equality with God' and into which, in his humanity, he entered for the first time, Jesus was now worshipped and confessed as divine Lord (Phil. 2: 6–11).[32] His resurrection disclosed him as the exalted Lord who merited worship—a point clearly made also by the evangelists in their Easter stories.

In Matthew's final chapter, first the female and then the male disciples worship Jesus (Matt. 28: 9, 17). Luke (Luke 24: 3, 34) and John (John 20–1, passim) recognize Jesus' divine sovereignty manifested in his new life. The risen Jesus' promise to be with the disciples right to the end of time (Matt. 28: 20) clearly hints at the revelation of his status as 'God-with-us' (Matt. 1: 23). Through the ascension motif, Luke (Luke 24: 52; Acts 1: 9–11) and John (John 20: 17), among other things, associate the risen Jesus with the 'place' now known to be his—heavenly glory.

Lastly, for the first Christians Jesus' resurrection from the dead illuminated 'the fullness of God' that was in him (Col. 1: 19). The hymn cited in Colossians confesses his divinity immediately after it speaks of him as being 'the first born from the dead' and immediately before it celebrates his reconciling death on the cross. The very same hymn not only acknowledges Christ's divinity manifested in the new creation, established by his resurrection from the dead, but also celebrates his role in the original creation of the world and its conservation (Col. 1: 16–17).[33] The Easter revelation of Christ's divine status quickly led his followers to name him as agent of creation, sharing in the essential property of God as creator of the universe (1 Cor. 8: 6; Heb. 1: 2–3; and eventually John 1: 3).

2. With the crucifixion and resurrection, Christians grew also into a fresh understanding of God. The first Good Friday and Easter Sunday revealed God in (a) suffering, (b) new life, and (c) unconditional divine love. This is not to say that pre-Christian Judaism failed to associate these themes with God. Even a rapid reading of the Psalms, Isaiah, Jeremiah, and Hosea would give the lie to that. But, in a startlingly fresh way, through these themes, Jesus' destiny focused and fixed the specifically Christian doctrine of God.

---

[32] See L. W. Hurtado, *Lord Jesus Christ: Devotion to Jesus in Earliest Christianity* (Grand Rapids, Mich.: Eerdmans, 2003), 108–18.

[33] On this hymn see M. Barth and H. Blanke, *Colossians* (New York: Doubleday, 1994), 193–251, esp. 213–24.

First, suffering: in developing the opening ideas of 1 Corinthians, Paul nine times brings God together with the 'word of the cross' (1 Cor. 1: 18–25). Left to their own devices, the horrendous disgrace of the crucifixion was the last place where Jews or others might expect to find God revealed, as we remarked above. Paul does not exaggerate when he calls it a scandal and a folly to recognize in the atrocious and shameful death of Jesus the high point of divine revelation and salvation (1 Cor. 1: 18, 23–5). Those who would not rethink the strict monotheism of first-century Judaism found claims about Jesus' divine sonship simply unacceptable. What Christians acknowledged in the crucifixion made things even worse. It was weirdly offensive to see the face of a crucified man as the human face of God.

Second, the language Paul took over from early Christians shows that the resurrection of Jesus to *new life* essentially shaped their vision of God (e.g. Rom. 8: 11; 1 Cor. 6: 14; 2 Cor. 4: 14; Gal. 1: 1). God was the Resurrector, the God who had raised Jesus to new life and who would raise the other dead to new life. The Old Testament consistently illustrates how the Israelites named 'life' as a central attribute of God.[34] The resurrection of Jesus led his followers to enlarge this notion and worship God as the One who not only gives life but even raises the dead to new life. Paul drew the conclusion that those who failed to acknowledge God as the Resurrector of the dead were essentially 'misrepresenting' the deity (1 Cor. 15: 15).

Third, the Old Testament has much to say about the initiatives of the divine love.[35] Yet these initiatives were enacted through others, above all through such prophetic emissaries of God as Jeremiah, Ezekiel, and Hosea. In the story of Jesus' crucifixion and resurrection, Christians perceived the initiative of self-giving divine love which led God to be personally involved in our sinful history (Rom. 8: 3)—even to the point of an appalling death on the cross: 'God shows his love for us in that while we were yet sinners Christ died for us' (Rom. 5: 8). This prior and unconditional divine love toward human kind caused God to send his Son (Gal. 4: 4–6),[36] whose free and obedient acceptance of a violent death at the hands of a wicked world revealed, as nothing else could, God's loving self-giving on our behalf (Rom. 8: 31–2; see 2 Cor. 5: 18–19; 1

---

[34] See G. von Rad, G. Bertram, and R. Bultmann, 'Zaō, zōē', TDNT ii. 843–61.
[35] See K. D. Sakenfeld, 'Love (Old Testament)', ABD iv. 375–81.
[36] On Gal. 4: 4–6, see Martyn, *Galatians*, 384–92.

John 4: 10). This divine self-giving, manifested supremely in the events of the first Good Friday and Easter Sunday and communicated through the Holy Spirit (Rom. 5: 5), eventually drew forth the lapidary statement 'God is love' (1 John 4: 8, 16).

Such then in summary is what it means to claim that the resurrection of the crucified Jesus disclosed God in a fresh and startling way—through the focus of suffering, new life, and unconditional love. With this triple focus of the Easter revelation, we come to its 'trinitarian' face.[37]

3. Even before John set down the story of Jesus' passion, death, and resurrection in terms of the Father, the Son, and the Holy Spirit (see Chapter 4 above), Luke and Matthew, in their different ways, had already drawn attention to the trinitarian face of the crucifixion and resurrection. Matthew chose to insert into the setting of the disciples' final encounter with the risen Jesus the later formula of baptism 'in the name of the Father and of the Son and of the Holy Spirit' (Matt. 28: 19). The evangelist found it appropriate to interpret the Easter revelation in a trinitarian key. According to Luke, the risen Christ communicated to his disciples 'the promise of the Father' that they would be 'clothed with power from on high' (Luke 24: 49), a promise which was realized by the coming of the Holy Spirit at Pentecost (Acts 2: 1–4). Luke interpreted this coming in a trinitarian fashion as Christ being 'exalted at the right hand of God', receiving 'from the Father the promise of the Holy Spirit', and 'pouring out' on believers the visible and audible effects of the Spirit (Acts 2: 33).

Years before any of the evangelists wrote, Paul ended a letter to the Corinthians with a solemn farewell about 'the grace of the Lord Jesus Christ', 'the love of God' the Father, and 'the fellowship of the Holy Spirit' (2 Cor. 13: 13).[38] In an earlier letter to the same community, a letter that began with Christ's crucifixion (1 Cor. 1: 18–25) and reached its climax with his resurrection (15: 1–28), Paul wrote of the Spirit, the Lord (Jesus Christ), and God (the Father) (1 Cor. 12: 4–6).[39] The apostle had most to say about his own revelatory encounter with the

---

[37] See G. O'Collins, *The Tripersonal God* (Mahwah, NJ: Paulist Press, 1999), 50–82.
[38] On 2 Cor. 13: 13, see M. J. Harris, *The Second Epistle to the Corinthians* (Grand Rapids, Mich.: Eerdmans, 2005), 937–42.
[39] On 1 Cor. 1: 18–25, see Fitzmyer, *First Corinthians*, 151–61; on 1 Cor. 12: 4–6, see ibid. 462–5.

risen Jesus and its missionary consequences when writing to the Galatians. That letter began with God the Father (1: 1) and his Son (1: 16; 2: 20), and then talked about the Holy Spirit (3: 2–5, 14; 4: 6, 29; 5: 5, 16–25; 6: 1, 8), while continuing to speak of the Father and the Son (e.g. 4: 4–6). In other words, Paul gave a strong trinitarian tone to a letter which drew conclusions from the crucifixion and resurrection of Jesus.

To be sure, applying 'trinitarian' to the revelation communicated through the resurrection of the crucified Jesus could be misleadingly anachronistic. It was to be centuries before the divinity of Christ (who is 'of one being' with the Father) was officially clarified at the First Council of Nicaea (325) and the divinity of the Holy Spirit was clarified at the First Council of Constantinople (381). Nevertheless, John, Matthew, Luke, Paul, and the pre-Pauline tradition had already discerned in the events of Christ's dying and rising some kind of pattern that disclosed the Father, Son, and Holy Spirit. The experience of God enjoyed by the first Christians took a triune shape.

4. The revelatory impact of his resurrection from the dead threw new light on Jesus and God. Yet Easter also disclosed that God had already initiated the resurrection of human beings and their world (Rom. 8: 29; 1 Cor. 15: 20, 23; Col. 1: 18). In raising and transforming Jesus in his human condition, God was seen to have begun the work of finally transforming the rest of creation and the rest of history. In the time between Easter and the end of the world, Jesus' dying and rising had brought into existence the community of the Church (Eph. 5: 25–7). Chapter 11 below will take up the fundamental question of the creation of the Church.

Three chapters have now displayed the essential features of divine self-revelation. We move forward now to human faith, the precise coordinate of revelation. What is faith like? What brings it about and what might serve to show its reasonableness?

7

The Faith that
Responds to Revelation

The Epistle to Diognetus, a letter written in the second or third century by an unknown Christian to an unknown recipient, declares: 'No living human being has seen God or known him. He himself has provided the *revelation* of himself. But he has revealed himself only in *faith*, by which alone we are permitted to see God' (8. 5; italics mine).[1] This anonymous letter catches the reciprocity between the divine self-communication and human faith.[2] God's revelation does not, as it were, hang in the air; it reaches its goal when human faith recognizes and accepts the divine self-communication in Christ. The experience of God's revelation in Jesus Christ called forth the faith of the founding fathers and mothers of the Church, and continues to call forth faith in those Christians who belong to the stage of dependent revelation.

How might we provisionally describe the response of faith?[3] Since revelation offers a vision of Someone (upper case) to whom we should

---

[1] 'Diognetus, the Epistle to', *Oxford Dictionary*, 487.

[2] Paul illustrates this reciprocity: 'for in it [the gospel] the righteousness of God is *revealed* through *faith*, for *faith*' (Rom. 1: 17); see also Rom. 16: 25–6.

[3] On faith, see A. Dulles, *The Assurance of Things Hoped for: A Theology of Christian Faith* (New York: Oxford University Press, 1994); 'Faith', *Oxford Dictionary*, 598–9; G. Lanczkowski et al., 'Glaube', *TRE* xiii. 275–365; I. von Loewenclau et al., 'Faith', in E. Fahlbusch et al. (eds.), *The Encyclopedia of Christianity*, ii (Grand Rapids, Mich.: Eerdmans, 2001), 261–74; K. Rahner, *Foundations of Christian Faith: An Introduction to the Idea of Christianity*, trans. W. V. Dych (New York: Seabury Press, 1978).

give our total allegiance and of whom we can also give some account, we can speak of faith as involving both 'believing in' and 'believing that'. A trusting and obedient adherence to Jesus Christ (*fides qua creditur*) allows believers to express something of who he is and what he has revealed, giving their assent to truths about God that have now been disclosed (*fides quae creditur*).[4] This version of faith obviously corresponds to the two models of revelation explained in Chapter 4: revelation primarily as the experience of a personal relationship with God through Jesus Christ which initiates a confident commitment of one's life to Christ, and revelation secondarily as propositions about God that are now disclosed and known to be true, or the confession of faith. This commitment and confession (both made possible by God) support a confidence that one's future here and hereafter is safe in the hands of God.

This 'believing in' and 'believing that' also involve accepting the foundational witness to the experience of God coming from the Old Testament and the New Testament. When experiencing in faith who God is and what God is like, believers today depend on the prophetic and apostolic witness. In particular, the first Christians and their leaders, the original recipients and bearers of the normative revelation in Christ, will play for all time an indispensable role in understanding and interpreting Jesus, his teaching, and all the events in which he was involved. Faith in the Founder (upper case) entails trusting the founders (in lower case), whom Jesus called and chose. It is also through them that the experience of his self-revelation is mediated now.

With such preliminary positions in place, fundamental theologians need to discuss what some put under the rubric of 'the epistemology of religious belief'. What justifies the response of faith when it experiences the divine self-revelation? Is faith a 'leap in the dark' that disdains any reasons drawn from history, philosophy, personal experience, or any other sources?[5] Or is it a conclusion based on overwhelmingly clear

---

[4] Paul mentions *both* 'the obedience of faith' (= the obedience which is faith, the faith by which (*fides qua*) we obey the Lord) (Rom. 16: 26) *and* the 'believing that' or *fides quae*: 'if you *confess* with your lips *that* Jesus is Lord and *believe* in your heart *that* God raised him from the dead, you will be saved' (Rom. 10: 9).

[5] Franz Werfel (1890–1945) spoke for this position when introducing his work on the shrine of Lourdes, *The Song of Bernadette*: 'For those who believe no explanation is necessary. For those who do not believe no explanation is possible.'

evidence that any intelligent, properly informed, and fair-minded person would accept? Or should we embrace some mediating position, which recognizes the role of evidence but goes beyond the evidence in a way that involves 'objective' factors (above all, the witness of Christian believers and the 'inner testimony' of the Holy Spirit) and subjective factors (e.g. the desires, joys, fears, and anxieties that make up the inner life of human beings)?

Three positions

Faith without reason

We can focus the first position in terms of the resurrection of Jesus which some accept in faith and others deny. In his *Beyond Resurrection* A. J. M. Wedderburn remains firmly agnostic about the post-resurrection appearances of Jesus, the historicity of the empty tomb, the new life of the risen Jesus, and any final resurrection for his followers.[6] He concludes with a picture of Jesus having offered his life to God and invites us to do the same; we should embrace a vulnerable, this-worldly faith and life modelled on the example of Jesus.[7] Like some others, Wedderburn appears to share a presupposition about faith and its alleged lack of 'support' which helps to decide his agnostic position on the resurrection. He praises 'the vulnerability of a faith that does not find the protection of firm proofs of its validity in the resurrection stories'.[8] It seems that any legitimizing of faith through making a case for God's victory over death would tamper with the purity of an unprotected faith. The fewer the reasons, the more genuine the faith?

Forty years ago such theological convictions about faith also seemed to control the way in which Willi Marxsen argued biblically and historically about the resurrection. Faith is simply a venture, a commitment made in answer to a call. Any alleged legitimizing of Jesus' claims by reaching reasoned conclusions about the event of the resurrection would be incompatible with this venture. It is not just

[6] London: SCM Press, 1999.
[7] Ibid. 317–18.
[8] Ibid. 220.

that faith goes beyond the evidence; it excludes the evidence. Rational appeals would distort faith. To believe after scrutinizing and accepting the testimony of those witnesses who met Jesus gloriously alive after his death would render impossible a trusting commitment to Jesus' challenge.[9]

Wedderburn and Marxsen converge in championing a vulnerable, unsupported faith, which partly predetermines their views of the resurrection. Marxsen, however, elaborates more clearly a closely connected and relevant presupposition: about the historian and the believer. From the outset, Marxsen resolutely holds apart matters of information and the call to faith. The historian deals with matters of information and alone has the task of deciding whether some alleged past event really happened. According to Marxsen, 'the historian's answer to the question of whether Jesus rose from the dead must be: "I do not know; I am no longer able to discover".' Even if historians were able to answer this question positively, such 'isolated talk about the reality of Jesus' resurrection' would constitute a statement apart from faith and remain simply 'the report of a somewhat unusual event'.[10]

We meet here a sharp distinction between the historian and the believer, what many see as an unwarranted separation of the cognitive side of faith from the decision to commit oneself—a radical isolation of faith from (historical) reason. This separation glosses over the fact that historians can be believers (or non-believers); in these cases the same individuals think and believe (or disbelieve). Such people would not be flattered to be described as 'schizophrenic' thinkers, as if their belief (or non-belief) were radically separated from their historical reason and knowledge.

In 1998, after reading an article I had published on the resurrection of Christ, a certain Mr J. wrote to me and, among other things, flatly stated that the 'the resurrection of Christ has nothing to do with the existence and history of human beings on our planet'. He added: 'it is a matter of faith.' He spoke for all those who firmly separate reason and faith and consider thinking about history and trusting

[9] W. Marxsen, *The Resurrection of Jesus of Nazareth*, trans. M. Kohl (London: SCM Press, 1970), 150–4.

[10] Ibid. 22–3, 30, 110, 118–19, 140. With strict tenacity Marxsen follows through on his position, and with breathtaking understatement can brush aside the resurrection as a 'somewhat unusual event'.

in God to belong to autonomous zones. They sometimes take their cue from what Immanuel Kant wrote in the preface to the second edition of *The Critique of Pure Reason*: 'Thus I had to deny knowledge in order to make room for faith.'[11] Quite logically my correspondent and those whom he represented remove the resurrection from the historical existence of human beings. They understand faith in the risen Christ to belong to a 'storm-free zone' and to be quite untouched by any investigations they might care to make into history and by any conclusions they reach about matters of history. As a matter of 'trust', my correspondent went on to say, the resurrection is not something which can 'be discovered and described by human beings'. Here we seem to glimpse part of the grounds for his position: those realities which human beings can 'discover and describe' belong exclusively to history and do not concern the realm of faith.

It is worth observing that, like others who argue that the commitment of faith has nothing to do with human reason and its exercise (e.g. in discovering and describing historical matters), Mr J. could not help using reason to support his claim that questions of faith and questions of reason are totally separate and autonomous. With all due respect to him, this position appears perilously close to being self-contradictory. He uses human reasoning to justify separating faith from reason. Furthermore, one might also remark that, on any showing, 'the resurrection of Christ' must have something 'to do with the existence and history of human beings on our planet'. Unless Jesus had lived on our planet and died on a particular day in history, no one could have started talking about his resurrection from the dead. In that basic sense, any claims about his resurrection have something to do with the existence and history of human beings. Add too that fact that, since all our languages belong to 'the existence and history' of human beings, the very fact that we speak about the resurrection of Christ brings it into the orbit of human existence and history.

Despite these obvious flaws in his argument, that correspondent served, nevertheless, a useful purpose by alleging that the 'faith, trust, promise, and hope' which he found in the resurrection have nothing to do with human history and historical reasoning. He spoke for one common, yet extreme, position.

---

[11] I. Kant, *The Critique of Pure Reason*, trans. P. Guyer and A. W. Wood (Cambridge: Cambridge University Press, 1997), 117.

Over three hundred years ago Blaise Pascal offered a subtle and sophisticated version of faith which seemingly stepped aside from reason: 'it is the heart which perceives God and not the reason. That is what faith is: God perceived by the heart, not by reason.' Pascal gave his contrast between 'heart' and 'reason' an exquisitely modulated expression: 'the heart has its reasons of which reason knows nothing.'[12] Nevertheless, Pascal modified this 'not-by-reason' and 'reason-knowing-nothing' approach to the making of faith. As we observed in Chapter 4, he repeatedly suggested that sufficient but not over-whelming light characterizes the divine revelation that calls for human faith. The available signs and evidence can elicit faith, but they are not so compelling as to take away cognitive freedom.[13] Perhaps Pascal pulled his weight best on faith's response to revelation when he remarked: 'we shall never believe, with an effective belief and faith, unless God inclines our hearts.'[14] In describing the making of faith, one should never let the 'inward witness of the Holy Spirit'[15] by which 'God inclines our hearts' slide out of sight. We return below to the theme of faith taking place in human hearts through the power of the Holy Spirit.

Faith based on evidence

In a lyrical phrase St Paul wrote of faith as 'knowing the glory of God on the face of Jesus Christ' (2 Cor. 4: 6). Some argue that there is good evidence supporting this knowledge; those who put aside any prejudices and examine the evidence will be persuaded by it. Faith in Christ will be the conclusion of the convincing evidence at one's disposal.

For years Wolfhart Pannenberg has led those apologists who argue that historical research, more or less by itself, can justify and engen-der faith. The resurrection of Jesus focuses this claim that rational argument verifies faith. Pannenberg has never wavered in his convic-tion that to accept Jesus' resurrection is to make a judgement on the

---

[12] *Pensées*, trans. A. J. Krailsheimer (Harmondsworth: Penguin Books, 1966), nos. 423–4.

[13] Ibid., nos. 394, 427, 429, and 461.

[14] Ibid., no. 380; see no. 382.

[15] J. Calvin, *Institutes of the Christian Religion*, 1. 7. 4; trans. F. L. Battles, i (Philadelphia: Westminster Press, 1960), 78–80.

basis of historical evidence. Back in the 1960s he wrote: 'whether or not a particular event happened two thousand years ago is not made certain by faith *but only by historical research*.'[16] He argued that historians, seen by many as threatening Christianity and its Easter faith, could and should pass a positive judgement on the evidence for Jesus' resurrection. In particular, the appearances of the risen Christ make the resurrection as reliably attested as any event in the ancient world. With his list of witnesses (1 Cor. 15: 5–8), Paul intended to provide proof for the fact of Jesus' resurrection, 'a convincing historical proof by the standards of that time'.[17] Pannenberg also defended the discovery of the empty tomb as historically factual: it served to confirm the visions of the risen Lord. 'How could Jesus' disciples in Jerusalem', he wrote, 'have proclaimed his resurrection if they could be constantly refuted merely by viewing the grave in which his body was interred?' The Easter message 'could not have been maintained in Jerusalem for a single day, for a single hour, if the emptiness of the tomb had not been established as a fact for all concerned'.[18]

As for the resurrection-event, which lay behind the Easter appearances and the discovery of the empty tomb and which constituted a transition from being an earthly reality to being a risen reality, it occurred 'once at a definite time' and in a definite place (Jerusalem). Hence Pannenberg will not tolerate a less than historical qualification for the resurrection. 'There is no justification', he writes, 'for affirming Jesus' resurrection as an event that really happened, if it is not to be affirmed as an historical event as such.' Since the resurrection, he argues, actually took place at a definite time in the past, it should be called historical and can be established by the research of the historians.[19]

One immediately obvious objection to Pannenberg's case is this: if he is right, historians should be much more prominent among the ranks of those who accept the resurrection of Jesus. Through their profession they should be peculiarly competent to assess the evidence in favour of the Easter appearances and the discovery of the empty tomb being actual events in the past. This should put historians into a

---

[16] W. Pannenberg, *Jesus: God and Man*, trans. L. L. Wilkins and D. A. Priebe (London: SCM Press, 1968), 99; italics mine.
[17] Ibid. 89.
[18] Ibid. 100.
[19] Ibid. 99, 113.

privileged position for concluding that the resurrection of Jesus is an event that really happened and thus coming to faith. But, in fact, we do not find historians featuring disproportionately high on the list of believers.

Pannenberg's response to this objection was anticipated by his requiring historians to approach the question of Jesus' resurrection with a truly open mind and not with the prior conviction that the dead cannot be raised by God. Too many historians share this bias and so rule out in advance the resurrection, betraying a one-sided orientation towards the typical at the expense of the historical and a conviction that any resurrection is simply excluded by the rigid laws of nature. Pannenberg criticized such historians by insisting that modern science has broken with a deterministic worldview: the 'laws of nature' leave open the possibility of unfamiliar, even unique (or the only one of their kind), events which are not determined by these laws. He argued that too many historians fail their profession because their background theories (about the impossibility of resurrection and other unique events) prevent them from investigating claims about Jesus' resurrection.[20]

Pannenberg was confident that Jesus' rising from the dead can and should be verified by historical investigation. This made Easter faith, the heart of Christian faith, more or less the necessary conclusion of rational argument. Nevertheless, even though Pannenberg insisted on faith being grounded upon historical evidence from the past, he introduced other considerations when he elaborated on the way in which the first disciples understood what the resurrection of Jesus revealed. Since they already hoped for a general resurrection at the end of history, they were in a position to grasp something new: that the general resurrection and the end of all history had been anticipated by Jesus' personal resurrection. Thus the truth of God revealed in the resurrection was rightly understood by the disciples. Yet, even though solid historical evidence supports Pannenberg in crediting Jesus' disciples with such prior hopes for a general resurrection, how can people two thousand years later accept and share in those prior hopes and expect a future fulfilment for human beings in a general resurrection? Pannenberg argued that such a hope for future

---

[20] Ibid. 97–8.

resurrection proves its meaning and truth by being acted upon and standing 'the test today in the decisions of life'.[21] In other words, accepting now the prior expectations of the first disciples, which vitally shaped their full interpretation of Jesus' resurrection, comes through living with hope. Thus, when Pannenberg expounds the genesis of faith, a key element in his total picture of accepting the resurrection and the revelation it brought goes beyond establishing historical truth and includes the exercise of trusting hope—an inner, personal factor.

Years later Pannenberg reflected further on the role of trust in the making of faith: '*mere* historical knowledge *by itself* is inadequate precisely because it fails to grasp the deeper meaning of the history, its bearing on our salvation and therefore on each of us personally. Simple historical knowledge, then, needs to be supplemented by confident trust that grasps the true meaning, the "effect" of the history of Jesus, namely, the forgiveness of sin.' Thus Pannenberg understood an 'external' historical knowledge of Jesus' life, death, and resurrection to be necessary but insufficient to ground faith. By itself such knowledge fails to grasp the 'deeper', 'intrinsic', and 'true' meaning of Jesus' history: 'a purely external historical knowledge does not fully grasp the historical basis of faith. For the sake of the *intrinsic significance* of the history of Jesus, for the sake of its meaning as promise, knowledge of the history has thus to move on to trust in the God who is at work in this history.'[22]

To sum up: scrutinizing the historical evidence, which supports belief in Christ's resurrection and faith in him, has its value and indispensable role. Such scrutiny feeds into a cumulative case for faith and, negatively speaking, can show up the weaknesses in various counter-explanations: for instance, theories about what happened in the aftermath of the crucifixion and burial of Jesus. But largely limiting ourselves to an examination of the evidence can encourage the notion that faith is more or less decided by human reason weighing the evidence, historical and otherwise, and can slide over

---

[21] W. Pannenberg, *Jesus: God and Man*, 99; see also ibid. 107, and id., *What is Man? Contemporary Anthropology in Theological Perspective*, trans. D. A. Priebe (Philadelphia: Fortress Press, 1970), 41–53.

[22] W. Pannenberg, *Systematic Theology*, trans. G. W. Bromiley, iii (Grand Rapids, Mich.: Eerdmans, 1998), 136–72, at 143; italics mine.

the reality of faith as a free commitment. There is enough evidence to make a proper claim on us, but not enough to take away freedom. Reasoned argument, while relevant to religious belief, is not a sufficient condition for acquiring it, or—more accurately—receiving it.[23] Experience constantly shows how the mere force of arguments rarely, if ever, suffices by itself to convert someone to Christian faith. If the (historical) reasons were sufficient to establish the resurrection and further grounds for faith, faith should be the utterly convincing verdict for all those willing to weigh the evidence and draw the obvious conclusions from it. By unilaterally attending to the evidence, however, we would risk identifying *faith (and its knowledge)*[24] with the *evidence for it* and *knowing the evidence for it*.

But here, as elsewhere in life, we know more than the evidence. In close personal relationships, for instance, the evidence at our disposal is not all that we know. Knowing those whom we love is much more than simply knowing a certain number of facts about them, 'facts' which the available evidence might readily establish. 'Knowing' people goes well beyond merely 'knowing of' them or 'knowing about' them. Knowing them can be expressed as experiencing them directly, deeply, and enduringly, as we shall see later about people who come to know Jesus.[25]

Before leaving this second approach to the making of faith, let us note the attractive view of William Wainwright about reason being influenced and guided by appropriate emotions.[26] Unquestionably, a well-disposed heart allows people to perceive the value and force of arguments for faith. Wainwright goes further by arguing that reason functions properly only when informed by a rightly disposed heart. Some object here that sinners, whose hearts have not been rightly disposed, feature prominently among those who heard Jesus' call to faith. That continues to be the case: many whose lives have not been

---

[23] While Paul pictures faith as something exercised by human beings, it remains a gift. of God. Hence the apostle writes of faith 'coming' to us (Gal. 3: 23, 25).

[24] On the knowledge brought by faith, see 2 Cor. 4: 6; Ephes. 1: 9, 17–19; Col. 1: 9–10.

[25] Every now and then we learn of some celebrity being named as the father of a child born out of wedlock and, despite his initial disclaimers, being proved to be such by a DNA test. The evidence establishes his paternity, but—far from furthering life-giving interpersonal relationships—it signals their breakdown. On the basis of such evidence, people do not 'know' or experience each other in a deeply enriching way.

[26] W. J. Wainwright, *Reason and the Heart: A Prolegomenon to a Critique of Passional Reason* (Ithaca, NY: Cornell University Press, 1995).

guided by appropriate emotions experience dramatic conversions, in which they embrace in faith the divine revelation and salvation brought by Christ. Nevertheless, Wainwright points us toward something not to be ignored in any adequate view of the making of faith: the role of inner dispositions.

Thus far this chapter has set itself to develop a conversation with Wedderburn, Marxsen, Mr J., Pascal, Pannenberg, and Wainwright. Let me turn now to set out the complete set of factors that I hold to be involved in the making of faith.

The objective and subjective factors

Christian faith arises through a convergence and collaboration of objective and subjective factors. Objectively it involves both the outer, public testimony of the believing community and the internal 'witness' of the Holy Spirit. First, faith 'comes from what is heard' (Rom. 10: 17; see Gal. 3: 5), when people testify that the self-communication of God has taken place normatively through a specific series of events, in the experiences of a specific set of people, and—in particular—through the person of Jesus Christ. The community of believers recall in their Scriptures and re-enact in their worship these events; they witness to the leading persons in the foundational period of revelation—above all, to Jesus himself. The revelation to which they testify offers a new vision of the world, of how human beings should behave, and of what they can hope for. This revelation answers the three questions that Kant raised at the end of his *Critique of Pure Reason*: 'All interest of my reason (the speculative as well as the practical) is united in the following three questions: What can I know? What should I do? What may I hope for?'[27] But why accept this call to faith? What is involved in doing so?

The faith to which the witnesses point enjoys its rational credentials. As we saw in Chapter 2, one can make a reasonable case for the existence of a powerful and loving God. Drawing on the historical testimony of the Gospels, people can be attracted to the personality of Jesus, and sense the life-giving quality of his message. They can see how Jesus resonated with the joys, hopes, and fears of his audience; he gave them consolation in their sufferings. He answered their existential questions

---

[27] Kant, *Critique of Pure Reason*, A805/B833, trans. Guyer and Wood, 677.

and taught them a truly human, if demanding, way of life. As we saw in the last chapter, there are good arguments to support the truth of his resurrection. Then the generous lives (and heroic deaths) of many of his followers can illuminate and nourish any initial attachment to Jesus and his teaching.[28] A cluster of historical reasons drawn from the foundation and subsequent history of the Church yields evidence encouraging faith. Although not exclusively rational, Christian faith points to plausible testimony and reasons (both historical and philosophical in the widest sense of those terms) when confessing what it believes about certain events as special acts of God and certain figures as bearers of special revelation.

Nevertheless, faith *goes beyond the evidence* since it involves a loving commitment to the person of Christ. It is reasonable but not merely rational. Such a 'going beyond the evidence' also characterizes what happens when people enter into such a deep relationship as marriage that shapes their lives forever. To be sure, shared values, common interests, and mutual expectations can make a commitment to 'this person' a reasonable option. There is 'evidence' that marriage with this person will work out well. Nevertheless, it would be insulting for a young man to propose marriage on the grounds that 'I have made a series of background checks on you, and all the evidence makes our marriage a compelling conclusion'. Human beings do not make such loving and successful commitments for life simply and solely on the basis of evidence.

When faith comes into existence, an objective, if invisible, agent leads people beyond the evidence. God 'inclines their heart', as Pascal put it. There is an interior divine illumination that accompanies the external presentation of the Christian message. The Book of Acts tells the story of Paul's first convert in Philippi, a woman named Lydia; 'the Lord opened her heart' as she listened to the apostle's words (Acts 16: 14). The apostle himself writes of the Holy Spirit 'revealing' interiorly 'the things of God' and enabling one to interpret them (1 Cor. 2: 10–13),[29] and giving people the freedom to share the vision

---

[28] This was a major theme G. O'Collins and M. Farrugia, *Catholicism: The Story of Catholic Christianity* (Oxford: Oxford University Press, 2003).

[29] See J. A. Fitzmyer, *First Corinthians* (New Haven: Yale University Press, 2008), 170, 179–82; A. C. Thiselton, *The First Epistle to the Corinthians* (Grand Rapids, Mich.: Eerdmans, 2000), 252–67.

of faith (2 Cor. 3: 17–18). It is when God 'shines' in the hearts of human beings that they can know 'the glory of God in the face of Jesus Christ' (2 Cor. 4: 6).[30] The 'inner' testimony of the Holy Spirit opens people to accept the 'outer' word of Christian witnesses. It is always due to the divine initiative when revelation comes and lets human beings experience the presence of the living God (see Matt. 16: 17).

On the *subjective* side, personal experiences, dispositions, questions, and needs play their role in the genesis of faith. Take the profound, intimate questions that touch the deepest needs and final values of human existence. Sooner or later all people face the question: 'what is the purpose of living if I am going to die?' Sooner or later they experience the fact that even the best 'goods in life', being incomplete and transient, can never fully satisfy them. Faith invites people to rethink their aims and values, so that they can discern religious truths and, in particular, the truth about Jesus. Faith offers the chance of answering fundamental questions about the nature, meaning, and destiny of our own existence and that of the whole cosmos. Faith promises to validate itself in practice by leading believers into a deeply satisfying union with God and one another.

To sum up: the experience of coming to faith involves *objective* realities (the testimony of the believing community and the gift of the inner light of the Holy Spirit), and *subjective* factors (the needs and dispositions of the human heart). This complex and cumulative experience allows things to 'hang together', and yields a coherent and meaningful vision of Christ that can underpin our existence and worship. Faith makes sense of life in all its complexities and sufferings.

As an 'insider' to the life of Christian faith, I have been describing the factors involved in coming to faith and exercising faith. At this point some narratives may provide vivid and convincing narratives of such a move to faith.

We argued above (Chapter 4) that John is the Gospel of revelation *par excellence*. It presents a series of 'case studies' that show Christ the Revealer at work in rousing human faith. Individual encounters with him distinctively shape the narrative of the Fourth Gospel. Through

---

[30] The human acceptance of God's self-communication is a divine work to be compared with the original act of creation, 'let there be light'. See M. J. Harris, *The Second Epistle to the Corinthians* (Grand Rapids, Mich.: Eerdmans, 2005), 337–9.

such encounters the evangelist brings on stage a range of people who feel various needs and face various challenges. The reader can see how Christ acts toward them, discloses himself to him, and leads them to faith. Given that revelation and the faith it elicits constitute key themes for fundamental theology, this discipline should turn naturally to John for illumination and support. Fundamental theology's reflections on faith will be enriched when it attends to the 'case studies' of coming to faith that John provides.

A narrative theology of faith

When exploring John's narrative theology of faith, we can reflect first on the representative problems affecting those who encounter Jesus. We can then explore how these encounters unfold in bringing about faith.

Representative problems

Sometimes the individuals who meet Jesus are given names, like Andrew (1: 35–42), Nicodemus (3: 1–15), Martha (11: 17–27), Mary Magdalene (20: 11–18), and Peter (21: 15–19). Sometimes they are simply called a Samaritan woman (4: 1–42), a royal official (4: 43–54), a man who has been disabled for thirty-eight years (5: 1–18), a woman taken in adultery (7: 53–8: 11),[31] or a man born blind (9: 1–41). In the case of all these people, we can spot representative problems and recurrent needs of human beings. Religious issues about salvation and the identity of Jesus puzzle Andrew and Nicodemus. The Samaritan woman, having been married five times and now living with another man, clearly has a problem in the area of irregular domestic situations.[32] A different family

---

[31] Most scholars agree that the episode of the woman taken in adultery was inserted later in the text of the Fourth Gospel. Yet it witnesses, in its own vivid and compelling fashion, to Jesus; see A. T. Lincoln, *The Gospel According to John* (London: Continuum 2005), 524–36.

[32] Some commentators want to interpret the Samaritan woman merely symbolically: for instance, with her marital relationships referring to gods worshipped by the Samaritans. But Andrew Lincoln argues persuasively that 'there is no need to choose between a more literal or a more symbolic interpretation'. Indeed, the symbolic interpretation, if it is 'to work effectively', needs the literal interpretation 'in which the woman is viewed as morally suspect'. The symbolic meaning for

problem affects the royal official: his little son is very seriously ill and seems to be on the point of death. A physical disability has condemned an anonymous man to spend his life helplessly lying next to a pool in Jerusalem. When another anonymous person, the woman caught committing adultery, meets Jesus, she is about to be stoned to death. When Martha encounters Jesus, she has just suffered a painful family tragedy: her beloved brother Lazarus has died. Jesus discloses himself to Mary Magdalene after she has seen him die on the cross and is now shocked by the suspicion that grave robbers have taken his body from the tomb where he was buried.

In these and other cases, Jesus discloses himself to those who suffer a pressing personal need that affects them personally and often affects their families as well. Some encounter him because they have gone looking for him (e.g. Nicodemus and the royal official). One person seemingly blunders into the presence of Jesus (the Samaritan woman). Another is dragged or driven into his presence (the woman caught in adultery). Others encounter Jesus because he himself comes to them (e.g. the man crippled for thirty-eight years and the man blind from birth). Andrew and his anonymous companion are directed towards Jesus by John the Baptist.

It does not seem to matter much to the evangelist *how* Jesus meets these typical figures. The only important thing is that they find themselves in his presence and then respond to his initiative and come to faith. Except for the disabled man in 5: 1–18, all the individuals allow Jesus to take over and exercise his revealing and saving activity. Andrew and his companion allow Jesus to lead them away for a quiet afternoon together. Nicodemus lets Jesus introduce some surprisingly new themes. The Samaritan woman lets Jesus not only raise the touchy topic of her irregular married life but also gradually reveal himself to her and bring her to faith. These meetings with Jesus regularly feature people being prompted by Jesus to rethink their vision of life in new and unexpected ways.

By telling the story of various encounters with Jesus, John encourages the fundamental theologian to draw an initial conclusion about the revelation that elicits faith. The saving self-revelation of Christ characteristically takes place in the apparently 'negative'

Lincoln concerns above all a betrothal scene, in which Christ as bridegroom seeks his bride, the new people of God (ibid. 170, 172–4, 176).

setting of some deep need or painful problem. I say 'characteristic-ally', since one could recall, for instance, the exchange between Jesus and Philip (14: 8–10). This is a moment of revelation (that should deepen faith), but one can hardly allege that Philip finds himself in the grip of a particular and serious personal crisis. He is rebuked for having failed to grasp that Jesus, in his person and activity, is totally taken up with revealing the Father: 'Whoever has seen me has seen the Father.' Like all the disciples and others, Philip has 'never seen the form' of the Father, but the One whom the Father has sent has completely represented him and disclosed him (5: 37–8). Hence Philip can be rebuked for not recognizing in faith that Jesus acts as and is in his own person the very revelation of the Father.

The dynamism of the encounters

Examining in detail several of the encounters in the Fourth Gospel might let fundamental theologians glimpse the evangelist's sense of *how* the self-revelation of Christ reaches and is accepted by indivi-duals who come to faith. If they all bring some nagging or even tragic problem to their meeting with Jesus, what happens when he reveals himself to them? Do they always have clear expectations when they meet Jesus? Does this self-disclosure necessarily take place quickly? What characterizes the meeting as it turns into an event of revelation and the birth of faith? Let me reflect on Jesus' encounters with Nicodemus, the Samaritan woman, the royal official, and the disabled man lying by a pool in Jerusalem.

(a) Nicodemus meets Jesus because he has gone looking for him (3: 1–15).[33] Admittedly he comes 'by night'. As a Pharisee, a ruler of the Jews and a teacher in Israel, Nicodemus shows himself sensitive to his own reputation and importance. Afraid of compromising himself publicly, he decides to visit Jesus under the cover of darkness. What expectations does Nicodemus have? He has already reached some limited conclusions about Jesus: 'Rabbi, we know that you are a teacher come from God; for no one can do these signs that you do, unless God is with him.' The question has become: in what sense has Jesus 'come from God'? Nicodemus has apparently fitted Jesus into

---

[33] See ibid. 146–57.

some traditional categories, based on such figures as Moses and the prophets. He wants reassurance and confirmation about Jesus being merely a divinely endorsed teacher sent by God, and does not expect a challenging message about Jesus being the incarnate Son of God who has descended from heaven (3: 13).

What happens in the dialogue suddenly goes far beyond the limited agenda Nicodemus has proposed. Jesus abruptly assures him: 'Amen, amen, I say to you, unless one is born again, he cannot see the kingdom of God.' Jesus speaks in a disturbing way by proposing a radically different perspective on his own mission and identity. He then spells out this unexpected invitation to enter the kingdom as involving new birth through water and the Holy Spirit. Is Nicodemus ready to submit to God's Spirit that, like the unpredictable and invisible wind, 'blows where it wills'?

Nicodemus knows what can happen and what cannot happen. The words 'how' and 'can' recur in his three questions and suggest a limited view of God's power: '*How can* a man be born when he is old? *Can* he enter a second time into his mother's womb and be born... *How* can this be?' It is disturbing to be called when one is 'old' to start once again from the beginning. Is it possible to do so? As Lincoln puts it, he 'sees only impossibilities rather than divine possibilities'.[34] Nicodemus is a professionally religious man, a rigid individual who has life under control but who also feels an ill-defined sense of some personal need. He visits Jesus of his own accord, and seems to betray a feeling that something needs to be changed in his life. But for the time being he has only a limited trust in the power of the Holy Spirit.

The story of Nicodemus' encounter with Jesus trails off (after 3: 13 or after 3: 15). There is no clearly indicated ending in the text of the Gospel. A change does come over Nicodemus but it will come slowly. It comes precisely in terms of public courage, the very quality Nicodemus has seemingly lacked. First, he disagrees with 'the chief priests and the Pharisees' and defends Jesus' right to a proper hearing (7: 50–1). Then, after the crucifixion he turns up with an enormous quantity of myrrh and aloes (19: 39). He sees to it that Jesus is buried like a king. Although he originally visited Jesus under cover of darkness, by

---

[34] Ibid. 151.

acting truly and courageously he has finally come to the light (3: 21) and joins those who believe in Jesus.

Four points about divine revelation and its correlative, human faith, emerge from the Nicodemus story. First, in revealing himself, Jesus disturbs the limited agenda that Nicodemus brings to their meeting. Second, he invokes the Holy Spirit as a crucial protagonist for those who open themselves to the revealing and saving activity of God. The inner witness and activity of the Spirit are essential for the passage to faith. Third, Nicodemus himself moves slowly in his journey towards accepting what Jesus offers him. This (slow) movement sets Nicodemus apart from the next three cases we consider. While saying nothing about what happened subsequently to the Samaritan woman, the royal official, and the disabled man in Jerusalem, the Gospel traces, albeit sketchily, Nicodemus' pilgrimage to full faith. Fourth, the revelation of Christ dramatically changes Nicodemus and his way of behaving: from a cautious enquirer he becomes a courageous, public follower of Jesus.

(b) It looks like an accident that the Samaritan woman meets Jesus (4: 1–42).[35] If he had not been so tired, he might have gone with his disciples into Sychar to buy food. She herself could have come to draw water earlier or later in the day. The midday encounter at Jacob's well might seem a perfectly chance meeting. But what begins like a random exchange ends very differently.

Unlike the encounter with Nicodemus, it is Jesus this time who takes the initiative and opens the dialogue: 'Give me a drink.' To begin with, their interchange centres on something which is not only simple and basic but also an elemental necessity for human beings and their world: water. The first part of the dialogue ends with Jesus' promise: 'Those who drink of the water than I will give them will never thirst; the water that I will give them will become in them a spring of water welling up to eternal life' (4: 14). Attentive readers appreciate this symbolism of water as that life-giving relationship with God mediated by the Spirit, whom Jesus will give.

The encounter at high noon abruptly moves on when Jesus says to the woman: 'Go, call your husband.' Jesus touches on her previous history involving five husbands and present domestic arrangements.

---

[35] On the meeting with the Samaritan woman, see ibid. 167–82, esp. 192.

She has had five husbands, and now lives with a man who is not her husband. But she does not break off the conversation with Jesus in embarrassment. Little by little she lets him lead her on, right to the point when he no longer speaks merely of living water but reveals himself as the living Messiah. She does not hoard this good news but, with the joy of a new believer, brings it at once to the people of Sychar. She has received the self-revelation of God and becomes then a catalyst for the faith of others.

Many Samaritans are so impressed by the woman's testimony that they quickly come to believe in Jesus. Later, others tell her that she is now redundant: 'It is no longer because of your words that we believe, for we have heard him for ourselves and we know that this is indeed the Saviour of the world' (4: 41–2). They no longer need the woman's witness to her own experience. They have experienced Jesus for themselves and they call him by a remarkable title that we find nowhere else in the New Testament, 'the Saviour of the world'. The woman has pointed them to Jesus, and they have 'known'—that is to say, experienced in faith—Jesus and his 'word' for themselves.

Significantly, the Samaritans prevail on Jesus to 'remain' or 'stay' (*menein*) with them: 'they asked him to *stay* with them, and he *stayed* there two days' (4: 40). Now revealed to them, Jesus initiates a lasting relationship, the fruitful, redemptive result of accepting him in faith (e.g. 8: 31; 15: 4–7).

This episode of revelation has 'trinitarian' overtones, since it involves a worship of the Father, empowered by the Spirit and mediated by Christ (4: 23–4). In particular, the creative, life-giving power of God, the Spirit, is not confined but, as Jesus has already said to Nicodemus, 'blows where it wills' (3: 8).

As in his meeting with Nicodemus, Jesus introduces something unexpected and disturbing for the Samaritan woman—in this case by showing that he knows her home situation. She differs from Nicodemus, who comes to Jesus by night and remains for a time in darkness. Meeting Jesus in broad daylight, she responds quickly in the dialogue Jesus opens up, accepts the revelation of his identity, and immediately becomes a missionary who wants to bring that good news to others. Hers is a story of someone who begins the day expecting nothing and ends it as a deeply changed person. She has allowed Jesus to reveal himself to her and transform her life.

(c) John's Gospel moves at once to the story of an officer in the royal service, who leaves Capernaum and hurriedly seeks out Jesus in Cana (4: 46–53).[36] He encounters Jesus because he wants one particular thing: a cure for his sick son. He meets an initial challenge or even rebuff from Jesus: 'Unless you see signs and wonders you will not believe.' The royal official will not be deterred by this testing, and simply repeats his request: 'Come down before my little boy dies.' In a real sense, Jesus' rebuff is addressed more to those who read the Gospel and may think that 'signs and wonders' (which authenticate revelation) are always a preliminary, even a necessary preliminary, to faith. Jesus questions those who might want to base their faith in him on such signs. The official himself does not do this; he believes before he has seen any sign. Jesus' self-revelation and its claims should be perceived as credible, even without miracles.[37] The official does not rely on miracles that he has *already* experienced before coming to faith.

When he arrives, the official shows his trust that Jesus could work a miracle *provided* he comes in person to visit the dying boy. Now he accepts that Jesus' all-powerful word can heal at a distance: he 'believes the word that Jesus spoke to him and starts on his way' home. Through trusting Jesus, the official now receives not only what he has asked for (the cure of his son) but also much more as well. He and his entire household become believers. Meeting Jesus leads him to faith and to found a community of faith. He has become a missionary to his own family.

Faith in Jesus and his revealing word, as he says in the opening dialogue with the Samaritan woman, will bring life, even 'eternal life' (4: 14). The story of the royal official dramatizes this life-giving quality of Jesus' self-revelation and the faith that responds to it. The imminent *death* of a little boy threatens the happiness of a household (4: 47, 49), but through the word of Jesus he now *lives* (4: 50, 51, 53). The language of this brief story highlights a passage *from death to life*.

---

[36] Ibid. 183–90.

[37] Addressing Philip, Jesus allows believing because of 'works' as a second-best route: 'The words that I say to you I do not speak on my own, but the Father who dwells in me does his works. Believe me that I am in the Father and the Father is in me. But if you do not, then believe because of the works themselves' (John 14: 10–11). The evangelist, however, is well aware that even the most striking works, like bringing Lazarus back from the dead, will not compel belief; in fact, that episode becomes the occasion of a deadly plot against Jesus and against Lazarus (John 11: 47–52; 12: 9–11; see 12: 37).

The revelatory word of Jesus overcomes death and brings life. But to experience the life that Jesus brings, one must first trust him in faith. The story of the official and his child discloses at a family level what the Samaritans believed at the level of the human race by accepting the revelation of Jesus as 'the *Saviour of the world*'.

One seemingly minor detail in the story of the official, which throws light on the faith that responds to revelation, emerges when we notice how the story gives the official various names. He is called at first 'a royal official' (4: 46, 49), then 'the man' or rather 'the human being' (*anthrōpos*) (4: 50) and, finally, 'the father' (4: 53). He enters the story as what he is in public life—an official who carries out a public function. Then he becomes 'the man' who believes the word Jesus addresses to him. In meeting Jesus he loses, as it were, his public mask. He becomes simply a human being, face to face with the Lord. He is offered and receives the only gift that ultimately matters: 'the man believed the word that Jesus spoke to him.' Then he becomes 'the father'. His new faith has not reduced but rather reinforced his humanity. He is no longer merely an 'official' but now 'the father' who returns to his family and finds his son restored to health. Then 'all the household' come to believe. As in the case of the Samaritan woman, far from being a private, isolating force, faith speaks out, spreads itself, and builds communities of believers. What has been just a household becomes a household of faith.

(d) After the story of the royal official, John's Gospel switches its setting from Galilee to the pool of Bethesda in Jerusalem and to a man who has been disabled for thirty-eight years (5: 1–18).[38] The man lies there, incurable and incredibly helpless. During the early years of his crippled state he could hope for healing, but now his friends have abandoned him and he has given up on himself. The man has become an impotent slave of his own condition

He cannot move himself and go looking for Jesus, as Nicodemus and the official from Capernaum have done. Jesus simply turns up and stands there looking at the crippled man. In that great crowd of invalids (5: 4), Jesus picks out the one who seems most in need. The others can to some extent help themselves, but this man has been lame for so long that he cannot do anything for himself, and has lost all heart.

---

[38] See C. K. Barrrett, *The Gospel According to St John* (2nd edn. London: SPCK, 1978), 249–56; Lincoln, *Gospel According to John*, 190–200; J. P. Meier, *A Marginal Jew: Rethinking the Historical Jesus*, ii (New York: Doubleday, 1994), 680–4, 729–30.

What does the crippled man expect when he notices Jesus looking at him? Some food or some alms perhaps? Instead, Jesus tries to rouse a little hope by asking, 'Do you want to be healed?' The man reacts by making excuses for himself: 'Sir, I have no one to put me in the pool when the water is troubled. While I am going [there], another steps down before me.' The lame man's situation has been tragically para-doxical. He has lived so close to a pool which, through an inflow of water, every now and then possesses special powers of healing. Yet he has been so weak that he could not take the small step that might have healed him. Jesus has singled out the crippled man, tried to rouse some hope, and made him acknowledge his impotence. Now he heals him: 'Rise, take up your stretcher, and walk.' At that command, the man who could hardly move himself gets up, carries off his mat, and after so many years can resume a normal life. This healing has not come about because he has recognized Jesus, let alone requested a miraculous cure—as did the royal official. It is simply the power of Jesus' word that has effected an instantaneous healing.

But the story does not end there. The man is not yet fully healed through accepting in faith the self-revelation of Jesus. As John's Gospel subtly puts it, he does not 'know' Jesus (5: 13). Unless he really knows him, he will not be truly saved. Jesus once again takes the initiative and seeks him out, in order to heal him interiorly: 'See, you are well! Sin no more, so that nothing worse happens to you.'[39] Does the man now recognize his own sinfulness, come to 'know' or experience Jesus in faith, and spread that faith? Rather he goes to the religious authorities who have ignored the extraordinary healing itself, have accused him of infringing the Sabbath by carrying his mat, and want to know who told him to break the Sabbath in that way. He informs them that it was Jesus of Nazareth who was responsible for his cure. This strengthens their desire to kill Jesus (5: 18).

While it is not clear what motivates the man in going to the hostile authorities, John's Gospel mentions here for the first time murderous plans to do away with Jesus. This chilling news comes in the aftermath of a loving initiative from Jesus, which has succeeded in touching a crippled man's body but not his heart. Meeting Jesus and even being

---

[39] Here Jesus makes some connection between past sin and a physical disabil-ity. In the case of a man born blind, however, he will deny that this tragic handicap can be traced directly to anyone's sin (9: 3).

physically healed by him does not irresistibly rouse faith and transform a human life.

Some conclusions

Those in search of a narrative theology of God's self-revelation that rouses human faith will find a gold mine in John's Gospel. Rather than moving on to further examples, let me pull together five conclusions from the four cases that I have examined.

First, such serious problems as religious doubts (Nicodemus), a sickness in the family (the royal official), and personal sinfulness (the Samaritan woman and the disabled man in Jerusalem) create the conditions for the possibility of receiving revelation and coming to believe. Second, faith responds to the revealing words and deeds of Jesus; the cases of the Samaritan woman and the royal official show most clearly how revelation and faith go or should go together. Third, the revelation that Jesus brings is life-giving, as emerges clearly in Jesus' exchanges with Nicodemus and the Samaritan woman and the healing of the official's little son. Revelation and salvation are distinguishable but never separable. The word of Jesus is a word of life. Fourth, revelation is centred on and mediated through Jesus (all four cases) and, through involving the Father and the Holy Spirit, has a 'trinitarian' dimension (the encounters with Nicodemus and the Samaritan woman). Fifth, the offer of revelation must be received freely and experienced in faith. The disabled man in Jerusalem seemingly misses his chance; Nicodemus responds slowly; the Samaritan woman (along with others in Sychar) and, above all, the royal official respond very quickly to the grace of revelation that comes to them when they encounter Jesus.

In short, John's Gospel offers a superb narrative theology of faith initiated by Christ's self-revelation. Over and over again, in his encounters with individuals (and groups of people) Jesus presents himself as the Revealer and the Revelation of God and calls for the response of faith.[40]

---

[40] See C. Bennema, *Encountering Jesus: Character Studies in the Gospel of John* (Milton Keynes: Paternoster Press, 2009).

Of course, the topic of faith raises other questions: e.g. on faith and justification, on 'faith working through love' (Gal. 5: 6), and on faith as a gift creating the obligation to live in new ways. But these issues belong to doctrinal or dogmatic theology. Fundamental theology is limited to the task of describing and explaining, at least briefly, how and why human faith responds to divine revelation. For those who belong to the stage of dependent revelation, this response takes place through experiencing the living tradition of the Church. To that tradition and its functions we now turn.

8

Tradition and the Traditions

Responding with faith to God's self-revelation and shaped by their experience of this divine self-communication, believers from the start of biblical history lived out their experience by handing on to the next generation an account of what they had experienced. The patriarchs and their wives, prophets, apostles, and innumerable others in the history of the Old and New Testament remembered and told the story of their dialogue with God. Abraham, Sarah, and other half-glimpsed figures in the earliest period, prompted by their experiences of the divine self-manifestation, set going the whole narrative of the believing community. Later generations reframed the communal story by interpreting and building into it their new experiences of God's actions on their behalf and messages to them. Thus revelation initiated the whole process of tradition. 'In the beginning', one might say, was revelation, and revelation 'became flesh' and was embodied in the living tradition of God's people, a tradition that linked and links one generation of believers with the next.[1]

---

[1] On tradition, see Y. Congar, *Tradition and Traditions: An Historical and Theological Essay*, trans. M. Naseby and T. Rainborough (London: Burns & Oates, 1966); J. F. Kelly (ed.), *Perspectives on Scripture and Tradition* (Notre Dame, Ind.: Fides, 1976); 'Tradition', *Oxford Dictionary*, 1646–7; H. J. Pottmeyer, 'Normen, Kriterien und Strukuren der Überlieferung', *HFTh* iv. 124–52;

Some of these believers, inspired by the Holy Spirit, set down in writing this story and the various ways they had understood, expressed, and acted upon (or sinfully failed to act upon) their encounter(s) with God. These inspired Scriptures emerged *from* tradition, and were understood, interpreted, and 'activated' *within* the whole living tradition of the community. Much more will be said later about the relationship between tradition and Sacred Scripture, as well as about biblical inspiration and the primary role of Scriptures in the life of the Church. Here I wish only to point out how the inspired Scriptures originated from and within the tradition triggered by experiences (in faith) of the divine self-revelation.

Right from the outset it is important to remark on the way 'tradition' may designate either an action (the act of handing on, *actus tradendi*) or what is handed on (the 'content' of what is handed on, the *traditum*). Understood either as process or content, tradition, while spoken of in the singular, involves innumerable 'actors' and 'items'. The protagonists who actively transmit tradition include, as well as the invisible Holy Spirit (to whom we return below), official leaders, charismatic figures, and millions of believers of every kind. It is the whole Church that hands on tradition. The *traditum* itself includes all manner of beliefs, forms of worship, and ranges of practice. That raises the question: how do we know whether and/or to what extent this complex *traditum* remains faithful to and authentically expresses the foundational, apostolic experience of the divine self-revelation? This question will be taken up later. Here I wish only to alert readers to the two senses of tradition. The context should make it clear which one is intended: either the act of transmission or the content of what is transmitted.

After these preliminaries, this chapter can take shape around three issues: the human reality of tradition; the ecumenical convergence on tradition and its relationship with Scripture; the need to discern particular traditions and criteria for doing so.

K. Rahner and J. Ratzinger, *Revelation and Tradition*, trans. W. J. O'Hara (London: Burns & Oates, 1966); M. Rösel et al., 'Tradition', *TRE* xxxiii. 689–732. J. E. Thiel, *Senses of Tradition: Continuity and Development in Catholic Faith* (New York: Oxford University Press, 2000); D. Wiederkehr, 'Das Prinzip der Überlieferung', *HFTh* iv. 100–23.

The human reality of tradition

Inasmuch as the experience of the divine self-communication in Christ is a human phenomenon, it necessarily involves tradition. People sometimes attach the label 'traditional' to those rigid conservatives who crave the past, resent the present, and dread the future. In that sense 'traditionalists' are those who falsely idealize past history and treasure old experiences in an excessive and unrealistic fashion. Sometimes, however, 'traditional' becomes a selling point, evoking healthy habits and products that have long proved themselves. We can be encouraged to drink 'traditional ales' and 'traditionally brewed' beers, 'eat traditional Greek cuisine', and enjoy 'traditional Thai massage'. Such negative or positive use of the term might distract us from the way that tradition belongs essentially to the social and historical existence of all human beings.[2]

Human life is simply unthinkable without the element of tradition. Over and above being a religious phenomenon that marks Christianity and other world religions, tradition—and this is a fact sometimes ignored by those who write about it in a theological context—shapes the entire cultural existence of men and women. At this level 'tradition' is almost synonymous with a society's whole way of life or, in a word, with its culture. Let me briefly recall how tradition functions as a human reality and secures a society's *continuity*, *identity*, and *unity*.

Tradition fashions *the bond between successive generations* in a society. We receive from the past our language, laws, customs, beliefs, practices, and other symbolic realities that are generally accepted unquestioningly and provide Italy, Japan, Madagascar, or any other society with its characteristic cultural values. Even if members of a given society rarely stop to formulate and reflect on what they have taken over, they remain radically indebted to the past for their inherited values and expectations which give life its meaning and provide ideals to be striven for. Thus one generation passes on to another norms, attitudes, and behaviour patterns by which society

---

[2] Experts in the broad disciplines of cultural anthropology and sociology (e.g. Robert Bellah, Peter Berger, Anthony Giddens, Thomas Luckmann, Talcott Parsons, and their successors) frequently study tradition, even when they do not explicitly introduce the term as such.

has hitherto functioned and now seeks to perpetuate itself. Of course, the newcomers can challenge, reject, or modify traditions they have received, but they can never do so totally. Any such *complete* break with the past—*du passé faisons la table rase*—is never a genuine option. At least initially, these newcomers to an existing society are taught to live by the existing ways. Otherwise they would be incapable of adjusting, altering, and rebelling against what the previous generation has handed on to them.

In 1968 North Atlantic countries witnessed a massive rejection of tradition, especially among the student population. But then the 1970s saw many young people disillusioned with change and revolution. Around the same time large segments of the Muslim world began returning to traditional values and practices, which they felt to be threatened by secularizing trends. The pendulum swings backwards and forwards. But neither total revolution nor rigid tradition will ever finally dislodge the other. Permanence and a hunger for permanence seem as essential a feature of human experience as change and a yearning for change.

Back in Chapter 3, when expounding my fourteenth and last point about experience, I drew attention to the way in which experience repeatedly goes beyond our expectations and involves novelty. The new comes in on top of the old. But for this to happen the old must already be there. Even in the most novel and unexpected experiences that happen to an individual or a group, some permanent 'traditional' substratum is inevitably preserved—no matter how many factors are new. Thus change and tradition, so far from being mutually exclusive, stand in function of each other.

Besides effecting continuity within the flow of history, an inherited tradition and its closely related culture *identify* us here and now at our deepest levels. Our traditional values and conventions help establish our cultural identity as Italians, Japanese, Scots, or whatever, and thus effectively *unite* our societies. In short, tradition works as the principle of continuity, identity, and unity in any human society—between generations and within generations. Sometimes, to be sure, traditions may be demonically misused by unscrupulous politicians who aim to secure the identity and unity of a nation or a group, so as to promote an unworthy and even criminal project by retrieving some past victory and calling for continuity with this 'glorious' tradition. It is at our peril that we ignore the ways traditions may be exploited in an evil cause.

It is clear from positive and negative examples that tradition transcends not only individuals but also the present history of the group. It covers the collective experience of a group here and now, as well as all those expressions of experience which one generation transmits to another. This is to pick up on what was said about the collective subject of experience (in the last point about experience in Chapter 3). In receiving, changing, and handing on its tradition, a social group acts as the collective subject, interpreter, and administrator of the tradition. This collective subject experiences and hands on something that goes beyond the mere sum total of individual experiences: namely, its cumulative experience.

When we move now to discuss Christian tradition, we should not imagine that it simply conforms to the typical trajectory of tradition in 'ordinary' human affairs. Christians look back through their history and tradition to an enduringly normative point of reference, an unsurpassable climax in the first century of our era. Admittedly other groups and societies may cherish the memory of some foundational event: like their war of independence, the landing of the first settlers, or a glorious revolution which they believe to have shaped the subsequent course of their history. In ways that bear some analogy to the Christian model, people can cling to the spirit of their national tradition and seek to renew themselves through documents and traditions derived from the origins and/or radical transformation of their country's history. Yet no nation has security of tenure. It could go out of existence, or it may in some future time be recreated through events that will provide a radically new point of departure. Christians, however, believe the coming of Jesus Christ to be the lasting, normative climax of the divine self-communication, trust that the Church which he founded will not disappear in the course of human history, and—as we shall see—acknowledge the Holy Spirit as the invisible 'bearer' of their essential tradition.

Christian tradition

How then has Christian tradition functioned (or failed to function) when the period of *foundational* revelation ended with the apostolic age and gave way to the era of *dependent* revelation in which all subsequent believers have lived? The Church had been founded and the writing of inspired Scriptures (which recorded the foundational experiences and their normative interpretations of the divine self-communication through Christ and his Spirit) had come to a close. Through a multiplicity of particular traditions, the foundational witnesses 'handed on' to subsequent generations their original experience of God and the ways in which they lived out that experience: through the New Testament Scriptures; the celebration of baptism and the Eucharist; the practice of regular prayer and help to those in need; appointment of community leaders through the imposition of hands and the invocation of the Holy Spirit; and other early traditions.

From the second and third century numerous further traditions emerged and spread in the Christian Church: for instance, the biblical canon settled by recognizing *these* Scriptures as inspired, apostolic, and authoritative (rather than e.g. the Gnostic texts castigated by St Irenaeus); the threefold ministry of bishop, priest, and deacon; the holding of synods and councils (that produced at times such enduring creeds as the Nicene-Constantinopolitan Creed of 381); pilgrimages to the Holy Land and to the tombs of martyrs; the creation of various liturgical texts and practices in Eastern and Western Christianity (e.g. infant baptism); obligations about celibacy, fasting, and abstinence; the founding and spread of monastic life for men and women; prayers for the dead; the unfolding story of Christian art (e.g. Eastern icons), architecture (e.g. Romanesque and then Gothic cathedrals and churches), and liturgical music in East and West; developments in devotion to the Blessed Virgin Mary and other saints; particular structures for ecclesiastical government (e.g. the erection of dioceses in the West and eparchies in the East); worship of Christ that took form in devotions to his presence in the Blessed Sacrament, to his five wounds, and to his love expressed through the symbol of the Sacred Heart.

Along with such particular traditions, one should also note some traditions that were less than happy and sometimes downright scandalous: the formation of ecclesiastical tribunals for tracking down, examining, and punishing heretics; the granting of indulgences (or remittance of temporal punishment due to sins for which sorrow has been expressed and forgiveness received) that could be blatantly misused; multiple benefices or properties attached to ecclesiastical offices that led, for instance, to bishops enriching themselves and depriving whole dioceses of spiritual leadership; relationships between Church and state that left one or other of these bodies deprived of a proper independence in their own spheres; forms of papal leadership that indulged power and greed and failed to exercise an authentic pastoral ministry inherited from St Peter. Some of these particular and scandalous traditions seriously wounded the Church, helped spark the sixteenth-century Reformation, and raised the issue of tradition and Scripture for the Council of Trent.[3]

Toward an ecumenical convergence?

In its decree of 8 April 1546 (Bettenson, 275–6; DzH 1501–9; ND 210–15), the Council of Trent did not intend to give a complete exposé of tradition but wished to oppose the 'Scripture alone' (*sola Scriptura*) principle of the Reformers. After acknowledging 'the Gospel' (which approximates to what this book calls 'foundational revelation') to be 'the source [singular] of all saving truth and [all] regulation of conduct', it pointed to the written books and unwritten (apostolic) traditions (plural) as 'containing' this truth and regulation. Over against any attempt to make the Bible the only guide to revelation and faith, Trent maintained that the Church's tradition also preserved and disclosed 'the Gospel'. We can expect to find revelation expressed, recorded, and actualized through various traditions, as well as through the inspired Scriptures.

But what did Protestants intend by *sola Scriptura*? The explosion of publications which followed when Johannes Gutenberg invented the printing press in 1450 promoted the humanist renaissance, which numbered many Reformers among its leaders. Excitement over the Scriptures and their message of forgiveness, grace, and freedom

---

[3] On the Reformation and Trent, see R. Bireley, *The Refashioning of Catholicism 1450–1700* (Basingstoke: Macmillan, 1999); H. J. Hillerbrand (ed.), *The Oxford Encyclopedia of the Reformation*, 4 vols. (Oxford: Oxford University Press, 1996); R. Po-Chia Hsia (ed.), *A Companion to the Reformation World* (Oxford: Blackwell, 2004); id. (ed.), *Reform and Expansion 1500–1660* (Cambridge: Cambridge University Press, 2007); J. W. O'Malley, *Trent and All That: Renaming Catholicism and the Early Modern Age* (Cambridge, Mass.: Harvard University Press, 2000).

joined forces with a vigorous reaction against decadent traditions and various commandments of the Church. The Reformers, when they rediscovered central themes of the New Testament, turned against such human enactments as the laws of fasting, the rule of annual confession, the practice of indulgences, and the obligation of celibacy for religious and Latin rite priests. Understanding the Bible and not human traditions to be the only authoritative rule for faith, Luther made *sola Scriptura* a battle cry in the campaign to reform the Catholic Church.

The main thrust of the principle could be put as follows. Within the limits of the biblical text the Holy Spirit actively expresses the truth of revelation and brings into play the saving reality of Jesus Christ. This activity, which authentically blesses the Christian with the presence of the Lord, remains restricted to the interpretation of the Scriptures. Hence the Bible alone takes on the role of being the exclusive rule of faith. No other authority really counts. The 1963 Faith and Order conference was to sum up the scope of *sola Scriptura* this way: 'The Protestant position has been an appeal to Holy Scripture alone, as the infallible and sufficient authority in all matters pertaining to salvation, to which all human tradition should be subjected.'[4] By the time of this conference, which took place during the Second Vatican Council (1962–5), a sea change had been occurring over the question of tradition and Scripture and brought a movement toward an ecumenical convergence. Before discussing that change, let us recall some of the issues that came up in the sixteenth century and subsequently.

Different ecclesiologies

The controversy over tradition and Scripture involved divergent views of the Church. To make a massive and risky generalization, Protestants differed from Catholics by distinguishing or even separating the Holy Spirit from the visible, historical community with its inherited traditions and authoritative magisterium (or office of teaching the good news in the name of Christ). In the short or the long run, the rejection of the magisterium meant *either* giving an

---

[4] P. C. Rodger and L. Vischer (eds.), *The Fourth World Conference on Faith and Order, Montreal 1963* (London: SCM Press, 1963), 51.

exclusive autonomy to the Scriptures (interpreted through private enlightenment coming from the Holy Spirit or—and this came later—in dependence on the latest results of biblical research), *or* allowing reason to take full charge, as typically happened in the Enlightenment. Over and against such trends, Catholics believed that the Holy Spirit both supported the wider community with its traditions and empowered the bishops, including the Bishop of Rome, to teach authoritatively, as well as to guide and sanctify other believers. In other words, they acknowledged the Spirit's active presence to extend beyond the situation of individual believers reading the Scriptures, preachers expounding the Scriptures, and ministers using the Scriptures in administering the sacraments.

Exclusive norm of faith?

Apart from a basic divergence over ecclesiology, Catholics and other Christians (Orthodox and many Anglicans) put further questions to the *sola Scriptura* view that the Bible by itself should determine Christian faith and practice.[5] To begin with, the Bible itself nowhere claims to function, independently of tradition, as the exclusive norm of faith. Largely the product of the Jewish and apostolic traditions, the Bible would never have come into existence without them. Hence, if the community's tradition, along with the inspiration of the Holy Spirit, led to the formation of the Scriptures, one would expect tradition to remain active in interpreting and applying the Scriptures, in bringing about the experience of (dependent) revelation, and in guiding the response of faith. The Bible nowhere declares its autonomy, as if it had supplanted tradition, the very force that brought it into existence, and become the exclusive norm of faith, once the apostolic generation had died out and the period of foundational revelation had ended. Without wanting this result, do those who separate the Bible from tradition finish up diminishing its value and impact by taking it out of its natural setting?

---

[5] See A. Dulles, 'Reflections on "Sola Scriptura"', in *Revelation and the Quest for Unity* (Washington, DC: Corpus Books, 1968); W. Pannenberg, 'The Crisis of the Scripture Principle', in *Basic Questions in Theology*, trans. G. H. Kehm, i (London: SCM Press, 1974), 1–14.

Some Catholic and other apologists insisted, moreover, that it took (post-apostolic) tradition to recognize *these* Scriptures as inspired and trustworthy witnesses to (foundational) revelation and to exclude other books from the biblical list or canon. In other words, tradition was needed to clarify just where the authoritative Scriptures were to be found. Yet, here one should share Karl Rahner's view that recognizing the extent of the canon was in some ways a special affair that did not exemplify the general relationship between tradition and Scripture.[6] That general relationship is seen rather in two different settings: where the Bible was first formed through Jewish and apostolic tradition and where it was later interpreted and applied through post-apostolic tradition.

A workable norm?

Critics came to point out how the overwhelming majority of Protestant Reformers never in fact drew their belief and practice solely from their experience of the Scriptures. As was argued above, in any rejection of tradition some traditional 'substratum' is always preserved, no matter how many factors are new. Thus nearly all the Reformers maintained, for example, the traditional belief in the Blessed Trinity, even though (as was pointed out in Chapters 5 and 6 above) a properly articulated doctrine of the Trinity was worked out only at two fourth-century councils. Moreover, most Protestants did not appeal to the *sola Scriptura* principle and abandon infant baptism, a practice which does not enjoy a clear and compelling warrant in the New Testament.

The difficulty of basing belief and practice simply on the Scriptures became even more acute when modern biblical scholarship began in the seventeenth century with the work of such writers as Richard Simon (1638–1712). Once historical exegetes began confining the sense of Scriptures to their strictly literal meaning and/or offered historical reconstructions of how these texts arose, it became more problematic to support Christian faith and practice simply and solely on the basis of the Scriptures. What learned professor should one follow in acknowledging the 'literal' meaning or accepting the reconstruction

---

[6] K. Rahner, 'Scripture and Tradition', in K. Rahner et al. (eds.), *Sacramentum Mundi*, vi (London: Burns & Oates, 1970), 54–7.

of given biblical texts? Add to this the rise of modern hermeneutics (or theories about the 'right' methods for interpreting scriptural and other texts), launched by F. D. E. Schleiermacher (1768–1834) and Wilhelm Dilthey (1833–1911).[7] Do we understand texts by seeking to recreate the intentions and creative process of the author? Or can texts mean something more than what the historical authors intended? What theory of hermeneutics should one follow? We will return to issues of scriptural meaning and interpretation raised by modern critical exegesis and hermeneutics; these disciplines have made easy appeals to the 'plain sense' of the Scriptures problematic.

Some writers, including Protestant ones,[8] have pointed out that the Bible sometimes brings as much multiplicity and even division as unity. If the literal meaning of the biblical texts emerged with the simple clarity of basic mathematics, the Scriptures might have effected agreement in interpreting and expressing the Christian experience of the divine self-communication. But we *create*, as well as discover, meaning when we read biblical and other texts. Not only changing public contexts but also what individuals bring to the reading of the Scriptures (their deep questions, previous experiences, inherited assumptions, actual commitments, and whole personal history) affect the meanings they proceed to champion. Right from the early centuries of Christianity, protagonists of division and even

---

[7] See B. C. Lategan, 'Hermeneutics', *ABD* iii. 149–55.

[8] At the 1963 Faith and Order conference, Ernst Käsemann (1906–98) highlighted the diversity of ecclesiologies found in the New Testament; see his lecture 'Unity and Multiplicity in the New Testament Doctrine of the Church', printed in *New Testament Questions of Today*, trans. W. J. Montague (London: SCM Press, 1969), 252–9. In this lecture he remarked that '[the Holy] Spirit and tradition must not be identified, but neither are they mutually exclusive' (256). See also a 1962 lecture given in Westphalia, 'Thoughts on the Present Controversy about Scriptural Interpretation', where he interprets *sola Scriptura* as meaning that the Church should be 'under' and not 'above' the Word of God: 'the relationship of the community and the Word of God is not reversible; there is no dialectical process by which the community created by the Word of God becomes at the same time for all practical purposes an authority set over the Word to interpret it, to administer it, to possess it. Naturally, the community has always the task of interpreting the Word afresh, so that it can become audible at all times and in all places. In a certain sense it has also the task of administering it, inasmuch as it creates ways and means for the Word to make itself heard. But possess it—never. For the community remains the handmaid of the Word' (ibid. 260–85, at 261–2). This language about the Church and her magisterium listening to the Word of God and not being 'above it' recurs three years later in Vatican II's constitution on revelation, *Dei Verbum* (no. 10).

of such heresies as Arianism have supported their interpretation of (foundational) revelation by appealing to the Scriptures. The verdict of history seems clear. The principle of *sola Scriptura*, if taken strictly, can hardly promise to bring agreement about right ways to interpret, express, and live out the experience of the divine self-communication in Christ.

Moreover, it seems too much to expect the Scriptures by themselves to provide answers, especially full and convincing ones, to new challenges. Faced with the new questions, unexpected problems, and whole medley of fresh experiences that characterize the modern world, how should we interpret and express—and that means re-interpret and re-express—the foundational experience of God's self-communication that the Scriptures have recorded and interpreted? More briefly, how can the Bible by itself respond to issues that have arisen only after the close of the apostolic age? For instance, Greek philosophy raised questions about the 'person' and 'nature(s)' of Christ that the New Testament could not be expected to answer clearly. The authors of the New Testament and the traditions they drew on did not face such questions and hence could hardly be expected by themselves to provide the appropriate answers. These questions touched something utterly basic about the Christian experience: the right way to discern, interpret, and express what or rather whom the disciples had experienced in the life, death, and resurrection of Jesus Christ, along with the coming of the Holy Spirit. The questions were crucial, but the New Testament by itself could not readily provide the answers.

Inappropriate language

As we saw above, Trent spoke of 'all saving truth and [all] regulation of conduct' being 'contained' in the inspired Scriptures and 'unwritten [apostolic] traditions'. So long as Catholic theologians understood revelation as God manifesting certain (otherwise undisclosed) truths, they remained comfortable with such language. They were concerned to establish where various revealed truths were to be found, and from a 'quantitative' point of view could raise the question: even if the Bible is not 'formally sufficient' (inasmuch as it needs to be interpreted by tradition), is it 'materially sufficient' in communicating the truths of revelation? That is to say, does it 'contain' all the revealed truths, or are some of them (e.g. the immaculate conception and assumption of the Blessed Virgin Mary) 'contained' only in tradition?

Juxtaposing tradition and Scripture in this 'material' way degraded both tradition and revelation. Tradition became a mere vehicle for transporting revealed contents, and precisely as such turned into something extrinsic to revelation. Revelation itself became something to be transported from one generation to the next. After the apostolic generation (which had received all the truths of revelation but did not record all of them in the inspired Scriptures) had died out, later Christians had the duty of preserving and handing on through tradition the full list of revealed truths. Despite the passage of time, faithful tradition, as well as the survival of the Bible, enabled the Church to preserve all the truths revealed at the foundation of Christianity.

Furthermore, post-Tridentine Catholic theology read Trent's decree as if it were teaching two 'materially' separate and equally valid 'sources' of revelation, one being tradition and the other being Scripture. J. H. Geiselmann (1890–1970), even if some details of his case had to be corrected, firmly established that the 'two source' theory of revelation could not claim support from Trent. That council reserved the term 'source' exclusively for 'the Gospel', or the *one* message of salvation communicated by Christ.[9]

A propositional view of revelation lay behind the typical Catholic version of the tradition–Scripture issue. Once the shift came to an interpersonal model of revelation (see Chapter 4 above), the whole discussion was reshaped. Whether in the foundational or in the dependent stage, revelation primarily means a gracious call to enter by faith into a relationship with the tripersonal God. This presence of saving revelation comes about when human beings prayerfully read the Scriptures, hear sermons, receive the sacraments, face various challenges in their lives, and undergo other experiences.[10] Revelation is something which happens and is not, properly speaking, 'contained' in a book (the Bible) or in traditions that believers inherit from previous generations of Christians. If divine revelation consisted

---

[9] See Congar, *Tradition and Traditions*, 411–12; W. Pannenberg, *Systematic Theology*, trans. G. W. Bromiley, i (Grand Rapids, Mich.: Eerdmans, 1991), 26–33; J. Ratzinger, in Rahner and Ratzinger, *Revelation and Tradition*, 50–68.

[10] See Ch. 2 above and the work of Sir Alister Hardy on religious experience.

primarily in a body of truths, one might remain at ease with the old terminology. But since revelation is the living reality of a personal experience of God, it is not happily described as being 'contained' in anything, whether it be Scripture or tradition.

The move to Montreal

The 1963 Faith and Order meeting in Montreal expressed a shift in Protestant views on tradition and Scripture. Take, for instance, the case of Gerhard Ebeling. When maintaining that reflection on proclamation is the proper task of theology, he stated that theology should also be concerned with 'the proclamation that has already taken place' and wrote: 'the task which theology is given to do is identical with the gift it receives from tradition.' Hence 'the task of handing on this tradition ... is clearly constitutive of theology'.[11] It may seem surprising that a theologian who was so consciously loyal to the Reformation as Ebeling could approach theology in the spirit of 'tradition seeking understanding' (*traditio quaerens intellectum*). In a long essay '"Sola Scriptura" and Tradition', he stated clearly: 'the Scripture-principle necessarily involves a doctrine of tradition.'[12] The change that we see here was partly due to the contribution to hermeneutics of Hans-Georg Gadamer (1900–2002). This Protestant philosopher incorporated tradition into interpretation and explained it not as an obstacle but as a necessary context for the recovery of meaning. Tradition is 'the way we relate to the past' and the way 'the past is present'. Hence 'we are always situated within traditions'; tradition 'is always part of us'.[13] Wolfhart Pannenberg, in a long study 'Hermeneutic: A Methodology for Understanding Meaning', reflects the significance of Gadamer through his attitude to the principle of tradition.[14]

[11] G. Ebeling, *Theology and Proclamation*, trans. J. Riches (London: Collins, 1966), 22–3; see also 15–16, 25–31. Paul Tillich understood tradition to be an indispensable feature of human and Christian life: *Systematic Theology*, iii (Chicago: Chicago University Press, 1963), 183–5. On the place of tradition in modern Protestant theology, see Congar, *Tradition and Traditions*, 459–82.

[12] G. Ebeling, *The Word of God and Tradition*, trans. S. H. Hooke (London: Collins, 1968), 102–47, at 144.

[13] See H.-G. Gadamer, *Truth and Method*, trans. J. Weinsheimer and D. G. Marshall (2nd edn. New York: Crossroad, 1989), 282.

[14] W. Pannenberg, *Theology and the Philosophy of Science*, trans. F. McDonagh (London: Darton, Longman & Todd, 1976), 156–224, esp. 197–8.

The 1963 Faith and Order conference disclosed several lines of convergence with Catholic reflection on tradition, which were to be incorporated in Vatican II's 1965 document, *Dei Verbum.* Some or even much of the justification for what was endorsed in Montreal and Rome came from Yves Congar's *Tradition and Traditions,* which originally appeared in French in two volumes (1960 and 1963). He was the leading Catholic theological expert (*peritus*) at Vatican II, having a hand in drafting eight out of the sixteen documents. Let me pick out six lines of convergence.

(a) The *model of revelation* as the divine self-communication which invites human beings to enter a communion of life and love with the tripersonal God was decisive for the Montreal report, Congar, and *Dei Verbum.* Since all agreed that revelation is primarily a personal encounter with God (who is the Truth) rather than the communication of a body of truths, the heat went out of any 'quantitative' debates about some revealed truths being 'contained' in Scripture and others being possibly 'contained' only in tradition. Thus *Dei Verbum* treated the theme of tradition only after it had clearly laid down in its first chapter some teaching on God's *self*-revelation.

(b) Both the Montreal report and *Dei Verbum* adopted 'total' views of tradition as that *whole living heritage* which forms the 'object' handed on. From this point on, let me talk of 'the Tradition' or *Traditum* (with a capital T) when I use the word in this sense. Thus *Dei Verbum* declared: 'What was handed on by the apostles comprises *all those things* that serve to make the people of God live holy lives and increase their faith. In this way the Church, in its doctrine, life, and worship, perpetuates and transmits to every generation *all* that it is, *all* that it believes' (no. 8; italics mine). The Montreal report likewise described Tradition in global terms as 'the Gospel itself, transmitted from generation to generation in and by the Church'.[15]

The Montreal report leaned toward interpreting the essential *Traditum* as 'Christ himself present in the life of the Church'.[16] It preferred to move beyond the *visible*, human realities which make up the Christian life of faith and emphasize the (invisible) truth and reality of the risen Christ present among believers. That presence constituted the heart of the *Traditum*: 'what is transmitted in the

---

[15] *Montreal 1963*, 50.
[16] Ibid.

process of tradition is the Christian faith, not only as a sum of tenets, but [also] as a living reality transmitted through the operation of the Holy Spirit. We can speak of the Christian Tradition (with a capital T), whose content is God's revelation and self-giving in Christ, present in the life of the Church.'[17] Then the report echoed what Käsemann had said in his lecture at the conference about the Word by applying it to the Tradition: 'the Tradition of the Church is not an object which we *possess* but a reality by which are *possessed*.'[18] Understood this way, the Tradition comes to more than merely the visible sum of beliefs and practices which Christians hand on. It is the saving presence of Christ engaged in a process of self-transmission through the Holy Spirit in the ongoing life of the Church.

(c) This brings us to a third item in the converging lines of agreement: *the invisible role of the Holy Spirit*. If the people of God form the visible bearers of *Tradition*, the action of transmission takes place 'through the power of the Holy Spirit'.[19] Ultimately, as Congar insisted, it is Christ's Spirit who maintains the integrity of the Tradition and thus guarantees the Church's essential fidelity to the foundational experience of the divine self-communication in Christ.[20] *Dei Verbum* introduced what amounted to the same point: 'The Holy Spirit, through whom the living voice of the Gospel rings out in the Church and through it in the world, leads believers to all truth, and makes the word of Christ dwell abundantly in them' (no. 8).

Under (b) above, I noted the total view of the Tradition or *Traditum* which both *Dei Verbum* and the Montreal report endorsed. This one *Traditum*, however, is expressed through *many traditions* or *tradita*. The Montreal report illustrated how this expression in particular traditions takes place in the spheres of liturgy, doctrine, and life: 'Tradition taken in this sense is actualized in the preaching of the Word, in the administration of the sacraments and worship, in Christian teaching and theology, and in mission and witness to Christ by the lives of members of the Church.'[21]

[17] Ibid. 52.
[18] Ibid. 54; italics mine.
[19] Ibid. 52.
[20] *Tradition and Traditions*, 338–46.
[21] *Montreal 1963*, 52.

In this terminology the specific traditions become 'the expressions and manifestations in diverse historical forms of the one truth and reality which is Christ'.[22] Vatican II's decree on ecumenism, *Unitatis Redintegratio*, even if apropos of the Eastern churches it spoke of an entire heritage rather than the Tradition, suggested similarly how the one *Traditum* gets expressed in the many *tradita*: 'this whole heritage of spirituality and liturgy, of discipline and theology, in the various traditions, belongs to the full catholic and apostolic character of the Church' (no. 17).

(d) This actualizing and expressing of the one Tradition in the many traditions entails not only a rich diversity but also a recurrent problem. Granted that we never find the Tradition 'neat' but always embodied in various traditions, do all of those particular traditions always actualize authentically the essential *Traditum*? The Montreal report put the issue as follows: 'Do all traditions which claim to be Christian contain the Tradition? How can we distinguish between traditions embodying the true Tradition and merely human traditions? Where do we find the genuine Tradition, and where impoverished tradition or even distortion of tradition?'[23]

A year later, at the third session of the Second Vatican Council, Cardinal Albert Meyer of Chicago raised what was essentially the same issue during a debate on the text that was to become *Dei Verbum*. He pointed to the 'limits' and 'defects' which show up repeatedly in the history of the Church and its traditions. He offered some examples: the long neglect of the doctrine of the resurrection, an exaggerated casuistry in moral theology, a non-liturgical piety, and the neglect of the Bible. He asked that the text under consideration should admit the existence of such defects and invoke the Scriptures as the norm that always helps the Church correct and perfect its life.[24] In fact, Cardinal Meyer's suggested addition was not adopted. But the final text of *Dei Verbum* did insist that the Scriptures should constantly 'rejuvenate' theology and the life of the Church (no. 24).

(e) *Dei Verbum* also alerted its readers to the difficulty of using the inspired Scriptures as the only source of certainty in assenting to given

---

[22] *Montreal 1963*, 52.
[23] Ibid.
[24] *Acta Synodalia Concilii Vaticani II*, III/III, 150–1.

truths, or—to transpose the point into the precise terms of our question—as the sole means for establishing where the authentic Tradition is to be found among diverse traditions. *Dei Verbum* declared: 'the Church does not draw its certainty about all revealed matters through the Scriptures alone' (no. 9). The Montreal report expressed the same difficulty this way: 'Loyalty to our confessional understanding of Holy Scripture produces both convergence and divergence in the interpretation of Scripture... How can we overcome the situation in which we all read the Scripture in the light of our own traditions?'[25] In other words, inherited traditions and other presuppositions cause Christians to *create* meaning, as well as discover it, when they read and interpret the Bible. The quality of their faith and practice will always determine, at least to some extent, how they interpret the biblical texts. Hence it is neither feasible nor even possible to use the Scriptures as the *sole* criterion for sorting out defective and authentic traditions, so as to find the Tradition within the traditions. What other criteria can support the Scriptures in the task of discernment and interpretation?

Discerning the tradition within the traditions

Fundamental theologians have the task of proposing criteria for examining particular traditions, with a view to discerning those that authentically express the foundational revelation and so help the good news of Christ to remain living and effective in the life of the Church. Faced with an array of specific traditions, how can the present generation of believers judge that these traditions truly represent the experience and interpretation of the original revelation transmitted by the apostolic generation of Christians? Can we establish true continuity and an essential identity between the apostolic Church and the contemporary community of believers with their array of traditions?

In *An Essay on the Development of Christian Doctrine* (1845),[26] John Henry Newman expounded seven 'notes' or tests for distinguishing between faithful development and corruption. The faithful 'development

---

[25] *Montreal 1963*, 53–4.
[26] London: Longman, Green & Co., 2nd edn. 1878; 14th impression 1909.

of an idea' involves preservation of its type, continuity of its principles, power of assimilation, logical sequence, anticipation of its future, conservative action upon its past, and chronic vigour. In the *Essay on Development* Newman aimed at scrutinizing eighteen hundred years of history and to explain 'certain apparent variations' in the teaching of Christian Christianity.[27] If he succeeded in so dealing with a sufficient number 'of the reputed corruptions, doctrinal and practical, of Rome', that might 'serve as a fair ground for trusting her in parallel cases where the investigation had not been pursued'.[28] Newman's tests, I have argued, have enduring value for distinguishing between doctrinal traditions that represent genuine developments from those that are corruptions.[29]

In an essay 'Criteria for Discerning Christian Traditions', I proposed eight such criteria: (1) the Church's official magisterium; (2) universality, antiquity, and consent (the 'canon' from St Vincent of Lérins: 'what is believed everywhere, always, and by everyone, this is truly and properly Catholic'); (3) the 'sensus fidei' (which, unlike the Vincentian canon, focuses on the present rather than the past); (4) continuity with the apostolic Church; (5) the Nicene Creed and the Apostles' Creed; (6) apostolicity; (7) the Scriptures; and (8) the risen Lord.[30] A few words about some of these criteria is in order.

Apropos of (1), Catholics enjoy in the Church's magisterium a criterion for receiving what previous generations have passed on to them and for discerning what the Spirit could be saying now to the churches. The magisterium will guide choices in that permanent dialogue between inherited traditions and new experiences. Nevertheless, this criterion does not suffice by itself. On given issues the magisterium may pronounce only after many years have elapsed. In the meantime believers will have to decide: does this or that tradition misrepresent or deviate from the Gospel? Moreover, the magisterium is only a proximate criterion, which points beyond itself. The Pope

---

[27] Ibid. 7.
[28] Ibid. 32.
[29] G. O'Collins, 'Newman's Seven Notes: The Case of the Resurrection', in I. Ker and A. G. Hill (eds.), *Newman after a Hundred Years* (Oxford: Clarendon Press, 1990), 337–52.
[30] G. O'Collins, 'Criteria for Discerning Christian Traditions', *Science et esprit*, 30 (1978), 295–302; reprinted with modifications in R. Latourelle and G. O'Collins (eds.), *Problems and Perspectives of Fundamental Theology*, trans. M. J. O'Connell (Ramsey, NJ: Paulist Press, 1982), 327–39; and in O'Collins, *Fundamental Theology* (London: Darton, Longman & Todd, 1982), 208–24.

and bishops in their magisterial role do not constitute the ultimate criterion but are bound to adhere to Christ's saving revelation.[31] As *Dei Verbum* puts this subordination, 'the task of authentically interpreting the Word of God, whether in its written form or in the form of tradition, has been entrusted to the living teaching office (magisterium) of the Church alone... This magisterium is not above the Word of God but serves it' (no. 10).

The Vincentian canon (2), which overlaps with the fourth, fifth, and sixth criteria, calls for various modifications to make it read, for instance, as follows: 'what has been believed everywhere, always, and by everyone *precisely as coming from the foundational revelation communicated through Christ*, this is truly and properly Catholic.' Yet readers should be alerted to further limits in the canon. For example, even if we were to take 'everyone' in the sense of the moral unanimity of practising believers, what of prophetic minorities in the Church who challenged some inherited traditions and eventually, but only eventually, have been proved right in their discernment of the gospel demands? The number of persons holding an idea need not guarantee its objective character; otherwise majorities could never be wrong. Newman put his finger on a further problem raised by the words 'always' and 'everywhere': 'What is meant by being "taught always"? Does it mean in every century, or every year, or every month? Does "everywhere" mean in every country, or in every diocese? And does "the consent of the Fathers" require us to produce the testimony of every one of them? How many Fathers, how many places, how many instances constitute a fulfillment of the test proposed?'[32]

With the needed adjustments, the Vincentian canon, however, classically recalls the intersubjective nature of inherited Christian truth and life, which should play a role for those discerning particular traditions. Any judgements and decisions about such traditions should be checked against the collective experience of earlier Christians. Certain trajectories and movements can suggest ways in which the enduring presence of Christ's Holy Spirit has shaped different Christian traditions. The canon might be rephrased this way: 'What

---

[31] Vatican II, Dogmatic Constitution on the Church (*Lumen Gentium*), no. 25.
[32] Newman, *An Essay on the Development of Christian Doctrine* (London: James Toovey, 1845), 12.

we can discover to have been believed and practised as part of the good news *at least* sometimes, in some places, and by some Christians, if it promises once again to be *life-giving*, that can truly and properly direct our discernment of present traditions and experiences.' Understood this way, the canon acts as a means of 'retrieval', a principle that guided reforms (e.g. in the liturgy) introduced by the Second Vatican Council.[33]

The criterion of the *sensus fidei* (3) looks to the present, spiritual sensitivity found in the whole body of believers. Here and now the Holy Spirit guides their instinctive discernment in matters of faith. Constituting the body of Christ, they enjoy, as *Dei Verbum* put it, an 'intimate sense' of the 'spiritual realities which they experience' (no. 8). Thus the Holy Spirit, by shaping the corporate mind of the Church, provides a further criterion for testing and scrutinizing inherited traditions.[34]

As regards criteria (7) the Scriptures and (8) the risen Lord, let me return to them in a moment. Thus far I have invoked the notes of Newman and some of my own earlier work to press a conclusion: fundamental theology has the responsibility of developing principles by which to assess inherited traditions and establish whether or not they express the foundational revelation that comes to us from the apostles. Let me now present four criteria that will pull their weight in this work of discernment.

To discern the Tradition within the traditions, we might ask *four questions*: first, does some particular tradition (e.g. in church governance or liturgy) contribute to our being led more clearly by the Holy Spirit and Christ? Second, does it help us to worship together better? Third, is our decision about this or that tradition illuminated and supported by prayerful reflection on the Scriptures? Fourth, does this decision inspire us to a more generous service of the needy?

---

[33] On the Vincentian canon, see Bettenson, 91–3; T. Guarino, 'Vincent of Lerins and the Hermeneutical Question', *Gregorianum*, 75 (1994), 491–523; O'Collins, 'Criteria for Interpreting the Traditions', in Latourelle and O'Collins (eds.), *Problems and Perspectives of Fundamental Theology*, 327–39, at 329–33; M. Parmentier, 'Vinzens von Lérins', *TRE* xxxv. 109–11; and *Oxford Dictionary*, 1712–13.

[34] See Ormond Rush, *The Eyes of Faith: The Sense of the Faithful and the Church's Reception of Revelation* (Washington, DC: Catholic University of America Press, 2009).

These four questions persistently overlap: the common worship of Christians (question two) is unthinkable without its being nourished from biblical readings and their thoughtful exposition (question three). Likewise eucharistic worship involves the first question, inasmuch as it includes the 'remembering' (*anamnesis*) of Christ's life, death, and resurrection and the 'invocation' (*epiclesis*) of the Holy Spirit. While recognizing how the questions overlap, let us see what each might contribute toward discerning the values or disvalues of particular traditions.

The first question puts the work of discernment within the experience of growing, through the Holy Spirit as adopted brothers and sisters of Christ, into the life of God. Do some inherited traditions (e.g. traditional liturgical and catechetical customs and texts) help us to experience more vividly what Christ has brought us: the forgiveness of sins, the new life of grace, and the hope of glory? Do these traditions facilitate the sanctifying work of the Spirit?

Our second question centres on common worship. Do particular liturgical practices and texts help the worshipping community to give glory to the Father, the Son, and the Holy Spirit? Do such traditions enhance the experience of those being baptized and confirmed and, in particular, those sharing actively in the celebration of the Eucharist? To adapt a classical axiom, 'the law of praying' (*lex orandi*) is 'the law of discerning' (*lex discernendi*) the traditions we have inherited.

Thirdly, the Bible provides us with the normative biblical witness to the foundational revelation which created the Christian community. In the period of dependent revelation, the Scriptures must guide and nourish the Church and every aspect of Christian life. The concluding chapter of *Dei Verbum* began by endorsing a comparison between the Eucharist and the Scriptures which we find in the fathers of the Church and which has its deepest roots in Chapter 6 of John's Gospel. Like and along with the eucharistic body of Christ, the Scriptures are the bread of life that feeds us on our pilgrimage through this world (no. 21). That closing chapter offers a wonderful dream about the way in which the Sacred Scriptures should lead, foster, and strengthen the entire life of the Church. It goes without saying that the Scriptures are essential for evaluating current traditions. What conclusion should be reached when we put under the Word of God various traditions: for instance, about the organization of parishes, dioceses, and the worldwide Church?

We come, lastly, to the fourth question, which has a special, terminological link with the second. In the New Testament and the works of early Christian writers, *leitourgia* referred both to community worship and the obligation to meet the material needs of others. The double usage of this term suggests the essential bond between worship and social action through the service of the suffering. Those whom Jesus expected his followers to help included the hungry, the thirsty, strangers, the naked, the sick, and prisoners (Matt. 25: 31–46). This list of suffering people with whom Christ identified himself did not explicitly include a typical Old Testament pair of sufferers, widows and orphans. But the list was obviously open-ended. Christ's parable of the Good Samaritan powerfully illustrated what he wanted from all: the willingness to help any human being in distress (Luke 10: 30–7). The words of Jesus from Matthew 25 and Luke 10, along with the parable of the rich man and the poor Lazarus (Luke 16: 19–31), have influenced and disturbed the conscience of Christians down through the centuries. They should also influence their discernment of various traditional structures they have inherited from the past. Do these traditional structures support and embody Christ's call to minister to the destitute? Do they encourage us to recognize and serve the crucified Jesus in those who suffer terrible need?

These then are four daunting questions Christians should put to themselves when interpreting and evaluating the array of traditions that the previous generation has handed on to them. I am not alleging that the four questions can be answered easily and at once. But if we do not even ask these questions, it seems difficult, if not impossible, to discern faithfully the traditions that embody the true Tradition and what Christ is calling us to change, reform, or strengthen in all that we have received from the past.

Revelation, tradition, and Scripture

Before moving forward to two chapters on the Bible, it seems useful to pull matters together and outline a workable understanding of the relationship between revelation, tradition, and the Scriptures—an understanding provisionally sketched in Chapters 4 and 5 above. First, the apostles and those associated with them experienced the fullness of foundational revelation and salvation (through Christ and the Holy Spirit), and faithfully responded by expressing and interpreting this once-and-for-all experience by their preaching. In and through this preaching, the conferral of baptism, and the celebration of the Eucharist, they fully founded the Church. The apostolic age brought not only the founding of the Church but also the composition of the twenty-seven inspired books of the New Testament. Under the guidance of the Holy Spirit these books (which drew on personal experiences and memories as well as on oral and written traditions) fixed for all time the apostolic preaching as the normative response to the complete revelation of God in Christ and through the Holy Spirit.[35]

Secondly, the books of the New Testament, together with the inspired writings of the Old Testament, do not as such coincide with revelation. The difference between revelation and Scripture is the difference between a reality and a (written and inspired) record. We cannot simply identify revelation with the Bible, even if, as we shall see in a later chapter, we rightly speak of these Scriptures as 'the word of God'. In a normative way the Scriptures record the human experience of foundational revelation, as well as the ways in which men and women responded to, interpreted, and remembered that experience. This scriptural witness remains distinct from the experience of revelation itself, just as a written record differs from a lived reality.

Where foundational revelation came *before* the Scriptures, dependent revelation comes *after* the writing of these Scriptures ended. Hearing, reading, and praying the Scriptures can bring about now the experience of (dependent) divine revelation. The biblical texts help initiate what believers experience today of the divine self-communication. Yet once again in this period of dependent revelation, the Scriptures differ from revelation itself in the way that an 'inspiring' record differs from the lived event of dialogue with God.

Thirdly and similarly, tradition never literally coincides with revelation. As such, tradition can hand on revealed truths but cannot precisely 'hand on' the experience of revelation. It may prove revealing in the sense of recalling moments of revelation, interpreting it, and offering means to experience it. Thus revelation differs from tradition

---

[35] The sacred writers were not necessarily aware of doing all that. As we shall see in Ch. 10, the results of their activity cannot be simply measured by their conscious intentions.

as a lived experience is to be distinguished from the community's expression of that experience which is transmitted through history. To sum up: we cannot simply identify either tradition or Scripture as such with the experience of God's revealing and saving presence.

Fourthly, how should the post-apostolic tradition of the Church be understood and how does it relate to the Scriptures? All active members of the Church are engaged in the *process* of transmitting tradition and bringing about for others the experience of the divine self-communication. They do so by pondering the Scriptures, celebrating the Eucharist, administering and receiving the sacraments, preaching and evangelizing, composing sacred music, writing catechisms, teaching prayers, involvement in religious education, and through all the other customs, beliefs, and practices that make up the total reality of the Church and give Christians their continuity, identity, and unity. Seen as such an active process (*actus tradendi*), the tradition of the post-apostolic Church includes but obviously goes well beyond the Scriptures. Handing on, interpreting, and applying the Scriptures is only one, albeit major, part of tradition's activity.

Fifthly, in this active process there exists a *mutual priority* between tradition and the Scriptures. On the one hand, authentic tradition seeks to remain faithful to the normative account of Christian origins and identity that it finds in the inspired Scriptures. On the other hand, fresh challenges and a changing context require tradition to do what the Scriptures cannot do for themselves. It must interpret and apply them, so that they can become the revealing word of God to new readers and hearers today. In this way, tradition (and the Christian life to which it gives shape and force) not only forms an extended commentary on the Scriptures but also allows them to come into their own and let Christ speak to people.

Sixthly, in this whole process the members of the magisterium have a special but not exclusive role as 'carriers' of tradition and (subordinate) mediators effecting the lived event of revelation. Tradition as an action is thus exercised in a particular way by the bishops, inasmuch as they transmit matters of faith and Christian practice. By formulating statements of faith and taking practical decisions which affect the life of the Church, they introduce some fresh elements into the tradition that will be transmitted to the next generation of believers. The exercise of the magisterium influences and modifies what will be handed down.

Seventhly, the whole people of God will not transmit all that they received exactly as they received it. Language shifts occur, the flux of experience calls forth fresh interpretations and activities, and the emerging signs of the times offer their special messages to believers. Certainly an essential continuity is maintained, and that happens not simply because one generation hands on to the next the unchanged text of the Bible. The dependent revelation which is experienced now remains essentially continuous with the original, foundational revelation which the apostles received in faith. At the same time, the whole Church, no less than the members of the magisterium, modifies to some degree that aggregate of beliefs, customs, and practices (tradition as 'object') which one generation of believers transmits to the next.

To draw all this together: understood *either* as the active process (*actus tradendi*) *or* as the object handed on (the *traditum*), tradition includes Scripture rather than simply standing alongside it. In both senses tradition is much more extensive than Scripture.

9

Revelation, the Bible, and Inspiration

The last chapter engaged itself with tradition and its complex relationship with the Scriptures. The Second Vatican Council's document on revelation, *Dei Verbum*, pointed to three essential moments in this link: tradition and Scripture 'flow from the same divine well-spring' (foundational revelation), 'in some fashion form together one thing' (dependent revelation), and 'move toward the same goal' (the final fullness of revelation and salvation) (no. 9). Having focused on tradition and its role vis-à-vis past, present, and future revelation, let me turn to the connections between the Scriptures and revelation; that will lay the ground to set forth some characteristics of biblical inspiration. So, first, what is the relationship between the Scriptures and revelation?

It should be pointed out, right from the start, that, despite its high doctrine of biblical inspiration, Christianity remains a religion of the word, not of the book. God's living word, above all in the form of the incarnate Word (the Revealer and the Revelation), takes precedence over the inspired book. Earlier (e.g. in Chapters 4 and 8) we have already distinguished between revelation and the Scriptures. The ways in which revelation goes beyond the Scriptures should become clearer in the course of this chapter.

The formation of the Bible

Let me begin by considering the *genesis* of the Bible, illustrating differences between revelation and the Scriptures. We will then be in a position to reflect on the *content* of the Bible in relationship with revelation.[1]

1. The Bible cannot be simply identified with revelation. As a living, interpersonal event, revelation takes place or happens. God initiates, at particular times and places and to particular persons, some form of self-communication. Chapter 7 drew from John's Gospel to show how such revelation could occur. The divine initiative achieves its goal and revelation happens when human beings respond in faith to God's self-disclosure.

As such the Scriptures are not a living, interpersonal event in the sense just described. They are written records which by the special inspiration of the Holy Spirit came into existence through the work of some believers at certain stages in the foundational history of God's people. The Scriptures differ then from revelation in the way that written texts differ from something that actually happens between persons—between human persons and the divine Persons.

In the long history of the Bible's composition, the gift of revelation and the special impulse to write the Scriptures were not only distinguishable but also separable. This is another way of expressing the difference that concerns us. Either directly or through such mediators as the prophets and, above all, Jesus himself, the special divine revelation was offered to *all* the people. God self-communication was there for everyone. The special impulse to write the Scriptures was a particular charism given only to those who, under the guidance of the Holy Spirit, composed or helped to compose the sacred texts.

---

[1] W. J. Abraham, *The Divine Inspiration of the Holy Scriptures* (Oxford: Oxford University Press, 1981); L. Alonso Schökel, *The Inspired Word*, trans. F. Martin (New York: Herder & Herder, 1965); 'Bible', *Oxford Dictionary*, 200–2; R. F. Collins, 'Inspiration', in R. E. Brown, J. A. Fitzmyer, and R. E. Murphy (eds.), *The New Jerome Biblical Commentary* (London: Geoffrey Chapman, 1989), 1023–33; T. M. Crisp, 'On Believing that the Scriptures are Divinely Inspired', in O. D. Crisp and M. C. Rea (eds.), *Analytic Theology: New Essays in the Philosophy of Theology* (Oxford: Oxford University Press, 2009), 187–213; C. Focant, 'Holy Scripture', in J.-Y. Lacoste (ed.), *Encyclopedia of Christian Theology* , ii (New York: Routledge, 2004), 718–25; T. M. McCall, 'Scripture as the Word of God', in Crisp and Rea (eds.), *Analytic Theology*, 171–86; J. W. Rogerson and J. M. Lieu (eds.), *The Oxford Handbook of Biblical Studies* (Oxford: Oxford University Press, 2006); S. M. Schneiders, 'Inspiration and Revelation', in *The New Interpreter's Dictionary of the Bible*, iii (Nashville: Abingdon Press, 2008), 57–63; B. Vawter, *Biblical Inspiration* (London: Hutchinson, 1972).

To be sure, the Scriptures were written for everyone. But the charism of inspiration was given only to a limited number of persons.

Even in the case of the sacred writers themselves, revelation and the charism of inspiration did not coincide. Opening themselves in faith to the divine self-manifestation was one thing, being guided by the Holy Spirit to set down certain things in writing was another. God's revelation impinged on their entire lives. In cases that we know of, the charism on inspiration functioned only in limited periods of their lives. The divine revelation was operative in Paul's life before and after his call/conversion (around AD 36). Around AD 50 he wrote his first (inspired) letter that has been preserved for us, and composed other letters during the 50s and into the early 60s. The divine self-communication affected Paul's entire history, the charism of inspiration only the last decade or so of his apostolic activity.

2. Reflection on the *content* of the Bible yields another angle on the difference I wish to express. The Bible witnesses to and interprets various persons, events, and words that mediated, more or less directly, the divine self-revelation. The Letter to the Hebrews acknowledges the Son of God as the climax in a series of mediators of revelation (Heb. 1: 1–2). A wide variety of events have manifested God and the divine designs: from an exodus, an exile, births of various children, through to a crucifixion and resurrection. Prophetic utterances, parables, creeds (e.g. Deut. 26: 5–9; Rom. 1: 3–4), hymns (e.g. Phil. 2: 6–11; Col. 1: 15–20), summaries of proclamation (e.g. 1 Cor. 15: 3–5), and—supremely—the words of Jesus himself serve to disclose the truth of God and human beings.

At the same time the Bible *also* records matters which do not seem to be connected, or at least closely connected, with divine revelation. The language of courtship and human love fashions the Song of Songs, an inspired book that, paradoxically, has no explicitly religious content. Alongside lofty prescriptions to guide the worship and life of Israel as a holy people, Leviticus includes many regulations about wine and food, about the sick and diseased (in particular, about lepers), about sexual relations, and about other matters that can hardly be derived from some special divine revelation. This book (which probably took its final shape in the sixth or fifth century) contains pages of rituals and laws, which usually look as if they came from old human customs rather than from some, more or less, dramatic divine disclosure. The Book of Proverbs puts together the

moral and religious instruction that professional teachers offered
Jewish youth in the period after the Babylonian exile. This wisdom
of the ages is based on lessons drawn from common human experience,
and is in part (Prov. 22: 17–24: 22) modelled upon the *Instruction of
Amenemope*, an Egyptian book of wisdom. Where religious faith
supports Proverbs' view of an upright human life, Ecclesiastes
seems to use reason alone to explore the meaning of human existence
and the (limited) value of our life which ends in the oblivion of death.

Admittedly, one might well argue that in human love, ancient
religious traditions, the experience of the ages, and the use of reason,
God is also at work to disclose the truth about our nature and destiny
and about the Creator from whom we come and to whom we go.
A theology that recognizes dramatic, special events as the *only* appropriate means and mediators of the divine would be a diminished
version of revelation. God can certainly use 'ordinary' channels to
communicate with human beings and shed new light on the divine
and human mystery.

Nevertheless, whole sections of the Bible (e.g. much of wisdom
literature) speak much more of the human condition and less vividly
of divine revelation. That the inspiration of the Holy Spirit operated
in the writing of these books is no immediate gauge of the 'amount'
of divine self-revelation to which they witness. On any showing, they
report and proclaim matters of revelation less intensely and closely
than other sections of the Bible. Simply from the presence of special
divine inspiration in the composition of a book, one cannot draw any
necessary conclusions about the degree to which God's self-revelation
shows through that book.

Add too the way many chapters of the Bible focus on the human
story of individuals and groups: for instance, certain sections of the
historical books in the Old Testament. Some of this material can seem
a long way from God's saving self-communication. Take, for instance,
the story of the concubine's murder and the subsequent revenge on the
Benjaminites (Judg. 19: 1–20: 48), Saul's visit to the witch of Endor
(1 Sam. 28: 1–25), and the death of Ananias and Sapphira (Acts 5: 1–11).
One might argue that such passages illustrate how people failed to
respond to the overtures of divine revelation. Stories of human failures, sins, and even atrocities were also things recorded under the
impulse of divine inspiration. But that fact does not as such guarantee

anything about their positive value for revelation. In short, an inspired record is one thing, revelatory 'content' is another.

The use of the Bible

In distinguishing between revelation and biblical inspiration, this chapter has so far directed attention to the formation of the Scriptures in the past. What does the relationship of revelation and inspiration look like if we turn to the role of the Scriptures in the life of Church today?

1. First of all, Christian experience witnesses every day to the way biblical texts convey the divine revelation. Passages from the prophets and the psalms, the words of Jesus from the Gospels, and reflections of Paul let the truth about the divine and human mystery shine forth. Such scriptural texts repeatedly bring an inner light to those who ponder them prayerfully. They can hear God speaking to them through these words. What was long ago written down under the guidance of the divine inspiration can become inspiring and illuminating today. To echo *Dei Verbum* (which quotes here St Ambrose of Milan), when we read the Scriptures, we listen to God (no. 25).

Christian experience also shows how less 'promising' parts of the Bible may enjoy such a revealing impact. At first glace, some scriptural texts can come across as 'primitive' (e.g. Saul's visit to the witch of Endor), 'boring' (e.g. the genealogies in 1 Chron. 1–9 or in the infancy narratives of Matthew and Luke), or so filled with hatred as to seem quite opposed to the revelation of divine love (e.g. Ps. 137: 7–9). Such passages can, however, act as negative 'foils' which bring out the true nature of divine revelation and our appropriate response to it. Saul's nocturnal visit to the witch is at the very least a cautionary tale: we should not try to enter that way into contact with the other world. In Psalm 137 we hear some exiled Israelites crying out for savage vengeance on their Babylonian and Edomite enemies. Their prayer for revenge works to illuminate God's loving concern for all (Jonah 4: 11) and Jesus' prayer that his executioners be forgiven (Luke 23: 34). As regards the biblical genealogies, they may not say much to many people in the North Atlantic world. But for some other cultures to lack knowledge of one's ancestors is to suffer diminishment in one's personal identity. In any case, given the chequered career of some who feature in biblical genealogies, including those of Jesus himself (Matt. 1: 1–17; Luke 3: 23–38), we could be helped to grasp more deeply the truth that 'God writes straight but with crooked lines'.

In short, experience shows how any biblical text can lead people to know the truth about God and the human condition. Normally the 'great' sections of the Scriptures have this revelatory impact. But thoroughly 'unpromising' scriptural texts can trigger or renew people's knowledge of God. This point has more relevance nowadays, since the lectionary for readings at the Sunday and weekday Eucharist contains a much broader selection from the Bible.

Before moving on from the revelatory power that the Scriptures exhibit in practice, let me add a few words about their heavily symbolic language. This language contributes to their power to evoke the truth and trigger moments of revelation. No book in the Bible surpasses John's Gospel in its symbolic force. One could test that assertion by opening oneself in prayer to the way it uses the cure of a blind man to present Jesus as the light of the world (John 9: 1–41). A sample passage from the Book of Revelation exemplifies how well its imaginative, symbolic language communicates the divine promise:

And I saw the holy city, new Jerusalem, coming down out of heaven from God, prepared as a bride adorned for her husband. And I heard a loud voice from the throne saying: 'Behold, the dwelling place of God is with human beings. He will dwell with them, and they shall be his people, and God himself will be with them. He will wipe away every tear from their eyes, and death shall be no more, neither shall there be mourning nor crying nor pain any more, for the former things have passed away.' And he who sat upon the throne said, 'Behold, I make all things new.'   (Rev. 21: 3–5)

Let me cite two further examples of biblical symbolism. The opening words of Second Isaiah are unrivalled in their power to console and generate trust in God's tender concern for those homesick for 'another' place where they shall truly be themselves (Isa. 40: 1–11). From the beginning of Christianity the highly symbolic story of the passion told by all four Gospels and culminating in Jesus' crucifixion at the place of the skull has invited all to 'look upon him whom they have pierced' (John 19: 37) and find in the events of Good Friday (and Easter Sunday) the climax of God's self-communication.

2. Having acknowledged the revealing power of the Bible, let me now call attention to some limits and qualifications. It is not and was not the only means for receiving divine revelation. Before the Hebrew Scriptures came to be written, God had already initiated the special revealing and saving history of the chosen people. Christians recognized in Jesus the climax of that revelatory and redemptive history, two decades before the first book of what came to be called the New Testament was written. Reading St Paul triggered Augustine's conversion. But it was a night of reading Teresa of Avila's autobiography that moved Edith Stein toward Christian faith and, eventually, martyrdom. An immense range of experiences can communicate to Christians the divine self-communication, even to the point of radically changing their lives. These experiences, at least initially, need not have anything directly to do with the Scriptures. The data gathered by Sir Alister Hardy's Religious Experience and Research Centre amply supports that conclusion (see Chapter 2 above).

God's revelation, as we shall see in Chapter 11, reaches non-Christians without their reading or hearing the Bible. To some extent at least, their religious environment and personal experience can mediate to them the truth of God and of our human condition. Only those out of touch with non-Christians and their world (and unaware of the testimony of the Bible itself[2]) will deny the evidence for the divine saving and revealing activity on their behalf. God speaks to them through means other than the Bible.

A final limit to be noted in the Bible's revelatory impact is a sad one. It is more than possible to read the Scriptures without being open to the Spirit. A merely 'scientific' knowledge of the Bible might yield little by way of knowing the God to whom the Scriptures testify. The question of scientific and spiritual exegesis will turn up in the next chapter. Here I simply wish to observe the regrettable fact that someone's extensive 'technical' knowledge of the Bible does not automatically guarantee for him or her that the Bible will become a vehicle of revelation. One may know the 'letter' but not the 'spirit' of the Scriptures.

3. To conclude: as an inspired text, the Bible illuminates constantly the divine and human mystery. It is indispensable for Christian

---

[2] See G. O'Collins, *Salvation for All: God's Other Peoples* (Oxford: Oxford University Press, 2008).

existence, both collectively and individually. Nevertheless, revelation or the living word of God proves a larger and wider reality than the Bible and is not limited to the Bible. It is an error to identify revelation with the Scriptures. God's living and authoritative word is not subordinated to a written text, even an inspired one. This fact explains and justifies the order in which *Dei Verbum* handles the matter. It clarifies the greater reality of revelation (Chapter 1) before turning to tradition (Chapter 2) and the inspired Scriptures (Chapters 3–6).

Nevertheless, three reasons justify calling the Scriptures 'the word of God' (*Dei Verbum*, 9).[13] a) First, unlike any other religious texts available for Christian (and, in the case of the Hebrew Scriptures, Jewish) use, they were written under the special guidance of the Holy Spirit. In a unique way, God was involved in the composition of these texts. (b)[13] Second, all the Scriptures have some relationship to *foundational* revelation—to those persons, events, and words which mediated God self-communication through to its fullness with Christ and his apostles. Even in the case of those books and passages of the Bible that focus less immediately and vividly on the divine revelation, some link can be found. Thus the love poems that make up the Song of Songs relate themselves to the history of revelation and salvation by invoking key personages and places in that history (Solomon, David, and Jerusalem). The bridegroom of these poems suggests Israel's God, who like a loving husband wishes to woo again a faithless wife (Hos. 2: 14–23).[13] (c) Third, in the post-apostolic period of *dependent* revelation any section of the Scriptures could become for human beings a living word of God. John's Gospel formulates its revelatory and salvific scope in terms that can be applied to the whole Bible: 'These things have been written so that you may believe that Jesus is the Christ, the Son of God, and that believing you may have life in his name' (20: 31; see 2 Tim. 3: 15–17). Our 'believing' completes divine revelation, and 'life' is the salvific consequence of accepting revelation.

The inspiration of the Bible

If it is an error to identify revelation *tout court* with the Scriptures, what are we to make of the divine activity of inspiration that produced the Scriptures, the unique record of the foundational

Jewish-Christian experiences of God and the human responses they evoked? By witnessing to collective and individual experiences of saving revelation and the new self-identity those experiences initiated, the Bible offers subsequent generations the possibility of sharing those experiences and accepting that new identity. The Scriptures are both an effect and a cause of the divine self-revelation. The record of what was experienced *then* helps to instigate and interpret the experience of God's self-communication *now*. Retrospectively the Bible records various experiences and realities. Prospectively these inspired writings can prompt religious experience in their later readers.

We might describe the essence of biblical inspiration as a special impulse from the Holy Spirit to set certain things down in writing. This distinguishes biblical inspiration from prophetic inspiration, the impulse to speak and act in certain ways that we examined in Chapter 4 above. Such prophetic inspiration to *speak* can, unquestionably, be closely connected with the biblical inspiration to *write*. Characteristically the Old Testament prophets were speakers (and actors) rather than writers. It was generally left to others to collect, expand, interpret, and publish their prophetic utterances. These (almost always anonymous) writers, as the immediate authors of the prophetic books of the Bible, enjoyed the charism of biblical inspiration. Nevertheless, their charism obviously presupposed that Isaiah, Jeremiah, and others had the prophetic inspiration to speak. It was natural for the Second Letter of Peter to describe the written texts of the prophetic writings as if they were the *spoken words* of the prophets: 'no prophecy of Scripture is a matter of one's own inspiration, because no prophecy ever came by the impulse of man, but men moved by the Holy Spirit spoke from God' (2 Pet. 1: 20–1). Both the spoken and written word, along with their interpretation, enjoyed a divine origin and authority.[3] The author of the Book of Revelation likewise blurred any distinction between the spoken (prophetic) word and the written word when he called his book 'words of prophecy' to be listened to (Rev. 22: 18).[4]

---

[3] See R. Bauckham, *Jude, 2 Peter* (Waco, Tex.: Word Books, 1983), 228–35; G. L. Green, *Jude & 2 Peter* (Grand Rapids, Mich.: Baker Academic, 2008), 229–34.

[4] See R. Bauckham, *The Climax of Prophecy: Studies on the Book of Revelation* (Edinburgh: T. & T. Clark, 2003); H. B. Huffmon et al., 'Prophecy', *ABD* v. 477–502, at 494–5, 500.

Hence, almost inevitably, the early Church understood the sacred writers to have the role of prophets, and later theologians like Thomas Aquinas interpreted biblical inspiration as prophetic.[5] However, precisely as such biblical inspiration is a God-given impulse to write rather than to speak. Therefore, from this point on, unless otherwise noted, 'inspiration' will be taken in that sense of biblical inspiration.

Since the books of the Bible have been written under a special impulse and guidance of the Holy Spirit, we can call God the 'author' of these books and the Bible itself 'the word of God'. Thus the effect of inspiration was to make their human words into the word of God, and allows us to call the Scriptures 'sacred'. God stands at their origin. But what form did this 'special impulse' take? Any answer affects what is meant by calling God 'the author'. Eight points enter our account of inspiration.

1. Various fathers of the Church and later theologians adopted the model of *verbal dictation* when describing inspiration. In this view the inspired writers heard a heavenly voice dictating the words which they were to set down. They obediently reproduced the text that was revealed to them. Christian art sometimes reflects this reduction of the inspired writers to the status of mere stenographers. In the Pazzi Chapel of the Basilica of Santa Croce in Florence, for instance, Luca della Robbia represents the evangelists in terracotta. An eagle has arrived from heaven to hold the text for John to copy down. A lion performs the same service for Mark. Some fathers of the Church likewise used images that minimalized the role of the biblical writers. In the second century Athenagoras described the Old Testament prophets as a flute played by the divine musician. Gregory the Great (d. 604) believed that the human authors enjoyed no more significance in producing the Bible than a pen in the hand of an author.

Such approaches interpret inspiration in a mechanical way which drastically reduces the human role in writing the Scriptures. The sacred writers ceased to be real authors, and became at best mere secretaries who faithfully took down the divine dictation. A set of tape-recorders could have served God's purposes just as well. In the verbal dictation view the divine causality counted for everything, the human causality for nothing or almost nothing. To experience

---

[5] See his treatise on prophecy in *Summa Theologiae*, 2a2ae, 171–4.

the gift of inspiration meant that the human authors did not deploy their own capacities as creative writers.

This interpretation of inspiration resembles those accounts of the incarnation that maximized the divinity of Christ at the expense of his humanity. Many classical Christologies presented schemes in which a credible human life got edged out for the sake of insisting that, in his divine nature, Christ was of one being with the Father. Given that the divine and human meet in the person of Christ and in the writing of the Scriptures, views of inspiration, no less than Christology, can go astray by one-sidedly stressing the divine component.

However, even as the humanity of Jesus with its historical characteristics and limitations has been properly acknowledged in most recent Christologies, so also the true role of those human beings who wrote the Bible has been increasingly respected. Just as the 'being divine' in Christ has been understood not to prevail at the expense of the 'being human', so God's special guidance in the process of inspiration has been seen to be compatible with genuine human activity and the individual characteristics of particular authors. In both cases we face a both/and, not an either/or. Jesus Christ is both true God and true man. The Holy Spirit and human beings work together to produce the inspired Scriptures. In neither case do we need to deny humanity in order to make room for divinity.

Verbal dictation theories mistakenly believe that affirming the Sacred Scriptures to be the inspired word of God entails denying that they are also a genuinely human word. They wrongly imagine God and human writers as competing rather than collaborating. Apart from this basic *theological* flaw, the verbal dictation approach cannot convincingly explain the many differences of form and style among the inspired writers. Did the Holy Spirit's style change from the years when Paul's letters were written to the later period when the Gospels were composed? If the human authors played no real part in the literary process, such differences could be due only to a mysterious, and even arbitrary, divine choice to vary the style and alter the form.

The naive model of verbal dictation may linger in the fantasy of unreflecting fundamentalists. But most Christian circles have made their peace with the genuinely human activity in the literary process that produced the inspired Scriptures.

2. Secondly, the inspired writers composed in various genres but not in all possible forms of literature. They wrote psalms, proverbs,

letters, gospels, apocalypses, and so forth. But the Bible contains, for example, no epic poetry (like Homer), no works for the theatre (like the ancient Greek dramas), no novels (in the modern sense), and no 'scientific' history (in the modern sense).

The last point may be the most important in this second, negative thesis. Christians have been prone to read biblical history through modern spectacles. Undoubtedly the historical books of the Old and New Testament convey much trustworthy information. The Gospels, for instance, provide a reliable guide to the last years of Jesus' life, as I argued in Chapter 5 above. But this well-founded conclusion should not be pushed to the point of treating the Gospels as if they were modern biographies or glossing over the fact that the historical books of the Old Testament belong to the genre of popular history.

In short, just as the Bible did not exemplify all the forms of literature available in classical times, it did not miraculously antici-pate future genres, like modern, 'scientific' history.

3. Some biblical authors deployed unusual resources as writers and produced works of literary power and beauty. The Bible has proved a great source of imagery, language, and 'inspiration'—not least in the area of music: for instance, in Gregorian chant, polyphony, the hymns of Martin Luther, the passions according to St Matthew and St John by Johann Sebastian Bach, the *Messiah* by George Frederick Handel, biblical operas, and other 'secular' biblical musical works.[6] The Scriptures, through their use by such writers as Dante, Shake-speare, Milton, and Bunyan, have also profoundly affected English and other modern languages.[7]

---

[6] See J. A. Greene, 'Music and the Bible', in B. M. Metzger and M. D. Coogan (eds.), *The Oxford Companion to the Bible* (New York: Oxford University Press, 1003), 535–8. Here one should not ignore the extraordinary impact of the Bible and, in particular, the Gospels on the visual arts: see e.g. the exhibition 'Seeing Salvation' held at the National Gallery, London (February–May 2000) and the accompanying catalogue, G. Finaldi (ed.), *The Image of Christ* (London: National Gallery, 2000).

[7] Besides the works of Robert Alter, see R. Atwan and L. Wieder (eds.), *Chapters into Verse: Poetry in English Inspired by the Bible*, 2 vols. (New York: Oxford University Press, 1993); D. Norton, *A History of the Bible as Literature*, 2 vols. (New York: Cambridge University Press, 1993); id., *A History of the English Bible as Literature* (New York: Cambridge University Press, 2000); L. Ryken et al. (eds.), *Dictionary of Biblical Imagery* (Downers Grove, Ill.: InterVarsity Press, 1998).

Nevertheless, the charism of inspiration did not mean that the *literary level* reached by the sacred writers was necessarily higher than that of other writers. This special divine impulse to write did not miraculously raise (but rather respected) the writing talents of those who received it. The first nine chapters of 1 Chronicles belong to the canon of inspired writings, but these dreary genealogies will not excite too many readers in the modern world. Inspiration could coexist with a dull form of writing. As such, this gift did not and does not automatically indicate anything about the literary standard of the product.

In his *Confesssions* St Augustine of Hippo recalls how disappointed he was when he first read the Bible, or rather the poor translation available in North Africa (3. 4–5). He found it to be no polished and cultivated text, and far from providing him with the lofty wisdom he desired. In particular, the earthy and immoral stories of the Old Testament did not match his expectations. It was only later that he came to appreciate the rich treasures, including literary treasures, of the Bible.

4. We should likewise be cautious about claiming that inspiration necessarily entails a uniformly *high religious power and impact*, which lifts the books of the Bible above non-inspired writings. Of course, the Gospels, the Psalms, the letters of St Paul, and many other books of the Bible continue to fire readers with their special spiritual quality. But experience shows how Augustine's *Confessions*, *The Imitation of Christ*, and the works of Teresa of Avila consistently enjoy a greater religious influence than the Letter of Jude, 2 Maccabees, and purity regulations from Leviticus. A striking spiritual impact is not necessarily an index that some text has been written under the impact of biblical inspiration, nor is its limited spiritual impact an index that *this* text has not been inspired by the Holy Spirit.

The limits that we find in the literary and even in the religious power of inspired writings stem from the fact that these books resulted from genuine human activity, albeit activity exercised under a special divine impulse. Inasmuch as they were human products, they inevitably reflected the limitations of a community's culture and of the writers' individual capacities.

5. Like the charisms of prophecy and apostleship, the gift of inspiration was *not strictly uniform*. Just as there were major and minor prophets and just as Peter and Paul clearly acted as more

significant apostles than some of those listed among the Twelve, so it seems reasonable to hold that the evangelists, for example, enjoyed a 'higher' degree of inspiration than was the case for texts like the Letter of Jude.

All the inspired authors received a special divine impulse to express and record something in writing. Yet there could be different degrees of the Holy Spirit's presence and activity on their behalf.[8] The divine impulse to write could prove stronger or weaker. Second, one would expect the nature of the theme—for example, the life, death, and resurrection of Jesus in the case of the Gospels—to have affected the degree of inspiration. In general, as the revealing and saving self-communication of the tripersonal God reached its climax with Christ's coming, a higher degree of inspiration would, we might expect, be associated with the written witness to that climax. Third, since divine gifts seem to be frequently proportionate to the human qualities of the recipients, a higher charism of inspiration would match a dramatic and cultured person like Paul of Tarsus.

6. A further *variation* concerns the *consciousness* of the inspired writers. Some like Paul (e.g. Gal. 1: 1–24) and the author of the Book of Revelation (1: 3; 22: 7, 9–10, 18–19), knew themselves to be specially guided by the Holy Spirit or at least to be writing with particular divine authority, but other biblical authors like Luke (1: 1–4) and the author of 2 Maccabees (15: 38) acknowledged the struggle involved in composing their works, claimed to have done their best with the sources available to them, but showed no clear awareness that they were writing under a special divine guidance. This was all the more striking in the case of Luke. In his Gospel and the Book of Acts he included a range of episodes in which the Holy Spirit acted strikingly in the lives of individuals and groups. Yet Luke never claimed to be prompted and guided in his writing by some such extraordinary impulse.

To be sure, it would be odd if the sacred writers never showed themselves consciously aware of being inspired. But neither the notion of biblical inspiration as such nor the data from the Old and New Testament support the conclusion that a special impulse

---

[8] See what I have written about the variety in God's causal activity (Ch. 2 above) and the qualitative differences that characterize the divine presence (*Salvation for All*, 208–14, at 213).

to write inevitably meant that all the sacred authors were fully aware of that divine guidance and authority coming to them. The Holy Spirit could (and can) be at work in many ways without the beneficiaries necessarily being conscious of this influence.

7. Often it would be more accurate to speak of 'special impulses' to write, since *many books of the Bible emerged from a long process* of oral and written tradition. They did not come from a solo author. Frequently the cast of those sharing in the charism of inspiration could be complex and varied. Inasmuch as they truly helped to shape and produce some part of the Bible, a special impulse of the Holy Spirit moved all of them to bring about the text.

The charism of inspiration, one should acknowledge, guided all those who contributed to the making of the historical book of the Old Testament and was not restricted to the final editor(s). Likewise the same charism touched all those Christians who handed on, as eyewitnesses or otherwise, the stories and sayings woven into the four Gospels. In the same way we should recognize the inspiration of the author(s) who created hymns subsequently incorporated into New Testament letters (e.g. Phil. 2: 6–11; 1 Tim. 3: 16).

8. Finally, *we should not compare the authorship of the Bible too closely with the work of modern authors.* First, unlike many contemporary authors, the biblical authors often drew on oral and written material that had already taken some shape and they did not fashion their books in a great blaze of creativity. Second, their aim was consistently religious: to communicate a message of faith and not to win success for their literary prowess. Some of them showed a remarkable grasp of language and an intensity of human feeling. But they did not wish to be judged either by the art of their expression or by their capacity to articulate and enter into deep personal experience.

The essential difference could be put this way. Modern poets, dramatists, and novelists normally write for themselves, often reflect their own personal background, and remain very much persons in their own right. The biblical authors, however, often wrote anonymously, drew on the general traditions and experiences of believers, and produced works to serve the community. Even if they were more, at times much more than mere mouthpieces of their communities (e.g. Paul), we would ignore at our peril the social setting, responsibility, and function of their writings.

The function of inspiration

Our eight points about biblical inspiration have clarified, hopefully a little, how the special impulse of the Holy Spirit worked through the historical and personal conditions of the sacred authors. Provided we recognize the real human role of these writers (point 1), we will be in a position to acknowledge various limitations in their activity (points 2 to 8). Admittedly what has been said so far about inspiration has attended to what the special guidance of the Holy Spirit did *not* involve. The biblical authors did not write in all possible styles; their works do not always enjoy a religious effect superior to that of all non-inspired texts; they were not necessarily conscious of being inspired; and so forth. It seems unreasonable to expect a direct and full description of the dynamics of inspiration, let alone a totally clear explanation of it. Such an account should not be looked for, once we acknowledge how this charism (which makes the biblical text both the word of God and the word of human beings) shared in the mystery of Christ, who was and is truly divine and truly human. If we cannot explain the mystery of the incarnation, we should not hope to explain the operation of inspiration in all its details.

Nevertheless, Karl Rahner's interpretation of inspiration points toward a positive and satisfying, if limited, account.[9] Without recalling and adopting in every detail his explanation, I want to present five considerations drawn from Rahner that indicate what made God the 'author' of the Scriptures and why we can call the Bible the word of God.

1. First of all, the charism of inspiration belonged to the divine activity in the special history of revelation and salvation which led to the foundation of the Church with all the elements (including the Scriptures) that constitute its total reality. Where the Old Testament books recorded various persons, events, and experiences that prepared the way for Christ and his Church, the New Testament recorded persons (above all, Jesus himself, and his apostles), events, and experiences

---

[9] K. Rahner, *Foundations of Christian Faith*, trans. W. V. Dych (New York: Seabury Press, 1978), 369–78; id., *Inspiration in the Bible*, trans. C. H. Henkey (New York: Herder & Herder, 1961).

(above all, the crucifixion, resurrection, and outpouring of the Spirit) that were immediately concerned with the founding of the Church.

2. Hence, God should be called the 'author' of the Scriptures, inasmuch as special divine activity formed and fashioned the Church. Creating the Church also involved 'authoring' the Bible.

3. Third, the charism of inspiration was communicated primarily to the community, and to individuals who belonged to the community. The social dimension of biblical inspiration has been noted under points 7 and 8 above.

4. Since God communicated the charism of inspiration precisely as part of the divine activity in bringing the Church into being, we can appreciate why that charism did not continue beyond the apostolic age. It overlapped with the unique, non-transferable role of the apostles and the apostolic community in (a) witnessing to Christ's resurrection from the dead and the coming of the Holy Spirit and (b) founding the Church. At the end of Chapter 5 above, we saw how the first Christians and their leaders, in their roles as resurrection witnesses and church founders, shared in the once-and-for-all quality of the Christ-event itself. The biblical authors and, specifically, the New Testament writers likewise had a once-and-for-all function, whether they were apostles like Paul or simply members of the apostolic community. Since the charism of inspiration belonged to the divine activity of establishing the Church, it ceased once the Church was fully founded. Inspired writing ended with the period of foundational revelation; in the period of dependent revelation the biblical texts prove richly inspiring (of which more in the next chapter), but the production of new biblical texts has ended.

To sum up the change: later generations of Christians bear the responsibility of proclaiming Christ's resurrection, keeping the Church in existence, and living by the Bible. But they neither 'directly' witness to the risen Christ (as did those who met him gloriously alive after his death), nor do they found the Church, nor do they continue to write inspired Scriptures.

5. Fifthly and finally, through the inspired record of their foundational experience, preaching, and activity, the members of the apostolic Church remain uniquely authoritative for all subsequent generations of Christians. Thus the priority of the apostolic Church was and is much more than a merely chronological one. In a later chapter we shall come back to this theme of apostolic authority.

Besides offering some, limited account of biblical inspiration, this chapter has set itself to distinguish between inspiration and the broader reality of revelation. Identifying inspiration and revelation is an endemic mistake. While one should say that the Bible is the word of God, it cannot be simply identified with revelation. It generates confusion to allege, as many do, that 'the Bible is the revealed word of God'. A similar and frequent mistake occurs when inspiration is identified with one of its major results, inerrancy (better called biblical truth). We move next to the truth of the Bible, along with its 'canonization' and interpretation.

10

The Truth, Canon, and Interpretation of the Bible

Before leaving the Sacred Scriptures, fundamental theologians need to address three questions: first, what is the truth of the Bible and where/how do we find it? Second, what account should they give of the formation and function of the 'canon' or authoritative list of inspired books? Third, how should Christians interpret their Scriptures? Obviously, each of these three questions could provoke a book-length reply. Yet fundamental theology may not use such an excuse and avoid them. Where the previous chapter focused more on the writing of the Scriptures in the period of foundational revelation, this chapter reflects on how Christian readers in the period of dependent revelation have experienced, understood, and been shaped by the Bible.

The saving truth of the Bible

Where this chapter speaks of 'saving truth', many Christians continue to speak of biblical 'inerrancy' or freedom from error(s). However, it is preferable to use a positive term, 'truth', since biblical truth not only aims positively at saving human beings (and not merely at keeping them free from error) but also relates to the person of Christ, who is Truth itself. It could be done, but it would be strange to picture Christ as 'Inerrancy itself'.

Along with this issue of terminology, one should notice the endemic and misleading tendency to identify biblical inspiration with the truth (or inerrancy) of the Bible. Rather than being identical, biblical truth is a major result or consequence of inspiration. The Bible was written under a special impulse of the Holy Spirit and, therefore, is true. Biblical inspiration enjoys other results and consequences: for instance, it produces texts that have nourished over thousands of years for Christian (and Jews) personal prayer and public worship. That result will surface later in this chapter when we engage with the interpretation of the Bible. Here, however, I focus on the particular result of truth and insist that the inspiration and truth of the Scriptures are not to be identified. This should become clearer below when I describe and explain biblical truth. What the previous chapter said in describing and explaining inspiration differs from what we should say about biblical truth.[1]

1. But, first of all, does the Bible everywhere communicate truth and exclude error? From the earliest centuries, difficulties, *inconsistencies*, and *errors* have been detected in the Scriptures—to the distress of believers and delight of unbelievers. In book twelve of his *Confessions* and elsewhere, we find St Augustine of Hippo already facing some of the challenges that ancient science and thought raised. The account of creation within a week, offered by the Book of Genesis, has looked simply incompatible with modern science and any Darwinian scheme of evolution. If the origins of the universe created problems, so too did its structure. The Psalms and other Old Testament books reflected in places the view that the earth is a flat disc (Isa. 42: 5; 44: 24) suspended over a cosmic ocean (Ps. 24: 2) or else supported by pillars stationed at the ends of the earth (Ps. 75: 3),

---

[1] O. Loretz, *The Truth of the Bible*, trans. D. J. Bourke (London: Burns & Oates, 1968); J. van Oorschot et al., 'Wahrheit/Wahrhaftigkeit', *TRE* xxxv. 337–78, at 337–45; A. E. Padgett and P. R. Keifert (eds.), *But Is It All True? The Bible and the Question of Truth* (Grand Rapids, Mich.: Eerdmans, 2006); I. de la Potterie, 'History and Truth', in R. Latourelle and G. O'Collins (eds.), *Problems and Perspectives of Fundamental Theology*, trans. M. J. O'Connell (Ramsey, NJ: Paulist Press, 1982), 87–104; id., *Vérité dans Saint Jean*, 2 vols. (Rome: Biblicum Press, 1977); id., 'La Vérité de la Sainte Écriture et l'histoire du salut d'après la Constitution dogmatique "Dei Verbum"', *Nouvelle Revue théologique*, 98 (1966), 149–69; G. Quell et al., '*alētheia*', in G. Kittel (ed.), *Theological Dictionary of the New Testament*, trans. G. W. Bromiley, i (Grand Rapids, Mich.: Eerdmans, 1964), 232–51; M. Theobald and J.-Y. Lacoste, 'Truth', in J.-Y. Lacoste (ed.), *Encyclopedia of Christian Theology*, iii (New York: Routledge, 2004), 1632–9, at 1632–4.

while the heavens are stretched out like a tent or a curtain (Ps. 104: 2; Isa. 40: 22), or a metal dome (Ps. 150: 1). Particular books of the Bible presented their special puzzles. How could the prophet Jonah have survived for three days in the belly of a whale, not to mention his passage into and out of the great fish?

Add too the fact that the Bible at times provides conflicting accounts of the same episode. How did the Israelites elude their Egyptian pursuers? In picturing their escape through the Reed (or Red) Sea, Exodus 14 has three versions to offer. First, Moses stretched out his hand and, as in the Cecil B. De Mille scenario, the waters piled up to let the Israelites pass through. Then the waters flooded back over the Egyptians (14: 16, 21a, 22, 27a, 28). In a second version, an east wind dried up the sea for the Israelites, while the Egyptian chariots got stuck. Then YHWH stopped the Egyptians with a glance and threw them into the sea (Exod. 14: 21b, 25–6). Thirdly, an angel of the Lord and a column of cloud that had been in front of the Israelites moved behind them, with the result that the Egyptians could no longer see their quarry, who thus happily escaped (14: 19–20).

Then who killed Goliath—David or a minor character called Elhanan (1 Sam. 17; 2 Sam. 21: 19)? Did the site of the Jerusalem Temple cost David 50 shekels of silver (2 Sam. 24: 24) or 500 shekels of gold (1 Chron. 21: 25)? In the New Testament, Matthew and Luke provide us with irreconcilable genealogies of Jesus (Matt. 1: 1–17; Luke 3: 23–38). Repeatedly it proves difficult, if not impossible, to harmonize into a single, coherent whole the different accounts that the evangelists provide of incidents in Jesus' ministry, passion, and resurrection. Were there two (Matt. 20: 30) or only one blind man (Mark 10: 46) healed by Jesus outside Jericho? Did the risen Christ appear in Galilee (Mark 16: 7; Matt. 28: 16–20; John 21) or only in and around Jerusalem (Matt. 28: 9–10; Luke 24; John 20: 11–29) or both in Galilee and Jerusalem? In short, factual inconsistencies and errors of an historical, geographical, and scientific kind turn up in the Bible.

Worse than that, various moral and religious errors appear in the biblical texts. Let me mention three. First, the innocent Job does not expect life after death, and cannot account for his unmerited suffering by invoking a 'post-mortem' vindication in the next life. Since death will release him from suffering (6: 8–13), he prefers death, which more or less means non-existence (3: 11–22; 7: 16, 21; 10: 18–22; 14: 18–22). Second, God gives Saul and his people the command to kill every human being and animal in the city of Amalek: 'Go and smite Amalek, and... do not spare them, but kill both men and women, infant and suckling, ox and sheep, camel and ass' (1 Sam. 15: 3). Such a *herem* or total destruction of enemies ordered (or permitted) by God forms a major feature of the first half of Joshua (e.g. 2: 10; 6: 17–21; 8: 26; 10: 28–9) but is also found in other Old Testament books (e.g. Deut. 21: 2–3). How can such instances of *herem* be associated with a loving God? Third, St Paul and other early Christians apparently expected the world and its history to be terminated speedily by the second coming of the Lord (e.g. 1 Thess. 4: 15–18).

2. Faced with such factual, moral, and religious errors, those who support biblical truth frequently recall three, interconnected items: (a) the *intentions* of the sacred writers, (b) their *presuppositions*, and (c) their *modes of expressions*. (a) Thus the authors of Genesis intended to teach some religious truths about the goodness and power of the Creator, the sinfulness of human beings, and so forth. They did not intend to teach some form of ancient 'science' about the origins of the world and the human race. It is unfair to accuse biblical (or other) writers of errors by ignoring the difference between the points they wished to communicate and those that lay outside such an intention.

(b) Second, biblical authors show the ways in which they shared with their Middle Eastern contemporaries false notions about the universe. But their acceptance of a flat earth, for instance, remained at the level of their presuppositions and was not a theme for their direct teaching. Similarly the notion that real life ceases at death formed a presupposition for the drama of Job and no more. If death ended all, how could an innocent man interpret and cope with massive and undeserved suffering? Job was not debating with his so-called friends 'is there life after death?', but rather 'since a good and powerful God exists, how can we explain evil' (*si Deus, unde malum*)?

(c) Ancient modes of expression and writing account for a number of alleged errors and inaccuracies. Modern historians would be expected to investigate the evidence and settle the issues. Who really killed Goliath? How much did King David pay for the site on which the Temple would be built? But the kind of popular, religious history found in the Books of Exodus, Samuel, Kings, and Chronicles could take final shape without any need being felt to tidy up inconsistencies and settle disputed details. Admittedly, the honesty of Hebrew historiography put it in a class by itself in the Middle Eastern world. It recorded David's shameful sins of adultery and murder, along with many other failures on the part of the leaders and the people. It showed itself clearly superior to the stereotyped and empty glorification of monarchs found in the records of some other nations.[2] Nevertheless, the religious significance of various events and personages mattered much more to Hebrew historians than any material exactitude. They did not feel a curiosity or sense of academic duty that would have pushed them into clarifying the record when various traditions reported conflicting details. They wrote history to legitimize their beliefs and institutions and to express a sense of their identity and continuity with the past.[3]

Attention to the literary genre removes such false problems as the manner of the prophet Jonah's survival inside the fish. The Book of Jonah is a piece of fiction, an extended parable that keeps for the last few verses its religious punch: God's loving concern extends to all, even to the wicked Ninevites. Any question about its truth or error will be decided only by agreeing or disagreeing with that religious message. To read Jonah as if it were a historical work condemns one to create artificial puzzles about the story-teller's details. Was Nineveh, for instance, really such a huge city that it took three days to cross (3: 3)?

We likewise save ourselves from further silliness by recognizing the kind of literature we deal with in the Book of Genesis. Its early chapters reflect on the nature of God and human beings, and in no sense give even an incomplete account of the 'pre-historical' origins of the human race.[4] If we ignore that fact, hopeless puzzles turn

---

[2] The Hebrew writers also differed from those in the surrounding world by pursuing a theology of history, by tying the chain of events to one and the same God, and by generally understanding the people as a whole to be the chief protagonist under God (even when the text presented the story of some king or prophet (e.g. Samuel or Elijah)).

[3] See M. Z. Brettler, 'Introduction to the Historical Books', in M. D. Coogan et al. (eds.), *The New Oxford Annotated Bible* (augmented 3rd edn. Oxford: Oxford University Press, 2007), 309–13 (Hebrew Bible); H. D. Preuss, *Old Testament Theology*, trans. L. G. Perdue, i (Edinburgh: T. & T. Clark, 1995), 208–51; J. van Seters, *In Search of History: Historiography in the Ancient World and the Origins of Biblical History* (New Haven: Yale University Press, 1983); E. Zenger, 'Eigenart und Bedeutung der Geschichtserzählungen Israels', in E. Zenger et al., *Einleitung in das Alte Testament* (2nd edn. Stuttgart: Verlag Kohlhammer, 1995), 124–7.

[4] A. Lacoque, *The Trial of Innocence: Adam, Eve, and the Yahwist* (Eugene, Ore.: Cascade Books, 2006).

up. When, for instance, Cain murdered Abel and was about to be sent away as 'a fugitive and wanderer upon the earth', God 'put a mark on Cain, lest any who came upon him should kill him'. So Cain left Eden for the land of Nod, 'knew his wife, and she conceived Enoch' (Gen. 4: 15–17). We would mistreat the story if we were to start asking: where did the others come from who might have threatened Cain's life? For that matter, where did his wife come from, if Adam and Eve were the parents of all human beings? Genesis is not a book about human origins that answers such questions.

3. Doubtless, respect for the intentions, presuppositions, and modes of expression used by the sacred authors goes some way toward mitigating the force of many difficulties and doubts, both serious and silly, about biblical truth. All of this concerns the *human* side of things. St Augustine makes a similar point about the *divine* intentions. Inspiration from the Holy Spirit had a religious purpose, and did not as such aim to advance 'secular' truth: 'we do not read in the Gospel [of John] that the Lord said: "I shall send you the Paraclete who will teach you about the movement of the sun and moon". He wished to make Christians, not astronomers' (*Contra Felicem Manichaeum*, 1. 10). But more needs to be added, so as to elucidate further the truth of the Scriptures. What has been said so far concerns the intentions, presuppositions, and literary styles of individual books. We should stand back and view the Bible as a whole. What is biblical truth in general?

4. Many people answer this question by introducing the *correspondence theory of truth*, a view that has deep roots in classical and medieval philosophy.[5] Truth is a function of human judgement. If what the intellect judges about reality (and hence causes us to say and write) conforms to reality (*adequatio intellectus et rei*), then we are in touch with truth. This pervasive way of understanding truth highlights the individual person's intellect, emphasizing the mind and judgement of the thinking subject. It evaluates the truth of propositions by their conformity with the 'facts'. But does this version of truth fit the Bible?

We would mistreat the scriptural texts if we tried to reduce them to a set of informative propositions, whose sole function was to make

---

[5] See R. L. Kirkham, 'Truth, Correspondence Theory of', in E. Craig (ed.), *Routledge Encyclopedia of Philosophy*, ix (London: Routledge, 1998), 472–5.

factual claims and state true judgements, religious or otherwise. The Bible forms no such catalogue of propositions which are to be tested for their truth or error. The Scriptures, while they do contain such true propositions as 'Christ died for our sins' (1 Cor. 15: 3), also include many exhortations, laws, prayers, poetic images, cries of joy, questions, and other items about which it is quite inappropriate to ask (at least in the sense of the correspondence view of truth): is this true or false?

The joyful cry 'alleluia' that turns up in the psalms is as such neither true nor false. Questions asked in the biblical story, like questions elsewhere, may be 'clear', 'pertinent', and 'meaningful', but they do not inform or describe and may not be classified under the headings of truth or falsity. To ask a question does not amount to saying anything true or false. Furthermore, exhortations delivered by the prophets, the apostle Paul, and others abound in the Bible. These exhortations may change attitudes and bring about right behaviour, but in themselves cannot be called true or false. It is the same with laws. Whether recorded in the Bible or in other texts, laws may be just or unjust, harsh or compassionate. Yet precisely as such they are neither true nor false. Lastly, poetic images (e.g. the heavens being like a curtain or tent) may be vivid and evocative, or trite and dead. But we cannot call such images as such true or false judgements.

Believers do violence to the Scriptures whenever they seek to reduce them to a set of (infallibly) true propositions. To be sure, all the verses of the Bible are inspired or written under the special guidance of the Holy Spirit. But that does not mean that all the verses of the Bible are in the business of making judgements that correspond to the facts. In *that* sense of truth, inerrancy is not co-extensive with inspiration. We cannot deal with the whole Bible as if it offered a series of propositions to be checked for their conformity with the facts and so declared true.

5. The *biblical notions of truth*, while not always proving utterly different from the pervasive correspondence view of truth, have their particular accents. They tend to be interpersonal, less one-sidedly intellectual, oriented toward action and transformation, progressive, and (for Christian believers) centred on Christ. In both Old and New Testaments the language of truth (whether expressed in the Hebrew *emet*, the Greek *alētheia*, or other terms) locks into the people's experience of God. In the Old Testament God is shown through

word and deed to be true—that is to say, consistently trustworthy and truly reliable: 'The Lord your God is God, the faithful God; with those who love him and keep his commandments he keeps covenant and faith for ever' (Deut. 7: 9). By their fidelity to the covenant, the people should prove themselves to be loyally conformed to the divine reality and hence persons of 'truth'.

According to the New Testament, the God who remains faithful and reliable and so is 'proved true' (Rom. 3: 1–7) is fully revealed through the person of his Son: 'the truth is in Jesus' (Eph. 4: 21); 'grace and truth have come through Jesus Christ' (John 1: 17).[6] Revelation may be summed up as one thing, the truth of salvation in Christ. The powerful presence of Christ and his Holy Spirit enables believers to 'do the truth' (John 3: 21) and to 'belong to the truth' (John 18: 37). The truth that sets them free (John 8: 32) does much more than conform their minds to reality. It transforms their entire person.

6. After this rapid survey of what truth can mean in the Old and New Testaments, let me propose five scripturally based and deeply important considerations. (a) First, biblical truth is *progressive*; it is gradually mediated and not communicated once and for all at the start. Earlier biblical authors faithfully recorded various items that reflect some unsatisfactory and downright erroneous views of God: for instance, the idea that God could order the total destruction of all the Amalecites and their livestock. Under the impulse of the Holy Spirit, the biblical authors recorded this and other instances of *herem*, which tell us something true about the Israelites and their image of God at that time. It was an image which they genuinely entertained, but it needed to be radically purified if they were to grow towards the true image of God who loves and cherishes all people that we find in Second Isaiah, Jonah, and other later traditions and books.[7]

Unless we recognize the progressive nature of biblical truth, we will find ourselves in the company of many people and even a few scholars who attempt to justify genocidal practices by arguing that God is,

---

[6] Here the Scriptures resemble that philosophical notion of truth associated with the work of Martin Heidegger (1889–1976), according to which something is true when it ceases to be hidden (*a-lēthēs*) and discloses itself. In this sense truth is the unveiling or throwing open of being.

[7] See G. O'Collins, *Salvation for All: God's Other Peoples* (Oxford: Oxford University Press, 2008), 64–78.

after all, the Lord of life and death. What the biblical authors recall at times is nothing less than an horrendous story: for instance, doing the divine will by killing all the inhabitants of town after town as the Israelites took possession of the promised land (Deut. 2: 31–3: 7); God destroying 70,000 people by sending a pestilence after David had ordered a national census (2 Sam. 24: 1–16; 1 Chron. 21: 1–14); the sacrifice of a daughter in thanksgiving to God for a military victory over the Ammonites (Judg. 11: 29–40). Hosea, along with inspiring and beautiful passages involving God, takes no exception to what will happen to the people of Samaria: 'Samaria shall bear her guilt, because she has rebelled against her God; they shall fall by the sword, their little ones shall be dashed to pieces, and their pregnant women ripped open' (Hos. 13: 16). There is a sad truth in what these and other passages record under the impulse of inspiration: namely, a picture of how Israelites thought at the time about God and about what God wanted from them. But their image of God called for massive purification; there was progress toward a fuller and more accurate truth about God reflected in later books that were to be composed under the inspiration of the Holy Spirit.

One might also find in such passages a further truth: namely, a warning about the lasting human temptation to make a savage deity in our image and likeness. National interests and security, or at least perceived national interests and security, have continued to encourage human beings and their leaders to picture God as ferociously 'with us' but 'against them' and so justify 'taking out' enemies even on a large scale. If the passages cited above show us how the Israelites portrayed God at an earlier stage, they also truly hint at the hostile feelings about others that believers down through the ages have often entertained and believed to be justified by God.

(b) My first consideration leads naturally to the second: the truth of the Bible is found in *the whole Bible*. We cannot properly speak of the truth of the Bible before all the biblical texts have been composed and then recognized as belonging to the canon (see below). In this sense we should not look for the truth of the Scriptures primarily in one passage, one book, or even in one Testament. Here as elsewhere, the truth is in the whole and not, strictly speaking, in one or other part, even the 'best' and 'most enlightened' parts.

(c) To state this unity in the whole more precisely, the truth of the Bible is primarily found in a person, Jesus Christ. He is the truth attested prophetically in the Old Testament and apostolically in the New Testament. Ultimately the Bible does not convey a set of distinct truths but has only one truth to proclaim, the personal disclosure of the tripersonal God in Jesus. 'Other' biblical truths or 'mysteries' with their distinct contents do nothing else than articulate the one primordial Mystery, which the apostolic generation of believers experienced and transmitted to later generations.

A twelfth-century Augustinian canon, Hugh of St Victor, witnessed to this union of the Bible in Christ: 'all divine Scripture speaks of Christ and all divine Scripture finds its fulfillment in Christ... because all divine Scripture forms one book, which is the book of life.'[8] In the sixteenth century William Tyndale expressed the same conviction: 'the scriptures spring out of God, and flow into Christ, and were given to lead us to Christ. Thou must therefore go along by the scripture as by a line, until thou come at Christ, which is the way's end and resting place.'[9]

(d) Fourthly, the biblical writings which record the preparation for Christ's coming and then the coming itself participate in the truth that he himself is. By testifying to the divine self-communication which reaches its climax in him and the various human responses to that divine self-giving, these writings help to communicate truly that saving and revealing event.

The texts (lower case) of the Bible share in the truth of the Text (upper case) that is Jesus himself. They set this divine and mysterious Text to words. He is the Word of God, in which the inspired words of the Scripture participate and to which they witness. When the biblical texts display and promote truth, they do so by sharing in the unrepeatable and unimprovable truth that is the person of Christ.

(e) Fifthly and finally, the Scriptures set up the conditions by which God speaks to us and enables us to acknowledge and practise the truth. In the last resort, the truth of the Bible is something to be lived. This truth is known by living in it and living by it. Biblical truth is to be experienced and expressed in action as much as (or even more than) it is to be seen and affirmed in intellectual judgements. Through doing and 'speaking the truth in love' (Eph. 4:15), we will

---

[8] *De Arca Noe Morali*, 2. 8–9; *PL* 176, cols. 642–3.
[9] *The Work of William Tyndale*, ed. G. E. Duffield (Philadelphia: Fortress Press, 1965), 353.

244 | TRUTH, CANON, AND INTERPRETATION OF THE BIBLE

be in a position to know and understand, at least partly and provisionally, what this truth is.

The canon of Scriptures

Talking about the unity of the whole Bible brings us to the question of the canon.[10] Fundamental theology can distinguish three basic questions with which it needs to engage, albeit briefly: the *formation of the canon*, the *closed nature of the canon*, and *canonical authority*.

1. One might describe the canon as a closed list of sacred books, acknowledged by the Church as inspired by God and enjoying a regulative value for Christian belief and practice. 'Canonization' presupposed and went beyond biblical inspiration or the special

---

[10] See J.-M. Auwers and H. J. de Jonge (eds.), *The Biblical Canons* (Leuven: Leuven University Press, 2003); J. Barton, 'Canon', in J. Bowden (ed.), *Christianity: The Complete Guide* (London: Continuum, 2005), 197–9; R. T. Beckwith, *The Old Testament Canon of the New Testament Church and its Background in Early Judaism* (London: SPCK, 1985); M. Z. Brettler and P. Perkins, 'The Canons of the Bible', in *New Oxford Annotated Bible*, 453–60 (Essays); R. E. Brown and R. F. Collins, 'Canonicity', in R. E. Brown, J. A. Fitzmyer, and R. L. Murphy (eds.), *The New Jerome Biblical Commentary* (London: Geoffrey Chapman, 1989), 1034–54; H. Fr. von Campenhausen, *The Formation of the Christian Bible*, trans. J. A. Baker (London: A. and C. Black, 1972); 'Canon of Scripture', *Oxford Dictionary*, 281–2; H. Y. Gamble, *The New Testament Canon: Its Making and Meaning* (Philadelphia: Fortress Press, 1985); M. Gilbert, 'Canon of Scriptures', in Lacoste (ed.), *Encyclopedia of Christian Theology*, i. 250–55; R. Gnuse, *The Authority of the Bible: Theories of Inspiration, Revelation, and the Canon* (New York: Paulist Press, 1985); M. Hengel, *Die vier Evangelien und das eine Evangelium von Jesus Christus: Studien zu ihrer Sammlung und Entstehung* (Tübingen: Mohr Siebeck, 2008); M. W. Holmes, 'The Biblical Canon', in S. A. Harvey and D. G. Hunter (eds.), *The Oxford Handbook of Early Christian Studies* (Oxford: Oxford University Press, 2008), 406–26; L. M. McDonald, *The Biblical Canon: Its Origin, Transmission, and Authority* (Peabody, Mass.: Hendrickson, 2002); id., 'Canon of the New Testament', *The New Interpreter's Dictionary of the Bible*, i (Nashville: Abingdon Press, 2006), 236–47; L. M. McDonald and J. A. Sanders (eds.), *The Canon Debate* (Peabody, Mass.: Hendrickson, 2002); B. M. Metzger, *The Canon of the New Testament: Its Origin, Development, and Significance* (Oxford: Clarendon, 1987; J. A. Sanders et al., 'Canon', *ABD* i. 839–66; A. C. Sundberg, 'The Bible Canon and the Christian Doctrine of Inspiration', *Interpretation*, 29 (1975), 352–71; id., *The Old Testament of the Early Church* (Cambridge, Mass.: Harvard University Press, 1964); A. B. du Toit, 'Canon', in B. M. Metzger and M. D. Coogan, *Oxford Companion to the Bible* (New York: Oxford University Press, 1993), 98–104; J. Trebolle, 'Canon of the Old Testament', in *The New Interpreter's Dictionary of the Bible*, i. 548–63.

guidance of the Holy Spirit in composing the Scriptures. In the Old Testament period inspired writings came into existence centuries before there was any question of a canon, be it a Jewish or a Christian one. Thus the exercise of the gift of inspiration preceded the later process of 'canonization'. In that process inspired books were recognized as such by the post-apostolic Church. Roman Catholics acknowledge in a decree from the Council of Trent (DzH 1502–4; ND 211–13) a definitive act of recognition which finally established a clear canon of inspired writings. When making this solemn definition of the canon, Trent confirmed the doctrine of the Council of Florence (DzH 1334–5; ND 208), which in its turn was based on teaching about the canon coming from local councils and Church fathers in the fourth and early fifth centuries.[11]

Fundamental theologians cannot be expected to trace the ins and outs of the history of particular books that were initially favoured but came to be excluded from the canon (e.g. the Epistle of Barnabas and *The Shepherd of Hermas*) or those that came to be included after serious doubts (e.g. the Letter to the Hebrews, the Book of Revelation, and the deuterocanonical books of the Old Testament). But some reflection on the criteria involved in selecting canonical books belongs on the agenda of fundamental theology. But before spelling out these criteria, we need to clarify the terms: protocanonical, deuterocanonical, and apocrypha.

The term 'protocanonical' or 'first-time members of the canon' applies to the thirty-nine books of the Old Testament which are universally accepted as inspired and canonical and correspond to the twenty-two books of the Hebrew Bible. The term 'deuterocanonical' (or 'second-time members of the canon') is a name for those seven books (plus further portions of other books) found in the Greek (Septuagint) version of the Old Testament but not in the

---

[11] In his 39th festal letter (of Easter 367), St Athanasius of Alexandria listed the 27 books of the New Testament; the Muratorian Canon, generally dated to the late second century (see Bettenson, 31–2; *Oxford Dictionary*, 1133), includes all the books of the New Testament, except Hebrews, James, and 1 and 2 Peter. As regards the Old Testament canon, Athanasius recognized the 22 books of the Hebrew Bible, which corresponded to the 39 protocanonical books of the Christian Bible. From the late second century St Melito of Sardis provided the earliest Christian list of Old Testament books; it was much the same as the 22 books of the Hebrew Bible. See D. Brakke, 'A New Fragment of Athanasius' Thirty-Ninth *Festal Letter*: Heresy, Apocrypha, and the Canon', *Harvard Theological Review*, 103 (2010), 47–66.

canon of the Hebrew Bible, and printed in Catholic Bibles. The seven books are Judith, 1 and 2 Maccabees, Sirach, Baruch, Tobit, and Wisdom. Some of these works, Judith, 2 Maccabees, and Wisdom, were composed in Greek, while 1 Maccabees, Sirach, and much of Baruch were composed originally in Hebrew. Written in Hebrew before 180 BC, Sirach was translated into Greek fifty years later; since 1900 two-thirds of the original Hebrew text has been recovered. Tobit was originally written in either Hebrew or Aramaic, but, apart from some fragments in those languages, only the Greek version remains. Some Protestant and all ecumenical Bibles include the deuterocanonical books, but normally call them the 'Apocrypha'— to be distinguished from the Apocryphal Gospels (e.g. 'The Gospel of the Hebrews', 'the Gospel of Mary', 'the Gospel of Peter', and 'the Gospel of Thomas'), works from the second or third centuries that no mainline Bibles include. For Catholic scholars and such Protestant scholars as Hans Hübner, who recognize the authority of some or all of the deuterocanonical books, being 'second-time members of the canon' refers to their being written in the second or first century BC (and hence after the protocanonical books) and to their being accepted in the canon of Christian Scriptures after a certain hesitation (coming from some Church fathers such as St Jerome, who expressed doubts about the full canonical status of the deuterocanonical books). The term 'deuterocanonical' is not intended to belittle their authority for Christians; the New Testament contains numerous allusions and verbal parallels to the deuterocanonical books of the Old Testament. In any case, around the Mediterranean world, Jews who became Christians brought with them the Septuagint, the Greek version of their Bible that had fed their spiritual lives. When citing the Old Testament and what came to be called protocanonical books, the New Testament authors often follow the Septuagint rather than the Hebrew original.

What then of the criteria for accepting some books into the canon and excluding others? Surprisingly perhaps, inspiration itself did not function as a criterion for early Christians when they selected or rejected sacred books. They understood the inspiration of the Holy Spirit to be widely and constantly present in the Church both during the apostolic era and later. Granted such a broad recognition of inspiration, an appeal to inspiration could not serve to establish the canon of sacred books. Moreover, both at the time of their writing and even more after the death of the authors, a claim to being inspired could not be readily checked and verified. How could other Christians know that *this* writer had been specially guided by the Holy Spirit unless they referred to other, visible criteria? Public criteria were needed—not least to counter the claims to have received special revelations and inspiration made by Gnostics in the second and third centuries. Three such criteria shaped the early Church's recognition of inspired writings: (a) *apostolic origin*, (b) *orthodox teaching*, and (c) *consistent usage*, particularly in the Church's liturgy.

(a) First, there was the historical criterion of apostolic origin. The Christian writings that complemented the scriptural books inherited by Jesus and his disciples and were to constitute the canonical New Testament came from the period of foundational revelation when Christ's apostles witnessed to his resurrection and founded the Church. To be sure, apostolic origin was often taken narrowly, so that the books that would make up the New Testament were all understood to be written by the apostles themselves or their close associates: Mark (connected with Peter) as author of the Second Gospel and Luke (connected with Paul) for the Third Gospel and the Book of Acts. In such terms apostles gave their authority both to the Jewish Scriptures (which they inherited) and to the new sacred books that they or their associates composed for Christian communities. Such a strict version of apostolic origin no longer works. Very few scholars agree, for example, that Paul wrote Hebrews or that Peter wrote 2 Peter. In any case hesitations about the 'apostolic origin' of Hebrews and 2 Peter, as well as the Book of Revelation, were expressed in early Christianity before Athanasius and others accepted these works into the list or canon of sacred writings.

Nevertheless, in a broader sense the criterion of apostolic origin still carries weight in sorting out canonical from non-canonical writings. Only those works that witnessed to Christ prophetically (the Jewish Scriptures) or apostolically (the Christian Scriptures) could enter and remain in the canon. Those works constituted an inspired record coming from believers who had experienced the foundational revelation that ended with the apostolic age. Only persons who shared in the events that climaxed with the crucifixion, resurrection, sending of the Holy Spirit, and foundation of the Church were in a position to express through inspired Scriptures their written testimony to those experiences. Later writings, even of such importance as the Nicene-Constantinopolitan Creed of 381 and the Chalcedonian Definition of 451, belonged to the period of dependent revelation, could not as such directly witness to the experience of foundational revelation, and emerged at a time when the charism of inspiration had ceased. Seen in this way, the criterion of apostolic origin still works to accredit canonical writing. Canonicity rests on apostolicity.

This conclusion rules out an analogy some have suggested between canonical and classic texts: the Scriptures function authoritatively for Christians in a way that parallels the authority of recognized classics in the Western and other cultures. Sallie McFague asserts: 'the Bible is not absolute or authoritative in any sense except the way that a "classic" text is authoritative.'[12] Francis Schüssler Fiorenza has drawn attention to a major flaw in this 'classic' interpretation of scriptural authority that hardly distinguishes the Bible from 'inspired' and 'inspiring' classic works of literature (and art). The classics exemplify in an inspiring way the deepest truths about human existence; in these books generation after generation of readers have recognized 'the truth of their own identity'. But it is 'the identity of Jesus' that is the basis for scriptural authority rather than the power of the Scriptures to elicit from one generation to the next compelling truths about the human condition. Schüssler Fiorenza recalls Krister Stendahl's observation: 'it is because of their authority as scripture that the Scriptures have become classics', and it is not that 'they have authority because they are classics'.[13]

In the light of the criterion of apostolic origin, one should add to Schüssler Fiorenza's argument by pointing out that the great literary classics may, like Homer's two epic poems and Dante's *Divine Comedy*, feature at the birth of a culture's literature, but not necessarily so.

---

[12] S. McFague, *Metaphorical Theology: Models of God in Religious Language* (Philadelphia: Fortress Press, 1982), 19. Incidentally, one should query the use of 'absolute' and 'authoritative' as synonymous alternatives. The Bible is authoritative but not 'absolutely' and in itself; its authority derives from the Holy Spirit, Christ, and his apostles.

[13] F. Schüssler Fiorenza, 'The Crisis of Biblical Authority: Interpretation and Reception', *Interpretation*, 44 (1990), 353–68, at 360–1. Others have interpreted the Scriptures as 'classic' texts: e.g. J. Coventry, *Christian Truth* (London: Darton, Longman & Todd, 1975), 45, 66. In dialogue with T. S. Eliot, H.-G. Gadamer, F. Kermode, and others, David Tracy developed at length an interpretation of the Scriptures as 'classics' in *The Analogical Imagination* (New York: Crossroad, 1981).

The dialogues of Plato and the works of Goethe, for instance, came long after Greek and German literature, respectively, were established. No 'canon' of literary classics can be declared to be closed. Outstanding writers may turn up today and in the future; their works will merit 'canonization' and inclusion among a people's classic texts. The inspired Scriptures, however, belong to the foundational period of Christianity. The biblical canon, as we shall see, is closed and cannot be enlarged.

(b) Second, there is the *theological criterion* of conformity to the essential message, 'the purity of the Gospel', 'the rule of faith', 'the Catholic faith that comes to us from the apostles', or call it what you will. Because it failed to meet clearly the test of orthodoxy, *The Shepherd of Hermas*, which was written perhaps in the early second century and hence might have made the grade in terms of time, was excluded from the canon. Other writings, like the Book of Revelation, were eventually included when their orthodox content was sufficiently recognized.

Of course, there was a certain circularity involved in applying this criterion of 'the rule of faith'. Since they fitted their understanding of Christianity, the faithful and their leaders judged certain writings (e.g. the letters of Paul and the four Gospels) to be orthodox, accepted them into the canon, and then proceeded to use them to test orthodoxy. At the same time, these Scriptures, inasmuch as they were written under the special guidance of the Holy Spirit, never simply mirrored what the Church community was but challenged Christians by picturing what they should be and should believe. In calling them and actually leading them to a fully transformed life, the Scriptures proved themselves in practice.

(c) Thirdly, constant use, above all in the context of public worship, also secured for the inspired writings their place in the canon of the Christian Bible. We can spot this operating in the case of Paul: when various communities received his letters, they treasured, reproduced, and read them at liturgical assemblies. These texts shared the apostolic authority of Paul's oral witness and teaching. By the time of the composition of 2 Peter, the letters of Paul seemed to have been collected (and misinterpreted by some on the issue of the final judgement being delayed) (2 Pet. 3: 15–16).

When reflecting on this third (liturgical) criterion it is worth recalling the case of 1 Clement. Around 170 AD it was still being read in the church at Corinth, along with Scriptures that were to belong definitively to the canon.[14] But this letter never entered the canon of New Testament Scriptures, later attested by Athanasius and others, since it failed to win lasting and widespread liturgical acceptance. That counted against its canonical status, even if it might be justified on the basis of the first (historical) criterion and second (theological) criterion.

2. Fundamental theologians, if they are to complete their task of dealing with basic issues about the Scriptures, need to reflect also on *the closed nature of the canon*. We called the canon above a 'closed collection' of sacred writings. It is relatively easy to organize three reasons for justifying the closed nature of the canon.

First, since the charism of inspiration ended with the apostolic age, there could be no later instances of inspired writings. The canon closed or rather being 'candidates' for canonical recognition and entry into the canon closed in the way a particular epoch of history—in this case the foundational period of the special history of revelation and salvation—has ended.

In the second place, unless the canon is closed and not the subject of modifications or additions, it cannot function as a canon: that is, as a truly normative rule for Christian belief and practice. Precisely as constituting a canon, these books, even if many of them (e.g. the letters of Paul) were written to meet particular needs and serve particular occasions, were and are acknowledged as forming together an adequate version of Christianity. If they do not sufficiently reflect the basic Christian experience and identity in response to the divine self-communication in Christ, they could not serve as an authoritative norm for Christian faith and life.

Third, the closed nature of the canon clearly ties in with the closed and normative nature of the apostolic age and charism. Just as the members of the apostolic Church shared in the unique, once-and-for-all character of the Christ-event, so too did their sacred writings—both those they produced and those they took over from their Jewish heritage. The inspired books shared thus in the unrepeatable role of the apostles and their associates.

---

[14] See 'Clement of Rome, St', *Oxford Dictionary*, 363.

The consequences of this argument are clear. On the one hand, to exclude some writings and thus *reduce* the canon (as Marcion did in the second century[15] and others later have done) would be to tamper with the richness of the Church's foundational experience of the divine self-communication, to minimize the diversity in the apostolic experience and witness, and, ultimately, to attack the divine fullness of Christ's person and work (see Col. 1: 19–20). On the other hand, enlarging the canon by adding such later writings as the Gnostic 'scriptures' would be tantamount to challenging the fullness of what Christ did and revealed with and through the apostolic generation. In the second century we find St Irenaeus of Lyons battling on two fronts in support of the emerging Christian canon. On one front, he defended the enduring authority of the Old Testament Scriptures against Marcion's total rejection of them. On the other front, he upheld the unique value of the New Testament Scriptures, especially the Gospels according to Matthew, Mark, Luke, and John, against Gnostic attempts to add further 'gospels' and other texts.

Granted the essentially closed nature of the canon, would it still be feasible to entertain the possibility of adding to the collection, for instance, some Jewish psalms and other prayers actually discovered in a Qumran cave or a missing letter of Paul that might be recovered by archaeologists? Such writings could satisfy the historical and theological criteria expounded above. Inasmuch as they would not substantially modify the total message expressed though the existing canon of Scriptures, they might win a place in the canon—under one condition, however. Such newly discovered texts from the period of foundational revelation would have to vindicate themselves through constant liturgical usage, a process that would take some time and has so far (in the case of several psalms from Qumran) not even begun.

3. Why should the canonical Scriptures enjoy normative authority for the Christian Church in general and her teachers and theologians in particular? What supports this *authority of the canon* and justifies giving permanent allegiance to the biblical texts as promising to preserve the Church's self-identity by constantly illuminating and enlivening her faith and practice?[16] The Church's fidelity to the

---

[15] See Bettenson, 41; 'Marcion', *Oxford Dictionary*, 1040.
[16] See J. Barton, 'Bible, its Authority and Interpretation', in A. Hastings et al. (eds.), *The Oxford Companion to Christian Thought* (Oxford: Oxford University

Scriptures rests on her fidelity to Jesus Christ as *the* Revealer and Saviour and her faith that the Holy Spirit gave special guidance to those involved in the production of the Scriptures. Apart from that faith, the Scriptures cannot credibly claim any normative value, becoming little else than 'mere' historical sources, the earliest records of the story of Israel and the origins of Christianity and an anthology of more or less edifying religious texts from the ancient Middle East. With a full faith in Christ and his Spirit, however, believers acknowledge the Scriptures as holy, sacred, and embodying divine authority,[17] and accept them as constituting the authoritative account and interpretation of Israel's history and of the formation of Christianity through Jesus Christ and his first followers. The official collection of foundational books witnesses to that special history of revelation and salvation which remains not merely a general interpretative framework but also the decisive point of orientation for all subsequent believers and theologians. Their attitude toward the authority of the whole Bible provides a litmus test of how theologians consider authority to function in and for their work. This calls for fundamental theologians, in particular, to give some account of how they understand canonical authority.

Press, 2000), 69–72; P. L. Culbertson, 'Known, Knower, and Knowing: The Authority of Scripture in the Episcopal Church', *Anglican Theological Review,* 74 (1992), 144–74; M. Goshen-Gottstein et al., 'Scriptural Authority', *ABD* v. 1017–56; R. Hammes, 'Authority of the Bible', in Metzger and Coogan, *Oxford Companion to the Bible,* 65–8; J. A. Keller, 'Accepting the Authority of the Bible: Is It Rationally Justified?', *Faith and Philosophy,* 6 (1989), 378–97; W. Pannenberg and T. Schneider (eds.), *Verbindliches Zeugnis,* i (Göttingen: Vandenhoeck & Ruprecht, 1992); H. Graf Reventlow, 'Theology (Biblical), History of', *ABD* vi. 483–505. S. M. Schneiders, 'Scripture as the Word of God', *Princeton Seminary Bulletin,* 14 (1992), 348–61; 478–89. Believers acknowledge the authority of the Bible because it rests on the authority of Christ and his Holy Spirit and because it promises to let them 'grow' (*augere*), a Latin word connected with 'authority' (*auctoritas*).

[17] Their faith in Christ underpins the New Testament authors' sense of the authority of the Old Testament Scriptures, which coincides for them with the authority of God. Thus they disclose the heart of their theological convictions through citations from their inherited Jewish Scriptures; see H. Hübner, 'New Testament, OT Quotations in the', *ABD* iv. 1096–104. The Letter to the Hebrews illustrates how Christians understood the Jewish Scriptures as divinely inspired and authoritative. Citing these Scriptures 37 times, Hebrews attributes all the passages to God, Christ, or the Holy Spirit, mentioning only two human authors—Moses (Heb. 8: 5; 12: 21) and David (Heb. 4: 7)—and even then referring twice to the divine 'author' (Heb. 4: 7; 8: 5).

The authority at stake is the *de jure* authority of the Scriptures, which means recognizing that the canonical Bible in and of itself constitutes the primary norm for determining the Church's faith and practice. Such authority in principle goes beyond mere de facto authority or the way in which the Scriptures as a matter of fact affect the life, worship, and teaching of Christians. Such de facto authority functions inasmuch as the Scriptures 'work' for us but does not allow them an independent authority to challenge and judge us and our society. To accept their *de jure* authority involves acknowledging that they legitimately invite an obedient hearing, because they derive from a foundational and authoritative past rooted in the missions of Christ, his Holy Spirit, and the apostles.

The *de jure* authority of the Bible derives from its historical origins in the mission of the Holy Spirit, a mission invisible in itself but visible in its effects, and the visible mission of Christ (with the passage of authority from him to his apostolic collaborators). In brief, the authority of the Scriptures is pneumatological, Christological, and apostolic; it derives from persons—the Holy Spirit and Christ with his apostles. Through the Scriptures, as well as in other ways, Christ, the Spirit, and the apostles remain powerfully and authoritatively present.

Interpreting the Bible

Before moving on from the Sacred Scriptures, fundamental theologians need to set out some principles for interpreting these Scriptures and using them in theology.[18] The role of the Bible for faith and

---

[18] See P. Beauchamp, 'Scripture, Senses of', in Lacoste (ed.), *Encyclopedia of Christian Theology*, iii. 1458–65; P. Bouteneff and D. Heller (eds.), *Interpreting Together: Essays in Hermeneutics* (Geneva: WCC Publications, 2001); M. Z. Brettler et al., 'The Interpretation of the Bible', in Coogan et al. (eds.), *The New Oxford Annotated Bible*, 471–97 (Essays); R. E. Brown and S. M. Schneiders, 'Hermeneutics', in Brown, Fitzmyer, and Murphy (eds.), *The New Jerome Biblical Commentary*, 1146–63; K. Froehlich and J. Barr, 'Interpretation, History of', in Metzger and Coogan, *Oxford Companion to the Bible*, 303–24; P. Gooder, *Searching for Meaning: An Introduction to Interpreting the New Testament* (London: SPCK, 2008); W. G. Jeanrond, 'Interpretation, History of', *ABD* iii. 424–43; B. C. Lategan, 'Hermeneutics', *ABD* iii. 149–54; R. W. L. Moberly, 'What is Theological Interpretation of

theology is nothing if not a basic issue that has repercussions right through systematic theology, moral theology, and further particular theological disciplines. Faced with the vast literature on biblical interpretation, let me suggest one scheme for interpreting and appropriating the Scriptures in life and theology: the *intentio auctoris* and the world of the past author; the *intentio textus* and the world/history of the text; and the *intentio legentis* and the world of the present reader(s).

1. The first task, which corresponds to the work of historical-critical exegesis, aims at understanding and clarifying the historical origin of the final form of the biblical texts and, above all, what their authors intended to communicate (= the original, literal[19] meaning and message). In the world in which they wrote and employing the resources of their culture and religious community, what did the sacred writers wish to communicate and 'fix' in their texts for the specific audience for which they wrote? Their meaning was generated and expressed by their choice of genre (e.g. a letter or a psalm), the goals to which they directed themselves, the judgements they made, the responsibility they assumed in asserting some truth-claims, the invitations they conveyed, and the commitments in which their texts involved them (e.g. an apostle's

---

Scripture?', *Journal of Theological Interpretation*, 3 (2009), 161–78; R. Morgan and J. Barton, *Biblical Interpretation* (Oxford: Oxford University Press, 1988); C. A. Newsom, 'Contemporary Methods in Biblical Study', in Coogan et al. (eds.), *The New Oxford Annotated Bible*, 497–505 (Essays); E. A. Nida et al., 'Translations', in Metzger and Coogan, *Oxford Companion to the Bible*, 749–78; G. O'Collins and D. Kendall, *The Bible for Theology: Ten Principles for the Theological Use of Scripture* (Mahwah, NJ: Paulist Press, 1997); J. C. O'Neill and W. Baird, 'Biblical Criticism', *ABD* i. 725–36; Pontifical Biblical Commission, *The Interpretation of the Bible in the Church* (Vatican City: Libreria Editrice Vaticana, 1993); id., *The Jewish People and their Sacred Scriptures in the Christian Bible* (Vatican City: Libreria Editrice Vaticana, 2001); id., *The Bible and Morality: Biblical Roots of Christian Conduct* (Vatican City: Libreria Editrice Vaticana, 2008); S. Prickett (ed.), *Reading the Text: Biblical Criticism and Literary Theory* (Oxford: Basil Blackwell, 1991); H. Graf Reventlow, *History of Biblical Interpretation*, i: *From the Old Testament to Origen*, trans. L. G. Perdue (Atlanta: Society of Biblical Literature, 2009); R. E. Schüssler Fiorenza, 'Feminist Hermeneutics', *ABD* ii. 783–91; D. Stuart, 'Exegesis', *ABD* ii. 682–8; A. C. Thiselton, *New Horizons in Hermeneutics* (London: HarperCollins, 1992); F. M. Young, 'Interpretation of Scripture', in S. A. Harvey and D. G. Hunter, *The Oxford Handbook of Early Christian Studies* (Oxford: Oxford University Press, 2008), 845–63.

[19] 'Literal' does not mean falling into the error of fundamentalism and taking texts 'literalistically', or in a wooden fashion that 'explains' parables (e.g. the Book of Jonah) or apocalypses (e.g. the Book of Revelation) as if they were historical or predictive texts, respectively.

mission). Obviously their meaning did/does not coincide in a simplistic way with the wording they adopted. The literary and religious conventions of the whole thought-world of biblical times, as well as what we might know about their particular life-setting, are indispensable guides in recovering what the sacred authors wanted to say when they used the words they did. Exegetes and interpreters must allow for a certain imprecision built into the 'original' intention and audience. We may not presuppose that the original meaning was always sharply defined as if it could be precisely recovered and exactly paraphrased. This is particularly true when we face poetic and imaginative texts (e.g. in the prophetic books). The original audience likewise was often not a single, clearly demarcated group, made up of hearers and readers of uniform convictions and needs.

We call this exegesis *historical*, because it tries to leap over the temporal and cultural gap between us and the original authors and return to the contexts in which the Scriptures were formed and fashioned. Obviously many difficulties attend this enterprise. Working in the twenty-first century, how can scholars recapture the intentions of authors who wrote twenty centuries ago or more and in a very different kind of world? Yet we may not ignore the basic human affinity between the biblical authors and modern interpreters and that mutual understanding brought by sharing in the same faith. A common faith can help contemporary readers enter the world and mind-set of the original writers.

We call this exegesis *critical*, because it requires professional knowledge of biblical languages and times, as well as a balanced judgement that can assess the evidence. The historical-critical method remains essential but insufficient; one should not overstate the case for it. Many of its conclusions remain tentative and may not be construed as 'assured results'. In fact, such conclusions range from the highly probable through the possible to the highly unlikely. Moreover, as with other texts, the biblical texts, once they were written and circulated, began to have their own history as people in different and later situations read and interpreted them.

2. As H.-G. Gadamer,[20] W. K. Wimsatt, and other philosophers and literary critics have insisted, all written documents enjoy a

---

[20] In *Truth and Method*, trans. J. Weinsheimer and D. G. Marshall (New York: Crossroad, rev. edn. 1989), Gadamer states a universally valid principle: 'not just

potential for developments in meaning (*intentio textus*) that go beyond the literal sense intended by their original authors when they wrote in particular situations for specific audiences (*intentio auctoris*). Texts can communicate to their readers more than their authors ever consciously knew or meant. Thus the biblical texts gained a life of their own, a 'reception history',[21] as they distanced themselves from their original authors and addressees, entered new contexts, and found later readers and hearers. This happened when the first Christians read their inherited Jewish Scriptures and when these Scriptures and the texts of what came to be known as the New Testament were read and applied down the centuries.

When, after many centuries of Christianity, we try to understand biblical texts, the 'effective history' of the text always influences us, whether we are aware of this or not. Interpreting, for example, the meeting between the risen Christ and Mary Magdalene (John 20: 11–18) will be affected by the celebration of her feast (22 July), by artistic representations of the scene (e.g. by Fra Angelico and Titian), by legends about her, by her being honoured by churches and colleges that bear her name, and, not least, by misguided identification of her with 'the woman who was a sinner' and anointed Christ's feet in Luke 7: 37.

Originally graced in their composition by a powerful input from the Holy Spirit, the Scriptures became richly *graced* as bearers of later illumination and redemption, mediated through their use in the liturgy, preaching, catechesis, theology, and whole life of the Church. Despite the sin, corruption, and ineptitude that disfigured the post-New Testament, dependent phase of revelation, the Holy Spirit continued to guide the interpretation and use of the Scriptures which the same Spirit had once and for all inspired in the foundational phase of revelation that closed with Christ and the apostolic Church.

---

occasionally but always, the meaning of a text goes beyond its author.' In repeating this point, he adds that texts also become independent from their original addressees: 'the horizon of understanding cannot be limited either by what the writer originally had in mind, or by the horizon of the person to whom the text was originally addressed.' Hence he argued that 'reconstructing what the author really had in mind' is at best 'a limited undertaking' (296, 395, 373).

[21] See M. Lieb, E. Mason, and J. Roberts (eds.), *The Oxford Handbook of the Reception History of the Bible* (Oxford: Oxford University Press, 2010). We might prefer here the term *Wirkungsgeschichte* (effective history or history or effects); it focuses more on the power and impact of the inspired text than on the receptivity of the readers.

Two thousand years of biblical reflection and interpretation have been marred by periods of neglect and decadent formalism. Yet the patristic witnesses, the followers of St Benedict and St Scholastica, the best of the medievals, the *devotio moderna* of Thomas à Kempis and others, the Reformers' return to the scriptural sources, and mystics in every age show the enduring vitality of the inspired texts. The history of the Church and her tradition have been shaped by and are to be evaluated by attention to and interpretation of those texts. One might even describe tradition as the Church's collective experience of the Bible.

Undoubtedly the rise of historical consciousness and the growth of literary criticism and other disciplines have opened new, valuable, and henceforth indispensable methods of exegesis. In scriptural studies we now 'know' much more, at least in the sense of having vast amounts of information at our disposal. But, despite all the journals, biblical commentaries, concordances, dictionaries, and translations, dare we claim that we understand and interpret the Scriptures better than Origen, Augustine of Hippo, Cyril of Alexandria, Hildegard of Bingen, Thomas Aquinas, Martin Luther, and Teresa of Avila? They knew by heart vast stretches of biblical texts, related them to one another, and through prayerful contact with these texts found in them light and life for their journey. It would be foolhardy to assert that twenty-first-century Christians have clearly progressed beyond all previous generations in their personal study, understanding, and interpretation of the Bible. Let me cite one among countless examples to illustrate the power of the biblical texts. Around the year 270 a wealthy landowner in Egypt heard read in church two verses from Matthew's Gospel (19: 31 and then 6: 34). Matthew's texts entered a new context and proved their potential when they inspired the young Egyptian to do something not intended by the first evangelist: he gave up his wealth, retired to the desert, and entered history as St Antony the hermit, one of the great figures at the origins of Christian monasticism.

3. Thirdly, what would I propose about the appropriate interpretation of the Scriptures today? Here the intention of the reader (*intentio legentis*) comes into play in activating potential meanings of texts produced by the sacred writers (*intentio auctoris*) and interpreted during two thousand years of reception history (*intentio textus*). Over and over again meaning occurs as readers discover, liberate, and

recreate the sense of the text in (and to some extent from) their own contexts.

Death long ago took away the original authors and their intended readers, but their communicative intentions created normative texts which continued to function in a long history of fruitful interpretation and actualization before reaching contemporary interpreters. In applying to the original writers, the texts themselves, and present-day readers the same term (communicative 'intention'), I recognize analogous, but not identical, functions. A difference remains between the original creators, their dynamic products, and contemporary recreators. Yet a convergence between their communicative perspectives allows us to apply to the writers, their texts, and their readers one and the same term ('intention'). Such communicative convergence excludes theories that flatly ignore the intentions of the original authors and attribute radical indeterminacy (or lack of intention) to biblical (and other texts). We return below to the issue of unchecked 'reader response/freedom', which would deny that biblical (and other) texts should exercise some control over their readers.

What then do I expect from contemporary readers of the Scriptures—in particular, from theological readers? In seeking to appropriate biblical texts by establishing their meaning and truth, they should act in the spirit of 'faith seeking understanding'.[22] They do their interpreting within the faith community and out of the faith that the Holy Spirit, despite human limitations and failures, both inspired the writing of the Scriptures and has guided their interpretation through the living tradition of the Church. As St Jerome insisted, the Sacred Scripture is to be read and interpreted in the same Spirit through whom it was written (*In Epistolam ad Galatas*, 5. 19–21; *PL* 26. 445A).[23] The Holy Spirit, who was at work in forming the biblical texts, continues to work in arousing faith through them; those texts which expressed various religious experiences 'then' will generate similar religious experiences 'now'. The Bible is truly what it is only when readers and hearers receive its impact and let its

---

[22] One should also add that this appropriation should be done in the spirit of 'worship seeking understanding' and 'justice seeking understanding'. We return to these two issues in the last chapter.

[23] Vatican II's *Dei Verbum* (no. 12, n. 9) refers to this passage in Jerome, but inaccurately gives the reference as *PL* 26. 417A.

consequences be worked out in their worship and practice. They 'perform' the biblical text and complete it.

Exegesis apart from the faith community means exegesis apart from the Spirit that gave the community those Scriptures, indwells the community, and facilitates the never-ending and life-giving appropriation of the Scriptures. Numerous biblical commentators, however, take their distance from any such confessional approach. They do their work in the name of descriptive, impartial, independent, and scholarly work proper to disengaged reason. Their ideal practitioners are free, rational, and enlightened spectators who are emancipated from all authority, open to a 'objective' grasp of things, and promise to provide us with the assured results of scholarship. What are their results like? Let us take one example: *Five Gospels: The Search for the Authentic Words of Jesus*, edited by R. W. Funk, R. W. Hoover, and the Jesus Seminar.[24] The work purports to take a neutral, unbiased, and properly sceptical stance in treating the four Gospels and one non-canonical Gospel (the so-called Gospel of Thomas). It presupposes that a religiously neutral, independent, and non-traditional interpretation of the Scriptures will prove a more reliable guide to Jesus and the biblical origins of Christianity than any interpretations coming from those who are confessionally committed and interpret the Gospels within a living tradition. Many outstanding exegetes, like Raymond Brown, James Dunn, and John Meier, have convincingly disputed detail after detail in the work of the Jesus Seminar. Theologians and others find much more reliable guides to the Gospels in the recent commentaries by Ulrich Luz and John Nolland (Matthew), Joel Marcus, Francis Moloney, and Adela Yarbro Collins (Mark), John Nolland and Robert Tannehill (Luke), Andrew Lincoln (John), as well as in recent books about the historical Jesus (by Richard Bauckham, James Dunn, Paul Eddy with Gregory Boyd, Craig Keener, John Meier, and Tom Wright). The central difficulty with the work of the Jesus Seminar is that their methodology expected far too much from merely 'objective' procedures, which might yield some particular results but no valuable insights into the life of the text as a whole.

Let us take an analogy from another discipline, literary criticism. A 'scientifically objective', disengaged approach might establish the

---

[24] New York: Macmillan, 1993; see reviews by R. B. Hays, *First Things*, 43 (May 1994), 43–8; G. O'Collins, *The Tablet* (17 September 1994), 1170.

date of the composition of *Macbeth* and various sources used by Shakespeare. But only a responsive, imaginative, and participatory approach that invests our own being in the act of appropriating the text will give some true perspective on the whole play and appropriate insights into the heart of the tragedy. Those who study great dramas in libraries but steadily refuse to attend the theatre and share in the living tradition of acting and production are hardly likely to become valuable critics of drama. Without a love for literature and a living affinity with it, we cannot expect to relate to the great texts and expound them in any worthwhile way. It is precisely such loving affinity that provides the proper and privileged condition for understanding and assessing great works of literature. In a similar fashion, merely 'objective' knowledge that refuses to let participatory knowledge also come into play when interpreting the Scriptures might produce some particular, historical findings. But it cannot take us very far, since such a 'merely objective' method chokes the voice of the biblical texts and declines to face them for what they are: extraordinary religious, ecclesial, and theological works. To ignore as an irrelevance the spiritual message of the Scriptures is a little like reading Shakespeare while sedulously ignoring the poetry and drama. This inappropriate method reminds me of scholars who used Homer's *Iliad* as a guide to the archaeology and history of Troy and steadfastly refused to face and read the first and perhaps greatest epic poem of Western literature for what it primarily was/is: a richly illuminating masterpiece on the enduring human themes of life, love, breakdown in relationships, violence, and death. Likewise a religiously neutral, disinterested, and 'objective' interpretation misuses the Scriptures by taking them as presenting mere historical puzzles and problems rather than as setting us in front of the supreme interpersonal mystery: the encounter between God and human readers. True and life-giving knowledge of God and ourselves is available only by personal participation and through relationship. The Scriptures are in the business of furthering such self-knowledge and knowledge of God.

Nothing of what I have just written should be construed as attacking the historical-critical method as such; it rightly concerns itself with the genesis and original meaning of our biblical texts. To aim, however, at making historical judgements from a wholly 'scientific' perspective is not only a technique for ignoring the real thrust of the texts but is also an illusion. Biblical scholars are always doing more than simply stating what some texts meant and paraphrasing them. After the work of Albert Einstein, Werner Heisenberg, Max Planck, and others, natural scientists have come to terms with the fact that observers (along with the instruments they choose) belong to the process of investigation. All human knowledge, including knowledge in physics, chemistry, and the biological sciences, remains participatory and personal. There is an inevitable relationship between the observer and the observed. Even more in historical study, including the study of the Scriptures, the subject is necessarily and properly involved—with his or her questions, beliefs, values, inherited traditions, and presuppositions.[25] Historical understanding and interpretation always remain subjective, even when (or especially when?) historians and biblical scholars deny that this is so. Any search for the meaning of biblical and other texts is essentially conditioned by the situation of the one doing the searching.

A coda: hearing the word

To clarify further how respect for the present readers and their world does not allow for unchecked freedom, let me add a coda. Theologians and other readers should be faithful hearers of the Word, oriented primarily toward the scriptural texts rather than toward themselves, and primarily responsive to the meaning they discover and receive rather than to the meaning they construct and create for themselves. In doing so, they respect divine revelation's absolute priority over all human beliefs and judgements. They read the whole Bible with consent (not suspicion) and with the anticipation that, being imbued with the hidden presence of the infinitely true, good, and beautiful God, it may well say something to them that they have never heard before. They come face to face with the biblical text,

---

[25] See R. Bultmann, 'Is Exegesis without Presuppositions Possible?', in *Existence and Faith: Shorter Writings of Rudolf Bultmann*, trans. S. M. Ogden (London: Hodder & Stoughton, 1961), 289–96; G. Ebeling, 'The Significance of the Critical Historical Method for Church and Theology in Protestantism', in *Word and Faith*, trans. J. W. Leitch (London: SCM Press, 1963), 17–61.

and are 'answerable' to that text. St Augustine of Hippo exemplifies the exposure to the Scriptures all theologians need: in his extant writings he quotes about two-thirds of the Bible. His example calls on theologians to hear again the voice crying out: 'tolle et lege' (take and read).

What I am asking for here opposes the practice of those theologians who pay little attention to the Scriptures, or submerge them in their own closed systems, or else make biblical texts mean almost anything they want them to mean. They draw from the Scriptures what they have already decided to say. That risks turning the Scriptures into a series of Rorschach inkblots that call up merely individual, projective interpretations. This raises the question of the ethics of biblical reception. May we remake the text and invent meaning in our own image? Some build such practice into theory, claiming that texts of unavailable authors have no rights, belong absolutely to readers, and may be used in whatever way biblical interpreters, theologians, and other readers choose. In the name of excavating for a hidden subtext, some critics dismantle biblical and other texts, let meanings proliferate, and come up with an uncheckable range of alternative interpretations.[26] Any such total reader freedom turns its interpretations into mere reflections of a particular community's or individual's interests and experiences. It espouses an extreme form of reader response that constructs meaning without being rooted in the text it reads; meaning becomes simply what the reader makes of the texts. Theories of reader-oriented and reader-creative meaning that almost inevitably become reader-manipulative are even less appropriate in the case of the Scriptures. They also become self-destructive. Those who de-construct texts and interpret their meaning quite independently of the authors who produced them (as if meaning in no sense inheres in texts themselves) can and should face the same treatment. We readers, when reacting to such modern 'interpreters', can give free reign to our own projective interpretations, allow our experiences to dominate as we search for the subtext, and make their texts 'mean' whatever fits our purposes.

Readers of the Bible should listen and 'correspond' to the texts, through which they can hear the voices of the original authors, the

---

[26] See the anonymous editorial 'What's Wrong with Deconstructionism', *American Philosophical Quarterly*, 29 (1992), 193–5; and Thiselton's critical evaluation of Jacques Derrida in *New Horizons in Hermeneutics*, 103–32, 472–4, 582–92.

voices of scholarly and saintly interpreters down through the ages, and, above all, the voice of the Holy Spirit. Letting themselves be encountered by the Bible and expecting that the Bible will speak to them with authority, theologians allow the scriptural texts in all their strangeness and otherness to convey meaning, disclose truth, and authoritatively transform theological ideas, interests, and practice. In the words of St Ambrose of Milan, 'when we pray we address God; when we read the divine words, we listen to him' (*De Officiis Ministrorum*, 1. 20. 88). What ultimately counts is not what we say to God but what God says to us. Only those who let themselves be addressed and judged by the Bible will notice, for instance, where their routine appeals to certain scriptural texts may enjoy no more validity than ingrained habits fostered perhaps by some merely doctrinaire and inadequate tradition. Only those theologians consistently open to revelatory moments effected by the Bible will know their work to be a process in which their interpretations can never enjoy definitive status.

This chapter has taken up three topics that belong squarely to the agenda of fundamental theology, concerned as it is with the basics that affect all particular areas of theology. What we hold about the truth, canon, and interpretation of the Bible is clearly foundational for all that follows in systematic and moral theology.

Of the three themes, biblical interpretation is the most difficult and controversial. Whatever particular approach to biblical interpretation we prefer, it must attend to the original authors, the history of the reception of their texts, and the context and questions that contemporary readers bring to their interpretation of the Bible. It should also make room for both reason and faith, the right use of historical reason and the appropriate attention to the transformative guidance of the Holy Spirit. We need (1) some critical distance when we read in a scholarly way the text and (2) a readiness to our being read by the text and transformed by it. This is the difference between grasping the meaning of a text and being grasped by its meaning, or between finding the truth and being found by it. The two 'readings' of the Scriptures, while distinguishable, should not be separated. Scholars who read these texts should also read them within the believing community (which has received the texts into its normative canon), recognize the Scriptures as inspired by the Holy Spirit, and accept some kind of biblical unity in Christ. Historical exegesis, while rationally critical, should not entail reading the Scriptures without faith. Rightly understood, scholarly interpretation of the Bible is also an exercise of a shared and personal faith.

This chapter and its predecessor have continued to link the reception of the Jewish Scriptures and the writing of the Christian Scriptures with the founding of the Church. We move next to that event, the understanding of which is also fundamental for all theology.

11

The Founding
of the Church

Previous chapters have argued that through the canonical Scriptures the leaders and members of the first-century Church exercise on later generations of Christians the normative authority given to them by the crucified and risen Christ. Such a position presupposes answering a number of fundamental questions.

1. Did Christ intend to found the Church? Or—to put this question more fully—did the community of the Church result from the *outer* communication of Christ's own message (together with the apostolic proclamation of his resurrection from the dead) and the *inner* gift of God's love in the person of the Holy Spirit? Or was the Church an unfortunate corruption that came from Paul's notion of Christians forming 'the body of Christ' (1 Cor. 12: 27–8; Eph. 4: 12; Col. 2: 17)? Jesus had preached only the kingdom of God, but Paul and his associates set themselves to organize the Church. Both serious and more popular writers have at times brought this charge against Paul in their 'Jesus, yes, but Paul, no' agenda. Philip Pullman made the misguided creation of an authoritarian Church part of his case against the apostle in *The Good Man Jesus and the Scoundrel Christ.*[1]

2. During the twentieth century some scholars began detecting in Luke–Acts and the Pastoral Letters a deterioration into 'early Catholicism'. In coining and promoting this negative term they pointed to

[1] London: Canongate Books, 2010.

what they claimed to have happened in first-century Catholicism: a decline from the pure gospel of Jesus and Paul that occurred when hope faded for the *parousia* or second coming, and a structured church emerged dispensing salvation through ministerial ordination, institutionalized apostolic succession, set forms of doctrine, and re-established law.[2] The thesis of 'early Catholicism' enjoys at least the merit of accepting Paul as a reliable witness to genuine Christianity and not charging him with being the agent of a fatal, early degeneration. But scholars challenge the way the thesis questions or rejects Luke–Acts and the Pastoral Epistles, thus pruning the New Testament canon for its own purposes. Moreover, if embarrassment at the delay of the *parousia* played a major role in producing 'early Catholicism', such embarrassment left very few traces, apart from 2 Peter 3: 1–13.

3. Long before the particular thesis of 'early Catholicism' developed, one 'myth' of Christian origins pictured an original purity being corrupted in a story of decline (*Verfallsgeschichte*).[3] Human weakness and decadence spoiled the noble or even divine start the Christian movement first enjoyed. We find this 'myth' being endorsed in some surprising places like the *Leviathan* of Thomas Hobbes (1588–1679). In his version of Christian history as a story of decline, the simple, charismatic groupings of the earliest Christians gave way to hierarchical structures. The 'consciences' of the first believers 'were free, and their words and actions subject to none but the civil power'. 'Out of reverence, not by obligation', converts 'obeyed the apostles, who were distinguished for their 'wisdom, humility, sincerity, and other virtues'. As the number of believers increased, 'the presbyters' (who later on 'appropriated to themselves' the name and role of 'bishops') and, eventually, the Bishop of Rome asserted their authority, promoted a sense of obligation towards themselves, and tied 'knots' on 'Christian liberty'. Hobbes advocated the demolition of this 'ancient authority' and a return to 'the independency' of the earliest Christians: 'there ought to be no power over the consciences of men, but [only that] of the Word itself, working faith in each one' (4. 47).[4]

---

[2] See J. D. G. Dunn, *Unity and Diversity in the New Testament* (2nd edn. London: SCM Press, 1990), 341–66; J. H. Elliott, 'A Catholic Gospel: Reflections on "Early Catholicism" in the New Testament', *Catholic Biblical Quarterly*, 31 (1969), 213–23.
[3] See R. L. Wilken, *The Myth of Christian Beginnings* (London: SCM Press, 1971).
[4] T. Hobbes, *Leviathan* (New York: Macmillan, 1962), 498–9.

4. Where Robert Wilken wrote of 'the myth' of Christian origins, accuracy suggests speaking in the plural, of 'myths'. Some significant writers like F. C. Baur (1792–1860)[5] with his Tübingen school elaborated a conflict model when interpreting Christian beginnings. In a Hegelian dialectic, opposed views of faith met in a struggle that produced the compromise synthesis of the Catholic Church out of the thesis of Gentile Christianity (espoused by Paul) and the antithesis of Jewish Christianity (represented by Peter and James). Baur understood the dialectical character of history to have been exemplified by the Catholic resolution of a conflict at the start of Christianity. He also endorsed some elements of the *Verfallsgeschichte* view by arguing that the pure Pauline gospel had already been partially corrupted by the time the inauthentic Pastoral Letters were written.[6] Baur's thesis involved assigning very late dates for the composition of the New Testament, an extreme view that has been universally abandoned, along with the Hegelian straitjacket into which he forced early Christian history.

5. Walter Bauer (1877–1960) produced a variant of this conflict model. In his view, Christian 'orthodoxy' was merely the position that prevailed over other, equally valid traditions in the early Church.[7] Where some have proposed an 'original purity' model, as in (2) and (3) above, in their different ways Baur and Bauer proposed an 'original conflict' model. While Baur's dialectical reading of history lost its popularity, Bauer has enjoyed some latter-day followers who claim that 'alternative' versions of early Christianity (e.g. those that showed little interest in the death and resurrection of Jesus and endorsed radical egalitarianism) lost out and were suppressed by the 'orthodox'. The victorious 'orthodox' established the list of canonical books and marginalized and suppressed as far as they could the

---

[5] See 'Baur, Ferdinand Christian', *Oxford Dictionary*, 172–3.

[6] H. Harris, *The Tübingen School* (Oxford: Clarendon Press, 1975); P. C. Hodgson, *The Formation of Historical Theology: A Study of F. C. Baur* (New York: Harper & Row, 1966).

[7] W. Bauer, *Orthodoxy and Heresy in Early Christianity*, trans. the Philadelphia Seminar on Christian Origins (Philadelphia: Fortress Press, 1971; German orig. 1934). See also K. L. King, 'Which Early Christianity?', in S. A. Harvey and D. G. Hunter (eds.), *The Oxford Handbook of Early Christian Studies* (Oxford: Oxford University Press, 2008), 66–84; S. E. McGinn, 'Internal Renewal and Dissent in the Early Christian Church', in P. F. Esler (ed.), *The Early Christian World*, i (London: Routledge, 2000), 893–906.

apocryphal Gospels, which supported alternate styles of Christianity and which, in whole or in part, are alleged to have antedated the canonical Gospels.[8]

In spelling out a position on the foundation of the Church as something intended by Christ and guided by the Holy Spirit, fundamental theologians face controversial questions and must contend with a range of opposing views. Let us begin with Jesus and what we might glean from the Gospels about his intentions. Did he intend to found the worldwide Church?

The founder of the Church

Apropos of the earthly Jesus' intentions to found the Church, modern scholars (represented by exegetes like Raymond Brown and theologians like Walter Kasper) have moved to a middle ground between earlier maximalizing and minimalizing positions.

Maximalists and minimalists

Maximalists held that from the outset Jesus clearly aimed at founding the Church with all its structural components. Usually such a maximal approach rested on two presuppositions. First, the earthly Jesus was credited with more or less unlimited knowledge; he was alleged to have enjoyed (in his human consciousness) the vision of God

---

[8] See e.g. J. D. Crossan, *Four Other Gospels: Shadows on the Contour of the Canon* (Minneapolis: Winston Press, 1985); the four Gospels in question are the Gospel of Thomas, Egerton Papyrus 2, the Secret Gospel of Mark, and the Gospel of Peter. The Secret Gospel of Mark is now widely recognized to have been a forgery perpetrated by the late Morton Smith; the Egerton Papyrus 2, made up of two imperfect leaves and a scrap of papyrus, dates from the late second century. The apocryphal Gospels of Thomas and Peter are normally dated to the second or early third century AD, and contain imaginative developments from what we find in the four canonical Gospels. Attempts to fix early, even very early dates for their composition have not convinced the vast majority of scholars. See R. E. Brown and P. Perkins, 'Christian Apocryphal Gospels', in R. E. Brown, J. A. Fitzmyer, and R. E. Murphy (eds.), *The New Jerome Biblical Commentary* (London: Geoffrey Chapman, 1989), 1065–8. For Crossan's attempts to establish an early date for part of the Gospel of Peter, see G. O'Collins and D. Kendall, 'Did Joseph of Arimathea Exist?', *Biblica*, 75 (1994), 235–421, at 236–8.

enjoyed by the saints in glory (the beatific vision). That meant, among other things, precise and detailed information about everything that was to happen, including the emergence of Christianity in the aftermath of his death and resurrection.[9] Second, behind the maximal view there often seemed to lurk the fear that unless the earthly Jesus explicitly intended to found the Church with *all* its institutional elements, its origin would not be divinely authorized. Hence he was held to have planned and prepared (at least from the start of his public ministry) the establishment of the Church in all its details.

Minimalists stressed the difficulty of recovering very much reliable information about Jesus' words and deeds. They often argued that we have no access whatsoever to Jesus' interior states of mind, let alone to any possible intentions on his part to initiate a new religious movement. Claims about his motivation and aims were dismissed as illegitimate psychological constructions. All we know, to echo Alfred Loisy's famous dictum, is that Jesus preached the kingdom of God and what emerged was the Church.

Various arguments built up against the maximalizing interpretation. It is after all orthodox faith to believe that Jesus of Nazareth was (and is) truly divine and truly human. Being limited in knowledge and foreknowledge is precisely part of being genuinely human and not some unfortunate perfection from which he had to be miraculously delivered. Among other things, some limitation in knowledge makes it possible for human beings to act freely in the world. Free acts entail entrusting oneself to situations and a future which are to one degree or another unknown. Hence, in the name of Jesus' true humanity and genuine liberty (not to mention other reasons), theologians and official teachers have accepted real limitations in his knowledge and foreknowledge about matters like the foundation of Christianity.

It has been frequently pointed out against the minimalizers (represented classically by Rudolf Bultmann) that they had abandoned one unacceptable position for another equally unacceptable extreme. Granted that those elaborate reconstructions indulged in by many nineteenth- and twentieth-century 'lives' of Jesus were almost totally subjective projections of their authors, this does not justify heading

---

[9] On the thesis of the earthly Jesus enjoying in his human consciousness the beatific vision of God, see G. O'Collins, *Christology: A Biblical, Historical, and Systematic Study of Jesus* (2nd edn. Oxford: Oxford University Press, 2009), 266–9.

to the other extreme and rejecting any claims whatsoever about the motivation and intentions of Jesus. The absence of full information about his psychological states is not the same as the absence of all information about his intentions. At least here and there, the Gospels, as we will see, allow us to draw some conclusions about what Jesus aimed at doing.

Furthermore, the minimalizers finish up with a strange account of what God effected through the whole Christ-event. Jesus, the primary protagonist on the visible scene, preached the kingdom without the slightest idea or intention about what was to come with the rise of the Church. We are expected to accept that Christianity got under way without any conscious 'input' from Jesus himself. He founded this new religious movement and yet in no way wanted or intended to do so! Certainly we should not simply identify the rule of God with the Christian Church, but neither should we separate completely Jesus' proclamation of the kingdom from the emergence of the worldwide Church. Some data from the Gospels tells against any such rigid separation between the ministry and the post-resurrection situation.

Jesus and Gentiles

Jesus is recalled by Matthew (writing probably after AD 70) as having said that his primary mission was to reform Israel and call Jews back to God: 'I was sent only to the lost sheep of the house of Israel' (Matt. 15: 24)—a saying that stood in such manifest discontinuity with the early Church's sense of her universal mission that, so far from being invented in the post-Easter situation, it was fortunate not to have been suppressed out of embarrassment. This statement (that paralleled an instruction limiting the trial mission of the Twelve found in Matt. 10: 5–6) appears in an account of Jesus encountering a Gentile woman who lived in Gentile territory, 'the districts of Tyre and Sidon'. Mark 7: 26 identifies her as Greek and Syro-Phoenician.[10] In this

---

[10] J. R. Donahue and D. J. Harrington comment: 'A "Greek" (used only here in Mark) does not [necessarily] mean someone who is ethnically Greek but can be used as a generic term for a non-Jew. It also suggests someone who had assimilated Greek culture and language' (*The Gospel of Mark* (Collegeville: Liturgical Press, 2002), 233). On the story of the Syro-Phoenician woman, see D. A. Hagner, *Matthew 14–28* (Dallas: Word Books, 1995), 438–53; U. Luz, *Matthew 8–20* (Minneapolis: Fortress, 2001), 336–42; J. P. Meier, *A Marginal Jew: Rethinking*

story the woman, even though a Gentile, asked help for her tormented daughter. While Jesus took his mission of salvation primarily to his fellow Jews, he was ready, nevertheless, to respond to faith wherever he found it, and healed the woman's daughter instantly (Matt. 15: 21–8; Mark 7: 24–30). When a Gentile asked him for a miracle, he was willing to do so, and began breaking down the barriers that separated Jews and Gentiles.

The Gospels record further episodes in which Jesus responded to the needs of non-Jews, both specific individuals and groups. In Capernaum a centurion, a non-Jewish military officer in charge of 50 to 100 soldiers, appealed to Jesus for help when his son (*pais*, which could also be translated 'servant') fell desperately ill (Matt. 8: 5–13).[11] Apparently the centurion knew that, as a Jew, Jesus should not enter the house of a Gentile. But he was convinced that a word of command would be enough, since diseases obeyed Jesus just as soldiers obeyed their officers. Jesus was astonished at the way the centurion trusted his (Jesus') power to work the cure: 'truly I tell you, in no one in Israel have I found such faith.' The faith of this Gentile put Israel to shame, in the sense that his faith went beyond anything Jesus had so far experienced in his ministry to Jews.

Before healing the centurion's son by a simple word of command, Jesus—at least in Matthew's account—used the image of God's final banquet to warn what would happen at the end. Many 'outsiders' will enter the kingdom while many Israelites will be excluded: 'I tell you, many will come from east to west and will eat with Abraham and Isaac and Jacob in the kingdom of heaven, while the heirs of the kingdom will be thrown into the outer darkness.' This is a 'pointed threat rather than something irrevocable. It may well go back to Jesus.'[12] Thus the faith of the centurion, 'the first member of the gentile church',[13]

---

the Historical Jesus, ii (New York: Doubleday, 1994), 659–61, 674–6; J. Nolland, *The Gospel of Matthew* (Grand Rapids, Mich.: Eerdmans, 2005), 628–36.

[11] Since Roman troops were not stationed then in Galilee, he probably belonged to the forces of Herod Antipas, who seemed to have 'employed foreigners in his service' (M. A. Chancey, *The Myth of Gentile Galilee* (Cambridge: Cambridge University Press, 2002), 173–6). On the healing of the centurion's son, see D. A. Hagner, *Matthew 1–13* (Dallas: Word Books, 1993), 200–6; Luz, *Matthew 8–20*, 8–12; Meier, *A Marginal Jew*, ii. 718–27, 763–72; Nolland, *The Gospel of Matthew*, 351–8.

[12] Luz, *Matthew 8–20*, 9.

[13] Ibid. 11.

signalled how the final gathering of the nations had already begun in the ministry of Jesus.

With the centurion, as with the Syro-Phoenician woman, Jesus healed someone from a distance. It is *only* in these two cases of Gentiles that the Gospels record such 'remote' healings. Luke 7: 1–10 and John 4: 46–53 tell about Jesus healing at a distance a centurion's slave (Luke) or a royal official's son (John). Despite some differences, these healing stories seem to be variations on what Matthew records about the centurion's son.

Exorcisms formed a prominent part of the wonder-working activity of Jesus, and included not only the deliverance of the Syro-Phoenician woman's daughter but also a dramatic exorcism in favour of a demoniac who seems to have been non-Jewish and living in the Gentile territory of the Decapolis (Mark 5: 1–20).[14] Mark includes two further miraculous deeds that Jesus performed for Gentiles and in Gentile territory: the restoration of hearing and speech to a deaf-mute (Mark 7: 31–7) and the feeding of the 4,000 (Mark 8: 1–10). Earlier Jesus had fed 5,000 fellow Jews (Mark 6: 30–44). Now in a separate episode in Mark's story, he provided an abundance of food for a crowd who seem to have been Gentiles.[15]

A healing story that includes an 'outsider' and is found only in Luke is that of ten lepers being cleansed by Jesus (Luke 17: 11–19).[16] One of them, who unlike the other nine was not a Jew but a Samaritan, returned 'praising God', 'prostrating himself' at Jesus' feet, and 'thanking him'. Jesus said to this man whom he called a 'stranger': 'your faith has made you well (saved you)'—words which he also used with two Jews, a woman cured of a long-standing haemorrhage (Mark 5: 34) and a blind beggar who received his sight (Mark 10: 52). In all three cases the verb conveys the sense of the divine power at work to rescue someone from an evil force. Spiritual, as well as merely physical, 'saving' or 'making well' was involved. The Samaritan 'saw'

---

[14] On the Gentile identity of the possessed man, see J. Marcus, *Mark 1–8* (New York: Doubleday, 2000), 342, 347, and 353.

[15] Marcus, *Mark 1–8*, 482–97. Some scholars argue that the two feedings are alternative versions of one and the same feeding miracle that the evangelist has incorporated in his text in two different places; yet see Meier, *A Marginal Jew*, ii. 950–66, 1022–38, at 956–8.

[16] See J. A. Fitzmyer, *The Gospel According to Luke X–XXIV* (New York: Doubleday, 1995), 1148–56; Meier, *A Marginal Jew*, ii. 701–6.

what his healing implied, came to faith, and received salvation. In this fuller way, Jesus blessed a person who was doubly an outcast—as a leper and a 'foreigner'.

If Jesus' *healing ministry* reached beyond the frontiers of racial and religious separation, so too did his *message* of the kingdom. God's reign now and in the future was for everyone. Even if at times his message was addressed to a Jewish audience precisely as Jewish (e.g. Mark 12: 1–12), normally his words were directed to human beings precisely as human beings. Let me offer some examples.

First, it was in the light, not of Mosaic legislation, but of the creation of humankind that Jesus expressed his ideal for marriage and opposition to divorce (Mark 10: 2–12; see Gen. 1: 29; 2: 24). This teaching concerned not merely Jews but all men and women whoever they were.[17] Second, Jesus set about founding a new family or new final community. Looking around at a group sitting near him, he declared: 'whoever does the will of God is my brother and sister and mother' (Mark 3: 35). He did not specify as candidates for his new family 'all those Jews who do the will of God'. Any man or woman who did what God wanted to be done qualified for admission to the new community, and became, whether he or she knew it or not, truly related to Jesus, a 'family member in the kingdom of God'.[18] Such people did not have to come from the ranks of those who had accepted an explicit call to follow Jesus, as though he had said: 'whoever among my disciples does the will of God is my brother and sister and mother.' There are other such 'whoever' statements in which the evangelists present Jesus' proclamation of the kingdom to his Jewish audience. These statements have a generalized form that lifts them above and beyond their specific setting to apply to people anywhere.[19]

Third, the parables of Jesus display a universal power that takes them far beyond Palestine, the original setting in which Jesus preached them. They were and are stories told for everyone, not just for Jews. To be sure, there are Jewish touches in such a parable as that of the prodigal son: above all, the religious disgrace incurred when the boy begins working with unclean animals, the pigs, and so publicly abandons his

---

[17] Donahue and Harrington, *The Gospel of Mark*, 292–9.
[18] Hagner, *Matthew 1–13*, 358.
[19] See G. O'Collins, *Salvation for All: God's Other Peoples* (Oxford: Oxford University Press, 2008), 88–9.

commitment to the Mosaic law.[20] Nevertheless, any Jewishness is inci-
dental; the main thrust of the parable goes beyond any ethnic or
religious frontiers to answer the universal questions: what is God like?
And to whom does God show mercy?

Fourth, other areas of Jesus' teaching illustrate how it reached out
to everyone: for instance, the beatitudes, the Lord's Prayer,[21] the love
command (Mark 12: 28–34; Matt. 25: 31–46),[22] and his parable of
the Great Dinner and of those who after accepting an invitation—
surprisingly—make last-minute excuses for not coming (Luke 14:
15–24).[23] The host reacts by first sending a slave to bring in from
the streets of the town some poor, crippled, blind, and lame people.
The slave is sent out a second time to bring others from the roads and
footpaths near the town and so fill up the house for the great dinner.
In this parable Jesus challenges those in his Jewish audience who
consider themselves the elect and take it for granted that they will 'be
present at the great eschatological banquet'.[24] By refusing to accept
the message of Jesus, they exclude themselves 'from the joy of that
festive meal, in which Abraham, Isaac, Jacob, and all the prophets will
share'.[25] The parable relates primarily to an actual moment in Jesus'
ministry to his fellow Jews, the moment that offers them the chance
to accept firmly and definitively an invitation to the messianic
banquet. That ministry is also initiating the final kingdom, which
will embrace the Gentiles. The parable hints at successive calls, first
to the Jews and then to the Gentiles, by distinguishing between the
group invited off the streets of the town and the second group who
come from the roads and footpaths outside the town.

In interpreting this parable and similar material, we face the
persistent difficulty of distinguishing between the theological insights
of the evangelists (and/or their sources) and the historical record

---

[20] On the parable of the prodigal son, see Fitzmyer, *The Gospel According to Luke X–XXIV*, 1082–94; J. Nolland, *Luke 9: 21–18: 34* (Dallas: Word Books, 1993), 777–91; G. O'Collins, *Following the Way* (London: HarperCollins, 1999), 3–28.

[21] For commentary and rich bibliography on the beatitudes and the Lord's Prayer, see Meier, *A Marginal Jew*, ii. 317–36, 377–89 (beatitudes), 291–302, 353–66 (Lord's Prayer).

[22] See O'Collins, *Salvation for All*, 92–5.

[23] On the wedding banquet staged by a king for his son, Matthew's adaptation of this parable (Matt. 22: 2–14), see ibid. 96–7.

[24] Nolland, *Luke 9: 21–18: 34*, 752–9, at 752.

[25] Fitzmyer, *The Gospel According to Luke X–XXIV*, 1048–59, at 1053.

derived from the activity of Jesus himself. Nevertheless, what we have cited above from what Jesus did and said prefigured the Church's coming mission and message to the Gentiles. The evangelists and other early Christians were justified in understanding their mission to Jews *and Gentiles* as continuing and expanding what Jesus had begun during his earthly ministry.

Finally, a reasonable case can be made that Jesus not only anticipated his violent death but also interpreted it in advance as somehow proving redemptive for Jews and Gentiles alike. The strongest testimony for Jesus' understanding of his coming death, its saving impact, and its 'beneficiaries' comes from the Last Supper.[26] Through the words and gestures of the 'institution narrative' (Mark 14: 22–4 parr.; 1 Cor. 11: 23–5), Jesus offered a covenant sacrifice—a cultic, priestly act which he wished to be continued as a central practice in the community that he had gathered. His historical, once-and-for-all offering on the cross was to become a permanent reality when his community celebrated the Lord's Supper. He wanted to establish for countless others his continuing and effective presence in the sacrificial meal-fellowship that he had instituted with a small, core group of disciples.[27]

The call of the Twelve

By asking that the sacrificial meal-fellowship of the Last Supper be continued, Jesus presupposed an ongoing community organized in a way that would make that possible. His previous call of the Twelve, for which we have multiple attestation, also implied some such measure of organization for his community.

[26] On the Last Supper, see J. A. Fitzmyer, *First Corinthians* (New Haven: Yale University Press, 2008), 429–32, 435–45; id., *The Gospel According to Luke X–XXIV*, 1385–406; C. S. Keener, *The Historical Jesus of the Gospels* (Grand Rapids, Mich.: Eerdmans, 2009), 296–302, 557–62; U. Luz, *Matthew 21–28*, trans. J. E. Crouch (Minneapolis: Fortress Press, 2007), 364–85; Nolland, *The Gospel According to Matthew*, 1069–86; J. Marcus, *Mark 8–16* (New Haven: Yale University Press, 2009), 956–68; A. C. Thiselton, *The First Epistle to the Corinthians* (Grand Rapids, Mich.: Eerdmans, 2000), 848–91.

[27] For details see O'Collins, *Salvation for All*, 100–20; id., *Jesus our Priest: A Christian Approach to the Priesthood of Christ* (Oxford: Oxford University Press, 2010), 19–24.

The Gospels report how, from a wider group of his followers, Jesus chose a core group of twelve to proclaim the good news of the kingdom and to drive out demons (Mark 3: 13–19 parr.). He later dispatched them on a preaching and healing mission, with instructions about their *modus operandi* that obviously mirror not so much the pre-crucifixion period as the situation of the post-Easter itinerant missionaries (Mark 6: 7–13, 30 parr.). At the end Jesus celebrated the Last Supper 'with the twelve' and Judas is called 'one of the twelve' (Mark 14: 10, 17, 43 parr.)—something that seems inconceivable unless the earthly Jesus had already called that leadership group into existence. Matthew, who names this core group the 'twelve disciples' and the 'twelve apostles', repeats (and modifies) some of the instructions he finds in Mark and adds others (Matt. 10: 1–11). When 'sent' by Jesus, the Twelve will share in the authority he has received from God (Matt. 10: 40). In Matthew's Gospel the Twelve are not actually reported to have gone out proclaiming the message of the kingdom; in the post-resurrection situation they were commissioned (as 'the eleven', after Judas' defection and suicide) to make disciples of all nations, to baptize in the name of the Father and of the Son and of the Holy Spirit, and to teach all that Jesus had commanded them (Matt. 28: 16–20). Much of what we read here comes, at least in its wording, from the evangelist Matthew, but for our purposes one point is important. Talk in that closing scene of 'the eleven', as happens similarly in Luke 24: 9, 37, would not be intelligible unless this core group had been created during Jesus' ministry. The functions of the group involved some kind of leadership role.

Luke has Jesus himself give the name of 'apostles' to the Twelve (Luke 6: 12–16), repeats almost all the instructions from Mark (Luke 9: 1–5), tells of the trial mission of the Twelve (Luke 9: 6), adds a similar mission undertaken by a broader group of seventy-two disciples (Luke 10: 1–12), and inserts Jesus' reaction to the joyful report of the latter group's success (Luke 10: 17–20). Luke ends his Gospel with the risen Jesus commissioning 'the eleven and those with them' for a worldwide mission (Luke 24: 33, 47–9), for which they will be empowered by the gift of the Holy Spirit—a promise repeated by the risen Jesus to 'the apostles' at the start of Acts (Acts 1: 1–5). Luke's detail about the need for Judas' place to be filled (Acts 1: 15–26) implies that a group of twelve existed and had an office to fulfil. For Luke, the Twelve (apostles) are *the* authoritative witnesses to the original Christian faith, above all as testifying to Jesus' resurrection from the dead and what it brings. Like

Matthew 19: 28, Luke draws from Q or the sayings source a promise about the Twelve's future role in representing and judging 'the twelve tribes of Israel' (Luke 22: 30). Only 'the Twelve', in their function as representatives and judges, will sit on 'the thrones', while all are called to 'the banquet' in the new age (Luke 13: 29 par.; 14: 15–24 par.).

The Gospels show, then, multiple witness for the fact that at some point in his ministry Jesus chose twelve disciples from among the wider ranks of his followers and gave them some kind of authoritative office and leadership role. Mark attests the original call (Mark 3: 13–19) and subsequent mission of the Twelve (Mark 6: 7–13); Q reflects the existence of this core group (Matt 19: 28 par.), and so too does John 6: 70. Then they are 'in place' to function as the key group receiving a foundational appearance of the risen Christ, an event attested by a kerygmatic formula in Paul (1 Cor. 15: 5) and subsequently narrated in varying ways by the Easter chapters of the Gospels.[28] The Twelve are given by Christ authority to lead and teach in his name, an authority for which, as Luke and (in his own way) John (John 20: 22–3) indicate, they are empowered by the Holy Spirit. Their apostolic mission shared in and came from the mission of the Son and the Holy Spirit. The choice of the Twelve indicates how Jesus planned a community.

At this point, some scholars move on to discuss the place within the Twelve of Peter and, in particular, to argue that the saying 'you are Peter and upon this rock I will build my church' (Matt. 16: 18) comes from the earthly Jesus himself. If so, we would have the earthly Jesus speaking explicitly of his intention to found 'the church' (see also Matt. 18: 17). While it has been common to interpret Matthew 16: 18 as a post-resurrection saying, W. D. Davies (with D. C. Allison) and others like C. S. Keener have put the case for Matthew 16: 18 being an authentic saying from Jesus.[29]

---

[28] In writing here of 'a' rather than 'the' foundational appearance, I wish— among other things—to respect the roles of Mary Magdalene and Peter as primary Easter witnesses. On Mary Magdalene, see G. O'Collins and D. Kendall, *Interpreting the Resurrection* (Mahwah, NJ: Paulist Press, 1988), 22–38; and on Peter, G. O'Collins and D. Kendall, *The Bible for Theology* (Mahwah, NJ: Paulist Press, 1997), 117–30. On the existence and nature of the Twelve during Jesus' ministry, see J. P. Meier, *A Marginal Jew*, iii (New York: Doubleday, 2001), 125–97.

[29] For details see Keener, *The Historical Jesus of the Gospels*, 200, 247–9, 529–30.

Any time for the Church?

Given the evidence about Jesus gathering a community (headed by the Twelve), reaching out to Gentiles,[30] and establishing a eucharistic meal-fellowship that he wished to be continued by his disciples, it would seem reasonable to find in the ministry, death, and intentions of the earthly Jesus the origins of the worldwide Church that emerged in the aftermath of the resurrection and Pentecost. Yet some hesitate, on the grounds of the imminent end inculcated by some of Jesus' teaching. How could he have intended to create a lasting community if the kingdom of God was to come so soon (see e.g. Mark 8: 38–9: 1)?[31] Did Jesus envisage very little time indeed between the kingdom already present through his own person and preaching and the future kingdom which would begin when he returned to judge the world (see Chapter 5 above)? How could there be any time for some community founded by him to carry on his work?

While some of Jesus' sayings leave any timetable open (e.g. 'your kingdom come' in Matt. 6: 10 par.), other sayings highlight the imminent coming of God's kingdom: 'there are some standing here who will not taste death until they see that the kingdom of God has come with power' (Mark 9: 1). However we interpret such prophetic language, we should, nevertheless, take Jesus at his word when he stated that he did not know when the end was to occur: 'of that day or that hour no one knows, not even the angels in heaven, not the Son, but only the Father' (Mark 13: 32 par.). This is the only place in Mark's Gospel where Jesus refers to himself absolutely as 'the Son', and yet that saying goes against an early Christian tendency to glorify Jesus by frankly admitting his ignorance about the timing of the end. It is difficult to imagine this logion being created by the Christian tradition and attributed to the earthly Jesus. The saying was fortunate not to have been suppressed.

All in all, Jesus' preaching of the kingdom envisioned an interim period between his present ministry and the end. For instance, the parables of the Sower, the Growing Seed, and the Mustard Seed

---

[30] On the mission to the Gentiles, see ibid. 389–93, 602–3.
[31] On Jesus' eschatological sayings, see ibid. 361–71, 594–7.

(Mark 4: 1–9, 26–32) involve a time of growth before the fullness of the final kingdom arrives.[32] Likewise, the warnings of Jesus about disturbing and violent events to come open up some passage of time before the world history would end (Mark 13: 5–13, 14–27).[33] Such language allows for an interim period during which a community founded by Jesus could continue his work and celebrate the Eucharist.

Once satisfied with the case for Jesus having in some sense founded the Christian Church, fundamental theologians can move on to examine what the post-resurrection and post-Pentecost Church was like. Thus they can carry through their work in fundamental ecclesiology or doctrine of the Church.

The early Church

If there was an interim period before the end, the first Christians thought it would be short. They expected the risen Christ to return again shortly in glory to judge the world (e.g. 1 Thess. 4: 13–5: 11). Totally focused on Jesus, they fashioned their interpretation and proclamation of him by putting together two elements: on the one hand, their experience of the events in which he had been the principal protagonist and, on the other, the concepts, expectations, and practices that they found to be relevant and illuminating within Judaism. To articulate their convictions about Jesus and his role in fulfilling the divine purposes, they depended upon their Jewish heritage. Thus their initiation rite of baptism took over some values from the purification rites of Judaism, not least from the baptism for the forgiveness of sins practised by John the Baptist. The followers of Jesus continued to find in the Jewish psalms their main prayer book. Some or even many of them continued to worship as Jews and in the Jerusalem Temple until excommunicated from Palestinian and other synagogues in the course of the first century. At least initially, Jesus' followers were unsure about the need to continue to observe the Torah or Jewish law (especially about circumcision and dietary requirements) and about the conditions they should impose on

---

[32] On these passages see Marcus, *Mark 1–8*, 291–8, 322–31.
[33] See Marcus, *Mark 8–16*, 874–900.

Gentiles who accepted faith in the crucified and risen Jesus. Yet the first Christians differed from other devout Jews by administering baptism 'in the name of Jesus' (e.g. Acts 2: 38) and celebrating together the Eucharist (e.g. Acts 2: 42, 45).[34]

In the Acts of the Apostles, Luke tells the story of the origin and early spread of the Christian faith.[35] In the opening chapters Peter functions prominently as the head of the twelve apostles, the core group of public witnesses to Jesus' life, death, and resurrection. With his dramatic calling on the road to Damascus around AD 36, Paul enters the Acts of the Apostles in chapter 9 and takes over the narrative from chapter 15. When Paul returns to Jerusalem in chapter 21, he meets James and 'all the elders'. But there is no mention of Peter being still in Jerusalem. Acts ends with Paul arriving in Rome several years before he and Peter died there as martyrs (between AD 64 and 67). James, a relative of Jesus and the leader of the Mother Church, had already been martyred in Jerusalem (probably in AD 62).[36]

These first decades of the Christian Church featured a tension between two 'constituencies': the original Jerusalem Church with its vision of a Torah-observant community and the non-Torah-focused vision of Paul and others. The latter vision lifted the early Church beyond being merely a reform group within Judaism. To be sure, Paul cherished the Jerusalem community and showed his love by collecting money for them from other, wealthier (local) churches (e.g. 2 Cor. 8: 1–9: 15). Nevertheless, a worldwide identity of Christians in Antioch, Rome, and further centres was formed in a tensional relationship

[34] On the rise and early spread of the Christian Church, see H. Chadwick, *The Church in Ancient Society: From Galilee to Gregory the Great* (Oxford: Clarendon Press, 2001), 1–109; J. D. G. Dunn, *Christianity in the Making*, ii: *Beginning from Jerusalem* (Grand Rapids, Mich.: Eerdmans, 2009); P. F. Esler (ed.), *The Early Christian World*, 2 vols. (London: Routledge, 2000); F. Vouga, 'Urchristentum', *TRE* xxxiv. 411–36.

[35] See J. A. Fitzmyer, *The Acts of the Apostles* (New York: Doubleday, 1998); E. Haenchen, *The Acts of the Apostles*, trans. B. Noble et al. (Philadelphia: Westminster Press, 1971); R. C. Tannehill, *The Narrative Unity of Luke–Acts*, ii (Minneapolis: Fortress, 1990). While the substantial historical reliability of many of the narratives in Acts can be defended (Fitzmyer, *Acts of the Apostles*, 124–8), the speeches and missionary discourses (which make up nearly one-third of the whole book) appear to be Lukan compositions, albeit passages in which Luke draws on some historical details and may give the general sense of what was actually said (ibid. 103–13). The speeches and discourses cannot be taken to be verbatim reports; they exemplify repeatedly Luke's style and formulations.

[36] See 'James, St', *Oxford Dictionary*, 862.

with the Jerusalem community. Despite exaggerations and forcing history to fit a Hegelian pattern, F. C. Baur's conflict model of early Christianity embodies some truth.

Paul spearheaded missionary activity around the Mediterranean world and, among Jews and Gentiles, spread faith in Jesus as Lord and Saviour. Luke understood this original Christian expansion as opening up an indefinitely long period which would close when Jesus who had 'ascended into heaven' would appear again in glory (Acts 1: 11). In the meantime, as Acts repeatedly indicates, the risen Jesus (e.g. Acts 9: 10–16; 18: 9–10; 22: 17–21) and his Holy Spirit (e.g. Acts 8: 29; 10: 19; 16: 6) constantly guided and empowered Christian life and mission.

By the 60s or even earlier, the followers of Jesus had come to be called 'Christians' (Acts 11: 26). Through baptism (initially in the name of Jesus and then in the name of the Trinity (Matt. 28: 19)), they knew their sins to be forgiven, received the Holy Spirit, entered the community of the Church, and celebrated the Eucharist. When praying, they followed Jesus' example and teaching by calling on God as 'Abba' (Rom. 8: 15; Gal. 4: 6), and used not only the psalms but also the Lord's Prayer and other such prayers as the Benedictus and the Magnificat (Luke 1: 46–55, 68–79), which were originally in Greek like the rest of Luke's Gospel but were subsequently known by their Latin titles. They learned the teaching of Jesus that reached them through their apostolic leaders and their associates.[37] They confessed the risen and exalted Jesus to be Messiah (anointed Deliverer), Lord, and Son of God,[38] and, together with God the Father, to have sent them the gift of the Holy Spirit. They believed that the Spirit was offered to all peoples and that salvation no longer required circumcision and the practice of the Mosaic law in all its details (Acts 15: 1–35).

Paul's letters defend God's gift of salvation to all alike; justification is not gained through human efforts at fulfilling the Jewish law. Faith and baptism incorporate people into the Church the Body of Christ,[39]

---

[37] See R. Bauckham, *Jesus and the Eyewitnesses: The Gospels as Eyewitness Testimony* (Grand Rapids, Mich.: Eerdmans, 2006).

[38] See L. W. Hurtado, *Lord Jesus Christ: Devotion to Jesus in Earliest Christianity* (Grand Rapids, Mich.: Eerdmans, 2003).

[39] Paul did not invent the Church nor was he responsible for appropriating an old title for Israel by naming the Church as 'a people claimed by God for his own' (1 Pet. 2: 9). Alongside the image of the Church as the People of God, Paul added two new images: the Church as the Body of Christ (1 Cor. 12: 12–31) and as the

and put an end, at least in principle, to distinctions between Jew and Gentile, slave and free, male and female (Gal. 3: 26–9). Faith in God the Father, in Jesus as Son of God and divine Lord, and in the Holy Spirit (2 Cor. 13: 13) brings all believers together in the unity of baptism, the Eucharist, and a common life. The apostle insists that sharing in the one eucharistic bread and in the one cup means belonging to the one Body of Christ (1 Cor. 10: 16–17).

Against all those who allege that it was Paul who created the Church and Christian doctrines (normally disparagingly called 'dogmas'), one must insist that Paul joined an already existing Church, which already believed in Christ as risen from the dead, had received the Holy Spirit right from the first Pentecost, practised baptism, celebrated the Eucharist, proclaimed Jesus as divine Lord and Son of God, and called God the Father 'Abba' because Jesus had done so, Paul accepted and did not create these and other fundamental beliefs and practices of Christianity. What he sometimes did was to illuminate them and connect them with lasting theological insights. Thus he understood baptism to re-enact symbolically the death and resurrection of Christ; it meant being 'buried' with him in 'death', so as to be 'raised from the dead' to walk in newness of life (Rom. 6: 4).[40] Paul interpreted sharing in the Eucharist as 'preaching' the death of the risen Lord until he comes again (1 Cor. 11: 26).[41]

While emphasizing the holy unity of the baptized, the apostle's letters let us glimpse some moral and doctrinal failures of early Christians. Those, like Hobbes and others, who endorse the *Verfallsgeschichte* theory (about an original and noble 'purity' of Christian life and faith that, more or less quickly, went into decline) maintain this theory despite the evidence, not because of it. The First Letter to the Corinthians reveals how some suffered from factionalism, indulged doubts over the central truth of the resurrection, indulged fornication, incest, and drunkenness, and showed a selfish unconcern for poorer Christians. The reproaches coming from Paul challenge illusions about a hypothetical golden age of Christianity that practised

Temple of the Holy Spirit (1 Cor. 3: 16–17). On these two new images see Fitzmyer, *First Corinthians*, 202–5, 473–86.

[40] See J. A. Fitzmyer, *Romans* (New York: Doubleday, 1993), 429–43.

[41] See Fitzmyer, *First Corinthians*, 444–5; Thiselton, *The First Epistle to the Corinthians*, 886–8.

heroic ideals on all sides. From the outset the Church suffered from scandals and divisions. The Book of Revelation, with its opening letters to seven (local) churches, joins the apostle in testifying to the mixture of holiness and sinfulness that characterized Christianity from the beginning (Rev. 2: 1–3: 22).

Along with holiness and sinfulness, a missionary outreach characterized the early Church. The Acts of the Apostles and Paul's letters name with respect missionaries who spread the good news about Jesus as the Saviour of the world: Barnabas, Epaphroditus (Phil. 2: 25; 4: 18), Timothy, Titus, and, not least, Prisca (Priscilla) and Aquila. This married couple, when they lived in Ephesus and Rome, gathered believers in their home, and were also known to the Christians of Corinth (1 Cor. 16: 19; Acts 18: 2–3, 26). Paul calls this couple his 'fellow workers' (Rom. 16: 3). When listing other collaborators on his mission for Christ, he names Andronicus and Junia (another married couple?) as 'distinguished in the eyes of the apostles' (Rom. 16: 7).[42]

Early leadership

In concluding his Letter to the Romans, Paul begins with 'our sister Phoebe, a helper/deacon [not deaconess] of the church of Cenchreae', writes of those who 'work' to spread the good news, and greets twenty-six people, twenty-four of them by name. This final chapter of Romans raises the question: was the Church meant to be, as Hobbes and others have argued, a completely egalitarian community, free of any kind of subordination to office-holders and sacred authorities? Did the vision of Jesus and the spontaneous direction of the Holy Spirit exclude any institutionalized leadership, which unfortunately occurred in the subsequent transmission of a threefold ministry of bishops, priests, and deacons? Did that historical development betray Jesus' original dream of male and female disciples as co-partners variously empowered by the Holy Spirit to minister to the whole community? Or was there always some kind of leadership that rightly developed and was handed on to successive generations for the good of

---

[42] Some translate this phrase as 'distinguished among the apostles'; see Fitzmyer, *Romans*, 739–40.

all? We have already examined the evidence from the earthly ministry of Jesus and what his choice of the Twelve entailed. What do the Pauline letters indicate about leadership in the Church?

A dramatic encounter with the risen Christ made Paul himself an apostle who proclaimed the resurrection of the crucified Jesus (1 Cor. 9: 1; 15: 8–11; Gal. 1: 12, 16). Paul's forceful sense of his own apostolic authority comes across clearly, not least in his Letter to the Galatians. After founding local churches, he exercised remote control over them through his letters, messengers, and occasional visits. But how did he understand the authoritative ministry of others in the growing Church?

In his earliest letter Paul speaks vaguely of those who 'preside' in the Church (1 Thess. 5: 12). Writing to the Philippians, he addresses 'overseers' (*episcopoi*) and their 'helpers' (*diakonoi*), terms that are often translated, somewhat anachronistically, as 'bishops' and 'deacons' (Phil. 1: 1).[43] But how they originated, what rites made them into 'overseers' and 'helpers', and what they did is left obscure. In another letter Paul notes how, within the whole 'Body of Christ', God has appointed various persons to be apostles, prophets, teachers, workers of miracles, healers, helpers, administrators, and speakers in different kinds of tongues (1 Cor. 12: 8–11, 28–30; see Rom. 12: 4–8).[44] The apostle's language in 1 Corinthians has encouraged some to envisage a Spirit-filled community with no lasting institutions and ordained officials. But does Paul intend here to issue permanent prescriptions for church order by setting special, personal gifts of the Spirit ('charisms') above any institutions and offices? It seems rather that he intends to give some practical advice to the Corinthian community and help solve some particular challenges facing their unity in Christ. The eight ministries in 2 Corinthians 12: 28 become five in another list, from a later letter: 'his [Christ's] gifts were that some should be apostles, some prophets, some evangelists, some pastors, and teachers'

---

[43] As we saw above, in Rom. 16: 1 Paul names Phoebe as a 'deacon/helper'.

[44] On these verses see Fitzmyer, *First Corinthians*, 463–4, 466–73, 482–4; id., *Romans*, 646–51; Thiselton, *The First Epistle to the Corinthians*, 938–65, 1013–24. On 'prophets', 'teachers', and other ministries in Paul's letters, see J. D. G. Dunn, *The Theology of Paul the Apostle* (London: T. & T. Clark, 2003), 580–93; and M. Edwards, 'The Development of Office in the Early Church', in Esler (ed.), *The Early Christian World*, i. 316–29.

(Eph. 4: 11). The list now includes 'evangelists' or messengers/preachers of the good news (see Rom. 10: 8–17).

'Prophets' (listed second to apostles in 1 Cor. 12: 28 and Eph. 4: 11) are mentioned not only by Paul but also by Luke, who records details of their activity in the emerging Church (Acts 11: 27; 13: 1; 15: 32; 21: 10). At least for Paul, 'prophets' seems to have been something like inspired and gifted preachers.

The Acts of the Apostles also introduces 'elders/presbyter (*presbuteroi*), who along with the 'apostles' led the Jerusalem church under James (Acts 11: 30; 15: 2, 4, 6, 22–3; 16: 4). Used of authority figures in Judaism, 'elders' came to designate officials in the Christian communities, without Luke or anyone else indicating how that happened. Early in Acts, Paul and Barnabas are said by Luke to have installed 'elders' in local churches (Acts 14: 23). Yet neither in the certainly authentic letters of Paul nor in the Deutero-Paulines does the apostle ever speak as such of 'elders' in the churches to which he writes, let alone install such persons. When Paul visits Jerusalem for the last time, he meets 'all the elders' and James, but neither 'apostles' nor 'the Twelve' are mentioned (Acts 21: 18).

Earlier, Acts 6: 1–6 has reported the appointment of seven to 'serve' (*diakonein*) in administering the Jerusalem church. One of them (Stephen), however, works wonders and acts as an outstanding speaker (Acts 6: 8–10) before being put on trial and martyred. Another (Philip) becomes a wandering preacher and miracle worker (Acts 8: 4–40).

The foundation of many local churches by apostles and others brought a shift in leadership, when pastors (called 'overseers', 'elders', and 'helpers/deacons') took over from the missionary apostles and other evangelists (see e.g. Acts 20: 17, 28; Phil. 1: 1; 1 Pet. 5: 1–4). A range of New Testament sources reflects this movement from missionary to settled pastoral leaders (e.g. the Pastoral Letters to Timothy and Titus). Nevertheless, many details about the appointment of these pastors, their leadership functions, and their relationship to the travelling missionaries remain unclear.

The Pastoral Letters, when recording a more developed organization of ministries, speak of 'overseers' or 'bishops' and their qualifications (1 Tim. 3: 1–7; see Titus 1: 7–9), of the 'elders' or 'presbyters' to be appointed by Titus in 'every town' of Crete (Titus 1: 5–6; see 1 Tim. 5: 17–20), and of the qualities of 'deacons' (1 Tim. 3: 8–10, 12–13), and apparently also of deaconesses (1 Tim. 3: 14). At least in Titus 1: 5–7, 'overseers' and 'elders' seem to be overlapping and almost synony-mous categories. Luke also seems to take 'presbyters' and 'overseers' as equivalent (Acts 20: 17, 28). There is some indication of succession in teaching authority (2 Tim. 2: 2). Much is conveyed about the teaching, preaching, defence of sound doctrine, administration, and family behaviour expected from leaders. But, apart from some passing regulations concerning worship (1 Tim. 2: 1–2, 8) and several references to the 'laying on of hands' (1 Tim. 5: 22; see 4: 14; 2 Tim. 1: 6), nothing further is said about the liturgical life of the community and, for instance, about the roles taken by these leaders (or others) in baptizing, celebrating the Eucharist, and instituting others as their successors in leadership functions.[45]

All in all, the New Testament, while witnessing to some organized ministry and structured leadership, yields no standard terminology for ministerial leaders and no fully clear pattern about how they functioned. To the extent that we can glimpse something about their appointment, commissioning, or 'ordination' (to speak some-what anachronistically), it seems to have occurred through an 'imposition' of hands and an invocation of the Holy Spirit (e.g. Acts 13: 3; 14: 23; 1 Tim. 4: 14; 2 Tim. 1: 6). The threefold ministry of leadership in the Pastoral Letters ('overseers/bishops', 'elders/presby-ters', and 'helpers/deacons') offers an early intimation of the threefold leadership ('bishops', 'presbyters', and 'deacons') that developed in the second century—a ministry for which they would be ordained through invoking the Holy Spirit and imposing hands.[46]

An examination of the New Testament supports the conclusion: the Christian Church, both at the start (AD 30–70) and then later in the first century (AD 70–100), was characterized by a measure of organization. This organization, along with the basic equality of all the baptized, comprised the leaders (with their institutionalized offices) and the led (with their personal gifts). The early Christian communities were not simply and totally egalitarian—a conclusion widely shared by those engaged in bilateral and other conversations on church order in the light of the New Testament.

---

[45] On various officials in the early Church, see Fitzmyer, *The Acts of the Apostles*: on 'apostles' (196–7), 'overseers/bishops' (678–9), 'helpers/deacons' (345), 'elders/presbyters' (482–3), 'prophets' (481), and 'teachers' (496).

[46] On all this see Faith and Order Commission, *Baptism, Eucharist and Minis-try* (Geneva: World Council of Churches, 1982), 21–5 ('Ministry', 7–25).

Members of ecumenical dialogues provide a useful sounding board for fundamental theologians engaged with church order and leadership. Some of the participants in such dialogues argue that the New Testament does not single out *one* pattern of order as divinely ordained. The New Testament neither excludes non-episcopal forms of leadership (e.g. government through elders) nor imposes for all times and places a threefold ministry of leadership (of 'overseer/bishop', 'elder/presbyter', and 'helper/deacon') that may enjoy an early intimation in the Pastoral Letters. Some Christians hold for an apostolic succession in a ministerial form but without episcopal succession. There appears, however, to be substantial consensus that the New Testament supports some organized ministry, some structured leadership, and not a total egalitarianism in which individuals appeal straight to the Holy Spirit in justifying their ministry and mission.

How are we to evaluate the view of those who trust that the Holy Spirit mediates salvation and mission directly to the individuals but decline to recognize that the same Spirit guided Christians in the foundational period to develop certain forms of leadership and, later, to collect into a canon the Scriptures which reflect that development (in particular, Acts and the Pastoral Epistles)? This position can seem like accepting the guidance of the Spirit for individuals but not for the community. Moreover, its appeal to the dynamic of the Spirit comes across as a one-sided 'pneumatological' principle that breaks free from the 'christological' principle expressed in the establishment of the Twelve and the call of Paul to his apostolic ministry and embodied in the institutional order of the Church. The person and mission of the Holy Spirit, far from being independent, are inseparable from the person and mission of Christ. The chapter in which Paul celebrates most fully the gifts of the Spirit (1 Cor. 12) takes its place in a letter which, from start to finish, is centred on Christ. The shape of Paul's faith shows through when he asks, 'Am I not an apostle? Have I not seen Christ?' (1 Cor. 9: 1), rather than, 'Am I not an apostle? Have I not received the Spirit?'

Into the second century

Besides exploring the development of church order in the first century, fundamental theologians need to pay some attention to what developed in the second century. We find in St Ignatius of Antioch (d. *c.* AD 107) a key witness to the emerging structure of Catholic Christianity.[47] The first writer known to have used the expression 'the Catholic Church' (*Epistle to the Smyrnaeans*, 8. 2), this martyr upheld worldwide, 'catholic' unity in belief and conduct. On the local scene, 'Catholicism' meant obedience to a monarchical or single presiding bishop, supported by presbyters and deacons. The bishop was to preside at the celebration of the Eucharist, defend the centrality of Christ's bodily resurrection, and approve the marriage of Christians.

Irenaeus of Lyons (d. *c.* AD 200) championed bishops as faithful teachers in the Church, who succeeded one another when the ministry of the apostles gave way to a continuous line of ordained bishops.[48] In the worldwide Church, their succession could be traced back to the apostles—something Irenaeus did for the sees of Ephesus, Smyrna, and Rome, 'the greatest and oldest church' (*Adversus Haereses*, 3. 1–4). The bishops witnessed to 'the rule of faith', a summary account of the central biblical truths that preceded the Nicene-Constantinopolitan Creed, the Apostles' Creed, and other creedal epitomes of Christian belief. The rule of faith involved recognizing both the continuity of bishops (with their orthodox teaching) and the canonical Scriptures (in particular, the four Gospels). Thus the championing of bishops also entailed acknowledging the authority of the apostolic Scriptures and rejecting the new 'scriptures', produced after AD 150 by Gnostics on the margins of Christianity. Gnosticism drew on Jewish, Christian, and pagan sources to present salvation as involving not the resurrection of the body but an immortal, human spirit escaping from an evil, material world and returning to the heavenly world from which it had come.[49] The so-called *Gospel of Judas*, written around AD 180 and after

---

[47] See 'Ignatius, St', *Oxford Dictionary*, 822–3.

[48] See F. A. Sullivan, *From Apostles to Bishops* (Mahwah, NJ: Paulist Press, 2001); on Irenaeus see E. Osborn, *Irenaeus of Lyons* (Cambridge: Cambridge University Press, 2001).

[49] See P. Jenkins, *Hidden Gospels: How the Search for Jesus Lost its Way* (Oxford: Oxford University Press, 2001). As Jenkins insists, the Gnostic Gospels and other texts were composed much too late to illuminate Jesus and the origins of Christianity. Add too their frequently odd content, which disqualifies them in the eyes of many contemporary readers. See also A. H. B. Logan, 'Gnosticism', in Esler (ed.), *The Early Christian World*, ii. 907–28; A. Marjanen, '"Gnosticism"', in Harvey and Hunter (eds), *The Oxford Handbook of Early Christian Studies*, 203–20; and P. Perkins, *Gnosticism and the New Testament* (Minneapolis: Fortress Press, 1993).

its rediscovery published with huge publicity, expressed typically such a scheme of redemption.[50]

The teaching of Irenaeus could encourage us to rephrase the whole fundamental question about the origins of the Church and her order in terms of *apostolic* origins and the episcopal office as it emerged in the second century and has continued ever since. Do bishops relate to the apostles in a way that resembles (but is not synonymous with) the relationship in which the apostles stood to Christ, so that bishops form a sign of continuity with that apostolic faith in and witness to Christ which constitutes the life of the Church? Putting this question presupposes that one accepts that what comes from Christ through the apostles (in both the pre-Easter and post-Easter situation) makes the Church to be his Church. In other words, the story of Jesus and his apostles constitutes the original foundation and lasting identity of the Church. Hence the question also presupposes that one wishes to be 'apostolic'—that is to say, that one wishes to transmit the faith, proclamation, church order, and commitment to service drawn from Jesus and the apostles. The question, then, becomes: is the church community, constituted by the proclamation of the Word, the celebration of the sacraments, and ministry to the world, also genuinely 'apostolic' in being served by an ordained ministry and led by bishops? I say 'also', because the life and worship of the *whole* community, maintained by the Holy Spirit, remains the primary expression of 'the faith that comes to us from the apostles' (Roman Canon) and of continuity in that faith. In this sense of continuing to be apostolic in faith and life, apostolic succession is an attribute of the whole Church and extends beyond episcopal succession. That said, the issue remains: do members of the ordained ministry, in general, and successors in the episcopal office, in particular, *embody visibly* in structured forms *the Church's fidelity* to the apostolic faith, witness, and life in fellowship? Do that ministry and office belong among the necessary means for handing on and living the same apostolic faith in 'succession' or continuity?

---

[50] See R. Kasser and G. Wurst (eds.), *The Gospel of Judas* (Washington, DC: National Geographic, 2007); S. J. Gathercole, *The Gospel of Judas: Rewriting Early Christianity* (Oxford: Oxford University Press, 2007); N. T. Wright, *Judas and the Gospel of Jesus: Have We Missed the Truth about Christianity?* (London: SPCK, 2006).

Put this way, the question of the institutional Church moves beyond a question of first- and second-century sources to be examined by biblical scholars and fundamental theologians and becomes an issue of public credibility. No amount of scriptural and theological argument about continuity in apostolic faith in Christ will prove successful apologetically, without the visible witness to that faith being embodied in the life and worship of those exercising the ordained ministry and episcopal office.

In this context we might argue for a degree of subordination to authority figures by pointing to the way important interpersonal arrangements function. Work in hospitals, theatres, cockpits of jet airliners, military posts, and other scenes of joint human activity would turn dangerously chaotic if there were no one officially in charge. The functioning of surgeons, managers, directors, captains, chiefs, and generals obviously requires the subordination of those who are led to their leaders. In many areas of life we need someone in authority who gives orders (often requiring to be articulated after genuine and supportive dialogue) and takes final responsibility. Or is *only religious authority* (that 'hier-archy' in the proper sense denotes) to be ruled out, on the basis that any subordination in church order has been excluded by Jesus and the Holy Spirit? To accept superiors and subordinates (not to be confused with masters and slaves) in 'secular' affairs while excluding them in the 'sacred' zone of religion would posit an extraordinary gap between the order of 'nature' and that of 'grace'. On the question of leadership did Jesus reject it completely and so take a stand against such a 'natural' way of organizing people? Rather than rejecting all leadership in his community, Jesus encouraged new ways of exercising authority: the greatest needed to become the least and the servant of all (Mark 10: 41–5 par.).

In any case, it seems fanciful to hold that a worldwide church could be coordinated and even maintained in its communion, if all authoritative leadership and subordination were to be banished. A measure of institutionalization is necessary for survival. As some sociologists point out, religious authorities and institutions can foster rather than thwart the spiritual lives of individuals and groups.[51]

---

[51] See J. F. McCann, *Church and Organization: A Sociological and Theological Enquiry* (Scranton, Pa.: University of Scranton Press, 1993).

In such terms one can argue for the *necessity* of ordained leaders to maintain and interpret the teaching and living memory of Jesus and his apostles. But no talk of such necessity dare ignore the fact that the *credibility* of such leaders requires them to embody in their lives the faith that comes from Jesus and his apostles.

The kingdom and the Church

This chapter has presented reasons for acknowledging the origins of the Church in the ministry of Jesus, and, not least, in his call of the Twelve and outreach to Gentiles. Without taking back anything that has been argued, I want to conclude by noting a key distinction between the larger reality preached by Jesus, the kingdom of God already breaking into the world, and the lesser reality promoted by Paul: namely, the Church, already present in various communities around the Mediterranean. While speaking a few times of the (present and future) divine kingdom (only eight times in all), the apostle seems more concerned with his own apostolic ministry in the service of the Gospel (e.g. Rom. 15: 18–19; 2 Cor. 12: 12), which brings Jews and Gentiles to enter the community of the Church through faith and baptism.

Unquestionably, the kingdom and the Church should not be separated, whether we deal with the first century (and the development from Jesus to Paul) or with the world today. But we forget at our peril that the Church is there to serve the kingdom, and not vice versa. This distinction matters essentially for the chapter which now follows—on the situation of those who have not (or have not yet) embraced Christian faith and baptism.

12

World Religions and Christ the Revealer and Saviour

Previous chapters have tracked the results of the self-revelation of the tripersonal God: the faith, tradition, and Scriptures of the worldwide Church to which that revelation gave rise. But the Church does not exhaust the presence and activity of the risen Christ and the Holy Spirit. They are not simply absorbed into the Christian community and its life. What of the millions of others, especially adherents of world religions who form the majority in our multi-faith and multi-cultural human race? Fundamental theology may not ignore that question, which was implicitly raised when Jesus preached the divine kingdom. If the sovereign rule of God has broken into the world and is steadily overcoming the power of evil, what does that imply about all those human beings who have never heard of Jesus, have not embraced Christian faith, do not belong to the Church, but are affected by God's universal reign?[1]

[1] See G. A. Barker and S. E. Gregg (eds.), *Jesus Beyond Christianity* (Oxford: Oxford University Press, 2010); D. Burrell, *Faith and Freedom: An Interfaith Perspective* (Oxford: Blackwell, 2004); G. D'Costa, *Christianity and World Religions: Disputed Questions in the Theology of Religions* (Chichester: Wiley-Blackwell, 2009); J. Dupuis, *Toward a Christian Theology of Religious Pluralism* (Maryknoll, NY: Orbis Books, 1997); id., *Christianity and the Religions: From Confrontation to Dialogue* (Maryknoll, NY: Orbis Books, 2002); C. Geffré, *De Babel á Pentecôte: Essais de théologie interreligieuse* (Paris: Cerf, 2006); L. Jones (ed.), *Encyclopedia of Religion*, 15 vols. (Detroit: Macmillan, 2005); M. Juergensmeyer (ed.), *The Oxford Handbook of Global Religions* (Oxford: Oxford University Press, 2006); D. Kendall and G. O'Collins (eds.), *In Many and Diverse Ways: In Honor of Jacques Dupuis*

This chapter will respond in terms of the universal, dynamic presence of Christ and his Holy Spirit. That presence touches everyone and all cultures and religions. I offer here a vision of this worldwide situation, without being able to argue everything out in detail. To do so would require a book. Unlike the last chapter, which appealed to biblical and historical testimony, this chapter will introduce doctrinal traditions and some philosophical reflections. In their own way, these two chapters, by bringing together the Scriptures, history, tradition, and philosophy, witness to the nature of fundamental theology as being not only concerned with basic questions but also functioning as a frontier discipline. We begin with two preliminary considerations.

Two preliminaries

1. When fundamental theologians begin reflecting on world religions and their role in mediating divine revelation and salvation, they run up against a well-entrenched terminology that features various '-isms': in particular, 'Christo-centrism', 'ecclesio-centrism', 'exclusivism', 'inclusivism', 'pluralism', and 'theo-centrism'. Originally introduced to sort matters out, these abstract nouns now groan under the weight of their various meanings and at times finish up confusing rather than clarifying discussion. Hence I avoid them. One terminological issue remains, however, a nagging problem. With many others I dislike such negative labels as 'non-Christians' and 'non-evangelized'. We might produce a long list: Buddhists, Hindus, Muslims, and so forth. But how are we to name en bloc those of other religious traditions? One could write of them as 'God's other peoples' or 'others', understanding those terms in a positive sense.

(Maryknoll, NY: Orbis Books, 2003); G. O'Collins, 'Christ and the Religions', *Gregorianum*, 84 (2003), 347–62; id., 'Jacques Dupuis's Contribution to Interreligious Dialogue', *Theological Studies*, 64 (2003), 388–97; id., *Salvation for All: God's Other Peoples* (Oxford: Oxford University Press, 2008); A. Race and P. M. Hedges (eds.), *Christian Approaches to Other Faiths* (London: SCM Press, 2009); B. Sesboüé, *Hors de l'Eglise pas de salut: Histoire d'une formule et problèmes d'interprétation* (Paris: Desclée, 2004); F. A. Sullivan, *Salvation Outside the Church?* (New York: Paulist Press, 1992).

2. It seems relatively uncontroversial for Christian believers to emphasize the need to reflect on these others primarily in the light of *Christ* and not the Church. Some try to give new life to an old slogan that many now find to be both arrogant and inaccurate, 'outside the Church no salvation', and say 'without the Church no salvation'. In its negative ring, however, 'without' hardly improves matters. I will return below to the Church's role in mediating to others salvation and revelation. But for the moment let me insist that Christ and the divine kingdom remain the primary realities, and should be not only the starting point but also the central and permanent point of reference.

The doctrinal background

Before facing the question of Christ and the place for all peoples in the divine kingdom, fundamental theology needs to reflect on the incarnation of the Word of God or Logos, and borrow some terminology and doctrines from the classical Christology of the Councils of Chalcedon (451) and the Third Council of Constantinople (680/1).[2]

The situation 'before' the incarnation does not or should not pose much difficulty. Unless one wants to claim in a heterodox fashion that the created humanity of Christ really (and not merely intentionally or in the divine plan) existed from all eternity and hence did not truly first come into existence at his conception and birth (around 5 BC), one should recognize that it was only through his divine nature that the Logos was active in the creation and conservation of the universe and in the unfolding history of revelation and salvation. The human nature, to be assumed by the Logos, did not actually 'pre-exist' the incarnation.

When we maintain, however, that the person of the Logos 'pre-existed' the incarnation and 'was' active then, we need to recall that in

---

[2] On the incarnation see G. O'Collins, *Christology: A Biblical, Historical, and Systematic Study of Jesus* (2nd edn. Oxford: Oxford University Press, 2009), 174–201, 229–61; id., 'The Incarnation: The Critical Issues', in S. T. Davis, D. Kendall, and G. O'Collins (eds.), *The Incarnation: An Interdisciplinary Symposium on the Incarnation of the Son of God* (Oxford: Oxford University Press, 2002), 1–27.

the existence of the divine persons there is no 'before' or 'after'. The eternal 'now' of the existence of the divine persons means an unchangeable fullness of life, with no relations of before and after, no having-been and going-to-be. Hence we strain language when we speak of the Logos personally existing and being active 'before' the incarnation. But it is another question with the humanity assumed at the virginal conception. This did not antedate the historical event of the incarnation. In the case of the human nature assumed by the Logos, 'there was [a time] when this nature was not'—to apply the language of the Council of Nicaea (AD 325) to the humanity but not to the person of the Son of God. From this point of view, it would have made sense to have said at the time of exodus from Egypt, the Babylonian captivity, or the assassination of Julius Caesar in 44 BC, 'the incarnation has not yet taken place', and 'the human nature of the Son of God is not yet operating'. His historical humanity began its existence in the temporal order, whereas the person of the Son of God exists eternally and timelessly. As Thomas Aquinas put it, 'the human nature' of Christ is both created and began in time, whereas 'the subsistent subject' (who is Christ) is both uncreated and eternal (*Summa Theologiae*, 3a. 16. 10). Being truly human and created, Christ's human nature remains finite and limited and, therefore, incapable of states of being and operations that are strictly infinite and divine. This conclusion comes from the teaching of the Council of Chalcedon and the Third Council of Constantinople.

In the fifth century the Chalcedonian definition responded to a 'monophysite' view, which apparently held that with the union of the incarnation the human nature of Christ was absorbed by the divine nature. Against this, the Council taught that the two natures of Christ, while not 'separated' or 'divided', remain 'distinct' and with the 'character' proper to each nature 'preserved' (DzH 302; ND 615).

In the seventh century a 'monophysite' tendency was transposed to the level of Christ's will and actions. The wider error labelled 'mono-energism' acknowledged only a single operation in Christ, as if he had only one nature or principle of activity. This amounted to a 'monophysite' view of Christ's activity, as if his human action were absorbed by the divine principle of activity. The error labelled 'mono-thelitism' recognized only one will in Christ, as if his divine will had swallowed up or replaced his human will. Constantinople III applied the Chalcedonian teaching in the context of these new questions about the activity and will of the two natures of Christ. It taught that the incarnate Son of God enjoyed and enjoys a human and a divine will (the two wills being in perfect harmony with each other) and two 'energies' or 'natural operations'. Extending Chalcedonian teaching to the issues it faced, Constantinople III insisted that the two wills and 'natural operations' were neither separated from each other nor blended together (DzH 556–8; ND 635–7).

By rejecting 'mono-energism' and 'mono-thelitism', Constantinople III defended the presence in Christ of a complete human nature with its human operations, and so upheld in him a duality of activity and a unity of agent. Obviously the Council's focus of attention was not precisely on distinguishing (a) the ongoing 'post-incarnation', divine operations on the part of the incarnate Word of God from (b) the human operations of the same agent (whose actual human operations began with the incarnation and would be glorified at the resurrection). Nevertheless, the Council indicated the continuing presence in the *one* Christ not only of *two* wills but also, more generally, of *two* 'natural operations', which are distinguished and not blended or amalgamated.

In his *Summa contra Gentiles* Thomas Aquinas drew some conclusions in the light of Chalcedon. He both championed the oneness of Christ's person *and* recognized that Christ's 'divine nature [with its operations] *infinitely transcends* his human nature [with its operations]', while remaining inseparable from that human nature once it came into being at the incarnation (4. 35. 8). Later in his *Summa Theologiae*, Aquinas remarked that 'the [human] soul of Christ' and its operations, inasmuch as they are created, are not 'almighty' (3a. 13. 1). It is only through his divine nature that Christ is strictly almighty or omnipotent.

By using reduplicative (as, qua, insofar as, or inasmuch as) statements in the christological section of the *Summa Theologiae*, Aquinas helps to clarify some of the issues. Reduplicative statements indicate the manner in which or the capacity in which a particular predicate is attributed to a particular subject. Thus he distinguishes Christ *as* 'subsistent subject' or divine agent, on the one hand, from Christ '*as* (*secundum quod*) man', on the other. As man, Christ is a creature, is not eternal, and begins to exist (3a. 16. 10). Such reduplicative statements can be applied to the teaching of Constantinople III. Inasmuch as he is man, Christ's 'energies' and 'operations' are created and limited; inasmuch as he is God, his 'energies' and 'operations' are uncreated and infinite. In both cases following the strategy of Thomas' reduplicative statements allows us to see what is the case, by definition and necessity, about the dual natures and operations of the Son of God.[3]

We can apply all this to three classes of actions of Jesus during his earthly life and, in particular, during his public ministry. First, he ate, slept, spoke, wept, took children in his arms, and performed similar actions inasmuch as he was human. All in all, his human actions qua human remained limited to his immediate environment; he operated as a human being in Galilee, Judea, and nearby territory. Second, we have such 'mixed' activities as his miracles of healing: for instance the curing of a leper (Mark 1: 40–5). In exercising his human powers, Jesus reached out and touched the face of the leper; in exercising his divine powers, Jesus healed him at once. Third, the divine actions of the Son of God continued, by conserving in existence the universe and by leading all people toward their final destiny with God. The divine person, who appeared in the rabbi from Nazareth and was identical with his person, continued his divine work around the world and throughout the whole cosmos.

In the name of St Paul's cryptic remarks about Christ who, being first 'in the form of God', then 'took the form of a servant' and 'emptied himself' (Phil. 2: 6–7), some have argued that the Son of God literally stripped himself of the form or mode of being of God, or at least surrendered for the duration of his earthly life the exercise of all or some of the divine attributes: for instance, being all-powerful and all-knowing. This view runs up against serious objections. Can one member of the Trinity, even by free choice, become bereft of divine powers? Surely properties that belong essentially to God cannot be abandoned, even for a short period of time? If the second person of the Trinity ceases to have divine powers, he would cease to be God. But can a divine person cease to be divine?

---

[3] On Thomas's use of reduplicative statements in elucidating the incarnation, see E. Stump, 'Aquinas' Metaphysics of the Incarnation', in Davis, Kendall, and O'Collins (eds.), *The Incarnation*, 197–218, at 211–17. The Chalcedonian definition introduces an early intimation of the reduplicative strategy when it speaks of the Son being *homoousios* (one in being) with the Father 'as regards his divinity' and 'one in being with us as regards his humanity' (DzH 301; ND 614).

Moreover, the idea of one person of the Trinity divesting himself of his divine powers seems to imply tritheism, or a belief in 'three gods' who do not share one and the same divinity but function together in perfect harmony. At the incarnation, one of these 'three gods' is supposed to relinquish for a time omnipotence and other divine attributes, leaving the other two divine persons to carry on the business of keeping in existence the whole universe. Thus this theory of 'kenoticism' seems to dissolve the unity of the one God into tritheism, or acceptance of 'three gods' each with its own nature. Furthermore, the theory appears incompatible with the Council of Chalcedon's teaching that the properties or essential features of both the divine and the human nature are *preserved* in the incarnation (DzH 302; ND 615).

The 'kenotic' language of Paul invites us not to entertain an impossibility, a divine person setting aside temporarily divine attributes and activities, but rather to cherish the humble love shown by Christ when he assumed the limited operations and painful sufferings of our human condition. Unless he had 'emptied himself' in that sense, he could never have wept, prayed in fearful distress, and been crucified.[4]

The universal presence of Christ

Later in this chapter we will return to the theological logic of the incarnation and its climax in the resurrection. Let us now spell out the thesis of the universal presence of Christ and his Holy Spirit; it involves the claim that in some real sense all human beings are 'in Christ' and the Holy Spirit is 'in' all human beings—to extend the typical terminology of Paul about Christians being 'in Christ' and the Spirit being 'in them'. Let us hear first some witnesses from early Christianity.

1. In the second century of the Christian era, Irenaeus acknowledged the universal scope of the divine action for human salvation: 'the Word of the all-powerful God ... on the invisible plane is co-extensive with

---

[4] See further G. O'Collins, *Incarnation* (London: Continuum, 2002), 55–64.

the whole of creation', 'rules the universe', and 'has traced the sign of the cross on everything' (*Demonstratio*, 34). In the third century Origen also highlighted the universal saving presence: 'Christ is so powerful that, although invisible because of his divinity, he is *present* to every person and extends over the whole universe' (*In Ioannem*, 6; 15; italics mine). This was not to deny that Christ was present in a special, fuller way in the lives of the baptized. But that fuller presence did not mean an absence elsewhere.

The universal action of the Son had both a revealing and saving dimension. Irenaeus summed up his universal role in revelation as follows: 'from the beginning the Son reveals (*revelat*) the Father to all whom the Father desires, at the time and in the manner desired by the Father' (*Adversus Haereses*, 4. 6. 7). No one is left out when the Son discloses the Father. Yet the timing and manner of this universal revelatory activity depend on God and not on human beings. What matters *primarily* is God's searching for all human beings through his Son rather than any human search for God. As Irenaeus put matters: 'no one can know God, unless God teaches: that is, without God, God cannot be known' (ibid. 4. 6. 4). Salvation belongs inseparably to this revealing activity of the universally present Son/Logos. As well as holding that, from the very beginning and in every part of the world, the Son has in one way or another revealed the Father to every human being, Irenaeus saw that this revelatory activity involved salvation for the non-baptized. The Son, he wrote, 'came to save all' (ibid. 2. 22. 4; see 3. 18. 7; 4. 22. 2).

2. When developing for today what Irenaeus and Origen said or implied about the universal presence of the Son/the Word of God, we need to introduce some philosophical considerations about presence.[5] One theme is especially relevant: the differing qualities and modes of presence. An indefinite variety of form and intensity characterizes the presences we experience; 'presence' is a radically analogous term and reality. We never face a simple alternative: presence or absence. It is always a question of what kind of presence and what kind of absence, or how someone is present and how someone is absent. Every presence, short of the beatific vision of the final encounter with God, is always tinged with absence.

---

[5] On presence, see O'Collins, *Salvation for All*, 208–14.

Given the stunning variety and qualitative differences that characterize human presence, we should be ready to acknowledge an endless variety in the qualitatively different possibilities of divine presence and activity. To allege anything less would be strangely at odds with the loving freedom of an infinitely creative God. It seems strangely arrogant to limit possibilities in the case of the divine presence and activity. Let us now recall the strikingly new modes of divine presence to humanity and the world that the missions of the Son and the Holy Spirit brought. We begin with the antecedents of this new presence, the creation and conservation of the world.

3. From the time of Justin Martyr, Irenaeus and later Church fathers regularly identified Christ as the divine Logos (Word) or Wisdom, who, by creating and sustaining the world, intimately accompanies everyone and everything. They understood the Logos to permeate the body of the world. No place or person lies 'far from' God's creative Logos or Wisdom. The Logos was and is universally present to and related with everyone and everything.

In explaining this universal presence, Justin and Irenaeus portrayed the Logos as the unique source of religious knowledge—a knowledge shared in differently by Christians, Jews, and others. According to Justin, on the one hand, 'the seeds of the Word' are everywhere and in every person (*Second Apology*, 8. 1; 13. 5). On the other hand, even though 'the whole human race shares' in the Logos (*First Apology*, 46. 2), some people live only 'according to a fragment of the Logos'. Christians live 'according to the knowledge and contemplation of the whole Logos, who is Christ' (*Second Apology*, 8. 3). One can translate this language in terms of the endless variety and modes not only in the presence of the Logos but also in the knowledge that he communicates.

In his concern to protect the utter transcendence of God the Father, Justin developed the intermediary roles of the Son as Logos and 'Angel'. As Logos he mediates and is present in all creation. As Angel he revealed the divine will in the Old Testament theophanies (*Dialogue*, 56. 1. 4). He was the One who spoke to Abraham, Jacob, Moses, and others in various theophanies, which Justin in effect turned into Christophanies. Irenaeus, while not continuing the 'Angel' Christology of Justin, agreed that it was the Logos who was manifested to Adam in the garden and to Noah at the time of the great flood. In the third century Origen endorsed this view: the books of 'the law and the prophets' record the encounters between the Old Testament saints and the pre-incarnate Logos (*In Ioannem*, 6. 4. 19–22).

4. The incarnation, when the Logos became flesh, brought a further stage in his revealing and saving presence. This event put Christ in material solidarity with all human beings and their world. Present now in a bodily, human fashion, he offered and offers new possibilities for mutual, interpersonal relationships.

Joining Paul in identifying Christ as the last Adam (Rom. 5: 12–21; 1 Cor. 15: 21–2, 45–9), and thus head of the new humanity, means acknowledging him as present and related to all men and women, wherever they may be. Likewise acknowledging him to be the Reconciler of the world (Rom. 5: 10–11; 2 Cor. 5: 16–21), the divine Agent of creation and new creation (Col. 1: 15–20), and exalted Lord of the universe (Phil. 2: 9–11) entails recognizing his all-pervasive presence and activity in the whole created world. There neither is nor can be any situation 'outside' or 'without' Christ and 'outside' his free self-giving that effects, however mysteriously, a communion of life and love with him. One must allow for an endless variety of qualities and modes in this cosmic presence of Christ. To say less would seem incompatible with New Testament faith in him.

In this context it is worth recalling Colossians 1: 19 where God is the presupposed but unexpressed subject: 'it was the will [of God] that all the fullness dwell in him [Christ]'. Markus Barth and Helmut Blanke comment: 'the presence of God exists now only in Christ'.[6] To this we might add: the presence of God exists now 'christologically' and 'pneumatologically', and that presence, identified with Christ and the Holy Spirit, is found everywhere.

5. Chapter 5 above expounded Jesus' preaching of and activity for the reign of God. In his earthly ministry Jesus, implicitly but clearly, proclaimed himself as inseparably connected with the divine kingdom that was breaking into the world. He was and is the kingdom in person. With and through his personal presence (in his life, death, and resurrection), the rule of God has become already present and will come in its fullness at the end of all history. Since the kingdom of God touches everyone, the revealing and saving presence of Christ, the heart of the kingdom, must do the same. No human beings,

---

[6] *Colossians*, trans. A. B. Beck (New York: Doubleday, 1994), 21.

whether they are aware of this or not, can escape living in the presence of Christ. Whatever occurs, occurs in the presence of Christ. Whoever acts, acts in the presence of Christ, even if he or she does not discern and acknowledge his presence.

6. In his life and death Christ drew near to all human beings in their sufferings. His presence made him fatally vulnerable; it cost him his life. The body of Christ on the cross expressed for all time his mysterious but truly redeeming presence to those who suffer anywhere and at any time. His death on Calvary between two criminals symbolized forever his close solidarity with those who suffer and die, an identification with human pain expressed also by the criteria for the last judgement (Matt. 25: 31–46). The final blessings of the kingdom will come to those who, without recognizing Christ, meet his needs in the people who suffer by being hungry, thirsty, strangers, naked, sick, or imprisoned. Pascal's reflection ('he is in agony to the end of the world') has classically articulated the crucified Christ's enduring presence in the mystery of all human suffering.[7] To express the worldwide presence of Christ in all who suffer, we could well say: *ubi dolor, ibi Christus* (wherever there is suffering, there is Christ).

7. Christ's resurrection from the dead ushered in a dramatically new, life-giving sharing of his presence, or—to put it another way—a situation in which his loving, reconciling presence remains definitively and universally present. This post-Easter presence is reflected in Luke's liking for the language of life when speaking of the resurrected Christ (Luke 24: 5, 23; Acts 1: 3), and in John's subsequent identification of Jesus with life itself (e.g. John 11: 25; 14: 6). Risen from the dead, Christ is actively present everywhere as the source of eternal life for everyone. This new presence meant that Christ was not merely *with us* (through creation and incarnation) and *for us* (through his ministry and crucifixion) but also *in us*, in all three ways inviting us to respond to his presence.

His personal self-bestowal, made possible through a glorious transformation that lifts his humanity beyond the normal limits of space and time,[8] has effected a presence which St John typically describes as 'Christ-in-us and we-in-Christ' and St Paul as 'we-in-Christ'.

---

[7] *Pensée* 616, trans. A. J. Krailsheimer (Harmondsworth: Penguin Books, 1966).

[8] This universal presence of Christ, not merely thanks to his divinity but also as a glorified human being, will be discussed below.

Where John's Gospel represents this new presence as mutual indwelling, Paul usually depicts it as our dwelling 'in Christ' as in a corporate personality.[9] In an unprecedented way the risen Christ, through the mission of the Holy Spirit, enables all human beings to share in his saving presence and live 'in him'. This presence is real and effective, but need not be a felt presence. It can remain a hidden presence— throughout the lives of innumerable human beings.

Christ's universal presence and the religions

The new, saving, revealing presence of the post-resurrection Christ differs according to human beings' location in the world of various cultures and religions. For the baptized, the Church's worship, teaching, and whole life bodies forth the living presence of the risen Christ. She forms the visible verification of his invisible but actively real presence. He exercises, for instance, the primary ministry in and through all the sacraments. Whenever the sacraments are administered, the risen Christ is personally and effectively present. In commenting on John's Gospel, Augustine summed up this sacramental ministry and presence of the risen Lord: 'when Peter baptizes, it is Christ who baptizes. When Paul baptizes, it is Christ who baptizes. When Judas baptizes, it is Christ who baptizes' (*In Ioannem*, 6. 7).

In other cultures and religions the risen Christ is also redemptively present in varying ways and degrees. To echo Irenaeus, Christ's invisible and powerful presence is spread everywhere. In other religions he is also actively 'there', even before any contact with the gospel message has taken place. These other religions have proved a matrix in which his saving revelation has been effectively present and so has mysteriously but truly brought people to live 'in him'. Here we might cite what Augustine wrote about the world's six ages of 'hidden saints' (*De Catechizandis Rudibus*, 22. 40) and 'prophets' among the Gentiles (*Contra Faustum Manichaeum*, 19. 2). 'Prophecy', he declared, 'was extended to all nations' (*In Ioannem*, 9. 9). These 'hidden saints', 'prophets', and—we should add—founders did not

---

[9] Very occasionally Paul varies his normal usage and writes of 'Christ/Jesus in me/us' (e.g. Gal. 2:20).

and do not operate independently of Christ. Without knowing this, they have been agents of Christ and helped people to a mysterious, real existence in him. This language of 'saints', 'prophets', and 'founders' should be understood analogously. Here, even more than within Christianity itself, one size does not fit all. There is, for instance, a difference of kind and not merely of degree between Christ as Founder (upper case) of Christianity and the founders (lower case) of various world religions.

But what of those founders (e.g. Siddartha Gautama) who lived centuries before the birth of Christ? How could one talk of such pre-Christian founders as 'agents of Christ' and, for that matter, how could one justify what Paul (1 Cor. 10: 4),[10] John 12: 41,[11] and various fathers of the Church (see e.g. Justin and Irenaeus above) wrote about Christ's presence and activity during the story of the Old Testament? In terms of a reduplicative strategy (see above), we can say that, even before the incarnation, the person of Christ was actively present and affected such founders inasmuch as he was/is divine, but obviously not inasmuch as he was/is human. His humanity came into existence only around 5 BC.

Add too that some founders or at least *some* of what (earlier or later) founders taught and did could dissuade us from recognizing them as being (or as being persistently) 'agents of Christ'. To some extent they may have been agents of evil. Some of what they did and taught could and did lead people away from any mysterious presence of Christ. But proper judgements here call for detailed investigations of the lives of such founders. In any case, we should remember that many Christian leaders, acknowledged as agents of Christ, have undertaken, commended, or at least tolerated things (e.g. the practice of torture and the institution of slavery) that have taken them and others away from Christ.

As regards the universal presence of Christ, we can extend the language of Luke about 'the unknown God' (Acts 17: 23)[12] to speak of the unknown Christ who has been and is active everywhere, for

[10] On this verse see J. A. Fitzmyer, *First Corinthians* (New Haven: Yale University Press, 2008), 382–4; A. C. Thiselton, *The First Epistle to the Corinthians* (Grand Rapids, Mich.: Eerdmans, 2000), 727–30.

[11] On this verse A. T. Lincoln writes: 'since Christ as the pre-existent Logos shared God's glory (cf. 1. 1, 14; 17. 5), all previous sightings of God's glory were also visions of Christ's glory' (*The Gospel According to John* (London: Continuum, 2005), 358).

[12] On this expression see J. A. Fitzmyer, *The Acts of the Apostles* (New York: Doubleday, 1998), 607.

everyone, and in the history of all cultures and religions—albeit often hiddenly. He may be unknown, but never absent. He has mediated revelation and salvation through particular historical events and persons, and continues to mediate to all the revelatory and saving self-communication of God. He proves effectively present in all creation and history, and yet not in a way that depersonalizes him and reduces him to being a mere 'Christ idea' or universal principle. Revelation and salvation are communicated personally—through the divine person who became incarnate as Jesus of Nazareth, died, and rose from the dead.

Many object to such a vision of Christ being present truly, but less visibly, in the lives of those who adhere to other religions. Such critics often belong to two sharply different groups. Some decline to share the generous and justified views of Justin, Irenaeus, Augustine, and other Church fathers about everything (and that includes the religions of the world) being under the influence of Christ. They argue that the adherents of world religions can be saved, *despite* their religion, ignoring (or denying) the possibility of Christ ever acting in and through the 'saints' and 'prophets' who shaped and shape such religions. Other critics dismiss the idea of a more vivid and powerful presence of the risen Christ in the Church as an arrogant claim that Jesus, more or less arbitrarily, favours some over others. Such an objection does not reckon with the way in which the love of Jesus resembles human love by not being exercised in an identical way towards all cultures, religions, and individuals. The risen Jesus lovingly interacts with the whole world, and that means that he interacts in ways that are different. He is absent from nobody, but he interacts differently with everybody.

Beyond question, this affirmation may seem to many 'others' overbearing and even appalling. They give their allegiance to other religions, or to none, and even vehemently reject claims about Jesus being present everywhere and lovingly interacting with everybody. Here we might recall three points. First, this claim is personal and not institutional; it maintains the universal impact of Jesus himself and not of the Christian Church as such. Second, we should not forget that some other religions (e.g. Islam and some forms of Hinduism) honour Christ and include him in one way or another in their faith. They do not endorse the universal significance of Christ being proposed here, but they certainly do not deny all significance to him.

Third, while Christians should not ignore the claims of other religions, they should not play down or misrepresent their own claims about Jesus being universally present to mediate revelation and salvation everywhere. In my experience, adherents of other faiths find such dissimulation, even when adopted by Christians for 'the best of reasons', dishonest and disrespectful toward partners in inter-religious dialogue.

An image from the Book of Acts provides a way for concluding more imaginatively this section. Paul pictures God as the One 'in whom we [human beings] live and move and have our being' (Acts 17: 28). This image of living, moving, and having one's being *in God* has its closest analogue for human beings during the first nine months of their existence. They live, move, and have their being within their mother, on whom they radically depend for life, sustenance, and growth. She is their total, all-determining environment. I do not allege that Luke gives a 'maternal' colour to the notion of God being the One in whom we live, move, and have our being.[13] But the text is obviously open to being connected with the situation of human life in the maternal womb. The image may also be applied to the risen Christ, whose all-encompassing presence forms the 'place' in which the entire human race, including those who do not yet explicitly acknowledge his presence, live, move, and have their being.

A medieval mystic, Julian of Norwich, expressed Christ's presence as follows: 'Jesus is in all who will be saved, and all who will be saved are in Jesus.'[14] This sense of mutual indwelling went hand in hand with Julian's wonderful sense of 'Christ our Mother'[15] and with Julian's hope for the salvation of all. She prayed and expected that all would be saved through Christ, who is the Mother of all human beings without distinction.

---

[13] Fitzmyer rightly dismisses theories that the 'Lucan tricolon' was drawn from Greek philosophical writing or was 'modelled on words' of the poet Epimenides. It was simply 'an old and frequent pattern in the Greek language' (*The Acts of the Apostles*, 610).

[14] Julian of Norwich, *Showings*, ch. 31, trans. E. College and J. Walsh (New York: Paulist Press, 1978), 276.

[15] In a striking paradox she wrote: 'our Saviour is our true Mother, in whom we are endlessly born and out of whom we shall never come'; ibid. (ch. 57), 292.

The transformation of Christ

The claim made above about the risen Christ being actively present to everyone and in every place should be brought into sharper theological focus. (a) Does he do this inasmuch he is divine? (b) Or inasmuch as he is both divine and human? For those who accept his divine identity and nature, answering (a) positively would be uncontroversial. But what of (b)? Could it be that his glorified human nature is also now involved whenever and whenever Christ interacts with any human being anywhere on this planet?

At first glance, such ubiquity would seem incompatible with the limits of being and operating proper to a human being, even a human being that has been transformed through resurrection from the dead. Such ubiquity appears to go far beyond the normal limits of space and time, so as to converge with the kind of omnipresence that mainstream Christian theology and philosophy have reserved for God and God's power and knowledge.

Nevertheless, two considerations encourage a positive response to (b). First, being gloriously raised from the dead lifts Christ's humanity beyond the usual limits characteristic of human existence in and for itself (*in se*). He lives now in glory, never to endure suffering and death again. That the resurrection from the dead *also* brings a far-reaching transformation in his human activity 'for others' or 'for us' (*pro nobis*) seems plausible. During his earthly ministry, inasmuch as he was human, he could affect and help only those with whom he enjoyed direct contact. If qua human he interacted with people near the Sea of Galilee, he could not do that simultaneously for people in Jerusalem, and vice versa. Resurrection from the dead makes Christ universally available—also inasmuch as he is human. To be present humanly, albeit through a glorified human nature, in indefinitely many places does not appear to be necessarily a divine attribute that would belong to Christ only in virtue of his sharing in the divine nature. The world population may have passed the six billion mark in October 1999, but to be available to all those people does not entail a state of being or an operation that is strictly infinite.

Second, while one should follow Aquinas in holding (see above) that Christ's divine nature and its operations infinitely transcend his human nature and its operations (and—we should add—continue to do so in the aftermath of the resurrection), we must ask: can and does Christ operate now in virtue of his divine nature alone, without any involvement of his glorified human nature? To be sure, the operations of his humanity, even in its glorified state, remain limited and can never match the omnipotent activity of the divine nature. But, since resurrection means that Christ's humanity has been elevated to share in the divine life to the maximum degree possible for a created being, can we imagine his glorified humanity being 'left out' when the divine person of Christ interacts with people everywhere on our earth?

This question becomes even sharper when we recall the language of Luke and John about the role of Christ in the sending of the Holy Spirit. During his Pentecost discourse, Peter explains the phenomena that the people in Jerusalem have just observed: 'God has raised up Jesus and of that we are witnesses. Being therefore exalted at the right hand of God and having received from the Father the promise of the Holy Spirit, he has poured out this that you both see and hear' (Acts 2: 32–3). In a scene from the first Easter Sunday, John portrays the risen Christ imparting the Holy Spirit to the disciples (John 20: 22). In his last discourse Christ had promised to do just that: 'when the Paraclete comes whom I will send you from the Father, the Spirit of truth who proceeds from the Father, that One will bear witness about me' (John 15: 26). Does this outpouring (Luke) or sending (John) of the Spirit 'from the Father' involve only the divine nature and powers of Christ? Or does it also involve his crucified, resurrected, and gloriously transformed humanity? Surely we should say that Christ, inasmuch as he is divine *and human*, jointly with the Father 'sends' and 'pours out' the Spirit?

The permanence of Christ's humanity

Some have answered the question we have raised about the post-resurrection operations of Christ's humanity by maintaining that the humanity assumed by the Son of God at the incarnation ceased to be with his death and burial. In rising from the dead, the incarnate Son surrendered or left behind his humanity. After an excursion into our world, he abandoned his humanity in a kind of 'throwaway' scenario that suggests a Gnostic-style escape from created reality.[16] Or should believers insist on the (now glorified) humanity remaining forever and remaining active forever? Some authors, such as Peter Forrest, raise the question of the *permanence* of the humanity assumed in the incarnation. Forrest, albeit briefly and not very satisfactorily, answers the question in the affirmative. Why should we maintain that the incarnation is not a temporary state and will never be undone, so that the Incarnate One will remain human forever and will remain humanly active forever? It is a question of some continuity between a pre-resurrection and a post-resurrection human nature, a continuity made possible by the fact that Christ's human existence, while wonderfully enhanced, does not disappear with the resurrection.

Mainstream Christians might appeal here to three additions to the Nicene Creed of 325 made by the First Council of Constantinople in 381. This latter council confessed that the 'Lord Jesus Christ' (who had 'suffered death, was buried, and rose again on the third day') now 'sits at the right hand of the Father', will come again 'with glory' to judge the living and the dead, and of his 'kingdom there will be no end'. Various Gospel passages underpin these three creedal statements; in particular, the evangelists attest a continuity between the pre-Easter and post-Easter Jesus in his revealing and redemptive activity 'for us' (*pro nobis*). The Jesus who built up his history as a human being (that is to say, through the human nature assumed at the incarnation) is the same risen Jesus who meets his disciples and commissions them for their mission, and, 'sitting at the right hand of the Father', intercedes for them as the eternal High Priest.[17] His

---

[16] If the humanity of Christ, even if dramatically transformed, did not continue into his risen state, it would be strangely difficult to maintain faith in his resurrection from the dead. Claims about 'resurrection' would amount to claims about the eternity of the Word.

[17] See Heb. 7: 24–5. The eternal activity 'for us' exercised by Jesus as High Priest takes place through his glorified humanity; it is his humanity that makes his priesthood possible. One might say: no eternally operating humanity, no eternally exercised priesthood. We could put this positively: like and together with his humanity, the priesthood of Christ will have no end. See G. O'Collins and M. K. Jones, *Jesus our Priest: A Christian Approach to the Priesthood of Christ* (Oxford: Oxford University Press, 2010), 241–2, 265–70. For Thomas Aquinas, Christ was and remains forever *the* priestly mediator, in virtue of the humanity that he assumed at the incarnation and that was glorified through the resurrection; see G. Emery, 'Le Christ médiateur: L'Unicité et l'universalité de la médiation salvifique du Christ Jésus suivant Thomas d'Aquin', in G. Augustin et al.

history which, thanks to his human nature, could be lived for others rose with him in a resurrection that initiated a new life for others. The eternal significance of his history (recorded and interpreted by the evangelists) goes hand in hand with the eternal significance of the humanity assumed at the incarnation.

The permanent existence and significance of Jesus' humanity, at which the Easter chapters of the Gospels hint, are more fully spelled out in the letters of Paul, the Book of Acts, and the Book of Revelation. What they have to say about the enduring presence and activity of the risen Jesus would be unthinkable if his humanity had disappeared with his death and resurrection. In a concise formula, Paul sums up what happened to Jesus (who is both divine Lord and human being) for our sake and to our advantage: 'he was handed over for our sins and raised for our justification' (Rom. 4: 25). Paul moves from what has happened to what permanently happens: 'Christ Jesus, who died, was raised, is at the right hand of God, and intercedes for us' (Rom. 8: 34).

In the Lukan scheme, the risen Jesus needs to be withdrawn from the visible scene before the Holy Spirit comes (Luke 24: 50–1; Acts 1: 9–11). The ascension does not, however, mean either that Jesus has disappeared or that his humanity has lapsed into nothingness. The human (and divine) Jesus remains dynamically present in and for the Church. Luke moves easily from cases of guidance by the Holy Spirit (Acts 8: 29; 10: 19; 16: 6) to cases of guidance by the risen and ascended Lord (Acts 9: 10–16; 18: 9–10; 22: 17–21). The Book of Revelation does likewise. After an inaugural vision and commission, the exalted Christ (Rev. 1: 9–20), who 'was dead' and 'now is alive forever' (Rev. 1: 18), addresses 'messages to the seven churches' (Rev. 2: 1–3: 22). These messages are understood to be the Spirit speaking through Christ to the visionary John (Rev. 2: 7, 11, 17, 29; 3: 4, 13, 22). The Christ of the Book of Revelation receives not only divine (e.g. Rev. 5: 11–14) but also human (e.g. Rev. 1: 5) attributes. Revelation does not convey any impression that with his resurrection from the dead, his humanity has been either annihilated or absorbed into his divinity.

The New Testament proclaims, in particular, that Christ's resurrection has inaugurated the general resurrection to come at the end

(eds.), *Christus—Gottes schöpferisches Wort: Festschrift für Christoph Kardinal Schönborn zum 65. Geburtstag* (Freiburg: Herder, 2010), 337–55.

(e.g. 1 Cor. 15: 20–8). The passage in 1 Corinthians to which reference has just been made could hardly be clearer about the risen Jesus and his impact on everyone. The One who does and will do this is the same as the Jesus who was crucified (1 Cor. 1: 10–2: 2) and certainly not 'merely' the divine Word of God who has left behind his human being and its properties. In and through his glorified humanity, the risen Jesus remains the agent (or rather joint agent with the Holy Spirit), who will raise human beings to eternal life with God. Karl Rahner put this even more broadly: 'the Word—by the fact that he is man and insofar as he is this—is the necessary and permanent mediator of all salvation, not merely at some time in the past but now and for all eternity.'[18]

To sum all this up. Without assuming a human nature, the Son of God could not have lived and completed a human history. Likewise, unless he maintained, albeit in a glorified state, his bodily humanity, we could not talk about his resurrection from the dead. But in fact the human condition he assumed at the incarnation persists eternally in his new, exalted state, and does so for the eternal salvation of all human beings. Both in his earthly lifetime and in his risen life, what occurred at the incarnation persists—for the salvation of human beings, all of whom are touched by his power and will meet him when he comes in glory to judge the living and the dead.

The universal presence of the Holy Spirit

Above we spoke not only of the Holy Spirit acting with Christ, but also of all human beings existing 'in Christ' and of the Holy Spirit existing 'in all human beings'. This brings us to the second panel in the diptych about the situation of those who adhere to religions other than Christianity or to no religion at all. For those who challenge the presence of the Spirit in the life of all human beings, the short answer, at least for those who accept Christ's universal presence, might be: the presence of the Spirit accompanies and enacts the presence of the

[18] K. Rahner, 'The Eternal Significance of the Humanity of Jesus for our Relationship with God', in *Theological Investigations*, iii, trans. K.-H. and B. Kruger (London: Darton, Longman, & Todd, 1967), 35–46, at 45.

risen Christ which is a universal presence. Since the co-Sender of the Spirit (the risen Christ) is always inseparably there with the Sent (the Holy Spirit) and since Christ is present everywhere and in every human life, the Spirit must also be present everywhere and in every human life. People do not have to be aware of living in the presence of Christ and the Holy Spirit for this to be the case. *Being present* does not as such imply *being known to be present*. A longer answer should begin with the function of the Spirit in and for the Church.[19]

1. As the 'soul' or vital principle of the Church (see 1 Cor. 6: 19), the Holy Spirit mediates the dynamic presence of Christ to his disciples through the sacraments, Scriptures, preaching, teaching, and other ministries of this new Easter community. It is the Eucharist that shows best the primary thrust of the Spirit's mission. With the eucharistic invocation (*epiclesis*) and the words of institution, the Spirit descends upon the gifts of bread and wine to change them and bring about the most intense and real presence of Christ for the Church and the world. Through the second *epiclesis* the Spirit is invoked to transform the worshipping community by strengthening their identity as believers, who call God 'Abba', share in Jesus' loving relationship to the Father, and serve his suffering brothers and sisters.

While being the primary agent in carrying out the mission of the Church, the Spirit also works to transform everyone and everything in the world. Baptism, the Eucharist, and other outward signs of the Church's life do not circumscribe and limit the operations of the Spirit. In its invisible mission the Spirit offers everyone the possibility of being changed by the saving grace brought through Christ's dying and rising from the dead. The Spirit communicates life to everyone and illuminates the pilgrimage of all humanity towards God, a pilgrimage which will bring human beings everywhere to make up the one body of Christ. In the New Testament, Luke and Paul witness to the impact of the Holy Spirit beyond the Christian community.

2. In his scene of the first Pentecost Luke gathers together representatives 'from every nation under heaven' to witness the outpouring of the Spirit who calls all people into the community of Christ (Acts 2: 5–11). Luke will then provide specific instances of the worldwide activity of the Spirit. In particular, the story of a Roman

---

[19] See G. O'Collins, *Jesus our Redeemer: A Christian Approach to Salvation* (Oxford: Oxford University Press, 2007), 200–17.

centurion, Cornelius, illustrates how someone who is neither Jewish nor Christian can experience the intimate presence of God—even in a most significant vision (Acts 10: 1–11: 18).[20] In a public way that repeats Pentecost, the Holy Spirit falls upon Cornelius and his party. Jewish Christians, who have come with Peter to meet Cornelius and the others, recognize that this manifestation corresponds to their own experience of the Spirit; Gentiles can also receive, even publicly and in a striking way, the Holy Spirit. This happens before any of them have been baptized. In Luke's view, divine visions and the manifest presence of the Spirit are not limited to actual members of the Christian community.[21]

3. Paul's language in Romans 2: 14–16 encourages us to recognize the Holy Spirit at work in the hearts and lives of Gentiles. The Spirit writes on the hearts of these 'outsiders' and enables them to practise the essential requirements of the divine law. Thus they can live 'according to the Spirit' and not 'according to the flesh' (or dominated by selfish passions and incapable of submitting to God's law).[22] Moreover, the Spirit imparts life and hope of fulfilment not only to all human beings but also to the entire created world. The Spirit is the divine principle of the new order created by God through Christ, or the universal, enabling power by which to live (Rom. 8: 1–30). Thus the invisible mission of the Spirit extends far beyond the visible members of the Church to be powerfully present in the whole of creation.

4. When we move to what later Christians said in applying the witness of Luke and Paul, one particularly instructive example turns up in 1 Corinthians 12: 3: 'no one can say "Jesus is Lord" except by the Holy Spirit.' In the context of the letter Paul was perhaps offering advice about interpreting episodes of ecstatic prayer. The Corinthians could be sure that those who cried out 'Jesus is Lord' were doing so under the impulse of the Holy Spirit. Possibly the reference was to a very short 'creed' used on the occasion of baptism. Yet it seems more likely that Paul had in mind a confession made in times of persecution. Through the agency of the Spirit, believers were empow-

---

[20] On the whole episode see Fitzmyer, *Acts*, 446–73; R. W. Wall, *The Acts of the Apostles*, in *The New Interpreter's Bible*, x (Nashville: Abingdon Press, 2002), 162–72.

[21] On the full importance of the whole Cornelius episode, see O'Collins, *Salvation for All*, 149–52.

[22] See J. D. G. Dunn, *Romans 1–8* (Dallas: Word Books, 1988), 98; J. A. Fitzmyer, *Romans* (New York: Doubleday, 1993), 305–12.

ered to confess Jesus as 'my/our/the Lord' (see Matt. 10: 17–19), rather than apostatize and declare under pressure that 'Jesus is cursed' and 'cursed is the Lord'.[23]

When commenting on this passage in the fourth century, an anonymous author who eventually came to be distinguished from Ambrose of Milan and known as 'Ambrosiaster' wrote: 'whatever truth is said by anyone whosoever is said by the Holy Spirit' (*quidquid enim verum, a quocumque dicitur, a Sancto dicitur Spiritu*).[24] In the form of 'everything that is true, no matter by whom it is said, is from the Holy Spirit' (*omne verum, a quocumque dicatur, a Spiritu Sancto est*), this expression turns up eighteen times in the works of Thomas Aquinas.[25] In the late twentieth century John Paul II gave the expression a twist that was fresh but that put it back in the original context of prayer, albeit authentic prayer that can go up to God anywhere and not simply prayer within a meeting of ecstatically gifted Christians.

In his 1979 encyclical *Redemptor Hominis* (the Redeemer of the human person), John Paul II supported 'coming closer together with the representatives of the non-Christian religions' through 'dialogue, contacts, and *prayer in common*' (no. 6; italics mine). In October 1986 he boldly broke new ground by doing just that, and going off to Assisi with the Dalai Lama and other heads or representatives of the world's religions to pray for peace. Some Catholics, including some members of the Roman Curia, judged harshly this event in Assisi, as if it somehow betrayed Christian faith in Jesus. The Pope replied to his critics in his Christmas address to the Roman Curia, delivered on 22 December 1986. He echoed and adapted the dictum of Ambrosiaster and Aquinas to speak not of truth but of prayer: 'every authentic prayer is called forth by the Holy Spirit.' For good measure he added that the Spirit 'is mysteriously present in the heart of every person'.[26] That same year the universal activity of the Holy Spirit had already been firmly put on the agenda of papal teaching.

---

[23] See Thiselton, *The First Epistle to the Corinthians*, 916–27.

[24] *In Epistolam S. Pauli ad Corinthios Primam*, 12. 3; *PL* 17, col. 243B; the passage is also found in CSEL 81, pars 2, 132.

[25] e.g. *Summa Theologiae* IIa–IIae. 172. 6, arg. 1. Like others, Thomas thought that the saying came from Ambrose of Milan.

[26] *Acta Apostolicae Sedis*, 79 (1987), 1082–90, at 1089. The full text of the address was published by the Secretariat of Non-Christians (renamed in 1988 the Pontifical Council for Interreligious Dialogue), *Bulletin* 64/22/1 (1987), 54–62. The key passages are found in ND, nos. 1049–52.

John Paul II dedicated a long encyclical letter, *Dominum et Vivifi-cantem* (Lord and Giver of life), published at Pentecost 1986, to the Holy Spirit active in the life of the Church and in the whole world. According to God's plan of salvation, the 'action' of the Spirit 'has been exercised in every place and at every time, indeed in every individual'—an action which is 'closely linked with the mystery of the incarnation and the redemption' (no. 5). That is to say, the universal activity of the Spirit is inseparably connected with what the Son of God did for all human beings by taking on the human condition, by dying and rising from the dead, and by sending the gift of the Holy Spirit from the Father.

As a Roman Catholic, I found this papal teaching not only illumi-nating and helpful in the inter-faith context of our world but also genuinely developing what Paul and Luke propose about the religious situation of those who are not (or not yet) Christians. I welcomed as a further development of New Testament teaching what I was to read in a 1990 encyclical *Redemptoris Missio* (the mission of the Redeemer). There John Paul II insisted that, while manifested 'in a special way in the Church and her members', the Spirit's 'presence and activity' are, nevertheless, 'universal'. He understood the Spirit to operate 'at the very source' of each person's 'religious questioning'. He went on to write: 'the Spirit's presence and activity affect not only individuals but also society and history, peoples, *cultures and religions*' (no. 28; italics mine). Here we read two momentous statements.

First of all, the Holy Spirit actively operates in and through the questions that sooner or later arise for everyone. Where did I come from? Where am I going? What is the meaning of life? What do suffering, sin, and evil mean? What will come after death? Who is the God in whom I live, move, and have my being? As far as John Paul II was concerned, the Holy Spirit is actively present not only when anyone prays authentically but also whenever anyone faces the pro-found religious questions of life. One might draw on Ambrosiaster and Aquinas to coin a new expression: 'every truly religious question, no matter by whom it is raised, is from the Holy Spirit' (*omnis quaestio vere religiosa, a quocumque moveatur, a Spiritu Sancto est*). The Spirit is the mysterious companion and religious friend who raises the deep and necessary questions in the life of every human being.

Second, the Pope appreciated how the presence and activity of the Holy Spirit also affect the wider human society and all human 'history, peoples, cultures, and religions'. In other words, the Spirit acts in and through the cultures and religious traditions of our world. This activity is inseparable from the revelation and salvation that Christ has brought about; it is an activity that aims at bringing all people, sooner or later, to Christ. But in the meantime the Spirit is present and operative in and through all that is true and good in various cultures and religions around the world.

This vision of the universal presence of the Holy Spirit presupposes a rich view of the nature of personal presence. Here too we should not think in terms of a sharp alternative: the Spirit is either totally present or completely absent. That would be to forget the vast variety of ways in which personal agents are present. Personal presence can assume many forms and exhibit great variations in intensity. What is true between human beings is all the more true of the various ways in which the Holy Spirit is present to human beings as individuals and in their various cultures and religious traditions. To be sure, the Spirit is present in a special and intense way within the Christian Church. But that does not allow us to say: 'outside the Church there is no Holy Spirit.' There is no such thing as being 'outside the Holy Spirit'. No place, person, culture, or religion is simply 'outside' the Spirit. Where there is the kingdom of God, there is the Spirit; and the kingdom of God is everywhere, just as 'the Spirit of God is at work everywhere'.[27]

Witnesses to this conviction have turned up among Christian believers, right down to modern times. Cardinal Henry Edward Manning (1808–92), for instance, wrote in 1875: 'it is true to say with St Irenaeus, "*ubi ecclesia ibi Spiritus* (where the Church is there is the Spirit)", but it would not be true to say, "where the Church is not, neither is the Spirit there". The operations of the Holy Ghost have always pervaded the whole race of men from the beginning, and they are now in full activity even among those who are without the Church.'[28] Bishop John V. Taylor (1914–2001) called the Holy Spirit 'the Go-Between God', that is to say, the One who acts as a kind of divine broker, subtly reaching everywhere and creating true relationships. The Holy Spirit, he wrote, is 'that unceasing, dynamic communicator and Go-Between operating upon every element and every process of the material universe, the immanent

---

[27] Y. M. J. Congar, *I Believe in the Holy Spirit*, trans. D. Smith, ii (New York: Seabury Press, 1983), 218.

[28] *The Internal Mission of the Holy Ghost* (New York: P. J. Kenedy, 1975), p. v.

and anonymous presence of God'—in short, the 'creative, redemptive action at the heart of everything.'[29]

The faith of others and the Church

Fundamental theologians who propose the universal presence of the risen Christ and the Holy Spirit as conveying revelation and salvation to all human beings must tackle *two related questions*: what should be said about the faith with which those who are other than Christian respond to God's self-revelation? Does this faith put them into any relationship with the visible Church? Chapter 7 considered the faith of those who respond to the divine self-communication as they experience it in the special history of revelation and salvation centred on Christ. But what might fundamental theologians say about the faith of those who belong to the general history of revelation and salvation, especially in the light of the basic dynamism of the human spirit that creates the possibility of religious experience (see Chapter 3 above)?

1. Chapter 4 above took up the Letter to the Hebrews and, especially its section on the witnesses to faith (11: 1–12: 2), to develop a picture of the faith with which the recipients of God's 'general revelation' can respond or fail to respond to that revelation. God calls and enables them to enter a personal relationship of faith. Without that faith they cannot 'please God' (Heb. 11: 6). What is at stake for their life and ultimate salvation is such 'God-pleasing' faith, much more than any beliefs about God and human existence that they may have worked out for themselves.

But, like the presence of Christ and the Holy Spirit in their lives, an endless variety of forms and intensities can characterize the concrete reality of the faith of those who belong to the general history of revelation and salvation.[30] One size does not fit all. Their faith expresses itself through a vast diversity in forms of worship and prayer, service of God and neighbour, and doctrinal articulations.

---

[29] J. V. Taylor, *The Go-Between God* (London: SCM Press, 1972), 64.
[30] See J. R Hinnells (ed.), *The Penguin Dictionary of Religions* (London: Allen Lane, 1984); id. (ed.), *The Routledge Companion to the Study of Religions* (London: Routledge, 2005).

Some of those forms call for purification and correction. Yet interreligious dialogue and serious study of those other religions has shown and will show a rich treasure of truth and goodness in those faiths. In a few cases, their lived faith coincides in part with that of Christians. Obviously, this holds true of Jewish believers, who share with Christians thirty-nine books of Sacred Scripture and whose faith functioned as the matrix in which Christianity arose. It holds true also of Muslims, whose holy book, the Koran, includes Abraham and other Jewish figures, not least Jesus himself, whom they honour as a prophet to the Hebrew nation but not as the universal prophet, Muhammad himself.[31]

2. As regards the second question, the Church and 'others', the universal reign of God must be the decisive point of reference. The Church exists for the kingdom and at its service, and not vice versa. The kingdom of God extends beyond the limits of the visible Church and is universally present and at work. A sign and sacrament of that wider, universal reality, the Church should be constantly oriented not toward itself but toward Jesus Christ and the divine kingdom that was already inaugurated with him and is steadily growing toward its final fullness.[32]

It is significant for me as a Roman Catholic that official teaching from the Second Vatican Council (1962–5) and its aftermath has become more cautious about the relationship of 'others' to the Church and about the Church's role in mediating grace to those who are not baptized Christians. The mystery involved in the unfolding plan of God to be revealed to all and to save all must be respected.[33]

The Church mediates grace to its members and does so, principally, through the proclamation of the Word and the sacraments, the centre of which is the eucharistic celebration. The Church intercedes for 'the others' and witnesses to them, not least through works inspired by love. The eucharistic prayers distinguish between invoking the Holy Spirit to maintain the holiness and unity of the faithful and interceding for 'others' (intercessions that do not take the form of an *epiclesis* of the

---

[31] See C. T. R. Hewer, *Understanding Islam: The First Ten Steps* (London: SCM Press, 2006), 18–20 (on Abraham), 182–5 (on Jesus).

[32] See J. Dupuis, *Christianity and the Religions: From Confrontation to Dialogue*, trans. P. Berryman (Maryknoll, NY: Orbis Books, 2002), 195–217.

[33] See John Paul II's 1979 encyclical *Redemptor Hominis*, 9–10; A. Mazur, *L'insegnamento di Giovanni Paolo II sulle altre religioni* (Rome: Gregorian University Press, 2004).

Holy Spirit). Here 'the law of praying' should encourage theologians not to blur the distinction between the Church's role for mediating revelation and salvation to her members and doing so for 'others'.[34]

At the same time the power of prayer ('for others' or for anybody) should not be underplayed as if prayer were a 'merely moral' cause. The power of intercessory prayer should not be written off in that way. All baptized Christians are called to intercede for the whole world. Through their prayers the revealing and saving self-communication of God can reach others. Christians have received the astonishing gift of faith in Jesus Christ, a gift that creates a serious responsibility towards 'others'—to be carried out not only through words and deeds but also through persevering prayer.

A coda: the omnipresence of the risen Christ

That the Holy Spirit is 'in' all human beings should be relatively uncontroversial. By sharing in the divine nature, the Spirit is unlimited in power and presence and exists intimately in everything and everyone. By giving everything and everyone existence and activity, the Spirit remains in causal contact with all created beings that exists. But what of the risen Christ and all that we have presented above about all men and women being 'in Christ'? Does the resurrection mean that, as human and not merely as divine, he is now universally present and active, just as the kingdom of God is universally present with power? Is that the conclusion we should draw from the language of Colossians about 'the fullness of God' now dwelling in Christ in a 'bodily' fashion (Col. 1: 19; 2: 9)?

A positive response to these questions may recall for some readers the theory developed by Martin Luther of 'ubiquitarianism', according to which the body of Christ is, to some extent, omnipresent.[35]

---

[34] See Dupuis, *Christianity and the Religions*, 210–12.

[35] See J. Baur, 'Ubiquität', *TRE* xxxiv. 224–41; H. Hudson, 'Omnipresence', in T. P. Flint and M. C. Rea (eds.), *The Oxford Handbook of Philosophical Theology* (Oxford: Oxford University Press, 2008), 199–216; G. Hunsinger, *The Eucharist and Ecumenism: Let Us Keep the Feast* (Cambridge: Cambridge University Press, 2008), 28–34; C. Michon, 'Omnipresence, Divine', in J. Y. Lacoste (ed.), *Encyclopedia of Christian Theology*, ii (New York: Routledge, 2004), 1153–5.

This position emerged as a reaction to those who, on the grounds of Christ's 'sitting at the right hand of the Father', denied that Christ could also be really present with his body and blood wherever and whenever the Eucharist was celebrated on earth. Luther argued, more on the basis of the incarnation than the resurrection, that the union of the two natures in the one divine person of Christ communicated a supernatural mode of being to his human nature, so that omnipresence could be one of its properties. Luther explained the eucharistic presence through the ubiquity of Christ's body.

This chapter has argued rather on the basis of the *resurrection* and what the risen life involved in terms of a new manner of being and acting for Christ's glorified humanity. To adapt Paul's language about the risen body, 'what is sown in weakness is raised in power' (1 Cor. 15: 43), we might say about Christ: 'what is sown in localized presence is raised to universal presence.' His humanity has been lifted beyond the normal limits and boundaries of human activity to fulfil the all-determining, final history inaugurated by the resurrection. What Paul states about the crucified and risen Christ's role in completing the work of 'the kingdom', a work that affects 'all' people and 'all' things' (1 Cor. 15: 20–8; the passage uses 'all' ten times), seems to rule out the view that this universal activity takes place solely through Christ's divine nature, with his human nature being 'left out'. Paul develops his position precisely on the basis of Christ being raised from the dead, as 'the first fruits of those who have died'. To be sure, the apostle does not introduce the language of 'two natures' and use the strategy of reduplication. Nevertheless, what he states seems incompatible with any claim that he is speaking only about Christ *as divine* Lord who is omnipresent with his knowledge and power.[36] In Paul's vision of the world's final history, the risen Christ is present everywhere, and—so it seems—not simply through his divine nature.

Add too Paul's teaching about Christ being raised from the dead through the power of the Holy Spirit (Rom 8: 11)[37] and being transformed to become himself a 'life-giving spirit' for everyone

---

[36] On these verses, see Fitzmyer, *First Corinthians*, 567–77; Thiselton, *The First Epistle to the Corinthians*, 1222–40.

[37] See Fitzmyer, *Romans*, 491–2.

(1 Cor. 15: 45).[38] This implies an enhanced presence and power of Christ's glorified humanity to make this universal activity possible. Admittedly, such universal presence and power stops short of the strictly unlimited presence and infinite power that belongs only to the divine nature of God. But, if we are to honour what Paul teaches in 1 Corinthians, we should agree that in some real sense the risen Christ, as divine *and human,* is present and active everywhere.

---

[38] On these verses see Fitzmyer, *First Corinthians,* 597–8; Thiselton, *The First Epistle to the Corinthians,* 1281–5.

13

Theological Styles and Methods

Before this book ends, it needs to come to grips with a final, all-pervasive issue: namely, ways for doing theology or, to put this more solemnly, theological method. Obviously the given style and method will have an impact on how anyone develops systematic theology, moral theology, and other branches of theology. As a basic, foundational issue, theological method belongs to the themes that fundamental theologians should tackle. Any rethinking of fundamental theology would not be a finished thing unless it takes a stand on styles and methods of theology in general.[1]

---

[1] See e.g. A. Dulles, *The Craft of Theology: From Symbol to System* (New York: Crossroad, 1995); G. Ebeling, *The Study of Theology*, trans. D. A. Priebe (Philadelphia: Fortress Press, 1978); J.-Y. Lacoste, 'Theology', in J.-Y. Lacoste (ed.), *Encyclopedia of Christian Theology*, iii (New York: Routledge, 2004), 1554–62; G. O'Collins, 'Theology, its Nature and Methods', in *Retrieving Fundamental Theology: The Three Styles of Contemporary Theology* (Mahwah, NJ: Paulist Press, 1993), 16–39; W. Pannenberg, *Theology and the Philosophy of Science*, trans. F. McDonagh (London: Darton, Longman & Todd, 1976); G. Pozzo and R. Fisichella, 'Method', *DFTh* 670–90; C. Pramuk, 'Making Old Things New: Imagination and Poetics in Theological Method', *Sophia: The Hidden Christ of Thomas Merton* (Collegeville, Minn.: Liturgical Press, 2009), 31–74; K. Rahner, 'Questions of Fundamental Theology and Theological Method', *Theological Investigations*, v, trans. K.-H. Kruger (London: Darton, Longman & Todd, 1968), 3–93; id., 'Reflections on Methodology in Theology', in *Theological Investigations*, xi, trans. D. Bourke (London: Darton, Longman & Todd, 1974), 58–114; K. Stock et al., 'Theologie, Christliche', *TRE* xxxiv. 263–343; J. Wicks, *Doing Theology* (Mahwah, NJ: Paulist Press, 2009).

A classic and widely influential work by Bernard Lonergan (1904–84), *Method in Theology*,[2] might have set the agenda for this concluding chapter. One could devote these final pages to summarizing Lonergan's account of the operations performed by theologians as they practise or should practise theology. Then, in the light of the many reactions to Lonergan's substantive proposals for theology and religious studies, one might, nearly forty years later, re-imagine these proposals for the practice of theology in the twenty-first century. I prefer, however, to take another path in this chapter, by first offering a vision of three approaches to theology and then making some practical suggestions for theologians who may have lost their way or perhaps never clearly found their way.

Three styles of theology

At a time when John Henry Newman has drawn renewed attention, his 1859 article 'On Consulting the Faithful in Matters of Doctrine' may be adapted to suggest three distinct but not separate approaches to theology, which consult, respectively, the scholars, the suffering, and the worshippers in matters of Scripture and doctrine.

1. The cultivated use of reason bulks large in the first style of theology which has predominated in the universities, colleges, and faculties of Europe and North America. The heirs of a tradition that stretches back through the Enlightenment, the Renaissance, and the medieval universities to Plato's academy, the exponents of this style pursue the meaning and truth of Christian revelation. Through research, rigorous thinking, and serious dialogue with academic colleagues in their own and other disciplines, they pursue fresh knowledge and new insights.

This North Atlantic style of theology is fashionable among well-educated persons or at least by those who aspire to be well educated. To echo and adapt Newman once again, it is a style that encourages us to consult the experts in matters of theology. Learned experts, including not only believers but also non-believers, are the desirable dialogue partners.

---

[2] Minneapolis: Winston Press, 1979; orig. edn. 1972. For an introduction (with bibliography) to Lonergan, see M. Lamb, 'Lonergan, Bernard', *TRE* xxi. 459–63; and F. G. Lawrence, 'Lonergan, Bernard', *New Catholic Encyclopedia*, viii (2nd edn. Washington, DC: Catholic University of America Press, 2003), 772–5.

This first way of doing theology characteristically finds its sources in the writings from the past: in the Bible; in the works of Greek, Latin, and Syrian fathers; in church documents; in the texts of medieval and Reformation theologians; and in other traditional texts that indicate how Christians, with various degrees of authority, have understood and interpreted the data of revelation. In their passion for truth, the protagonists of this style of theology take up dialogue and debate with their intellectual contemporaries. Yet the normative voices and texts generally remain those of the past.

2. Theology studies what in the last resort can only be lived. Hence a desire to promote justice and the common good shapes a second style, best exemplified by liberation theology. It is a practical way of doing theology, concerned to struggle against the massive injustice found everywhere and to change the world. It regularly asks itself: what does our theology lead us to do or leave undone? While it aims to stimulate, interpret, and critique action in the present, this style of theology also bears witness to a Jewish-Christian tradition that reaches back to the history of ancient Israel and the prophetic denunciation of social evil and oppression. It draws inspiration from Jesus' solidarity with the marginalized and outsiders of his society.

This kind of theology thrives on contact with the poor and powerless: the Christian poor of Latin America, the non-Christian poor of Africa, India, and elsewhere, and the disintegrating victims of Western consumer societies. The second style of theology encourages us to consult the poor and the suffering in matters of faith, doctrine, and morality.

Reading such outstanding liberation theologians as Gustavo Gutierrez and Jon Sobrino indicates their respect for the normative voices of the past: above all, the Scriptures and official church teaching. Nevertheless, this style of theology typically looks to the contemporary situation: in particular, to the millions of victimized non-persons of our world. Its primary *locus theologicus* is found in the suffering people of today.

3. Prayer and worship form the context for the third style of theology which finds its classic home in Eastern Christianity.[3] Instead of being naturally located in a university (the first style) or in a poor

---

[3] Hans Urs von Balthasar (1905–88) was a Western theologian whose focus on prayer, beauty, and worship put him in the company of many Eastern theologians, such as Sergius Bulgakov (1871–1944), Paul Evdokimov (1901–70), and Pavel Florenskij (1882–*c*.1943).

barrio (the second style), this third style works out of the setting of the Church at public prayer. It bears witness to the triune God, revealed and reflected in liturgical celebration.[4] Where the first style of theology focuses typically on truth (understood more theoretically) and the second on justice and the common good, the third style centres on the divine beauty.

This third style of theology encourages theologians into consulting worshippers in matters of faith and doctrine. According to the geographical situation, these worshippers will be Christians (e.g. in much of eastern Europe) or non-Christians (e.g. in many parts of Asia). Rather than looking to learned experts (the first style) or suffering victims (the second style), the third style of theology aligns itself with persons at prayer. It looks not only at solemn, official worship but also at expressions of popular religiosity in feasts, pilgrimages, devotions, icons, and other things that mirror underlying beliefs, attitudes, and experiences of God.

Finally, the third style does not ignore the present and past. Traditions, inherited from the past, bulk large for Eastern Christians who, like the rest of believers, must worship now or not at all. All the same, the future plays a special role for their prayer and theology. With the exalted and heavenly Christ presiding, worship anticipates the final glory of heaven. Through prayer, icons, and architecture, an eschatological future with God shines through.[5]

4. Thus far I have sketched academic, practical, and contemplative styles of theology.[6] There are further ways of comparing and contrasting these styles; let me mention seven. First, the classic language about the

---

[4] A 1990 document of the International Theological Commission 'On the Interpretation of Dogma' calls the liturgy 'the living and comprehensive *locus theologicus* of faith', constituting with prayer 'an important hermeneutical locus for the knowledge and transmission of the truth' (*Origins*, 20 (1990), 1–14, at 6, 11).

[5] The typical 'time focus' of each style could also be clarified through the theme of experience (see Ch. 3 above). The first style seeks to understand and explain someone else's experience, above all the past, apostolic experience of God's full self-revelation in Christ. The second style takes as its point of departure our present experience of physical suffering and further evil. The point of departure for the third style is the experience (especially, the liturgical experience) of the beautiful and the human longing for complete fulfilment in the future.

[6] After distinguishing three styles of theology, I should add that all theology operates through thought, speech, and writing. Differences emerge, however, inasmuch as thought, speech, and writing primarily serve knowledge and understanding (style one), action (style two), and prayer (style three).

impulse of faith that produces theology can be adapted to illustrate the different emphases in these three styles. Faith expresses itself as and in knowledge, action, and worship. Hence we might contrast faith seeking 'scientific' knowledge or understanding (*fides quaerens intellectum scientificum*, the first style) with faith seeking social justice (*fides quaerens iustitiam socialem*, the second style), and with faith seeking adoration (*fides quaerens adorationem*, the third style). In all three descriptions, the word 'seeking' (*quaerens*) has an essential function. Faith seeks a knowledge and understanding that in this life will never be conclusive and exhaustive. It seeks a just society that can never completely come in this world. It seeks an adoration of God that will be fully realized only in the final kingdom.

Second, faith, love, and hope offer an alternative vision of what has just been suggested.

Faith seeking understanding characterizes the first style of theology; love seeking a more just society expresses the second; and hope seeking to anticipate liturgically the final vision of God suggests the third.

'Truth' offers a third way of profiling the three styles of theology. In the Fourth Gospel Pontius Pilate asked '*What* is truth?' and did not wait for an answer. In the context of this chapter we might ask: *where* is theological truth? The Socratic method, exemplified originally in Plato's dialogues, could encourage us to deploy all the resources of our human reason illuminated by faith and look for truth *within ourselves*—through the working of our understanding and judgement. As distinguishable from this first style of theology, the second style hopes to find and live human and Christian truth working with and for *other people*. The place of truth for the third style is above all *in God*, the Father, Son, and Holy Spirit. Thus the characteristic place of truth for the three styles of theology is, respectively, in our reasoned judgement, in our practice, and in our praise of God.

Philosophical theories of truth offer here a scheme for 'placing' the three styles of theology. The first style can be associated with the correspondence theory of truth, for which truth is found in the intellect when its judgements correspond to the 'facts'. The second style may be associated with pragmatic theories of truth, for which truth is verified in action or verified in its consequences. The third style, which wishes to fit what God has revealed into a beautiful, comprehensive pattern of meaning and view of the universe, suggests the coherence of truth.[7]

Fourth, one could enlarge an adage, 'the law of prayer is the law of belief' (*lex orandi lex credendi*), that goes back to Prosper of Aquitaine (d. c. 463),[8] and speak of theological truth emerging through the laws of believing, living, and praying (the *lex credendi* for knowledge, the *lex vivendi* for behaviour, and the *lex orandi* for worship). The *lex credendi*, which looks back to and draws on authoritative texts for faith, guides and illuminates the study and knowledge required by the first style of theology. The *lex vivendi* yields truth through a life spent serving powerless and suffering people. The *lex orandi* enables the faithful to grow in the divine life communicated through baptism, fostered in worship, and to be consummated at the end. The academic, practical, and contemplative styles differ by approaching truth as primarily something (or Someone), respectively, to be known or believed (*lex credendi*), done (*lex vivendi*), or worshipped (*lex orandi/adorandi*).

Fifth, 'the triple office' (*munus triplex*) of Christ as priest, prophet, and king/pastor, while rooted in the Old Testament and deployed occasionally by the fathers of the Church and medieval theologians (e.g. Thomas Aquinas), came into its own with John Calvin in the sixteenth century, John Henry Newman in the nineteenth century, and the Second Vatican Council in the twentieth.[9] Taking the order as prophet, king/pastor, and priest, one can apply this scheme of 'the triple office' to theologians as another way toward elucidating the three styles open to them. They can speak out as prophetic interpreters of revealed truth (style one). They can work pastorally for the good of those who suffer (style two). They can allow their share in

---

[7] See R. L. Kirkham, 'Truth, Correspondence Theory of', in E. Craig (ed.), *Routledge Encyclopedia of Philosophy*, ix (London: Routledge, 1998), 472–5; K. Simmons, 'Truth', in D. M. Borchert (ed.), *Encyclopedia of Philosophy*, ix (2nd edn. Farmington Hills, Mich.: Macmillan, 2006), 534–42.

[8] In a fuller form, 'let the law of prayer establish the law of belief' (*legem credendi lex statuat supplicandi*), the adage comes from the *Indiculus*, a dossier on grace Prosper drew from Augustine of Hippo. From the need to pray for everyone (1 Tim. 2: 1–4), Prosper concluded to the universal need for grace (DzH 238–49; ND 1907–14; at DzH 246; ND 1913).

[9] See G. O'Collins and M. K. Jones, *Jesus our Priest: A Christian Approach to the Priesthood of Christ* (Oxford: Oxford University Press, 2010), 127, 149–54, 208–22, 234–8.

Christ's priestly ministry to promote prayer and worship (style three). In other words, a given theologian may prove more a prophet, or a king/pastor, or a priest.

Far from being freelance operators, theologians are called to be prophets, kings/pastors, and priests at the service of the whole Church. Hence one might describe in ecclesial terms the threefold role open to them. They can represent and personify the Church at study (*ecclesia ratiocinans*, first style), the Church at work for those who suffer (*ecclesia laborans*, second style), or the Church at prayer and worship (*ecclesia orans et adorans*). The varying character of their ecclesial engagement gives their particular theology its special quality.

Sixth, theologies can be evaluated by the way they typically interpret and appropriate the Scriptures. For the three styles of theology, the Bible is, respectively, a book for study, action, and prayer. The first style studies the biblical text and asks: what did it mean? What does it mean? The second style finds in the Bible a practical programme for life and asks: how do the Scriptures challenge us? What should they lead to do and/or leave undone? The third style takes up the Bible as *the* guide to worship and asks: how does it turn into and nurture private prayer and public liturgy? Some exponents of the three styles clarify their preferred approach to interpreting the Scriptures. Even when they do not explicitly present their biblical hermeneutics, their particular style of theology will be reflected in their use of the Scriptures.

Seventh, it is tempting to range widely and discover support for one's thesis in unlikely places. Let me then, without pushing matters strongly, mention two such places: one traditional and the other from the Second Vatican Council. Medieval (and some later) philosophy spoke of 'transcendentals', those properties which belong to a being just because it is a being and which thus 'transcend' the categories (e.g. essence, quality, time, and space) frequently used for classifying things. The full list of transcendentals has varied, but three of them bear application in the context of this chapter: truth, goodness, and beauty. The first style of theology searches for truth, the second for the good that justice demands to alleviate human suffering, and the third for the divine beauty encountered in common worship and personal prayer. The Constitution on Divine Revelation from Vatican II, *Dei Verbum* (the Word of God) speaks of the Church 'in her teaching, life, and worship' handing on to 'all generations all that she herself is, all that she believes' (no. 8). This triple scheme of 'teaching, life, and worship' enjoys some analogy to my three types of theology. The intellectual type expounds and hands on true teaching. The practical type concerns itself particularly with the Church's life in its struggles on behalf of the suffering. The contemplative type finds its inspiration in the Church's worship.

Risks and possibilities

Thus far this chapter has set itself to expound positively each style of theology, as well as to compare and contrast them. Experience suggests a word of warning. Developed one-sidedly and by itself, each of the three styles can fail to be fully faithful and Christian.

1. The cultivated use of reason that distinguishes the first style may produce a sterile erudition which avoids facing public issues that may involve far-reaching changes. Its academic exponents can fail to be outward-looking and remain blind to problems that cry out for remedy in the Church and the world. Endorsing a 'neutral' theological standpoint, they may be tempted to remain socially, politically, and ecclesiastically somewhat 'apart'. Since the Holocaust and the failure of leading academic theologians in Germany under the Third Reich, many theologians admit that such *praxisferne Theologie* (theology distanced from praxis) is no longer acceptable. But the first style's concern for scientific precision frequently risks losing contact with life and worship.

Can those scholars who neither encounter God in prayer nor actively reach out to suffering human beings hope to contribute to progress in theology? At times they indulge a studied scepticism that delights in doubts and refuses to hold positions, or they may promote hypotheses that enjoy very little hard evidence. They abstain from prayer and service of the suffering, activities which could have anchored them in the reality of the human condition.

2. The second style may fail to test its conclusions stringently in the light of the authoritative voices of Scripture and tradition. Some kinds of commitment to suffering people can end up in an activism, violent or otherwise, that has forgotten its roots in Christian faith and worship.

3. When taken to extremes, the third style may neglect sound scholarship (style one) and social commitment (style two). It can turn into a flight toward timeless worship, cut off from serious study and concern for a world in pain. This would involve ignoring how sharing in the eucharistic body of Christ should involve a radical commitment to the suffering body of Christ in the world (see 1 Cor. 11: 17–34). In the case of all three styles of theology, a unilateral cultivation of one style risks producing deficient or even deplorable results.

4. Positively speaking, Christian theology will happily survive and serve the people of God to the extent that it is open to and can even combine the three styles. We need Wolfhart Pannenberg and Karl Rahner (style one), Jürgen Moltmann and Gustavo Gutierrez (style two), and Hans Urs von Balthasar and Paul Evdokimov (style three). Of course, classifying these and other theologians in this way risks glossing over the variety of ways in which their work developed. In Rahner's case, for example, we ignore at our peril how his theology was rooted in his Jesuit spirituality. At the same time, however, characteristic elements allow us to categorize theologians as some-what more oriented towards the truth (style one), the good (style two), or the beautiful (style three).

Christianity needs an inclusive approach that allows these three styles to complement and mutually enrich each other. Different images of Christ himself match the three styles. Titian's painting of the boy Jesus (now in Dresden) shows him in the Jerusalem Temple long ago, engaged in dialogue with contemporary theologians (style one). The tortured Christ of Latin American iconography presents the second style through the One who identifies with the wretched of the earth and remains 'in agony until the end of the world' (Blaise Pascal). The Pantocrator of Eastern Christian churches pictures Christ now reigning in majestic beauty and to come at the end of time (third style). Christ is not confined to the past, the present, or the future. He is 'Jesus Christ yesterday, today, and the same forever' (Heb. 13: 8): the Christ of the Scriptures and the tradition, the Christ whose passion continues today, and the Christ who will come in glory. In Christology and other branches of theology we should be open to three styles of approach that attend, respectively, to 'what is past, passing, and to come' (W. B. Yeats, 'On Sailing to Byzantium').

A theologian from Manila once expressed to me in Filipino his hopes for a theology that 'knows how to walk (*na marunong lumakad*), knows how to sit (*na marunong umupo*), and knows how to kneel (*na marunong lumukod*)'. His three requirements can be aligned with my three styles of theology. We need theologies that know how to sit studying the past (with the famous *Sitzfleisch* of German scholars), that know how to walk the streets with the poor, and that know how to kneel in adoration of the Saviour who is come.

Some guidelines

The first half of this chapter has been largely descriptive. In the second half I wish to turn prescriptive and offer eight pieces of advice. These guidelines could be summed up as: be scriptural, be historical, be philosophical, be provisional, be ecumenical, be local, be converted, and be prayerful.

Be scriptural

Scripture should not only be *the* norm but also the primary inspiration for all theology. Some talk of the Scriptures as the very soul of theology, a life-giving force which 'inspires' order and growth and without which theology would be dead. Others speak of the Scriptures as the highest normative principle for theology. No other theological sources, not even the most solemn teaching coming from official teachers in the Church, can claim to be written under the special guidance of the Holy Spirit. This gives the Scriptures their specifically authoritative character as 'the Word of God', as texts that not only have human authors but also God as their 'author'.

Being scriptural involves being attentive to all that interpreting the Bible involves (see Chapter 10 above) and attentive, in particular, to the 'reception history' of the Scriptures down the centuries. That history includes the living reception of the Scriptures in Christian liturgy, personal prayer, art, architecture, patterns of behaviour, and shining examples of lives based on the Bible, and should not be limited to what the fathers of the Church, medieval teachers, reformers, and preachers of all ages have left in writing. The glorious calligraphy and glowing illustrations of finely ornamented biblical manuscripts, for example, also belong to this history of 'reception', along with the works of Origen, the sermons of Augustine of Hippo, the biblical and theological works of Thomas Aquinas, and the commentaries of John Calvin.

To trace through the centuries something of this broad reception of such key texts as Colossians 1: 15–20 and Philippians 2: 6–11 can enrich theologians' grasp of who Christ is and what he has done for human salvation. Undoubtedly, the demands of time set limits on how much research theologians can undertake into twenty centuries of 'reception history'. But some attention is called for. The *Hermeneia* series of commentaries provides a fine example of scholars examining and expounding biblical texts not only in their original setting but also in the light of how Christians subsequently interpreted the texts and expressed them in life.[10]

Being biblical should involve theologians in reading scriptural commentaries and not merely the text of the Bible itself. On the desks of some fellow theologians, the Bible is regularly in evidence and sometimes in its original Hebrew and Greek. Yet rarely if ever do I see a contemporary commentary on the desk of some fellow theologian. Too many theologians seem indifferent to scriptural scholarship and simply bypass the biblical experts when drawing on the Scriptures. This continues to be the case in an age when they could draw on many excellent scriptural commentaries. I found it possible, when writing *Salvation for All: God's Other Peoples*,[11] to enlist help from outstanding commentaries that covered almost every book of the Bible from which material came for the book. Some writers have lamented the lack of creative theology as we move further into the third millennium. Could one major cause of that situation be the reluctance of many theologians to learn from the many biblical commentaries which are at their disposal?

Some theologians enlist support from biblical scholars, but limit themselves to reading only one or two authors. That practice risks taking over into theology the adventurous and even maverick opinions advanced by a particular biblical scholar or by a small group with its own special agenda. To some extent Edward Schillebeeckx

[10] See e.g. Ulrich Luz, *Matthew 1–7*, trans. W. C. Linss (Minneapolis: Augsburg, 1989); id., *Matthew 8–20* and *Matthew 21–28*, trans. J. E. Crouch (Minneapolis: Fortress Press, 2001 and 2007).
[11] Oxford: Oxford University Press, 2008.

did just that in his 1974 work on Christology.[12] The same regrettable tendency on the part of some theologians to consult only one or two biblical scholars and naively adopt their views showed up in a detailed study by Nunzio Capizzi of the use of Philippians 2: 6–11 in some contemporary works in Christology.[13]

Be historical

As an Italian philosopher, Benedetto Croce, famously remarked, 'all history is contemporary history'. Chapter 8 above, when dealing with the human reality of tradition, pointed out how tradition fashions the bond between successive generations. It makes possible the presence of the past. It is thanks to tradition that all history is or can be contemporary history. Hence the advice 'be historical' equivalently calls on theologians to 'be traditional'. Tradition conveys to each generation the collective experience of previous generations, the cumulative experience of the history through which they have lived. To ignore or belittle tradition is to ignore or belittle history.

Being historical and being traditional should shape the work of theologians within the Christian Church. A history and a tradition stretching back to apostolic times give the Church her identity as a community that continues to proclaim 'the faith that comes to us from the apostles'. In that sense, being historical and being traditional in one's theology imply being apostolic; historical consciousness[14] involves apostolic consciousness. If faith 'comes from hearing' (Rom. 10: 17), theology also comes from an attentive listening to the great witnesses of Christian history and tradition.

[12] R. E. Brown (*Catholic Biblical Quarterly*, 42 (1980), 421–3), in his review of Schillebeeckx's *Jesus: An Experiment in Christology*, trans. H. Hoskins (New York: Seabury, 1979), regretted Schillebeeckx's one-sided reliance on N. Perrin, S. Schulz, T. J. Weeden, and others—that is to say, a reliance on what F. Kerr (*New Blackfriars*, 60 (1979), 549–52) called the 'extremely fragile and arguable hypotheses of his [Schillebeeckx's] favourite exegetes'. In their reviews R. H. Fuller (*Interpretation*, 34 (1980), 293–6, at 293) and A. E. Harvey (*Journal of Theological Studies*, 51 (1980), 598–60, at 604) also noted the way in which Schillebeeckx, even if claiming to be doing his own exegesis, in fact followed the quite dubious views of a few exegetes.

[13] *L'uso di Fil. 2, 6–11 nella cristologia contemporanea (1965–93)* (Rome: Gregorian University Press, 1997).

[14] See Lonergan, *Method in Theology*, 175–234.

Be philosophical

All theology will remain low on clarity and substance unless it puts what it gleans from the Scriptures and history/tradition into dialogue with philosophy. From the time of Justin Martyr in the second century, philosophical views of God, the created world, and the divine interaction with the world have assisted the interpretation and appropriation of the biblical witness. In general, philosophical reason sharpens the questions to be asked, helps to organize approaches to the material, partly illuminates the nature of human beings and their world, and brings conceptual clarity to bear on biblical texts, which by and large are pre-philosophical. It also throws some light on what happens when we read and interpret the Scriptures. By developing insights into the nature of knowledge, meaning, and truth, philosophy elucidates to a degree that spiritual dynamism operating when we read and hear the Scriptures. Let me introduce four areas which exemplify the role of philosophy.

First, how do you know that you know in theology? Issues of the epistemology of theology turn up everywhere: for instance, on the question of 'evidence' for the resurrection of Christ. What counts as evidence here? What might justify claims about the resurrection? In general, what criteria apply to theological enquiry?[15] In *Method in Theology* Lonergan brings his philosophy of human knowing to bear on such questions.

Second, theological discussion of the personal pre-existence of Christ (who existed 'in' eternity 'before' he assumed a life 'in' time) cries out for dialogue with philosophers. What are time and eternity? How might an eternal, pre-existent person take on an existence in time? In particular, from the days of Augustine (d. 430) and Boethius (d. *c.* 524) down to the present, philosophical minds have examined and debated the nature of time and eternity. Some use of what ancient and modern philosophers have proposed about time and eternity would have enhanced considerably the value of K.-J. Kuschel's discussion of Christ's pre-existence, *Born Before All Time: The Dispute over Christ's Origin*,[16] but none of that philosophical enquiry made a appearance in this book.

---

[15] See G. O'Collins, 'Historical Evidence and its Limits', in *Easter Faith: Believing in the Risen Jesus* (London: Darton, Longman & Todd, 2003), 25–50.
[16] Trans. J. Bowden (London: SCM Press, 1992). An account of the vigorous philosophical debate on time and eternity that went on through the 1980s, in the

Third, in the 1970s and 1980s biblical scholars (like Martin Hengel, Xavier Léon-Dufour, C. F. D. Moule, E. P. Sanders, and Heinz Schürmann) carried on a vigorous debate about the intentions of Jesus when faced with death. Some (like Anton Vögtle) argued for a rather minimalist position, others (like Rudolf Pesch) for a stronger, even 'maximalist' interpretation of the pre-crucifixion intentions and expectations of Jesus.[17] This (largely biblical) debate would have been sharpened by introducing the philosophical distinction between event and act: that is to say, by distinguishing between (a) the language of causality, which asks *how* the central agent contributed to some occurrence and its results, and (b) the language of intention, which asks *why* the agent acted in the way he or she did.

Fourth, philosophy copes also with questions about language and religious language. Can literal, analogical, metaphorical, and symbolic language yield some true knowledge of God? And, in any case, what are the differences between such uses of language? In religious reflection (first style), practice (second style), and worship (third style), language is used in non-literal, extended ways. We may speak metaphorically, applying such common terms as bread, light, lamb, shepherd, and priest to Christ. He is the bread of life, the light of the world, the lamb of God, the good shepherd, and the high priest. He is both like and unlike the bread, light, lambs, shepherds, and priests of our experience. His own symbolic language about a lost coin, a lost sheep, and a lost son (Luke 15: 3–32) expresses and 're-presents' truths about the invisible God and the divine designs in our regard. We are guided toward ultimate realities by symbolic language, even more than by abstract concepts. Faced with analogies, metaphors, and symbols, theologians must listen to the philosophical experts on language and religious language.[18]

---

decade before Kuschel published the original (German) edition of his book in 1990, is provided by B. Leftow, *Time and Eternity* (Ithaca, NY: Cornell University Press, 1991), and A. G. Padgett, *God, Eternity, and the Nature of Time* (New York: St Martin's Press, 1992).

[17] On this debate, as it developed from 1970 to 1993, see W. M. Becker, *The Historical Jesus in the Face of his Death* (Rome: Gregorian University Dissertation, 1994), 105–60.

[18] See W. P. Alston, *Divine Nature and Human Language: Essays in Philosophical Theology* (Ithaca, NY: Cornell University Press, 1989); O. Boulnois, 'Analogy', in Lacoste (ed.), *Encyclopedia of Christian Theology*, i. 27–30; F. Kerr, 'Language, Theological', ibid. ii. 876–81; A. P. Martinich, 'Metaphor', in Craig (ed.), *Routledge*

Contact with philosophers, who normally require precise language, can help theologians 'watch their language' in the presence of God and, at least, introduce the brief qualifiers that make all the difference. I found one contemporary theologian remarking that 'statements about God are not informative', when I presume he meant (but did not say): 'statements about God are not *merely* informative.' The 'merely' saves the situation. Otherwise, this theologian would be alleging something that looks self-contradictory: 'the only statement about God that is informative is my claim that statements about God are not informative.' Years before I read the same theologian on the subject of 'Modernism', an umbrella term for a rather diffuse Catholic theological movement at the end of the nineteenth and the start of the twentieth century.[19] He wrote: 'the Second Vatican Council vindicated the concerns and views of the Modernists'. Historical accuracy would require a qualifier: the Second Vatican Council vindicated *some* of the concerns and views of the Modernists. Contact with philosophers could encourage theologians to qualify what they write with 'some', 'merely', 'also', and other small but significant words. I am not calling for 'death by a thousand qualifications', but simply for a standard of careful precision that might be expected.

Be provisional

This injunction might have been phrased 'be apophatic'. Often translated as a call to 'negative' theology, an 'apophatic' approach points out the radical inadequacy of all attempts to describe the absolute mystery of God.[20] Any affirmation about God must be qualified by a corresponding negation and the recognition that God infinitely transcends our human categories and capacities. Short of the final vision of God, we 'see only dimly' and not yet 'face to face' (1 Cor. 13: 12). Insofar as they deal with the mystery of God, theologians

---

Encyclopedia of Philosophy, vi. 335–8; O'Collins, *Retrieving Fundamental Theology*, 98–107; J. M. Soskice, *Metaphor and Religious Language* (Oxford: Clarendon Press, 1985).

[19] 'Modernism', in *Oxford Dictionary*, 1104–5.
[20] See Thomas Aquinas, *Summa Theologiae*, 1. 13. 4.

cannot be too 'knowing' but must remain provisional, modest, and apophatic in what they say and claim.

This involves restraining the desire for a closure that works in the spirit of 'that's it', and remembering constantly the restless 'seeking' (*quaerens*) that should distinguish any style of theology. Far from ever reaching definitive solutions, an apophatic awareness always experiences a sense of incompleteness, a feeling that there is 'something more', and never loses its sense that what it does not know far surpasses the little truth it may have glimpsed.

Be ecumenical

The advice to 'be ecumenical' applies in the widest sense: to relations with Jews, Christians of different denominations, and all those others who are not Christians. The value of such an ecumenical outreach, which took various forms in their lives and work, shines through the theological contributions made by such notable twentieth-century theologians as Hans Urs von Balthasar, Karl Barth, Dietrich Bonhoeffer, Henry Chadwick, Yves Congar, Avery Dulles, Jacques Dupuis, Gerhard Ebeling, Hans Frei, John Macquarrie, Karl Rahner, Paul Tillich, and Tom Torrance—not to mention those who are still alive, like Sarah Coakley, Walter Kasper, René Latourelle, Jürgen Moltmann, Wolfhart Pannenberg, Janet Martin Soskice, Frank Sullivan, David Tracy, and Frances Young. Ecumenical relations affected all of these figures differently and at different points of their lives. But those who knew (or know) them or have read their biographies (or autobiographies) can verify my claim. To state that an ecumenical outreach enriched the work of all of them (and of others not named here) seems a relatively uncontroversial claim. Let me give one example. The openness Tom Torrance showed to the theology of Eastern Christians and to a Jesuit specialist in liturgy, Josef Jungmann, flowered in Torrance's contribution to thinking about the Eucharist and Christ's sacrificial self-offering in which the faithful share.[21]

The motivation for advising 'be ecumenical' varies according to the groups mentioned above. Any failure to attend to Judaism (today and in the time of Jesus himself) can only prove a very serious

---

[21] See T. F. Torrance, *Theology in Reconciliation* (Eugen, Ore.: Wipf & Stock, 1996); O'Collins and Jones, *Jesus our Priest*, 224–9.

impoverishment for Christian theologians. To go into detail would require an enormous parenthesis. But, in view of St Paul's metaphor about Gentile Christians (who were to make up the overwhelming majority in the Church) being wild olives grafted into the stock that is Israel (Rom. 11: 17–24), one must ask: how can anyone explore the theology of Christianity without paying serious attention not only to Christian origins in Judaism but also to the ongoing life of Christianity that is grafted into and shares the life and blessings of the chosen people? Then, given the way Jewish Scriptures live also in the Christian Church and its daily liturgy and given the way the Christian Scriptures cannot be adequately understood apart from their Jewish matrix, any theologian who wishes to be biblical must not ignore Judaism.[22]

As regards other Christians and Christian theologians who belong to other denominations, I remain a Roman Catholic because I find in that community the fullness of the Church founded on Christ and his apostles. But, following the lead of the Second Vatican Council, I have found very many elements of Christian faith and life in other communities and much that has enriched my theological thinking. To put this concretely: over many years what Barth, Chadwick, Moltmann, and Pannenberg have written served to challenge and nourish my theological development. From time spent at the University of Tübingen I remember with special gratitude two Lutheran professors, Ernst Käsemann (who lectured on Romans) and Gerhard Ebeling (who ran a seminar on Christ's resurrection). From my years at the University of Cambridge, I profited greatly from the teaching and seminar sessions of C. F. D. Moule, a devout and very learned Anglican scholar.

The last chapter of this book highlighted the presence of the risen Christ and the Holy Spirit in the lives, cultures, and religions of all men and women. This means that Christians, and—specifically—Christian theologians should expect that, in the faith and practice of every human being, Christ and the Spirit will, at some point, have something to say to them. The prayer life of Muslims, for instance, could well

---

[22] See e.g. the Pontifical Biblical Commission, *The Jewish People and their Sacred Scriptures in the Christian Bible* (Vatican City: Libreria Editrice Vaticana, 2001).

challenge the followers of Christ and make them rethink Paul's injunction to 'pray without ceasing' (1 Thess. 5: 17). A properly ecumenical spirit involves being always open to learning from all others and to hearing Christ and the Holy Spirit speaking through them. In short, being ecumenical amounts to being open *to* God *in* others.

Be local

In the late twentieth century theological concern became more focused on the need to 'be local': that is to say, the need to inculturate theology in particular settings. Theologians must grapple with the question: how can I express the Christian message through the traditions, symbols, and language(s) that shape my particular culture? What should I say about the presence of Christ in the history and culture of my country or continent, and about the way he challenges that history and culture? More and more theologians, instead of seeing the Church as centred in the West and represented elsewhere by satellite communities, have shifted their attention to the local churches spread around the world. That vision brings with it the pressing need to contextualize and indigenize the good news and its way of life for all cultures and peoples.

There is one Christ, one Bible, and one Church, but there are many cultures. Translating the Scriptures into contemporary cultures (so that every generation can appropriate and 'inhabit' the biblical narrative) calls for wide experience and innovative fidelity. Any given culture concerns the totality of life; it embraces a complex of secular and religious value-systems, ways of thinking, traditional lifestyles, and forms of celebration. The thorough inculturation of the biblical message depends, at least in part, from the success of theologians in discerning the potential (and failure) of a culture to be illuminated by the Scriptures and to serve as a vehicle for expressing the great narratives and metanarratives of the Bible. Such a capacity to discern requires a mastery of what one's own culture and biblical faith within that culture mean or could mean. Achieving such inculturation implies both faith and reason: both (a) a faith to believe that Christ with his Spirit are present in all human cultures and that, as centred on him, the Bible is a book for all cultures; and (b) a sensitivity in fashioning ways in which inculturation should function for any given period, people, and culture.

Be converted

From the days when I studied at the University of Cambridge, I recall what a retired farmworker from the fens of East Anglia said: 'if you don't believe, you won't see anything.' 'Be converted' could be rephrased as 'practise the Christian faith'; otherwise, you will not be attuned to God, fruitfully engaged with the divine mystery, and capable of seeing something of value. Personal faith and moral practice affect theologians, just as regularly attending the theatre affects the work of those who teach drama at colleges or universities. How could anyone effectively educate students in the work of Shakespeare, Chekhov, Ibsen, and other great dramatists if he or she never bothered to see plays in their own city, attend drama festivals, and participate actively in the community of playwrights, producers, actors, and critics?

In *Method in Theology* Lonergan emphasized the intellectual, moral, and religious conversion required by his approach: be attentive, be intelligent, be reasonable, be responsible, and be loving. Unconverted theologians remain theologians who will never develop and fulfil their vocation and mission. Equipped with the required degrees, they 'teach God' but without participating in God through an active faith and sharing in the living community of the Church. In this context some words by Clive James about a famous but 'unconverted' philosopher, Jean-Paul Sartre (1905–80), express a chilling warning about what might happen to philosophers and theologians. 'Debarred by nature from telling the truth for long about anything that mattered', Sartre was 'perverse whether he realized it or not'; this perversity 'made him the most conspicuous example in the twentieth century of a fully qualified intellectual aiding and abetting the opponents of civilization'.[23]

Be prayerful

I have always felt grateful for the way Pope Paul VI and Gerhard Ebeling rightly associated prayer with the practice of theology. In an

---

[23] C. James, *Cultural Amnesia: Notes in the Margin of my Time* (London: Picador, 2007), 671.

address to an international symposium on the resurrection of Jesus (1–5 April 1970), Paul VI exhorted those present to look for 'solutions by joining study and prayer'. He went on to cite St Augustine's advice to biblical scholars that 'they should pray in order to understand'.[24]

Ebeling concluded *The Study of Theology* by quoting Martin Luther's 'three rules' for theologians: 'Oratio, Meditatio, Tentatio' (prayer, meditation, challenge/temptation). Luther said to theologians: 'kneel down in your little room and pray to God with real humility and earnestness, that he through his dear Son may give you his Holy Spirit, who will enlighten you, lead you, and give you understanding.'[25]

---

[24] See E. Dhanis (ed.), *Resurrexit* (Vatican City: Libreria Editrice Vaticana, 1974), pp. xii–xiii; *Acta Apostolicae Sedis*, 62 (1970), 220–4; Paul VI quoted Augustine's *De Doctrina Christiana*, 3. 56.

[25] Ebeling, *The Study of Theology*, 167–9, at 167.

Epilogue

This book has aimed at relaunching the discipline of fundamental (or foundational) theology by clarifying its major themes: faith in a personal God and its justification; the essential features of the nature and destiny of human beings, understood above in terms of their experience; some of the essential features of revelation, both the general revelation available to all human beings and the special revelation centred on God's self-communication in the history of Israel and Jesus Christ; the fullness of revelation that came with the life and ministry of Jesus; the self-disclosure of the Trinity that reached its highpoint in the crucifixion, resurrection, and coming of the Holy Spirit; the response of faith to God's self-manifestation; the transmission through tradition and Sacred Scripture of that divine self-revelation; the nature of biblical inspiration and truth; the formation of the biblical canon and some principles for interpreting the Scriptures; the founding of the Church; the situation of world religions and the universal presence of the risen Christ and his Holy Spirit; theological styles and guidelines for practising any theology.

By setting out the major themes that give fundamental theology its characteristics as a distinct discipline, *Rethinking Fundamental Theology* attempted to establish the identity of a theological discipline that is related to but is distinct from apologetics, natural theology, philosophical theology, the philosophy of religion, and systematic theology.

As I warned in the Preface, each of the chapters in this work could be expanded to make a book in its own right. That meant being selective in the material assembled in each chapter, as well as proposing positions and perspectives that often could only be stated and not supported by detailed argument. For instance, after drawing from Hans-Georg Gadamer views on the function of tradition, on the way interpreters share in the historical continuum that they study, and on the concept of 'effective history' (*Wirkungsgeschichte*), I could have pressed on and discussed the criticism that came from Jürgen Habermas (*On the Logic of Social Sciences*, 1967) and the swift response of Gadamer, *Rhetoric, Hermeneutics,and the Critique of Ideology* (1967). Likewise in dealing with the founding of the Church, I might have discussed in detail continuing attempts to sustain Walter Bauer's thesis that Christian orthodoxy was merely the position that prevailed over other, equally valid, traditions in the early Church. Did a model of redemption as the flight of the spirit from the material world belong to any of various 'theologies' present in the New Testament or was that model an aberration introduced by second- and third-century Gnostic or Gnostic-tinged groups on the margins of the great Church? Thirdly, Bernard Lonergan's *Method in Theology* raises not only questions of theological procedures in general but also the specific question: how might Lonergan's method and, in particular, his reflections on 'foundations' reshape the whole discipline of fundamental theology in the third millennium?

But this book is already long enough. I am happy to leave to others to pursue further the three issues just mentioned and other questions that have emerged in the course of thirteen chapters. *Rethinking Fundamental Theology* does not presume to 'wrap it all up'.

If my book has offered a coherent vision of fundamental theology as a whole, it can help to relaunch the discipline around the world. I would find real satisfaction in achieving such a result.

Index of Names

348 | INDEX OF NAMES

Subject Index

Biblical Index

Printed and bound by CPI Group (UK) Ltd, Croydon, CR0 4YY